Politics in Africa

7 Cases

CONTRIBUTORS

J. Gus Liebenow
INDIANA UNIVERSITY

William J. Foltz
YALE UNIVERSITY

St. Clair Drake
ROOSEVELT UNIVERSITY

Leslie Alexander Lacy
UNIVERSITY OF GHANA

Richard L. Sklar
BRANDEIS UNIVERSITY

Crawford Young
UNIVERSITY OF WISCONSIN

Donald Rothchild
UNIVERSITY OF CALIFORNIA, DAVIS

Jeffrey Butler
WESLEYAN UNIVERSITY

A HARBRACE CASEBOOK IN POLITICAL SCIENCE
Under the General Editorship of Alan F. Westin, Columbia University

Politics in Africa

7 Cases

EDITED BY
Gwendolen M. Carter NORTHWESTERN UNIVERSITY

NEW YORK · CHICAGO · BURLINGAME
Harcourt, Brace & World, Inc.

The Harbrace Casebooks in Political Science

Under the General Editorship of
ALAN F. WESTIN, *Columbia University*

The Uses of Power: 7 Cases in American Politics
The Third Branch of Government: 8 Cases in Constitutional Politics
The Centers of Power: 3 Cases in American National Government
Power and Order: 6 Cases in World Politics
Politics in Europe: 5 Cases in European Government
Politics in Africa: 7 Cases
Politics in the Soviet Union: 7 Cases

Library of Congress Catalog Number: 66–15608

PRINTED IN THE UNITED STATES OF AMERICA

CONTENTS

Political Map of Africa, 1966

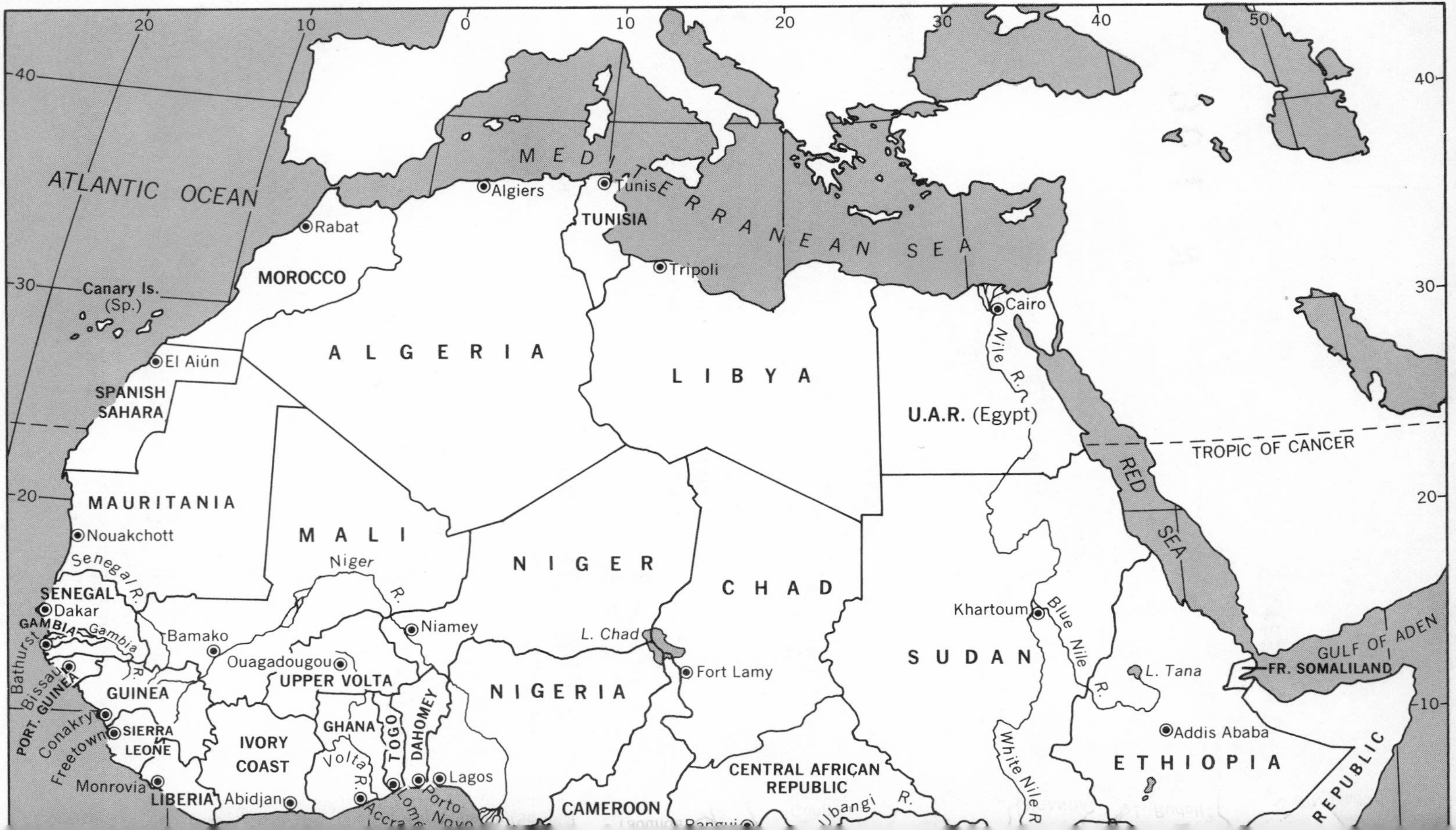

GULF OF GUINEA
Fernando Po (Sp.)
Príncipe (Port.)
RIO MUNI (Sp.)
São Tomé (Port.)
Annobón (Sp.)
EQUATOR
Libreville
GABON
CONGO
REPUBLIC OF THE CONGO
Congo R.
L. Albert
UGANDA
Kampala
L. Rudolf
KENYA
SOMALI
Mogadiscio
EQUATOR
L. Victoria
Nairobi
RWANDA
BURUNDI
INDIAN OCEAN
Brazzaville
Leopoldville
CABINDA (Port.)
L. Tanganyika
TANZANIA
Pemba Is.
Zanzibar Is.
Dar es Salaam
Luanda
L. Mweru
ATLANTIC OCEAN
ANGOLA (Port.)
Comoro Is. (Fr.)
MALAWI
L. Nyasa
ZAMBIA
Lusaka
Zomba
Zambezi R.
Kariba Lake
Salisbury
MOZAMBIQUE (Port.)
MOZAMBIQUE CHANNEL
MALAGASY
Tananarive
SOUTH-WEST AFRICA
RHODESIA (Br.)
Windhoek
(S.A. Mand.)
BECHUANALAND (Br.)
TROPIC OF CAPRICORN
Pretoria
Lourenço Marques
SWAZILAND (Br.)
Orange R.
Vaal R.
SOUTH AFRICA
BASUTOLAND (Br.)
Cape Town
0
10
20
30
20
10
0
10
20
30
40
50

INTRODUCTION

Until recently, comparative government has concerned itself chiefly with descriptions of mature state systems like those of Great Britain, France, and Switzerland, and with the contrasts between accepted democratic and totalitarian regimes. Now, however, the wealth of stimulating material available on the developing countries invites a new and broader analysis. The independent African-controlled states are particularly valuable for comparative study because these countries are attempting to shape to their own purposes and conditions the traditional parliamentary systems they have inherited from the colonial powers, notably Great Britain and France.

The tensions created by these attempts are particularly evident in the pressures for state unity and the counter-pulls toward regionalism in African countries. Although European-imposed state boundary lines are artificial—they often divide as well as combine ethnic groups—almost all African leaders are determined to build their nations within these boundaries; if they were not, there would be constant warfare to remake the map of Africa. Thus there is strong opposition to the attempts of the Somali Republic—which alone among African states has an ethnic nationalism comparable to that of nineteenth century European countries—to expand into a greater Somaliland through the revision of its boundaries with Kenya and Ethiopia. Similarly, President Kwame Nkrumah of Ghana has encountered powerful resistance to his Pan-African efforts. As is shown by the first case study in this book, "Which Road to Pan-African Unity? The Sanniquellie Conference, 1959," Liberian President Tubman's sober emphasis on maintaining existing state boundaries and stressing functional cooperation has become the predominant Pan-Africanist approach, rather than Nkrumah's more radical idea of pressing for continental political unity.

Working against the efforts to establish and consolidate state unity, however, is the powerful opposing force of regionalism. Regional pressures may be either internal or external; that is, they may work either to divide existing states or to unite them with their neighbors. "The Politics of Separatism: Katanga, 1960–63" provides an outstanding example of the former, divisive, tendency. At the same time, there is strong resistance from many quarters to internal regionalism. The Katanga did not succeed in its efforts to establish a separate and internationally recognized state, and at an earlier point the British did not yield to pressures from the Ghanaian regions for a federal rather than a unitary constitution as a prerequisite for independence. That the transition to independence in the Congo (Leopoldville) was so troubled and turbulent is atypical in Africa: in general, former British and French territories made the transition to independence relatively smoothly, and have succeeded in maintaining their state cohesion thereafter. But the cases dealing with "Nigerian politics and the Sekondi-Takoradi strike" highlight the persisting problem of trying to maintain national unity in the face of various post-independence tensions, arising in the latter case from resistance to financial sacrifices demanded in the interest of national development. Thus, internal regionalism can become increasingly reinforced as a divisive factor by new economic strains and trade union demands.

"An Early Failure of Pan-Africanism: The Mali Federation, 1959–60" and "A Hope Deferred: East African Federation, 1963–64" illustrate the second type of regionalism—the effort, inspired by economic and Pan-African motives, to build larger unities through federal arrangements. As the cases show, these two efforts to establish larger federal entities were frustrated by the particular characteristics, aspirations, and felt needs of the separate state units. Thus the African experience tends to demonstrate that only under exceptional circumstances—when, for instance, ethnic bonds provide an additional unifying force as they did in the joining of former British and Italian Somaliland and of the former Southern British and French Cameroons—does the appeal of larger units override that of individual state unity.

"Nigerian Politics: The Ordeal of Chief Awolowo, 1960–65" illustrates yet another feature of contemporary African development: the interaction between political rivalries within regions and those on the national level. Political rivalry is especially significant in developing states where political ideology and state action inevitably mold every aspect of life, particularly the educational and the economic. In developing nations, the relative absence of nonpolitical ways to command internal or external financial support increases the importance of political power; in more mature polities, the impact of political struggles is likely to be less drastic because state unity is strong and the economic fruits of political power are less rich than those offered elsewhere in the community.

Both the drive to enforce state unity and the efforts of ruling groups to maintain their dominance contribute to the establishment of the one-party states so commonly found in independent African-controlled countries. However, the absence of an organized and politically active opposition does not automatically make these countries dictatorships or totalitarian states. In any case the African states are far from developed enough, either economically or in the organization of public force, to permit totalitarian rule. The most that can be imposed is authoritarianism. In several African states, where strong party rule is backed by preventive detention measures, these have an unhealthy effect on the free speech and action of intellectual and professional groups but much less impact on other sections of the community. The Ghana case can also affect other groups.

In African states like Senegal, Kenya, and Zambia, the existence of a dominant party does not preclude considerable interaction of varied points of view on policy and its implementation. Such one-party organization is more similar to national governments like the one formed in Great Britain during World War II than to that in the one-party states of the Communist world. One reason for this difference is their leaders' avowed desire to maintain some of the basic characteristics of democratic states, notably the independence of the courts, civil rights, and opportunities to express divergent views on public policy. "A Hope Deferred: East African Federation, 1963–64" brings out the fact that in Kenya and Tanganyika (now Tanzania), both one-party states, backbenchers openly criticized their leaders for not carrying to fruition the negotiations on East African federation.

In Nigeria, largest in population of all African states—it is commonly estimated that one African in six is a Nigerian—a federation made up of four units and representing three major political parties continues to function despite severe strains imposed by regional and political rivalries. It is a tribute to the restraint and political acumen of Nigeria's present leaders that the federation survived the crisis arising from the election of December, 1964, described at the end of "Nigerian Politics: The Ordeal of Chief Awolowo, 1960–65." The Nigerian experience also shows, however, that political oppositions in developing states can *cause* crises. In the formative years of new states—as, indeed, in the first decades of the United States—a dominant party with state-wide support may be a great advantage in building and maintaining a cohesive, stable state system.

"South Africa and the High Commission Territories: The Ganyile Case, 1961" introduces yet another issue of great significance in contemporary Africa. South Africa embodies what the African-controlled states most abhor: the domination of a white minority and the enshrinement in law of discrimination based on color. Opposition to this system animates South Africa's African nationalist movement, which from 1912 (when it was formed) to 1960 (when it was banned) resisted, though unsuccessfully, the ever increasing restrictions on Africans and other non-whites. The British-controlled High Commission Territories—Basutoland, Swaziland, and Bechuanaland, the first enclosed by South African territory and the latter two abutting on it—have been natural havens for Africans fleeing the Republic in fear of imprisonment or other reprisals for their nationalist activities. In the Ganyile case, the issue was the violation (whether deliberate or not) of British territory through the kidnapping by South African authorities of one of these refugees. Thus the case raises questions of the harboring of known enemies of an adjacent country; the possibility of retaliation by a much stronger power against weak African territories whose economies are totally dependent on it; and the degree to which the British government—and in the future the independent African governments of the three territories—will extend protection to South African political refugees. In addition, it concerns important issues of international law and the relations between white- and African-controlled countries.

The casebook approach to African politics is particularly revealing because the developing African countries are still—and will long be—in transition, reacting to particular challenges and opportunities. The cases show, for instance, how much politics depend on personalities; how strains can be cushioned or can lead to breaking points or repression; and how institutions developed in the European milieu are shaped by African desires or by circumstance. Never before in the history of the world have so many countries achieved independence within so short a period of time as in sub-Saharan Africa from 1957 through 1964. As these countries respond to ethnic and political rivalries, to the need to build cohesive state units, and to the requirements of economic and educational development, they provide not only a fascinating political panorama but unparalleled comparative material. The insight to be gained is significant for the study of comparative government as well as for an understanding of contemporary politics in the vast continent of Africa.

GWENDOLEN M. CARTER

1

Which Road to Pan-African Unity?

The Sanniquellie Conference, 1959

J. Gus Liebenow

Sanniquellie: The Setting for Action

The town of Sanniquellie is nestled in the northeast corner of Liberia, not far from the intersection of the boundaries of Liberia, the Ivory Coast, and Guinea. It is one of those "boom towns" that is becoming increasingly characteristic of Africa in the present period of rapid modernization. As in all communities with growing pains, chaos often predominates over planning and artistry. Yet Sanniquellie has had its visionaries, and the triumphal arch which straddles the highway at the edge of town is the work of one of its more prophetic district commissioners. One wonders whether he somehow knew that beneath this arch on their way to the Sanniquellie Conference of July, 1959, would pass three of the principal figures in the developing struggle for Pan-African unity. For that conference not only marked the reversal of Liberia's traditional role of isolation from the affairs of the continent but also saw drawn major battle lines that would remain for several years to come. On the one side were the proponents of continental political unity, headed by Ghana's Prime Minister Kwame Nkrumah and Guinea's President Sékou Touré. On the other side was Liberia's President William V. S. Tubman, who cautiously advised regional cooperation in economic and cultural affairs as a prerequisite to political cooperation and unity at the continental level.

Tubman's choice of Sanniquellie as the site for the conference was symbolic of changes in Liberia itself. As the President had noted in an address delivered five months before the historic events of July, "In less than fifteen years Sanniquellie has been transformed from an isolated, jungle-hidden, hard-to-reach town into one of the finest and most promising places in the nation."[1] Similarly, Liberia as a whole had changed from a sleepy—and, some critics would add, sleazy—country on the west coast of Africa into a rapidly modernizing state in which the problems of class and ethnic distinctions, insularity, and public corruption were at least being recognized and, in some instances, even attacked. One of the sources of this change was President Tubman, master politician of the dominant True Whig Party. Tubman has governed Liberia since 1944 and, through his Unification Policy, attempted to mold the Americo-Liberian aristocracy and the members of Liberia's more than twenty tribal groups into a single nation.

Another source of change—for Sanniquellie and for Liberia—was the discovery of iron ore. Sanniquellie stands at the foot of Nimba Mountain, one of the richest sources of high-grade iron ore in the world. One estimate is that 90 percent of the 4,000-foot mass is iron, and that it will yield more than 400 million tons of ore. From the day the first truckload of equipment arrived, the tranquillity and peace so long enjoyed by the Gio and Mano tribal people were completely vanquished. To a town of a few hundred people were added thousands of workers each year from all parts of Liberia and from neighboring countries. Prior to the discovery of iron, an occasional missionary had been the only non-African seen by most of the tribal people. Now the American and European engineers, geologists, and construction supervisors who came to work for the Liberian-American-Swedish Mining Company (LAMCO) formed a sizable subcommunity within greater Sanniquellie.

Even more significant for Sanniquellie has been its new contact with the outside world. Before the Second World War, the two-hundred-mile trip to Monrovia, Liberia's capital, was a journey of five or six days by foot, hammock carry, and automobile. Now the new motor road, the building of which began in 1945 with American foreign aid funds, has reduced the journey to a matter of hours. Within a few years following the events of July, 1959, the ore itself would be transported by rail along an even more direct route to the coast, near Buchanan.

Despite the drama of the past few years, it is doubtful that the inhabitants of Sanniquellie were fully prepared for the events of July, 1959. Before the visit in 1945 of "Borbor Shad"—as the tribal people affectionately call President Tubman—most inhabitants of the town had never seen a Liberian head of state. Now, as the long line of mud-stained limousines pulled up to the arch, the inhabitants were to see dismount not only their President, but two other African leaders who within a few brief years had become almost legendary figures throughout the continent. To the three thousand spectators who lined the streets of Sanniquellie, the name of the younger

---

[1] E. Reginald Townsend, ed., *President Tubman of Liberia Speaks* (London: Consolidated Publications, 1959), p. 291.

West Africa, 1966

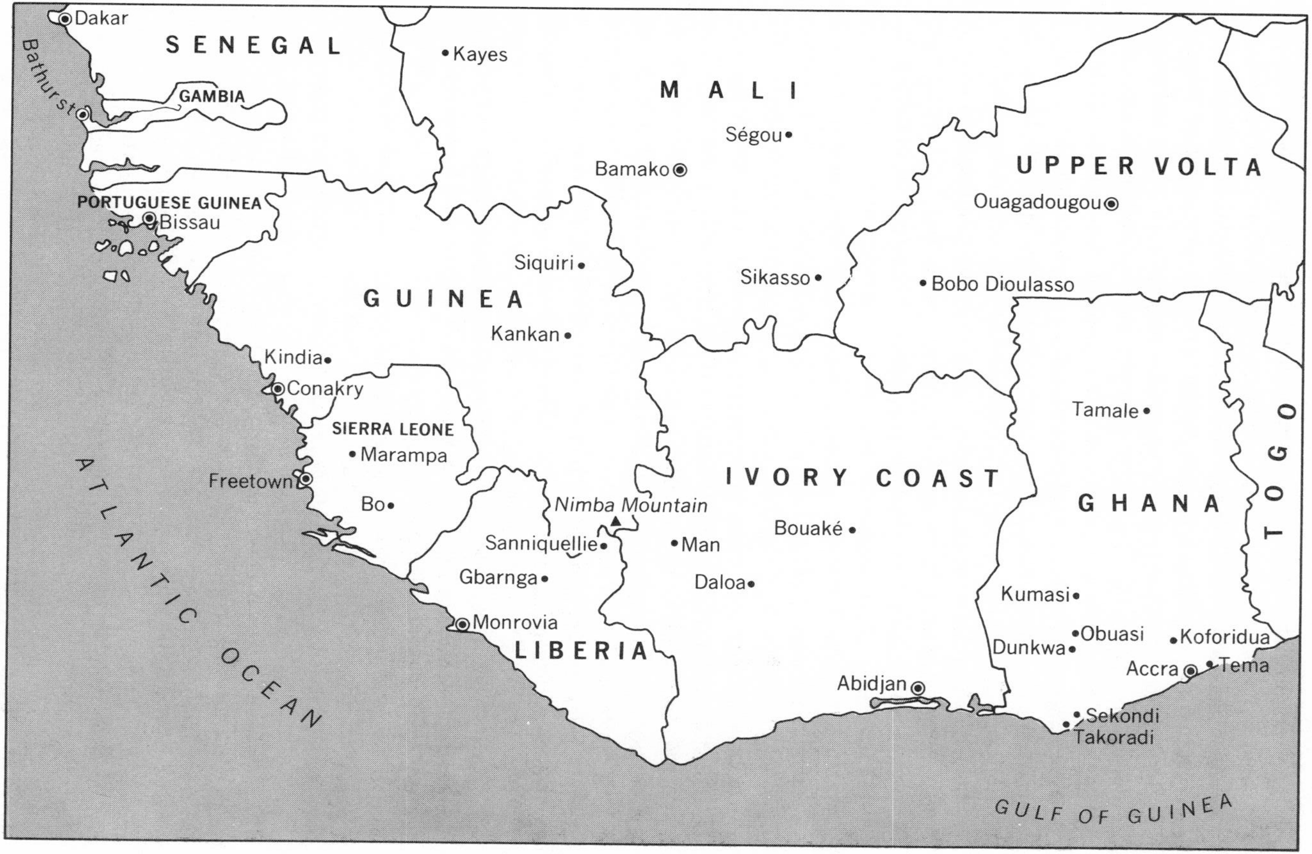

man was probably the more familiar even though he had achieved international fame only the year before by defying President Charles de Gaulle of France. In opting for Guinean independence during the referendum on the constitution of the Fifth French Republic, with its provision for a French-dominated, Franco-African community, Sékou Touré overnight had acquired the status of a giant. Although the Guinean President was only thirty-six years old at the time of this meeting—Tubman was sixty-three—youth and virility seemed for once to take precedence among a people who venerate the aged. Many of the workers at Sanniquellie were Guineans, and as a national hero Sékou Touré seemed to project a composite image: his work as a trade union and party leader revealed him as a modernist, but his claim that his grandfather was Almamy Samoury, the last of the tribal leaders to challenge the French conquerors in the nineteenth century, gave his authority a traditional base as well.

For the purpose of the meeting, however, it was the third man whose credentials were most respected by Africans around the continent. He was Kwame Nkrumah, Prime Minister of Ghana, proclaimed by many as spiritual leader of the modern independence movement in Africa and as chief apostle of Pan-African unity. His fight for unity began long before he became the leader of the Convention People's Party and brought his country to independence in 1957. During his student days in Pennsylvania at Lincoln University and in London, where he studied for the bar, he had fired the enthusiasm of fellow West Africans for his cause. In 1945, when he was thirty-six, he was elected one of the joint secretaries of the Pan-African Conference at Manchester, England. Thirteen years later, in April, 1958, he convened a Conference of Independent African States in Accra and tried to persuade Africa's other leaders that independence without unity was meaningless.

It was to consider the question of how to achieve this unity that the "Big Three" of African politics came to Sanniquellie. The conference could not, as the Liberian *Listener Daily* pointed out in its editorial of July 10, 1959,

> be interpreted otherwise than one which will make history, because it is a meeting to which all Africa and the world at large will be looking forward with unusual interest and enthusiasm, in view of the fact that these three leaders can rightly be regarded as the "Big Three" of Africa.

If they were to agree, which road to Pan-Africanism would they choose?

Pan-Africanism

Pan-Africanism, the notion that all Africans are brothers and should be members of a common nation, is a relatively new idea in international relations. It is an idea, too, that finds even its most ardent champions in sharp disagreement in regard to how the unity of Africa's 300 million people is to be accomplished. Cleavages within Africa are many, and they run deep in the social fabric. The barriers that geography has posed, as well as the centuries of disparate and uneven exposure of Africa's peoples to each other, to Islam, to Christianity, to European colonial rule, and to other forces, have left Africa a fragmented continent. Differences of religion, language, and race, and of political, economic, and social values accepted by its people divide each of the thirty-five states (with the possible exception of Somalia) that by 1965 had been created out of the ashes of European colonial rule. Even more acute perhaps are the divisions that permeate the territories still remaining under European or local white resident control.

Yet there are few African leaders of importance who do not advocate some form of Pan-African unity. The basic question has always been how and when this unity is to be achieved. At one extreme are those who feel that the issue is a simple one: political unity now. To this group the continued "Balkanization" (splitting up) of Africa spells economic backwardness and threatens the loss of recently achieved political independence. At the other extreme are those who insist that African political unity is desirable only following a much wider measure of regional, economic, social, and cultural cooperation among the people of the existing African states. To this latter group political unity now would inevitably favor those areas which are already economically advanced, and unity could only be accomplished, it is argued, by a further erosion of democratic institutions in Africa.

African unity is not only a novel and complex concept to most Africans; it is also a concept whose origins lie primarily in developments which occurred outside the African continent. One germ of the idea can perhaps be found in the efforts of Englishmen in the eighteenth century and of white Americans in the early nineteenth to repatriate liberated slaves to Sierra Leone and Liberia respectively. It was assumed—mistakenly—that any place in Africa was home for people of African ancestry, and that it mattered little, for example, that Yoruba were deposited for settlement in Sierra Leone rather than Nigeria. A subsequent and much more significant version of the kinship of all persons of African ancestry developed among Negroes in the United States and the West Indies during the first few decades of the present century. The "Back to Africa" movements of W. E. B. Du Bois and Marcus Garvey received much publicity and fanned many hopes. In the end they attracted few Negro adherents in the New World, and their reception in Africa itself was decidedly mixed. On an intellectual rather than an activist plane, however, the concept of "Négritude" found a welcome on both sides of the Atlantic. The originator of "Négritude"—the notion that all persons of Negro ancestry had a common spiritual and cultural heritage—was a West Indian named Aimé Césaire. The concept later found a ready champion in Léopold Senghor, who became in 1960 the poet-President of Senegal.

As a political concept, Pan-Africanism remained vague until 1945. In that year, at the Sixth Pan-African Conference, held at Manchester, the torch of Pan-Africanism was seized by Africans themselves. For the next fifteen years, the struggle for African independence and for unity following independence were inextricably linked together in the minds of many African nationalists. As most of colonial Africa stood on the threshold of independence in 1959, the issue of how to combine independence with African unity was at its most urgent point.

Liberia's Traditional Role in Africa

If the town of Sanniquellie seemed an unusual site for an international conference, Liberia itself was an improbable candidate, in the 1950s, to play host to a meeting on Pan-African unity. During much of Liberia's history, the descendants of the freed American slaves who settled the colony had regarded Africa as a somewhat hostile environment. The Mandingo, Grebo, Kru, Vai, and other original inhabitants attempted to push these settlers of 1822 into the sea, and their efforts persisted well into the period following the republic's declaration of independence in 1847. From the standpoint of the indigenous population, the Americo-Liberian tactics of conquest, treaty-signing, and territory-claiming on the basis of journeys of "discovery" placed them in the same category as the European powers who were extending their control elsewhere in Africa. Time and again the subject Kru or Grebo had to be subjugated all over again.

The European colonial powers proved equally unfriendly neighbors to the Americo-Liberians. Britain and France, moving in from their respective dependencies of Sierra Leone, Guinea, and the Ivory Coast, whittled away Liberian claims to territory. As recently as the 1930s, moreover, they charged that slavery was practiced in the country, and they attempted to limit the independence of the republic itself by recommending that Liberia be placed under the League of Nations Mandates System. Wherever and whenever they could, the colonial powers minimized official and unofficial contacts between Liberians and residents of neighboring countries. Roads in Sierra Leone or Guinea stopped a few miles short of the Liberian border, and the establishment of consular and other relations dates mainly from the postwar period. Nigerians, Guineans, and other Africans came to accept the stereotypes of Liberians presented to them by the colonial civil servants and to accept the myth that it was the example of the alleged failure of self-government provided by Liberia that delayed the independence movement elsewhere in Africa. Other African leaders sensed that Liberia's ties with America were stronger than those with Africa, as evidenced by the term

"Americo-Liberian" and the heavy reliance Liberia had placed since 1924 upon the Firestone Plantations Company and other American companies, as well as upon the United States government, for economical and financial aid.

Liberia's fears of its African neighbors were reciprocated as developments of the Second World War indicated that Liberia's relations with the European colonial powers were becoming less and less stable. The acceleration of economic development and the expansion of educational facilities in the colonial areas were leading to increased political awareness and demands for independence in those areas. Liberia's leaders, who had consciously avoided development of the hinterland in order to forestall demands by the tribal majority for a reversal of their relationship with the Americo-Liberian minority at the coast, realized that a change in strategy was required. President Tubman's Unification Policy and his Open Door Policy of encouraging foreign investors to exploit Liberia's resources were supposed to bring about a gradual evolution, not a dramatic revolution, in the country's political and social fabric.

The charge that Africa's oldest republic was "soft on colonialism" had been voiced many times by Africans from other West African countries. This point of view was perhaps unintentionally supported by the oft-quoted, plaintive statement made by Charles T. O. King at the time of Ghana's independence in 1957. Ambassador King, the son of a former President of Liberia, lamented, according to the New York *Times* (March 24, 1957),

> that his country lagged materially behind the new nation of Ghana because it had always been independent and had never reaped the advantages of colonialism.
>
> "It is the difference between the home of a man who has had to accomplish everything by his own sweat and toil," Mr. King said, "and that of a man who has enjoyed a large inheritance.
>
> ". . . The material differences . . . are clear to see," he said. "Ghana had better roads, better schools, better harbor facilities, a more highly developed industry, agriculture, and public revenue.
>
> ". . . The United States did not care about a colony on the coast of Africa," he said, "and we were left alone and struggling, to vegetate in the midst of developing European colonies.
>
> ". . . By contrast . . . the liberal colonial policy of Britain was to extend great efforts to develop her colonial holdings, and build them up materially."

As independence movements gained momentum in territories adjacent to Liberia, the doubts became greater. The lack of enthusiasm regarding the sudden achievement of independence by Guinea in 1958 was communicated in an editorial in the government-owned *Liberian Age* on October 3, 1958. It commented:

> There is a tendency among imperial powers to say that African leaders are communists when they demand independence. . . . What are the facts about Guinea? Its Premier is a staunch Trade Unionist who controls his territory through the unions. But apart from this Mr. Touré was educated in communist countries. He has been labelled in many circles as [a] "Marxist-trained" unionist. What everyone is watching now is, will Guinea remain with France or go the communist way as an independent country? Whatever is her answer, we in this country must be on guard. And France should really not do anything to force the Africans into a tight corner.
>
> Most patiently we would like to see a Guinea that is stable since part of that territory is also Liberian territory which we have sought by peaceful means and negotiation to regain.

A little later the Secretary of Defense expressed in his *Annual Report, 1960,* the official apprehensiveness concerning the accomplished or pending independence of all three of Liberia's neighbors.

> With the attainment of independence of our sister African brothers contiguous to our borderline, problems which were never thought of are arising and have to be grappled with every degree of efficiency and alertness. Not only are the problems of the crossing into our territories of citizens of other States involved but also the question of national ideologies, some of which are divergent to ours and destined to threaten and uproot the very foundation upon which our democratic institution was founded. To ensure that the situation just referred to will be averted and not permitted to take a foot hold in Liberia we have to strengthen and increase our border control units and give more attention to border problems as they arise from day to day.

It was apparent, in fact, that the independence of its neighbors, and of Guinea in particular, presented the leaders of Liberia with a crisis of the first magnitude. The True Whig Party of Liberia and the Parti Démocratique de Guinée (PDG), the ruling parties of the two states, upheld drastically divergent philosophies. The Liberian ruling class clearly sought to preserve its dominant position in its country by combining economic modernization with control of the political and social consequences of industrialization as far as the tribal majority of the hinterland was concerned. The Guinean party leaders, on the other hand, sought the rapid political, social, and economic mobilization of all segments of society within a socialist state. In creating a new society, the PDG was seeking to eliminate ultimately all vestiges of tribalism and traditionalism, a course of great appeal potentially to Liberia's tribal people, many of whom had kinsmen on the Guinean side of the border. Moreover, the dynamic Guinean party favored an activist foreign policy on the part of Africa's independent states to complete the task of liberating and uniting the rest of Africa, whereas the Liberian leaders had long held aloof from intra-African politics.

Less threatening to the True Whigs, but still a subject for concern, was the slow but steady progress of Sierra Leone towards independence. The origins of that state were similar to those of Liberia: Sierra Leone, and especially Freetown and its surrounding area, had served as a refuge for freed British slaves during the eighteenth and nineteenth centuries. Unlike Liberia, however, the political struggle in Sierra Leone between the settler minority (called "Creoles") of Freetown and the tribal majority of the interior had been resolved by the British in favor of the tribal majority. Although the governing party in Sierra Leone under Milton Margai was conservative and supported by traditionalists, it was nevertheless a tribal-based party which successfully dominated the Sierra Leone counterpart of the Americo-Liberian community in Liberia.

Liberian Reaction to the Ghana-Guinea Union

The prospect of independent neighbors was one thing, but the prospect that two or more of Liberia's neighbors might join larger federations of states in West Africa, thereby intensifying Liberia's isolation from the rest of Africa, was another. In November, 1958, Liberia heard with alarm the announcement of the Ghana-Guinea Union, which was to form the basis of a future Union of West African States. The initiative for the Ghana-Guinea Union was provided by Ghana's Kwame Nkrumah, who sweetened the proposal by offering simultaneously to lend Guinea £10 million for development purposes, to offset the disastrous consequences of the sudden withdrawal of French capital at the time of independence. The declaration, made on November 23 and printed in the December 10 issue of *Ghana Today,* was vague regarding the details of fusing the political institutions of the two states and the timing of the introduction of a joint currency and flag. The declaration, nevertheless, did attempt to provide a historical precedent for the action of Ghana and Guinea:

> Inspired by the example of the thirteen American colonies which, on the attainment of their independence, constituted themselves into a confederacy which ultimately developed into the United States of America. . . . We the Prime Ministers of Ghana and Guinea . . . have agreed to constitute our two states as the nucleus of a Union of West African States.
>
> Conscious of the fact that an aspiration for closer union is shared by all the peoples of our Continent, we appeal to the Governments of the Independent States of Africa, as well as to the leaders and peoples of the territories still under foreign rule, to support us in our action. In this same spirit, we would welcome the adherence to this Union of other West African States.

In concrete terms, this meant that the militant Kwame Nkrumah could become a neighbor of President Tubman. Although Tubman was aware of the aid and comfort the militant declaration provided dissident elements within the True Whig Party, he was visibly annoyed by what he regarded as a breach of protocol. Neither Nkrumah nor Touré had consulted him in advance regarding the move, despite the fact that only a few weeks before the latter had been given a hero's welcome in Monrovia, where he had gone to discuss boundary and other problems with President Tubman. Rather than denouncing the union—a move which could be unpopular both at home and abroad—President Tubman declared in his November 27 press conference, reported the following day in the *Liberian Age,* that "those African nations and peoples who desire to become a part of such a union have every right to do so without let or hindrance." As for Liberia, however, President Tubman emphasized that he would stand by what he had said two weeks earlier in his annual message to the legislature. In that message he indicated:

> There are some African states that seem to favour and argue for a federation of Africa; others for a United States of Africa; and still others who advocate the United States of West Africa; but we advocate that type of African unity, and West African unity and solidarity in particular, which is based upon treaties and conventions of friendship, amity, navigation, trade and other alliances on the basis of mutual respect and equal consideration for all.
>
> Not only does it appear to us that this would be the safer course for African States with and among themselves, but also with other nations with whom they need to have friendly intercourse. For no European, Asian or African nation can exist exclusively unto itself, nor only in friendship with the community of nations within their respective continents; nor is there any federation or United States of Asia, Europe or the Americas; such a proposition is, in our opinion, unrealistic and a utopia.

To follow up the approach suggested here Liberia in the next month did negotiate a treaty of friendship, commerce, and navigation with Guinea.

It was not until early in January, 1959, that President Tubman realized that the Ghana-Guinea Union could not be easily brushed aside. What goaded the Liberian President into action was a casual remark of the Ghanaian Prime Minister during a triumphal tour of India, in which he suggested that "it would be in the best interest of Liberia to join the Ghana-Guinea Union." As the *Liberian Age* reported on January 2, 1959, the Liberian Ambassador to Ghana, Wilmot David, was forthwith instructed to present a protest in Accra, capital of Ghana, stating that the Liberian government "has never attributed to the Ghana Premier either the ability or the capacity to determine better than the Liberian Government which [i.e., what] is in its best interests."

Positive action was clearly called for to prevent further attempts by the Ghanaian and Guinean heads of government to appeal directly to the

Liberian people. The idea of Pan-Africanism was already catching fire among the younger Americo-Liberians, the educated tribal people of the hinterland, and the African immigrant community in Monrovia. To keep its concepts from serving as a rallying cry for militant university students, younger educated tribal dissidents, disappointed office-seekers, and other domestic critics of the True Whig regime, the Liberian government had to shift to the offensive, even if it meant a departure from Liberia's characteristic aloofness from African affairs. As recently as Independence Day, July 26, 1957, President Tubman had shunned the mantle of unilateral leadership. He stated then that the question of African leadership,

> in my considered opinion, has been or is being skillfully manoeuvered deliberately at this time to separate and weaken the ties of friendship which should exist among all African States, and have the African States leave the proverbial substance for the shadow. In this connection I have observed that there seem to be three schools of thought on this subject. There are those who feel that Liberia should assume leadership based on the fact that she is the oldest African Republic and is riper in political experience; but it will require more than age and political experience to assume leadership of Africa. There are others who hold that Ghana should assume that role because she is physically more developed and embraces larger territories. It will require more than development and larger territory to assume leadership of Africa. And there are yet those who opine that Egypt with its rich traditions dating back to the remotest antiquity, should do so. It will require more than rich traditions of antiquity. It will require, in my opinion, the aggregate of all three of these and more besides. It will require the aggregate of the best of all that Liberia, Ghana, Egypt, Tunisia, Ethiopia, the Sudan, Morocco, South Africa, Nigeria, the Federation of Nyasaland and all other African Territories and States possess, moulded together, to assume the leadership of Africa, compounded in such a manner as to represent the divisibility of Africa indivisible.[2]

The Functional Approach to Pan-Africanism: Associated States of Africa

To counter the dramatic quality of the Ghana-Guinea Union declaration, the Liberian head of state decided to present an alternative plan to achieve African unity. In an issue of the Liberian *Official Gazette* of January 26, 1959, the Acting Secretary of State, J. Rudolph Grimes, declared that,

> taking into consideration differing economic systems, differing political allegiances and preferences, differing cultural backgrounds and differing social customs; and not wishing to superimpose any artificial unity upon

[2] Townsend, pp. 185–86.

> these differences, it is the opinion of the Liberian Government that the peoples of Africa should resolve to achieve close association and cooperation, without prejudice to their national or international identities.

Instead of a political union of states, Liberia was to propose a permanent organization, to be known as the Associated States of Africa, to deal with the common economic, educational, social, and other nonpolitical problems of the independent and soon-to-be-independent states.

President Tubman was thus arguing for the "functional" approach to cooperation, i.e., for political unity to take place only *after* the various functions performed by separate governments had gradually been delegated to a supranational organization. His model then was not the American one of 1787, dear to the heart of Nkrumah, in which a strong central political force displaced the political authority of the smaller states. It was, rather, the one currently being pursued in Western Europe, in which political unity was to be sought only after various economic functions, previously controlled separately by France, Western Germany, Italy, and the Benelux powers, had been surrendered step-by-step to a supranational agency—the Common Market.

The organization President Tubman proposed would deliberate, *not* act as a superlegislature, on problems concerning Africa as a whole. It would be entrusted with the settlement of intra-African disputes. Another important aspect of Tubman's proposal, which ran counter to the views of Prime Minister Nkrumah, was the suggestion that *continental* cooperation should be pursued gradually through the vehicle of *regional* authorities, which would be created within the association to deal with problems of health, scientific research and training projects, cultural exchange, and tariff reduction. That President Tubman was seeking a broad consensus on his association was revealed in his statement of February 5, 1959, in Sanniquellie, when he suggested that this approach to unity would probably be the "least objectionable to all the nations and peoples of Africa."[3]

The Political Approach to Pan-Africanism: Union of Independent African States

Temporarily, at least, Tubman had gained the initiative. For a time he remained silent, waiting for the idea of the functional and regional approach to unity to germinate. Then, on April 7 he proposed to Kwame Nkrumah and Sékou Touré that they meet with him to discuss their common problems and "the unity of the continent of Africa." This letter, published in the *Gazette,* apparently caught the leaders of the political-first approach off guard. Though five months had elapsed since their November declaration

[3] Townsend, p. 294.

on the Ghana-Guinea Union, it was still a union on paper only. Stirred to action, Nkrumah replied on April 20 that multilateral discussions could be more profitably pursued if the Ghanaian and Guinean leaders had first, on a bilateral basis, clarified their own position.

It was obvious that Nkrumah was concerned lest his proposal for a stronger political union be lost in a more open discussion of alternative plans for union. He was determined, therefore, that Ghana and Guinea should present a united front against the Liberian position. Perhaps, too, he had some doubts about the firmness of Sékou Touré's commitment to the Nkrumah version of Pan-Africanism. To achieve his ends, Prime Minister Nkrumah traveled to Guinea and seemed to achieve success there. On May Day the two leaders announced the creation of a Union of Independent African States (UIAS), which other independent states or federations would be free to join.

The impression the Guinean and Ghanaian leaders attempted to give was that they had now decided the matters that had been left vague in the announcement of the Ghana-Guinea Union the previous November. The UIAS was to have a union flag, an anthem, and a common citizenship that would eliminate the need for visas among citizens of its member states. A political organ composed of the heads of the states of the union was to determine common defense policy, while a common economic council would decide on general development policy. According to the May 14, 1959, issue of *Ghana Today,* efforts were also to be made to "coordinate historical research, teaching of languages and cultural activities designed to promote the harmonious development of African civilization."

On closer examination, however, the UIAS was something less than a prospective super state. There was to be no fusion of political and military institutions; each state was to maintain its "own individuality and structure," and the extent to which authority was surrendered was to be a matter of common agreement among the members. Although one state might ask another to undertake foreign representation in its behalf, there was no unified diplomatic service or foreign policy. Finally, although a Union Bank would issue and back the currencies of member states, this was a step back from the common currency proposal of the preceding November.

What happened to the great dream of political unity first? The Ghanaian Prime Minister gave no public impression that anything had gone awry. Indeed, as *Ghana Today* reported on May 27, Nkrumah declared upon returning by ship to Takoradi, Ghana's main seaport, that "the union between Ghana and Guinea is now established and unbreakable. It has laid the foundation for the unity and personality of Africa. It establishes the nucleus for a community of African States. We have dedicated our lives to that end."

President Touré, on the other hand, remarked to a correspondent from *West Africa* that the new union was similar to the Anglo-American alliance.

It was a close association of allies, not a fusion of political and other institutions.

Several other items in *West Africa* also suggested that Sékou Touré had insisted upon a watered-down version of unity and that Guinea was now finding Ghana's embrace somewhat less than irresistible. In September, 1958, when Guinea had stood practically alone, Ghana's offer of support had been welcome in the extreme. Now Guinea found itself wooed from several directions: Ghana; the Eastern bloc in the "Cold War"; and the newly formed Mali Federation, a short-lived union of Senegal and the then Soudan (now Mali), headed by Sékou Touré's former political associate Mobido Keita.[4] Moreover, being the poorer of the two partners, Guinea suspected that it would have to make the greater economic sacrifices. This was strongly suggested to the *West Africa* reporter who accompanied the Ghanaian party during the April visit to Guinea, which included a trip to the nearly completed alumina factory at Fria near the Konkouré River in Guinea. With Nkrumah's plans well under way to harness the power of the Volta River and make Ghana a leading producer of processed aluminum, the reporter, in discussing this problem in the issue of May 23, 1959, wondered,

> Can either Ghana or Guinea be persuaded to postpone their dreams of aluminium industries each converting bauxite through all stages into aluminium, and accept, for the time being, the idea of complementing each other, with Guinea exporting the alumina for conversion into aluminium in Ghana? No wonder Dr. Nkrumah was in a reflective mood, when next day he left, amidst much cheering, to sail back to Ghana.

Although President Tubman undoubtedly saw that the two militants were drifting apart, he was extremely annoyed—as he had been the previous November—by the efforts of the Ghanaians and the Guineans to make plans without consulting him. He reserved his wrath for the younger of the two leaders. When Sékou Touré wrote him on May 4 inviting him to join the union (as a fait accompli) and to accept the role of "Dean" of the Independent States as the union became a reality, President Tubman waited more than three weeks to respond. His letter of May 27 in the *Official Gazette* pointedly noted:

> Your advocacy of the President of Liberia as the Dean of the Independent African States seems plausible; but how can that be considered practicable when Guinea and Ghana have already for themselves developed a Constitution and a Flag for the African Independent States without reference to or consultation with the Government of Liberia?

[4] For a more detailed examination of the creation of the Mali Federation, see Chapter 2.

The "Big Three" Meeting at Sanniquellie

Despite President Tubman's annoyance at the actions of the two leaders, he chose to respond to Prime Minister Nkrumah's invitation to have the three leaders pursue multilateral discussions. Perhaps in recognition of the offense to President Tubman, Prime Minister Nkrumah made a concession that was to provide the Liberians with a decided advantage. The Ghanaian leader wrote on May 15:

> It is my view that the meeting should be held in Liberia, provided that you are willing to act as host. Further, I consider that we should, if possible, keep private those meetings at which serious discussions will take place. The great importance of our deliberations to our respective countries and to Africa will require that our discussions are held in an atmosphere of complete frankness and calm. For that reason, if you agree, it may be convenient for the serious discussions to take place outside Monrovia City itself. A statement can be issued to the public at the conclusion of our discussions.

Even before he had replied to the earlier letter of Sékou Touré, President Tubman on May 24 wrote back to Kwame Nkrumah:

> You suggest that the meeting be held in Liberia, provided I am willing to act as host. Since you recommend the meeting to take place in Liberia, it follows as a normal sequence that I will in that case become host.
>
> . . .
>
> Since it is felt that the conference should be held outside of Monrovia, I go along with you in this respect and will arrange a place outside of Monrovia for that purpose.

International courtesy would require that, as host of the conference, President Tubman also serve as chairman of the meetings. It followed, too, that the Liberian head of state would give the keynote address and propose an agenda to the conference—with his advisers and documents rather close at hand.

In addition, the President was to have a free hand in choosing the exact site for the conference. In that way he could get full political mileage out of his choice. Instead of selecting the facilities of Cuttington College at Gbarnga, about 120 miles from the coast, or even the nearer presidential estate at Totota, he decided upon Sanniquellie. The upcountry town had symbolic value because President Tubman had given his first speech regarding the proposed Associated States of Africa there in February. Moreover, he was expecting that his guests, who would enter Liberia at Monrovia, would have to travel the two hundred miles to Sanniquellie by car. During this long journey the Ghanaian and Guinean delegations could not help but be impressed with the facilities at the Free Port of Monrovia, the Firestone Plantations at Harbel, the German-financed DELIMCO mining operations near the Bong Range, the President's farm at Totota, the Seventh-Day Adventist Academy at Konala, the Agricultural Experimental Station at Suakoko, and the leprosarium and hospital facilities developed at Ganta by the American medical missionary and scholar, George Harley. If the developments along the road did not impress the guests, surely the long journey would at least dispel the notion that Liberian leaders were not fully in control of the tribal hinterland.

Undoubtedly, the terminus itself would be the most impressive sight. The LAMCO operations at Nimba would provide the best proof of Liberia's ability to bring about rapid economic modernization. And for Sékou Touré, in particular, the selection of Sanniquellie was extremely pointed, for in effect it provided international recognition for Liberia's claim to Nimba and its wealth—a claim somewhat disputed by Guinea. Furthermore, the long journey would serve to remind the Guineans that they depended upon the new Liberian highway and the Free Port of Monrovia to get many of the commodities of eastern Guinea into world trade, since the longer route from Guinea's interior to Conakry, its capital and leading port, was too expensive for a country short of vehicles and gasoline.

Gathering for the Conference

President Sékou Touré was the first to arrive in Monrovia, flying in to Spriggs Payne Field on the thirteenth of July via Liberian National Airways.[5] His party was the smallest of the three delegations. It included Saifoulaye Diallo, President of the National Assembly and, despite his noble Foulah ancestry, an early supporter of the outstanding party of French West Africa—the Rassemblement Démocratique Africain (RDA), which originally had a leftist orientation—and of Sékou Touré's associated PDG; Cisse Foda, Secretary of State for Foreign Affairs; Diallo Alpha, secretary-general of the Ministry of Foreign Affairs; and Madame Escalas, the President's secretary and translator.

Prime Minister Nkrumah, who preferred not to fly, arrived the following day on his yacht. His welcome at the Free Port was royal indeed, with a twenty-one-gun salute from Fort Norris and an inspection of a guard of honor. Similar to the welcome Sékou Touré would be receiving from his countrymen near Sanniquellie was the reception Nkrumah received in the Ghanaian community of Monrovia, mainly composed of several thousand Fanti fishermen. "Old Man Yankey," the leader of the group, poured libations and thanked God for bringing the *Osagyefo* (our deliverer) safely to Liberia. Shouts of "Free-dom!" filled the air. Several thousand enthusiastic flag-waving citizens cheered the three heads of government as they drove to

[5] The subsequent details of the arrangements for the conference are taken from the *Listener Daily*, July 10–20, 1959.

the Executive Mansion where they were to spend the night. Signs along the main streets proclaimed the unity of Africa and urged such sentiments as "May the Hinges of Our Friendship Be Always Oiled!"

The party that Kwame Nkrumah brought with him was small but significant. Perhaps the best-known member of the group was George Padmore, the Afro-West Indian author, who as a friend and tutor had helped to shape Nkrumah's thoughts on African nationalism and unity during the Ghanaian's student days in London. Along with Nkrumah, Padmore had served as the joint secretary of the Fifth Pan-African Congress of 1945. He emigrated to Ghana, became a Ghanaian citizen, and now served as Nkrumah's Adviser on African Affairs. Unofficially he was regarded as the principal theoretician of Pan-Africanism.[6] Also in the Ghana delegation was Ako Adjei, Minister of Foreign Affairs and a former fellow student of the Prime Minister's at Lincoln University; Krobo Edusei, Minister of Communications and long the *éminence grise* of Ghanaian politics, particularly in the troubled Ashanti area; A. L. Adu, permanent secretary in the Ministry of Foreign Affairs;[7] and J. H. Allassani, Minister of Guinean Affairs.

Not unexpectedly, the Liberians had the largest delegation. In addition to President Tubman and Vice-President William R. Tolbert, the group included J. Rudolph Grimes, Acting Secretary of State, a cousin of Mrs. Tubman and one of the ablest representatives of the "new look" among Liberian diplomats; Harrison Grigsby, Secretary of the Interior and the person most responsible for the administration of the tribal hinterland; Joseph Chesson, Acting Attorney General; Henry Ford Cooper, Ambassador Extraordinary and Plenipotentiary and one of the President's most reliable advisers on foreign affairs; Ernest Eastman, the bright young director of the State Department's Bureau of African Affairs; C. Abayomi Cassell and T. O. Dosumu Johnson, officially Advisers on African Affairs but also long-time "cronies" of President Tubman; Reginald Townsend, director of the Liberian Information Services; and Liberia's Ambassadors to Ghana and Guinea, Wilmot David and S. Edward Peal.

The twenty-car procession left the Executive Mansion at 8:30 A.M. on the fifteenth. The first stop along the way was the President's personal farm at Totota, where Prime Minister Nkrumah unveiled a statue of President Tubman which had been executed by an Ashanti sculptor, Yaw Boakye.[8]

---

[6] Padmore is the author of *Pan-Africanism or Communism?* (New York: Roy Publishers, 1956). He died before the end of 1959.

[7] Adu subsequently fell from favor and moved away from Ghana to become secretary of the East African High Commission.

[8] In an interview given to the correspondent of the *Listener Daily,* July 20, 1959, the sculptor described the statue. "It is six feet high with two lions beside it. The portrait of President Tubman is mounted on Charles Atlas (sic) with a miniature earth in his left arm. On each side, between the Statue and Charles Atlas, is the seal of the Republic of Liberia, the talking drums of Africa, a praying Angel, and a Moslem."

The meaning of the Statue and the other emblems, Mr. Boakye explained, is as

There was one further stop at Gbarnga, within sight of Cuttington College, where the three chiefs of governments stopped for refreshments and were welcomed by District Commissioner Charles H. Williams and a throng of over three thousand persons who lined the highway between the international control gate and the town. Since Liberia's school year runs from May to December, many of the welcomers were school children, assembled there by their principals since shortly after dawn. The motorcade traveled directly to the new district headquarters building, a rather garish piece of architecture which had cost the citizens of the district over $100,000 to construct. As reported in the *Listener Daily* of July 17,

> A characteristic feature of the occasion was the distribution of the flags of the three Independent States and, as the three leaders stood on the balcony of the Administrative Building, these were waved by the huge crowd in a very emphatic and spectacular manner. The "Big Three" did not fail to show their real appreciation of the gesture by waving, in turn, with their handkerchiefs.
>
> The royal form of welcome was followed by a medley of tribal dances which were executed by members of the crowd and for which they were lustily applauded. After a very enjoyable experience, President Tubman and his distinguished guests retired to the dining room where they engaged in light refreshment.

From Gbarnga to Sanniquellie, seventy miles distance, the fast-moving caravan passed under innumerable arches of wood and dracaena palms which the enthusiastic chiefs had erected for the occasion. The welcome at Sanniquellie exceeded in numbers and enthusiasm the one at Gbarnga. Included in the gathering were many Guineans and Ghanaians who were seeing their national leaders for the first time.

Although the three leaders were undoubtedly fatigued after their journey, they visibly enjoyed the display of "devil" dancing and the lavish spread of "country chop" and other Liberian dishes which had been prepared for the occasion. Indeed so successful a host was Commissioner Allen Williams that he was soon elevated to the post of Undersecretary of the Interior and regarded as one of the coming young leaders of Liberia.

The Sanniquellie Conference

The conference did not formally begin until the morning of the sixteenth. At that time the Liberian chief executive marshalled all the political skill he

---

follows: "President Tubman mounted on Charles Atlas reveals the wisdom and humility of the President. The lion succumbs and gives him honour. The talking drums of Africa stand for the noble achievements of the President to the world. The Angel and praying Moslem symbolize President Tubman's long life."

had developed through more than thirty-five years of infighting in Liberian domestic politics—where mere survival is itself a remarkable feat. The agenda had been carefully constructed to include the Algerian crisis and other matters not related to African unity, thereby ensuring that the conference would end with each faction represented having its share of victories.

It was inevitable that the Liberian host be elected chairman of the conference. President Tubman used the occasion of the welcoming speech to emphasize broad principles of interstate cooperation in the hopes of directing discussion to his own concept of functional cooperation among relatively sovereign states, rather than to the need for accepting political fusion of African states at this stage. His welcoming address, quoted in the *Listener Daily,* July 19–20, began as follows:

> Let me make it clear that we glory in the fact that this is not a meeting to plan and plot the subjugation and suppression of peoples or nations. It is not designated to consult upon and plan the strategy for waging a hostile political, social or economic campaign against any nation, groups of nations or race of peoples. Nor is it intended to be preoccupied with the attainment of any selfish national, political, social, or economic predominance of any one nation or groups of nations over any other nation or nations, nor any one of us over either of us. On the contrary, its primary objective is the quest for a formula or formulas to hasten and effect the liberation and independence of the subjected peoples of our continent; to bring unity and harmony, coherence and mutual understanding among ourselves and our brothers.

Undaunted, Prime Minister Nkrumah in his opening remarks (also quoted in the *Listener Daily*) stressed the point that independence and unity were two inseparable goals, and that one without the other was meaningless. Moreover, in order to achieve either, it was necessary to pursue political goals first. One was reminded at this point of the inscription at the base of his statue in Accra: "Seek ye first the political kingdom and all other things shall be added unto it." Since the formula succeeded so well when Ghana achieved independence from the British, why would it not also succeed for African unity? Only by political unity, the Prime Minister insisted, could Africa overcome the fact that as a people "we have been arbitrarily chopped up into bits and pieces and dissected by artificial boundaries giving rise to all sorts of irridentist problems." Nkrumah went on to say,

> I am sufficiently a realist to know that we cannot achieve overnight a perfect union. It is a formidable task which we have set ourselves and we require all our genius, determination and goodwill to bring it into being. But Gentlemen, I am confident that what the great United States and the Soviet Union have achieved we can also achieve. . . . I feel so strongly that we who are in the vanguard of this great historic mission

> must close our ranks and unite our forces in the closest bond of political unity, not only for our common good but as an inspiration to those countries like Nigeria, the Cameroons, Togoland and Somalia. . . . Let us send them a message of hope that we who are gathered here today have laid the foundation of a mighty edifice in which other African Countries on the attainment of their independence can find a place and enjoy with us peace, happiness, and prosperity, united in all matters of common interest.
>
> Gentlemen, let us not postpone this task of laying the foundation of West African Unity. We the leaders and representatives of Liberia, Guinea, and Ghana . . . must make the beginning NOW. We cannot delay. Time presses. We must start with what we have got. We must build with what we have. If we agree upon this, then this meeting will have been fully rewarded and Heaven will bless our efforts.

While Sékou Touré largely affirmed the hard line put forth by the Ghanaian Prime Minister, the results of the conference confirm unofficial reports that the Guinean leader played a pivotal role in the discussions, mediating between Nkrumah's and Tubman's radically different formulations of the proper means for achieving African unity. Since much of the debate was in English, Touré more than the other two had to rely upon his interpreter. Perhaps it was symbolic of his desire to remain above the fray that throughout the three days of informal discussion he retained his jacket and tie, whereas the other two leaders were seen in open-necked shirts while work was in progress.

Although the details of the jockeying and the exchange of ideas remain classified information, the declaration issued at the end of the meeting had a decidedly Tubman ring to it.[9] Kwame Nkrumah, who had devoted close to two decades to the quest for political unity in Africa, must have felt a profound sense of disappointment as the delegates, at the close of the conference, "formed a circle around the conference table and, clasping hands with each other, raised their hands three times in succession, repeating as they did so the words "Freedom and Unity."

The statements by the "Big Three" on the Cameroons, Algeria, racial discrimination, Southwest Africa, nuclear tests in the Sahara, and other matters not directly relating to African unity clearly reflected the more militant positions of Kwame Nkrumah and Sékou Touré. On each of these issues Liberia's leaders, in the past, either remained silent or took equivocal stands. These statements were obviously included to salve the wounds inflicted by other and more vital sections in the final communiqué.

On the central question of African unity, the Community of Independent African States proposed by the Sanniquellie Conference had none of the supranational characteristics of the Ghana-Guinea Union arrangements of

---

[9] The quotations and other information given below concerning the declaration and the close of the conference are from the September 1959 issue of *Liberia Today*.

November, 1958, or of May, 1959. There was no statement on common citizenship and currency. The common flag and anthem for the community were not to replace the individual flags and anthems of the member states. As in the United Nations,

> each State or Federation which is a member of the Community shall maintain its own national identity and constitutional structure. The Community is being formed with a view to achieving unity among independent African States. It is not designed to prejudice the present or future international policies, relations and obligations of the States involved.

As the editor of *Liberia Today* indicated in the September 1959 issue,

> In this nation-founding period, none of Africa's many George Washingtons wants to play second fiddle to any other [and the clause regarding "national identity"] reflects Liberia's desire to do nothing to compromise her special relationship with the United States. . . . This permits Ghana and Guinea to have a totally different attitude to Israel from that of the Arab-African States.

The victory of Tubman's functional approach was obvious. Although the Community was to set up an economic council, a cultural council, and a scientific and research council, no mention was made of more patently political organs. On the contrary, the declaration contained a number of statements indicating that political union was not intended. It stated:

> Each member of the Community accepts the principle that it shall not interfere in the internal affairs of any other member. . . .
>
> The acts of States or Federations which are members of the Community shall be determined in relation to the essential objectives which are Freedom, Independence, Unity, the African Personality, as well as the interest of the African Peoples. . . .
>
> Policy shall be based essentially on the maintenance of diplomatic, economic, and cultural relations, on the basis of equality and reciprocity with all the States of the World which adopt a position compatible with African interest and African independence.

The actual charter for the community was to be drafted at a conference in 1960 of all Independent African States and states having fixed dates for independence. The conference was never convened, however.

The Sanniquellie Conference was concluded on July 18. President Touré left by car for Conakry, crossing the border near Sanniquellie. Prime Minister Nkrumah and President Tubman's motorcades returned to Monrovia, and the Ghanaian leader returned home on his yacht. Perhaps as he departed the full implication of the conference had not yet become apparent to him. In view of the subsequent fate of his version of Pan-Africanism, his words of farewell were prophetic in a way he never intended:

> This declaration here today is more than an atomic bomb, for ideas are stronger than weapons of war. This continent of ours from now on can never be the same. It is changed forever. Let us in oneness of purpose and unity of spirit maintain the initiative which we have taken. If we do not stand firmly together this document will not be worthy of the time and energy we have put into it. Let the history which Sanniquellie has made stand forever.

The Aftermath

The full significance of the Sanniquellie meeting of 1959 could not be seen immediately even by the delegates who participated in the discussions. It took four more years and, finally, the signing of the Charter of the Organization of African Unity, to reveal the Sanniquellie Conference as the landmark it was. For the charter signed at Addis Ababa on May 25, 1963, was essentially a triumph of the functional approach to African unity put forward by President William V. S. Tubman of Liberia.

The Ghanaian attitude toward the 1959 meeting in the Liberian hinterland went through several transformations during the next few years. Initially, the Ghanaians treated it matter-of-factly, as another step in the general direction of African unity. The August 15, 1959, issue of *Ghana Today,* for example, saw the Sanniquellie statements as highly provisional. Its cover article began,

> The leaders of Ghana and the Republics of Liberia and Guinea have proposed a special conference in 1960. It will be attended by Independent States of Africa as well as others with fixed dates for independence and the aim will be to form a community of independent African States.

The failure to capitalize "community" indicated Ghanaian reluctance to regard the union proposed at Sanniquellie as a thing of substance.

The realization that other African leaders were beginning to regard the Sanniquellie Conference as a defeat for the Nkrumah version of unity required that the Ghanaians employ another tactic. This consisted of ignoring the Sanniquellie Conference and its implications entirely. Less than a month after the July 1959 meeting, Ghanaian silence regarding Sanniquellie was indeed noticeable at the Conference of Foreign Ministers of Independent African States in Monrovia. Foreign Minister Ako Adjei, who had accompanied Prime Minister Nkrumah to the meeting in the interior of Liberia, made no reference to the joint declaration of July 18 and only casually mentioned that he had even been to Liberia recently. The conference at Monrovia during August, moreover, was startling in that not a single resolution was proposed regarding the very burning question of African unity. When Ako Adjei was compelled publicly to refer to the Sanniquellie Conference, as he was at Addis Ababa for the Second Conference of Independent African States in June, 1960, he gave a rather curious interpretation of the name of the organization and of the events which took place in Sanniquellie:

> It is clear from this declaration of principles . . . that the Union of African States, which the three leaders discussed and agreed upon, is intended to be a political Union. Such a political Union, in their view, will provide the framework within which any plans for economic, social and cultural co-operation can, in fact, operate to the best advantage of all.
>
> To us in Ghana, the concept of African Unity is an article of faith. It is a cardinal objective in our national policy. We sincerely believe that the Independent African States can, and may some day, form a real political union—the Union of African States.[10]

The defeat at Sanniquellie compelled Kwame Nkrumah to push harder his approach to unity as an essentially political act. To indicate Ghana's commitment on this score, the republican constitution adopted in 1960 specifically provided for the surrender, in whole or in part, of Ghana's sovereignty to a Union of African States. At the end of 1960, furthermore, Kwame Nkrumah and the other more militant African leaders decided to counter the effect not only of Sanniquellie, but of the recently formed Brazzaville bloc, which brought together for purposes of functional unity most of the members (except Guinea and Mali) of the former French West and French Equatorial African Federations and Malagasy (formerly Madagascar). At the suggestion of the then Sultan of Morocco, Mohammed V, a meeting was called at Casablanca to discuss the Congo and other matters. It was an exclusive gathering, to which only Ghana, Guinea, Mali, Morocco, Egypt, Libya, Liberia, and representatives of the Algerian rebels were invited. If Liberia needed any indication of the way this particular gathering would deal with the problem of African unity, it was vividly provided by the declaration issued by the Presidents of Ghana, Guinea, and Mali on the eve of the Casablanca meeting. That declaration, issued at Conakry on December 24, proposed the enlargement of the Ghana-Guinea Union to include Mali. There were to be regular meetings of the three heads of state, and the promotion of a common economic and monetary policy. The three leaders also "deplored the attitude taken by certain African Heads of State whose recent stand is likely to jeopardize the unity of Africa and strengthen neo-colonialism."[11] Although that statement was intended primarily for the Brazzaville bloc, it also referred indirectly to the approach to unity advocated by President Tubman.

Even before the meeting in Conakry, however, President Tubman had indicated to Mohammed V that he felt that the exclusion of Nigeria, Senegal,

---

[10] Colin Legum, *Pan-Africanism* (New York: Praeger, 1962), p. 170.
[11] *Ibid.*, p. 175.

and Tunisia from the Casablanca Conference would cause a further breach in the African unity movement. The President in his press conference of December 29 (reported the next day in the *Liberian Age*) said that he "could not support a policy of picking and choosing among African nations especially when those countries [Nigeria and Tunisia] had troops in the Congo."

In any case, Tubman found it impractical to leave Liberia at that time and did not go to Casablanca. He knew that there were unstated reasons for the meeting, and that it constituted a "trap." To the surprise of no one, the Casablanca resolutions of January 7, 1961, came out strongly in support of the political-first approach, and the Congo situation—the supposed reason for the conference—was the last item on the agenda.

Whatever success the Casablanca participants achieved in clarifying their own ideological stance on Pan-Africanism and other issues, the conference unintentionally succeeded in intensifying the isolation of Ghana, Guinea, and Mali from the mainstream of thought among leaders in sub-Saharan Africa. The majority of these leaders emphasized functional unity, with political unity—if conceived at all at this stage—desirable only on a limited regional basis. President Tubman found himself in the center of the main stream that equates Pan-Africanism with functional cooperation. Following the Sanniquellie Conference, Tubman increasingly attempted to provide more specific content to his proposal, indicating more clearly the nature and purpose of the new community. In the Inaugural Address for his fourth term, given on January 4, 1960, and in subsequent speeches, he suggested that regional (rather than continental) councils be created to stimulate investment, facilitate regional exchange of commodities, and bring about the common training of African personnel for government, business, schools, and hospitals. He proposed calling these councils "Organizations for West African Cooperation." He further suggested that with United Nations support the states in West Africa could do much more by way of sharing their facilities of higher education.

To enlist support for his approach to African unity, President Tubman attempted to get each head of state or government who visited Liberia to subscribe to his point of view. The *Liberian Age* between July and December, 1960, recorded a steady stream of visiting African leaders (whose presence gave some support for the Tubman approach). Sir Milton Margai of Sierra Leone, President Philibert Tsiranana of the Malagasy Republic, and a Nigerian parliamentary delegation might have been expected to support Tubman's notion of a looser association of states. On the other hand, the commitment of the Congo's Patrice Lumumba, Mali's Modibo Keita, and Senegal's Léopold Senghor to this "soft" approach, as suggested in the joint communiqués at the end of each visit, was dubious. In fact, President Senghor in Ghana, several days after his visit to Monrovia, found himself being quoted as a supporter of the Nkrumah political-first approach.

The most startling apparent acquiescence to Tubman's point of view, however, was reported in the *Liberian Age* on May 30, 1960, during President Tubman's state visit to Guinea. A joint statement from Tubman and Sékou Touré indicated that "there exist no boundary disputes between their two countries and that they will recognize the same territorial limitations as existed before the independence of Guinea," and the two heads of state

> re-affirmed their complete adherence to the Declaration and Resolutions of . . . the Sanniquellie Conference in July, 1959. . . . In their determination to achieve African Unity, understanding and mutual cooperation, the two Presidents pledged themselves to recommend to all African States . . . to consider some inter-state Agreement for the permanent settlement of inter-African disputes and also for mutual defense.
>
> The two Heads of State further agreed that the forms of African solidarity should be developed through cooperation among the African States within specific fields of common interests.

Sanniquellie was not only significant in a general Pan-African sense; it also marked the beginning of a much more active role for the Liberian government in African affairs. Liberia tried to establish embassies in each new African state as it achieved independence. The Liberians strove, moreover, to assume the leadership of the African bloc in the United Nations, taking the initiative in condemning colonialism and apartheid in South Africa, and in furthering other African causes. This reversal of the traditionally isolationist Liberian role was dramatically confirmed in late 1960 when Liberia became the first African state elected to the Security Council of the United Nations. In view of the long-standing ties between Liberia and America, it was curious that Liberia should inadvertently find its campaign strengthened by United States reluctance to support Liberia. In this contest the Eisenhower administration in its last month of existence decided to support Portugal, which had only recently been condemned by the General Assembly for its colonial policies. Thus Liberia was somewhat freed of the charge that it was an American "satellite."

Liberia's greatest success in advancing functional unity for Africa came in the series of inter-African conferences leading up to the Addis Ababa meeting of May, 1963. The first of these meetings was in May, 1961, and President Tubman was once again operating on his home grounds. The Monrovia Conference of May, 1961, was initially proposed to eliminate the grouping of African states into the two blocs: the Brazzaville bloc, whose position had been solidified by the creation of the Union of African and Malagasy States and the Afro-Malagasy Economic Cooperation Organization; and the Casablanca bloc, which planned tighter political and economic unity. The Monrovia Conference in fact only succeeded in adding a third bloc, with membership that was drawn from both the preceding blocs (Libya, for example) as well as including states belonging to neither, such as Nigeria, Sierra Leone, Tanganyika, and Liberia. The Casablanca powers (with the exception of Libya) decided to withdraw at the last minute, although initially they had agreed to sponsor the gathering. Obviously both Kwame Nkrumah and Abdel Nasser realized they would be outvoted in such a large assembly of moderates. Some of the resolutions of the twenty-state conference were, in fact, obviously directed against the principle that one African leader should attempt to monopolize the position of leadership in the quest for African unity and peace.

Moreover, the resolutions of May 12 regarding relations among the states represented at Monrovia differed markedly from those agreed upon by the Casablanca powers in a meeting at Cairo the week before. Concerning noninterference in the internal affairs of members and subversion from neighboring territories, for instance, the Monrovia Conference recognized "respect for the sovereignty of each State and its inalienable right to existence and development of its personality." Most significant, however, was the statement in the resolution passed by the Monrovia Conference: "The Unity that is aimed to be achieved at the moment is not the political integration of sovereign African States, but unity of aspirations and of action considered from the point of view of African social solidarity and political identity."[12]

The 1962 round of inter-African conferences essentially constituted further sparring between the Monrovia and Casablanca groups. The former met at Lagos, in a conference to which all independent African states had been invited. The Casablanca group again decided at the last minute not to attend and instead held its own conference two weeks later. Although the Lagos conference did not formally approve the Liberian draft proposal to create an Organization of African and Malagasy States, the conference did accept the idea in principle, and it recommended that its foreign ministers consider the matter at a later date. Not to be outdone, the Casablanca bloc moved to establish an African Military High Command in Ghana and inaugurate an African Common Market.

Not until the Addis Ababa Conference of May, 1963, were the two opposing camps brought together to consider, among other things, the issue of African unity. On this occasion the leaders of the Casablanca bloc felt obliged to join the ever increasing number of states that adhered to the Monrovia group or, like Tanganyika, abhorred the division of Africa into blocs. The militants, however, were at a disadvantage, for their forces were in disarray. The Ghana-Guinea-Mali union had never advanced far beyond the blueprint stage; the secession of Syria had left the United Arab Republic a "union" of only one state; Guinea was engaged in an agonizing reappraisal of its ties with France and with the Soviet Union following the dismissal of

---

[12] *Ibid.*, p. 198.

the Russian ambassador on charges of interference in Guinean internal affairs; and, finally, the pragmatic cleavages between Sékou Touré and Kwame Nkrumah were becoming ever more apparent. Indeed, one of the side issues at the Addis Ababa Conference dramatized the tenuous character of the Ghana-Guinea alliance. The issue concerned the seating of Nicholas Grunitsky as the representative of Togo. Grunitsky had only recently succeeded the assassinated Sylvanus Olympio as President of Togo. Inasmuch as Nkrumah and Olympio had long been feuding, it was suspected by many African leaders that Ghanaians had played a role in Olympio's murder and that this was further evidence of Ghana's interference in the internal affairs of its neighbors. The possibility that Ghana might find itself entirely isolated at the conference became all too apparent when Guinea voted against its ally, Ghana, in rejecting the claims of Grunitsky to a seat at the conference table.

Nkrumah recognized that the sentiment at the conference was running against him. Although the speeches of Kwame Nkrumah indicated no deviation from his conviction that "African Unity is above all a political kingdom which can only be gained by political means,"[13] it was apparent that he had either to acquiesce in the decision of the majority to pursue functional unity or to suffer the consequences of isolation. As the figure in the cartoon of the French Revolution of 1848 was forced to say: "There is the crowd; I must follow them, for I am their leader."

Although many of the thirty delegations present at Addis Ababa contributed to the drafting of the Charter of the Organization of African Unity, it is watermarked "Made in Liberia." The Assembly of Heads of State, the Council of Foreign Ministers, the Secretariat, and other institutions created by the Charter are, in one sense, "political"—they do discuss political problems. But the charter does not bind member states to surrender their political authority in advance to these institutions at the continental level. The key words in the charter speak of the adherence of the Organization of African Unity to the principle of "the sovereign equality of all Member States," and the primary powers of its institutions are simply to discuss and to review. The unity sought for is still the unity of the future.

Hence, the course which President Tubman and the Liberian True Whigs had chosen in order to preserve their own domestic situation had now found acceptance among the majority of the leaders of the new Africa. For good or evil, the role that Sanniquellie played in this ultimate acceptance of the functional approach to African unity cannot be overstated. Coming as it did upon the eve of the Year of African Independence—1960—it had a profound effect upon the leaders of the new states, who recognized the popularity of the idea of Pan-Africanism among the intellectuals and the

[13] For a discussion of the main points of the conference, see Boutros Boutros-Ghali, "The Addis Ababa Charter," *International Conciliation,* No. 546 (January, 1964).

masses within their respective states. Sanniquellie gave them an alternative to the Ghana-Guinea Union model, which at the time of its dramatic announcement had seemed to clear all other considerations off the board. Sanniquellie also bought time for the leaders of the newest states, assuring them that the critical unity negotiations taking place in the future would be negotiations among relatively equal bargaining partners who had acquired experience in dealing with governmental problems and who knew what they would gain or lose by closer political union at the continental, or even the regional, level.

In the two years following the Addis Ababa Conference of 1963, the fortunes of those seeking political unity at the continental level waned considerably. The Organization of African Unity seemed to have the unintended effect of publicizing the divergent political views within the African community instead of bringing the states and blocs closer together. The OAU seemed singularly incapable of taking united action on purely intra-African problems such as the recurrent crisis of the Congo or the many boundary disputes (for instance, the one which threatened the peace between Somalia and its neighbors, Kenya and Ethiopia). Indeed, even the opportunity to meet and discuss their common problems was challenged by the French-speaking African bloc's threatened boycott of the Accra summit meeting planned for October, 1965. Pursuing a recurrent theme, it was now Upper Volta, Niger, and the Ivory Coast that charged Kwame Nkrumah with interference in their internal affairs. Only following Ghanaian assurances at a hastily called meeting of foreign ministers at Lagos that Ghana would guarantee the safety of delegates and send away dangerous refugees did the French-speaking bloc agree to attend the Accra meeting.

By the spring of 1965 the functional-regional approach was also in a somewhat uncertain state. On the credit side of the ledger were two events which occurred in May, 1965. The first extended the area of cooperation among the French-speaking states by the admission of Moise Tshombe's Congo (Leopoldville) to the ranks of those states which had been previously seeking a wider measure of economic, educational, and social cooperation through the Organisation Commune Africaine et Malagache (OCAM). The action of the OCAM bloc, however, had many complex overtones, and had to be evaluated in the context of the hostility of the more moderate French-speaking states to the policies of Ghana, the United Arab Republic, and Uganda regarding the Congo crisis.

The second event which appeared to enhance the prospect of functional-regional cooperation came with the announcement that Sékou Touré—undoubtedly to the extreme chagrin of his erstwhile ally, Nkrumah—had elected to join President Tubman, Sir Albert Margai of Sierra Leone (who had become Prime Minister upon the death of his brother, Milton), and Félix Houphouet-Boigny of the Ivory Coast in an agreement to create an interim organization leading ultimately to an Organization for West African

Economic Cooperation. According to *West Africa,* June 12, 1965, the interim organization was to be responsible for planning

> a multilateral system of economic cooperation of a regional character with a view to removing trade barriers and encouraging the harmonious development of the co-operating states in every field. [It would undertake studies regarding] economic development targets with specific reference to agricultural and industrial development, trade and customs problems, markets and marketing difficulties, monetary, financial and payments arrangements, fiscal systems in force in the four states, development of transport and communication facilities and existing barriers to economic cooperation.

This too, however, had to be placed in its proper perspective. Essentially it was precisely what President Tubman had been advocating for more than half a decade, and it was already provided for in previous agreements.

Indeed, the optimism engendered by the decision of four West African states to study and discuss ways of functional-regional cooperation was more than offset by the action taken by three East African states to undo the measure of functional-regional cooperation they had already achieved. By a series of acts in the spring of 1965, Tanzania (itself a political union between Tanganyika and Zanzibar), Kenya, and Uganda were indicating that they preferred to pursue independent courses of action in education, currency, customs, and other fields. Thus the whole structure of economic, cultural, and social cooperation embodied in the Common Services Organization was in jeopardy.[14]

The rather harsh conclusion that must be drawn is that the prospects for genuine unity within Africa were becoming increasingly dim despite the fact that everywhere in Africa Pan-Africanism as a vague symbol seemed to be flourishing. Unquestionably, however, the leadership of each of the new states was giving the concept a strictly domestic interpretation, and it usually meant little more than a desire to cooperate with one's African neighbors. It seemed to be difficult indeed to translate this vague commodity into the hard reality of concrete political or economic union.

With the single exception of the union of Tanganyika and Zanzibar in 1964, all other actual political unions (Ethiopia and Eritrea; Ghana and British Togoland; Italian and British Somaliland; the division of British Cameroons between Nigeria and the former French Cameroun; and the short-lived Mali Federation that joined Senegal and Mali) took place before one or more of the parties had achieved its independence. In the case of other proposed unions (the East African federation; the creation of a Greater Maghreb, joining Tunisia, Morocco, and Algeria; and the union of Senegal and Gambia), the discussion became noticeably muted after each of the proposed partners had achieved independence. Once a nationalist

---

[14] For a discussion of the Common Services Organization, see Chapter 6.

group has managed (often against great odds) to wrest the control of the machinery of state from a colonial power, it is reluctant to turn over the distribution of the fruits of that struggle to an "alien" group of Africans.

A long and protracted struggle against Britain and France might have served to weld the people of the several states into a common political group. Britain and France, however, capitulated to the nationalists as soon as they appreciated the strength of their political movements. Not only have they managed—with only a few exceptions, such as Guinea—to make the transition to independence a peaceful one; they have also continued to serve as the main source for investment capital, technical skills, and education for African nationals, and as the chief markets for African commodities. Under these circumstances it has been difficult to cast either Britain or France in the role of "the enemy at the gate," a role thought to be necessary for the consolidation of national feeling in other quarters of the globe. Despite the constant discussion of the "neocolonialist" threat, moreover, South Africa, Portugal, Belgium, the United States, and the Soviet Union have each proved to be ineffective as the "external menace" that would bring about Pan-African political unity.

The path to functional-regional unity has also proved difficult. Although language for the purposes of higher education and for administration has not been a barrier to cooperation among the French-speaking states and was not an obstacle to federation in East Africa, there is still relatively little communication, trade, or social exchange within West Africa across the arbitrary linguistic boundaries which colonial rule imposed upon that area. The differing colonial pattern is not a sufficient explanation for the failure of the new African states to cooperate in economic terms even though it must be realized that habit, subsidies for various commodities in French markets, and other inducements serve to perpetuate the preexisting colonial economic relationships. The fact is, however, that nature itself has made inapplicable for West Africa both the American example of union in 1787 and the present European Common Market. Regionally, African economies are more competitive than complementary. Neighbors are trying to eke out their share of the world's markets for the same minerals and the same agricultural commodities. The only areas in Africa with any immediate prospect of industrialization are—apart from Nigeria—areas in which European minorities continue to control the destinies of Africans (South Africa, Rhodesia, and Angola) and the crisis-ridden Congo, where unity within the state is a far greater issue than external cooperation. In the areas with limited prospects of industrialization, the local nationalist regimes have undoubtedly come to power on the promise of increasing economic benefits to the masses. It would take a courageous and militarily strong regime (which very few African states possess) to ask one's own people to forego the production of scarce resources because the short-term sacrifice might produce a long-term benefit for the citizens of all the cooperating states. The typical regime is too unstable to ask for economic self-sacrifice, as the late Sylvanus Olympio must have realized, and as Julius Nyerere of Tanzania apparently did realize, as he saw advantages go to the more industrialized Kenya economy within the developing East African market. This is not to argue that internal trade and investment will not increase within Africa, but that it will be some time before a stabilized Congo or an industrialized Nigeria or Ghana begins to make an appreciable change in the present economic relations between Europe and Africa.

It is a matter of speculation whether the imaginative forging of a political union of African states might eventually have brushed all economic and cultural arguments aside and made Pan-Africanism a reality. To those like Kwame Nkrumah who felt—and feel—that the only correct course is political-continental union now, however imperfect the details of such a union might be at the outset, the Sanniquellie Conference and its aftermath must stand as a betrayal of Pan-Africanism. It also is a matter of speculation whether Africa would be better or worse off had the will of Africa's foremost visionary—Nkrumah—prevailed over the wiles of one of Africa's foremost politicians—Tubman.

Study Questions

1. What were the domestic and international problems faced by the Liberian leaders in the 1950s that led to a reversal of Liberia's previous role in African politics?

2. Did Kwame Nkrumah and Sékou Touré pursue the political-continental unity approach for the same reasons? What eventually led Guinea to change its commitment and join forces with Liberia, the Ivory Coast, and Sierra Leone?

3. Does the American experience of 1787 provide a good analogy to African continental unity? In what way were the situations similar and in what way were they divergent?

4. How far does the charter of the Organization of African Unity go in unifying the new states of Africa?

5. Did the fact that African states had differing colonial experiences and became independent at different times influence the outcome of the quest for African unity?

Selected Bibliography

For further reading on the domestic political situation that conditioned the responses of the three principal countries involved in this study, see L. Gray Cowan's chapter on Guinea and my chapter on Liberia in Gwendolen M.

Carter, ed., *African One-Party States* (Ithaca, N.Y.: Cornell University Press, 1962); Cowan's case study on the Ghanaian struggle for independence, in John G. Stoessinger and Alan F. Westin, eds., *Power and Order: 6 Cases in World Politics* (New York: Harcourt, Brace & World, 1964); David Apter, *Ghana in Transition* (New York: Atheneum, 1963); and my chapter on Liberia in James S. Coleman and Carl G. Rosberg, Jr., eds., *Political Parties and National Integration in Tropical Africa* (Berkeley: University of California Press, 1964).

The general background of the African independence movement and the forces leading to the development of nationalism are well covered in Thomas Hodgkin, *Nationalism in Colonial Africa* (London: Muller, 1956) and Rupert Emerson, *From Empire to Nation: The Rise of Self-Assertion of Asian and African People* (Cambridge, Mass.: Harvard University Press, 1960).

A useful compendium, indicating the historical development of Pan-Africanism, its current problems, and the positions of various African leaders, is the American Society of African Culture, ed., *Pan-Africanism Reconsidered* (Berkeley: University of California Press, 1962). Documents relevant to the various conferences leading up to the establishment of the OAU and other commentaries by African leaders are contained in Colin Legum, *Pan-Africanism: A Short Political Guide* (New York: Praeger, 1962).

The continental-political-union-now position on Pan-Africanism is perhaps best appreciated through reading George Padmore, *Pan-Africanism or Communism?* (New York: Roy Publishers, 1956) and Kwame Nkrumah, *Africa Must Unite* (New York: Praeger, 1963).

For a more general treatment of the problems of unity and national integration at the suprastate level see Karl W. Deutsch *et al., Political Community and the North Atlantic Area* (Princeton, N.J.: Princeton University Press, 1957).

Acknowledgments

This manuscript is based partly on field research conducted in Liberia through the generous support of the Social Science Research Council and the Carnegie Seminar at Indiana University.

2

An Early Failure of Pan-Africanism

The Mali Federation, 1959-60

William J. Foltz

"It is high time for the world to take African political leaders seriously," began Léopold Senghor, presiding officer of the Federal Assembly of the Mali Federation. It was the evening of June 19, 1960, as the Assembly met in formal session to declare the recent union of Senegal and Soudan independent of France. The handsome building was packed with the representatives of Mali's constituent territories, and a choice position on the dais was given to the high level delegation sent by General de Gaulle to convey his blessing on the first of France's Black African colonies to achieve independence by amicable agreement. In his elegant French, the Senegalese leader and former professor lectured his audience on the importance of the new federal union that the two former colonies had joined in, and emphasized not only the joys, but the costs and burdens that independence would bring. "For it is now that our difficulties are born, that problems will arise."

In response to Senghor's words, the Federal Assembly approached its task in a dignified, matter-of-fact manner, applauding but refraining from any undisciplined outburst. When Modibo Keita, political leader of Soudan and Premier of the Federation, bluntly outlined the increased efforts and sacrifices that would be required of all Senegalese and Soudanese "to make our political and economic independence real," he was greeted with the same considered reserve. It fell to Lamine Guèye, the Senegalese dean of African politicians, whose only concession to his seventy years was a slight stoop in his tall frame, to rouse the joyous enthusiasm of the Assembly by triumphantly leading the unanimous vote for independence as the clock struck midnight, June 20.

Throughout the day the people of Dakar had echoed their leaders' restraint. The nineteenth had been like any other hot Sunday in June. The African population of the city had spent the day at the wrestling matches or gone to the countryside to help with sowing the peanut crop; the European residents had left the city for its beaches. Three hundred miles inland in Bamako, the capital of Soudan, the people had been treated to a succession of political meetings explaining the importance of independence for the Federation, but discipline and sobriety more than wild enthusiasm had been the order of the day.

It was not until the morning of the twentieth that the citizens of the independent Federation of Mali finally showed their emotions. Assembled in Dakar in front of what the day before had been the French High Commissioner's Residence, they burst into wild dancing applause as the Federation's flag—vertical bands of green, yellow, and red, with a matchstick figure of a black man in the center—was raised over what was now to be the palace of the Federation's president. At last a black chief of state was going to rule where previously a succession of French governors general and high commissioners had laid down the law for French West Africa.

Who the first African resident of the palace was to be had not yet been decided, although the Dakar crowd knew that Senghor and Modibo Keita were the obvious candidates. But in fact the palace was never to be occupied by a chief of state of the Mali Federation. Precisely two months after the day of independence, on the eve of the meeting to choose between the Senegalese and Soudanese candidates for the Federation's highest post, Senegal unilaterally declared the Federation dissolved and arrested the Soudanese leaders. When Léopold Senghor moved into the palace, it was as President only of the independent Republic of Senegal.

The breakup of the Mali Federation on August 20, 1960, put an end to one of nationalist Africa's cherished myths, that Pan-African unity would be easy to achieve once independence came. It also marked the beginning of the split between "moderate" and "revolutionary" Africa that was soon to be formalized in the creation of the Monrovia and Casablanca groups. Outside commentators promptly imposed their own interpretations on the unhappy events of Dakar. For the right-wing European press this offered one more proof (if it needed any more) that Africans were incapable of governing themselves. For the left-wing press, the breakup demonstrated the nefarious interference of European neocolonialism in African affairs. More detached observers, in Africa and elsewhere, put the finger on different factors: the incompatibility of Soudan's revolutionary and Senegal's reforming ideologies; personal quarrels between Federation leaders; intervention of traditionalist forces; and perhaps, most insistently, what Senghor has called African micronationalism, the feeling of each African political unit, no mat-

French West Africa, 1958

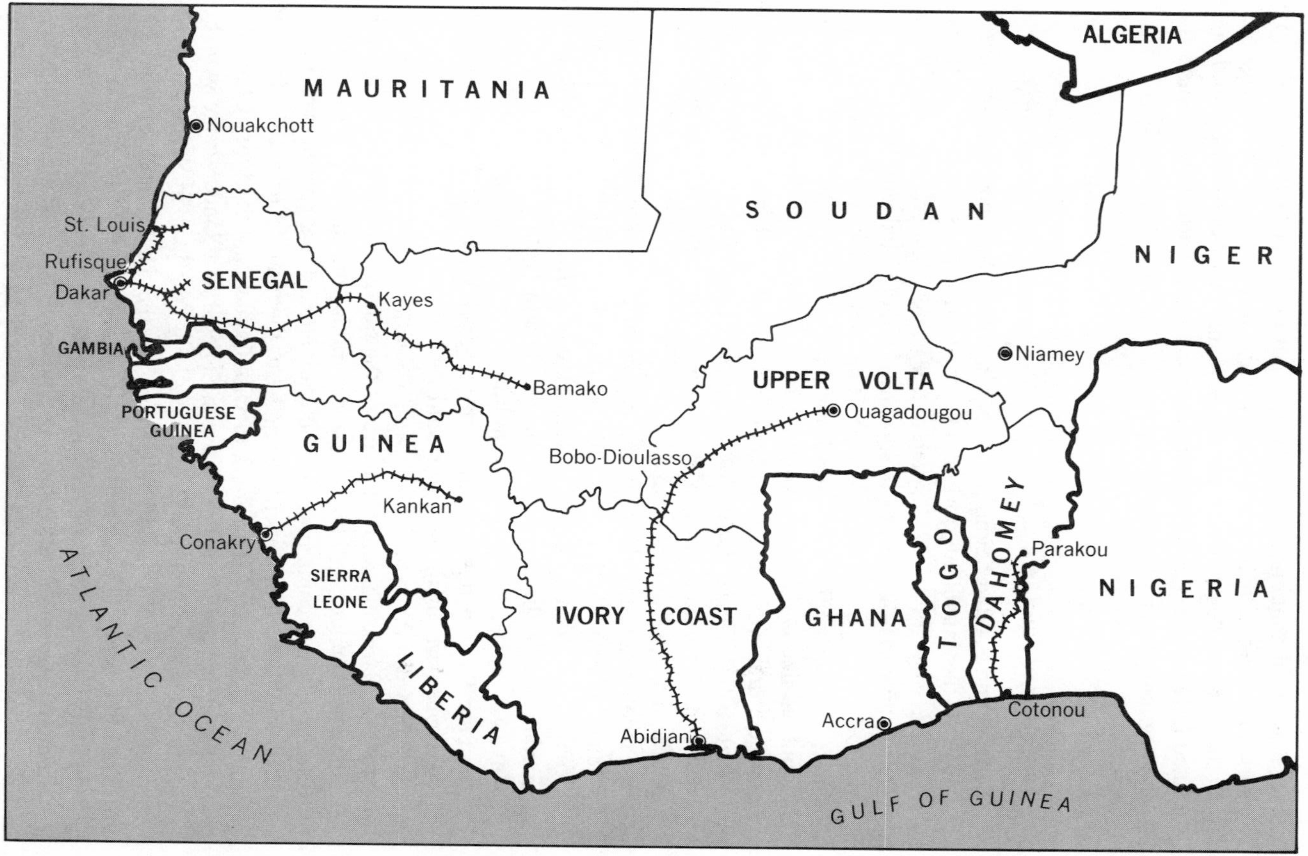

ter how small, that once the colonialist power was gone it was under no obligation to take orders from anyone. Modibo Keita accused the Senegalese and French of an illegal "coup de force," and Senghor retorted that he had acted only to forestall a Soudanese coup d'état. Perhaps we should start at the beginning . . . .

Senegal and Soudan

Senegal and Soudan belong to the same general Sudanese cultural area, and most of the inhabited portion of each territory is covered with typical savanna vegetation, i.e., scattered trees and high green grass during the yearly rainy season, turning to sere brown and dotted with brush fires during the December-to-June dry season. The Senegalese and Soudanese people share marked similarities in traditional social organization with neighboring countries like Guinea and Upper Volta, although locally important ethnic and cultural differences exist both between and within each territory. Whereas for Senegal the Wolof language is the lingua franca among its half-dozen major ethnic groups, Bambara is the lingua franca over much of southern and western Soudan.

Precolonial history brought the people of the two territories into sporadic contact. During the thirteenth and fourteenth centuries much of present-day Senegal was ruled by the Mali Empire controlled by the Malinke people of Soudan, and in the first half of the nineteenth century much of central Soudan was conquered by the Muslim holy man, El Hadj Omar Tall, who came from the Tukulor region of the Senegal River Valley. None of these political units was permanent, however, and throughout most of their history relations between the Wolof, Serer, and Tukulor of the Senegalese area, and the Malinke, Sarakolle, and Bambara of the Soudan, were marked by quiet indifference punctuated by occasional raids and limited wars. The great Dioula trading community of Soudan carried on commercial operations throughout much of eastern Senegal, but the main focus of their interest was in their trade across the Sahara or with Guinea and the Ivory Coast.

The first continuous link between Senegal and Soudan came with French conquest and commerce. From their long-time base in Senegal the French penetrated steadily inland to conquer in the 1890s most of what became French Soudan. They soon built the Dakar-Niger railway, linking first Kayes and then Bamako with the Senegalese port, and they established branches of French Senegalese trading firms in Soudanese towns along the railroad. With the rapid extension of peanut culture in Senegal in the early twentieth century, Soudanese seasonal laborers were imported annually to help in the peanut fields.

But the closest links established by the French between Senegal and Soudan were administrative and political. Dakar was made the capital of the administrative federation of French West Africa (Afrique Occidentale Française or AOF) in 1904, and from there the Governor General ruled the eight territories France had conquered in West Africa. Under the Fourth Republic, established in 1946, all the constituent territories sent representatives to the Grand Council of AOF, which met in Dakar to consider federation-wide problems. Moreover, the political leaders of these territories came into instant contact with each other as deputies to the French National Assembly in Paris. Of the Senegalese leaders, Lamine Guèye led the African members of the French Socialist Party (SFIO), and Léopold Senghor led the grouping of Overseas Independent deputies. Modibo Keita of Soudan emerged as one of the chief lieutenants of the Ivory Coast's Houphouet-Boigny, the leader of the African Democratic Rally (RDA), the most powerful of the three West African interterritorial political groups.

For all the common experience imposed upon them by the colonial regime, however, Senegal and Soudan brought to the Mali Federation substantially different political traditions. As Senghor once reminded the Soudanese:

> A different face on Colonization, a different treatment by the Colonizer . . . have augmented our differences. Without mentioning that our political education . . . has been different for fifteen years. All these differences have created divergent sociological conditions: habits, mentalities, and psychological reactions.[1]

The Mali Federation brought together two different political processes, each of which molded the behavior and expectations of its own participants in the Federal government. The differences proved too great to be overbridged.

Senegal

Nowhere in West Africa has French influence been more thoroughly implanted than in Senegal, and nowhere has it been more thoroughly combined with the predispositions of the African population. The first permanent French settlement, St. Louis, went back to 1659. By the end of the nineteenth century French citizenship and extensive political and civil rights were extended to all inhabitants of the four coastal cities, or "communes"—St. Louis, Rufisque, Gorée, and Dakar. These communes elected municipal authorities and sent representatives to a colonial council and a deputy to the French National Assembly. Although political assimilation was limited to the privileged few living in the communes, the interior regions were brought under a system of direct administration that almost everywhere destroyed or severely weakened traditional political institutions.

[1] This case study is adapted from William J. Foltz, *From French West Africa to the Mali Federation* (New Haven: Yale University Press, 1965). A detailed bibliography of African political sources appears in that volume.

Along with its political privileges, Senegal consistently ranked first among the French West African territories on all indicators of economic and social progress. By World War II, 10 percent of Senegal's children attended school; it had three secondary schools and the federal normal school. Before World War II Senegalese were almost the only French West Africans educated in France. Lamine Guèye was the first African Doctor of Laws and Léopold Senghor was the only African to receive the *agrégation* degree.

Although the French did not succeed in creating a nation of black Frenchmen in Senegal, much less of the master-servant relationship between the two races existed than elsewhere in Africa. Nor was this a recent product of political evolution. In the 1920s an American political scientist noted with some dismay that a white passenger had no special claim on a seat even in a first-class railway carriage and that African councillors "unmercifully criticized European officials."[2]

Senegalese politics grew out of the four communes and their tradition of self-government and representation in France. When political life was reborn in French West Africa after World War II, the coastal communes continued their political preeminence under the leadership of Lamine Guèye's Senegalese branch of the French Socialist Party (SFIO). His protégé, Léopold Senghor, broke from the SFIO in 1948 to form an opposition party, the Senegalese Democratic Bloc (BDS), based primarily on the newly enfranchised bush electors and on the new populations flooding the urban areas. To obtain their allegiance Senghor first sought the support of the notables of the interior and the various regional, ethnic, religious, cultural, and occupational protective societies that had grown up since the war. In particular he sought and obtained the backing of the Muslim leaders. Thus, the traditions of local responsibility and of intraparty bargaining among local leaders were well established. Although denied much power of initiative, these intraparty interest groups, called *clans* in Senegal, often set policy limits beyond which the territorial leaders could not go without risk of having their plans sabotaged on the local level.

The BDS of Senghor and his lieutenant, Mamadou Dia, grew in influence over the years by incorporating other political parties. When Lamine Guèye's Socialists finally joined it in 1958, it attained a position of overwhelming electoral preeminence under the name of Senegalese Progressive Union (UPS). While the party hierarchy was able to strengthen its hold over the local *clans*—particularly once it gained access to governmental patronage and coercive resources—the incorporation of new groups increased the number of cleavages within the party structure. The fight for influence between old Socialists and ex-BDS members had been particularly sharp in the cities where once the party of Lamine Guèye held sway.

Despite frequent appeals for "party solidarity" or "union behind our

[2] R. L. Buell, *The Native Problem in Africa,* I (New York: Macmillan, 1928), 980.

leaders," the UPS leaders accepted the open expression of diversity as a normal aspect of party life, so long as the electoral aims of the party were not compromised. Thus Mamadou Dia announced to a party congress: "all those assembled here, each and every one, [have] the right, precisely because we share common objectives, to come here and express the most diverse, the most varied opinions so that there will be no confusion [over points of view]." Structurally, the informal division of the party into competing *clans* and the importance of personalities made a monolithic facade impossible to attain.

The UPS leaders have also specifically recognized the right of opposition, though subject to the condition "that it be a *national,* and constructive opposition." This tolerance might not be extended to the point of permitting an opposition party to become a major electoral threat, but the Senegalese leaders believed it important to maintain the outward form of a competitive democracy. Chief among the opposition parties at this time was the PRA-Sénégal composed primarily of "Young Turks" who split with Senghor when he refused to push for immediate independence, as had Guinea, in 1958.

The UPS and particularly Mamadou Dia consistently emphasized the importance of economic development. For Dia, economic development was the key even to political progress. "[Economic] development signifies for us true independence, liberty, and human dignity also, for *we believe that there is no independence without development.*" Because of his concern for development, Dia refused to attack French commercial interests and to yield to pressures to replace all French technicians with Africans. As he expressed it, "The question of Africanization is . . . not political; it is technical." Understandably, this did not always please many of the younger UPS politicians looking for a lucrative government job.

Although they might ritually denounce colonialism in the abstract, the UPS leaders were quite generous when they referred to the French and their influence in Africa. As the Senegalese leaders put it, "It is up to us . . . to take up where the French left off, to give a soul to the spirit created, a little despite itself, by the colonial administration." They thus saw no immutable difference between their own interests and goals and those of France. Although they might seek independence, this was not to take them totally out of the French orbit. "Above and beyond constitutional independence, what we want to bring about is effective independence and the guaranteed cooperation that [France] offers." Caught between its African past and its French training, Senegal saw no reason not to enjoy the best of both worlds.

Soudan

Compared with its coastal neighbor, Senegal, Soudan was a political, economic, and cultural backwater throughout most of the colonial era. During this time its main claims to renown in the outside world were the storybook mystery of Timbuktu, the thousands of its soldiers who died at the Marne, and the inefficient and expensive Office du Niger rice- and cotton-growing scheme. Soudan was a great producer of food crops, fish, and livestock, and its merchants carried on trade throughout West Africa, but it produced little for international commerce. Although by geography and history it had been a "crossroads of West Africa," the commerce and communications lines of the colonial power treated it more as a dead end. Here French civilization was at its least radiant. Before World War II a maximum of 3 percent of school-age children attended school, and although several of these went to secondary school in Senegal, none were sent to France for advanced training.

Politics were not formally introduced into Soudan until after World War II, and they were at first dominated by traditional chiefs and their allies. The Soudanese Socialist Party, headed by Fily Dabo Sissoko, was supported and, in the beginning at least, influenced by the French administration. Its strength came from the rural areas completely under the thumb of the local chiefs and also from the older African civil servants who were beholden to the colonial administration for their jobs.

The Union Soudanaise, the territorial section of the RDA, was quite another matter. This party was led by young secondary school graduates, many of whom had participated in Communist Study Groups in the 1940s. It found its support among the non-tribally oriented masses of the towns, the traders, and those villages where the chiefs' authority was weakest. The Union Soudanaise had to battle not only against the Socialists, but against the colonial authorities. Of its 1959 political bureau at least three, including Modibo Keita, had spent time in French prisons, and many others, when serving as government functionaries or teachers, had been banished to the least desirable posts in the desert or in the farthest bush. The political intervention of the colonial authorities and particularly of the French army, which manipulated the votes of the many Soudanese veterans, was seldom subtle. Despite such handicaps, the Union Soudanaise steadily increased its support, thanks to its superb mass-party organization and its defense of the interests of many groups without regard to tribal lines. By late 1956, when the French finally made peace with the RDA, the ascendancy of the Union Soudanaise was apparent. It won two of the three Soudanese seats in the French National Assembly in the January 1956 election and a year later all but six of the seats in the Soudanese Assembly. By the time of the September 1958 referendum on the De Gaulle constitution of the Fifth Republic, the party of Modibo Keita was assured of general popular support, although it still encountered opposition from many local chiefs and from certain regions and ethnic groups.

The Union Soudanaise considered itself the "guide and organizer of the Soudanese people, so as to lead it as rapidly as possible in the path of liberation and well-being." Initiative and directives came from the party and were applied to the masses, which were mostly passive in the decision-making process. The party realized, however, that it could not be successful if the masses did not go along with its chosen course of action. For the party, the masses were the ultimate judge of the correctness of its political program.

A sympathetic Senegalese party (the PRA-Sénégal) described the Union Soudanaise as the party "which truly and democratically controls the Soudanese masses." Although control was a one-way process, it was considered "democratic" and effective because it was accepted by the masses and was in the masses' interest.

The strength of the party came from three related factors: collective leadership, organization, and discipline. The party insisted on strict application of the principle of democratic centralism. Once a decision was reached, everyone "must bend to the decision of the majority, whatever may be his appreciation of the worth of that decision, he must make that decision his very own and work for its success."

The party tried always to act as a united front, without fissure and without second thoughts. Once a program was launched, all criticism became "divisive activity," one of the worst—if not the worst—crimes a party member could commit. As the party's bylaws state, "Any attempt at demoralization, any divisive work or attack against the Party's candidates or leaders must be vigorously denounced to the Party's directing body."

The fundamental tenet of the Union Soudanaise's doctrine is the supremacy of the political in all things. "Priorité au Politique," its newspaper frequently proclaims. As politics was accorded all honors, so economics fell to the level of the minor arts. As one leader put it, "If the political line is correct, the economic side will take care of itself."

In Union Soudanaise doctrine politics was "rational," "logical," "constant," and, like the party and the masses, it could be organized and controlled. It was also all-encompassing. Every action and every organization had its political dimension. A good political program must be "rooted in reality," and must be "dynamic" and "comprehensive." It must "go in the sense of history and the interests of Africa." Needless to say, once the Union Soudanaise gained full power, it tolerated no opposition party.

The Union Soudanaise upheld the ideal of unity of the people as a reflection of the classlessness of traditional African society. It felt this unity had been threatened by the introduction of European economic and social forms, and after independence aimed to break down the divisive and individualistic structures that colonialism had implanted on African soil. Thus, independence should bring no relaxation of discipline.

The Union Soudanaise has argued that all opposition to the party and to the party's program somehow relates to "the fact of colonialism," which destroyed the natural collective unity of traditional African society. Its view of France's role in Africa was thus much less charitable than that held by the Senegalese leaders.

The Appeal of Federation

Differences between the two territorial political units certainly existed, but their leaders felt a common commitment to make federation work. On the Senegalese side, Léopold Senghor had made federation the cornerstone of his political program ever since 1948 when he first called for a revision of the constitution of France's Fourth Republic to replace the "Republic one and indivisible" with a "Republic one and divisible" through a federation between France and its overseas territories. With the growth and increasing political power of indigenous African political movements, Senghor revised his federalist ideas to put, as his party's banners proclaimed, "The African Community before the Franco-African Community." Behind this slogan lay a recognition of how important it was for Senegal, and particularly for its major city, Dakar, to continue to play the role of the capital and nerve center for the French-speaking West African territories that the colonial federation of French West Africa had allocated them. Dakar was the seat of most of the large trading companies operating throughout AOF; Senegal's nascent industries were intended to supply the whole federation, and Senegal contributed about two-thirds of the employees of the French West African governmental services. But, in Senghor's mind, federation was of more than immediate economic importance to him and his country. He realized how much his territory derived from its close association with France, and fully expected to retain the most beneficial aspects of that association after independence. However, he knew that Senegal's three million people and one-crop economy could hardly hope to deal with a prosperous, developing France on anything approaching equal terms. His goal was thus to lead a vaster ensemble of territories and peoples which would command the economic and political resources to make France sit up and take notice.

During the declining years of the Fourth Republic, Senghor skillfully used the political issue of federation to bolster his own political position both within Senegal and within the larger context of Franco-African politics. In 1956 when Houphouet-Boigny of the Ivory Coast, the leader of the RDA and Senghor's personal rival, backed the Guy Mollet government in Paris in its effort to allocate the powers of French West Africa's Grand Council to the individual territories, Senghor seized on the issue to champion the cause of "African unity" and to denounce his opponents for "Balkanizing," i.e., splitting up, Africa to render it impotent. This attack weakened Houphouet-Boigny's position within the RDA and attracted to Senghor the sympathy of many members of the RDA's more radical branches, notably in Guinea and Soudan.

But it was within the volatile context of Senegal's domestic politics that Senghor secured the most mileage from championing the cause of federation. In the crucial years, 1956 and 1957, when France for the first time made ready to allocate significant powers of internal self-government to its African territories, Senghor used the issue of federation to attract most of Senegal's young and dynamic intellectuals to his political party. He used these young men to build up his party structures in the interior and to sap the strength of Lamine Guèye's Socialist Party in Dakar and St. Louis. When in April, 1958, Lamine Guèye capitulated and agreed to play second fiddle to his one-time protégé in a single political party (the UPS), Senghor's domestic position seemed assured. Federation was one of those happy political slogans that a politician could both believe in and profit from.

Although Senghor was now clearly the dominant political figure in Senegal, he was not the only member of the UPS whose opinions counted. His long-time associate and the premier of Senegal's territorial government, Mamadou Dia, was a power in his own right. Although not personally identified with the cause of federation to the degree that Senghor was, Dia saw substantial economic advantages to linking Senegal with complementary African economies to provide a larger market and also raw materials for Senegalese industry and rice for the inhabitants of expanding Dakar.

The appeal of federalism to Soudan's leaders was of a somewhat different sort. Like Senghor, they fully appreciated the importance of having a larger political base from which to deal with the outside world, but they saw this confrontation from a different perspective: "It is not with dispersed troops that one effectively combats colonialism," Modibo Keita told a party congress. The Union Soudanaise extended its principle of reinforcing domestic unity to the level of interterritorial politics and saw African political unity as one of the main features of the flow of African history. To be for federal unity, they felt, was to be for political progress; to oppose it was to advocate political stagnation. Modibo Keita and his chief lieutenants had long advocated greater attention to federal political unity within the councils of the RDA, where they usually supported Guinea's Sékou Touré rather than Ivory Coast's Houphouet-Boigny. Although the Union Soudanaise retained the RDA initials after its name, that interterritorial formation had ceased by the fall of 1958, as we shall see, to have any influence over the Soudanese mass party.

Soudan's flourishing traditional Dioula commerce with neighboring states and its dependence on a coastal state for an outlet to the sea made its leaders' support of federalism the more logical, but these factors would not by themselves have been enough had not the whole political vision of its leaders concentrated on the problem of reinforcing political unity. In federal as in domestic affairs, the Union Soudanaise clearly gave priority to the political, and for them, the political had always an ideological aspect.

Their common commitment to federal unity helped the leaders of

Senegal and Soudan over perhaps the most trying period in their political careers, the period of De Gaulle's 1958 referendum. The constitution that was drawn up for the new Fifth Republic after De Gaulle's return to power in France pleased very few of the African leaders. By obliging the territories of French West Africa individually to accept or reject the constitution as a whole, De Gaulle was intentionally slighting what little interterritorial unity was left in the old colonial federation. Moreover, nowhere in the text was there provision for negotiating independence. The French chief of state announced that the African territories were free to accept his constitution and thus participation in the Franco-African Community or to reject it "with all the consequences that such a decision would entail."

Both Senegalese and Soudanese leaders termed the constitution a "disaster" when it was first published, but both were afraid of the consequences of voting "no." The French made it clear to the leaders of the Union Soudanaise and the UPS that they risked being totally eliminated from political power if they were to adopt such a course and fail. They played upon the sentiments of the conservative chiefs and veterans of the French colonial army in Soudan and upon the old Socialists of the Senegalese cities and the Muslim religious leaders of the Senegalese bush. Also, ostentatious movements by French troops stationed in each territory did little to reassure the leaders.

At the same time, both Senghor and Dia in Senegal and Modibo Keita and his aides in Soudan were faced by considerable pressure from younger and more radical elements in their own parties to vote for immediate and abrupt independence, as did neighboring Guinea, consequences or no. The leaders of both parties hit upon the same strategy for trying to quiet these activist voices: they argued that immediate independence would break off all chance of forging a larger federation, whereas if they adopted the strategy of first trying to build a strong federation within the Community they would then have the strength to negotiate a fruitful and peaceful independence agreement with France. Although some of the UPS young Turks split off to form the PRA-Sénégal party and to campaign for a "no" vote on the referendum, the strategy worked and both Senegalese and Soudanese leaders weathered the storm. The referendum was approved by 97 percent of the voters in each country.

Founding the Federation

The immediate effect of the referendum vote was to put pressure on the Senegalese and Soudanese leaders to produce some federalist action in a hurry.

The opening move for federation was made by Senghor and his political associates in several African territories, who on October 14, 1958, laid "a proposal for a federal constitution" before the other parties of French West Africa. The RDA, torn between its strongly federalist Soudan section and the adamantly antifederalist Ivory Coast section, was obliged to yield the initiative to its rival. The split within the RDA burst into the open on November 12, when Gabriel d'Arboussier, head of the small Senegalese RDA section, circulated a proposal for a primary federation to all the French West African heads of government. Most embarrassingly for the RDA, his proposal was virtually identical in principle to that issued earlier by Senghor's friends. Federalist fever was clearly in the air, and in quick succession the assemblies of four French West African territories—Senegal, Soudan, Dahomey, and Upper Volta—chose formally to empower their governments to join in a federation. The Ivory Coast, its political dependency, Niger, and Mauritania, whose predominantly Moorish populations wanted to stay clear of Black African problems, said nothing.

Thus began a period of intense activity in which federalists and their opponents multiplied formal missions to coordinate activity and informal attempts to persuade the hesitant. At first the federalists seemed to carry the day. The Senegalese and Soudanese transcended party differences to call jointly a meeting of all West African federalists at Bamako on December 29 and 30, 1958. The four territories that had formally chosen to federate sent representatives, and Mauritania sent observers. The status of the Voltaic delegates was unclear, however, since they had been obliged to pay their own fares and accordingly, some argued, could not represent the territory "officially." Despite such inconsistencies the proceedings conveyed a surprising impression of unity of purpose and resolution in which party, sectional, and personal differences were muted.

Perhaps most significant was the conference's decision to appeal to political leaders of all parties and groups "to unite their efforts to bring about political unity within each State, as a guarantee of the Federation's cohesion and development." The motion's significance lay first in its author, Doudou Guèye, a leader of the Senegalese RDA. Here was a minority group asking to be absorbed in the territory's dominant party, a loyal RDA man putting himself at Senghor's service.

The conference concluded with a resolution to meet in a Federal Constituent Congress at Dakar two weeks later, and despatched official delegates to explain its position to the Ivory Coast and to Mauritania, in an attempt to bring all of French West Africa (save Guinea, now ruled out of the system) into the primary federation. Neither mission met with success. Houphouet-Boigny maintained his intransigence, and the Mauritanians maintained their noncommittal attitude which, in this case, amounted to a de facto rejection of the Federation.

The focus of attention shifted rapidly from Bamako to Dakar, where the Grand Council of AOF formally declared the old French West African colonial federation at an end and gave over its hall to the federalists. Under the presidency of Modibo Keita, the new Federal Constituent Assembly was to translate the political option of the Bamako Conference into a new constitution binding those states that accepted federation.

The Constituent Assembly had to be hastily arranged, but the two dominant delegations from Senegal and Soudan worked smoothly together, and events proceeded with considerable éclat. Although Sourou Migan Apithy, the Dahomeyan Premier, had refused to come, the Dahomeyan delegation seemed firmly under the control of Alexandre Adandé and Emile Zinsou, both convinced federalists. The Voltaic delegation arrived this time with full official powers, and its hitherto hesitant leader, Maurice Yameogo, bristled with protestations of federalist faith. Both the Senegalese and Soudanese delegations had carefully included opposition members who accepted the idea of federation. The Senegalese UPS leaders, particularly, took pride in presenting Gabriel d'Arboussier of the RDA as one of their own, while the Soudanese included two second-ranking members of the Socialist opposition. Thus domestic political unity was enhanced by the campaign for interterritorial unity.

The actual work of the Assembly took only three days. The draft constitution for the Federation of Mali was approved without public discussion and by acclamation of the assembled delegates. Whatever bargaining had gone on behind the scenes seemed to be of minor moment compared to the simple political fact that, as one orator put it, "Africa had reestablished itself." The most memorable aspect of the Assembly was its conclusion, when the majestic figure of Modibo Keita led the delegates in swearing three times "to defend everywhere the Mali Federation, to become tireless pilgrims and preachers of political unity, and to accept the ultimate sacrifice for the realization of African unity." The emotions aroused by the solemn oath were overwhelming. Even those in the public gallery joined in, including pickets protesting the Senegalese government's policies toward trade unions.

The document that emerged from this extraordinary session went considerably beyond the initial proposals for granting executive power to a federal government. The federal premier was to be chosen by majority vote of the Federal Assembly, without formal reference to the territorial delegations. Although everyone expected much informal consultation to take place off the assembly's floor to permit the individual territories to voice objections privately, the principle of a strong federal executive, independent of formal territorial control, was accepted without question.

The powers of the federal government were to extend to all the spheres that had been controlled by the French Government General in its heyday. Furthermore, it was to have charge of foreign representation, within the limits laid down by the Federation's membership in the French Community.

Perhaps most encouraging for the future of the new federation was the easy spirit of compromise that animated the different territorial delegations.

Soudan, the most populous territory, had originally wanted representation proportional to population, but raised no objection to giving all territories equal representation. Thus, each territorial assembly was to choose twelve deputies to the unicameral Federal Assembly, and each territory was to contribute two men to the federal cabinet. On the Sengalese side, Senghor himself proposed the name, Mali Federation, thus reviving Soudanese memories of the medieval empire of Mali whose center had been in Soudan. More concretely, Senegal agreed that federal revenues should be derived principally from customs and excise duties, that is to say, from the operations of the port of Dakar.

Aside from their efforts to establish a strong federal authority, the Constituent Assembly's overriding concern seems to have been to leave the door open to the other West African states of the French Community. The preamble of the constitution states: "This Federation remains open to all autonomous states of West Africa which desire to join. . . ." This insistence on maintaining "une Fédération ouverte" was underlined in all the major speeches concluding the session. Part of the open invitation to other members was just good politics in the sense that it built up the promise of the new federation and reassured waverers in Dahomey and Upper Volta that they were riding the wave of the future. Of at least equal importance was the feeling that the Mali Federation was to be the nucleus for the recreation of the French West African primary federation destroyed by the referendum. The four-party federation was to be just the beginning.

The Reaction

While the federalists were winning all the headlines, their opponents, both in Paris and Africa, were not asleep. In Africa, Félix Houphouet-Boigny, the Ivory Coast RDA leader, saw Mali as both an economic and political threat. The Ivory Coast depended on more than 100,000 migrant workers from Upper Volta to raise its coffee and banana export crops, and both Upper Volta and Dahomey were important clients for Ivory Coast commercial houses. Even more important, however, Houphouet-Boigny had long fought Senghor on the federalism issue, and Mali's success would have severely weakened the Ivory Coast leader's prestige and power in West African politics. In France De Gaulle was concentrating on making a success of the new French Community set up by the referendum and wanted a strict minimum of complications to compromise the success of his venture. Since Houphouet-Boigny had staunchly supported De Gaulle's African policies while many of the original proponents of federation did not, his words carried considerable weight in Paris. To the extent that African politics could be viewed as a choice between the "moderate" policies of Houphouet-Boigny and the "adventurous" policies of Senghor and Modibo

Keita, both equally "African" in origin and content, the French government tended to support the approach of the former.

Nor was the Ivory Coast leader caught without an alternative policy to support. On December 5, 1958, following his return from Paris, Houphouet-Boigny had announced his preference for maintaining direct political links between the individual territories and France while establishing a loose "conseil d'entente" consultative arrangement for "economic harmonization" among the West African territories that were members of the Community. Houphouet-Boigny had the backing not only of the French government but of his own Ivory Coast political party, the PDCI, and of the major Ivory Coast commercial interests as well. He moved swiftly to turn the balance in his own direction.

First, the combined political weight of the Ivory Coast leader and the French administration was brought to bear against Upper Volta. On January 28, 1959, the Voltaic Assembly had approved the Mali federal constitution without a dissenting voice, but with several important individuals absent. Since this vote did not oblige Upper Volta to join the Federation, its significance was not entirely clear. In the month following this action, pressure from the Ivory Coast increased. A PDCI delegation visited the major Voltaic trading centers stressing the importance of Abidjan as a commercial outlet and reminding the Voltaic leaders of how important the Ivory Coast was as a place of employment for Voltaic labor. A delegation of chiefs from Niger paid a formal call on the Morho Naba, traditional leader of half of Upper Volta's people, and reportedly warned him of the dangers to all chiefs implicit in the activities of the radicals in Dakar and Bamako. Considerable restlessness was noted among Upper Volta's many ex-servicemen, all dependent on pensions from the French army. It is commonly assumed that during this period considerable Ivory Coast funds found their way into Voltaic pockets.

Precisely which of these pressures was decisive is not certain, but the cumulative effect was overwhelming. On February 28 at a hastily called midnight meeting of the Voltaic Assembly, the bare quorum (39 out of 70) who were present approved Prime Minister Yameogo's draft constitution which made no mention of the Federation. Despite the federalist charge that in fact only 22 members were present and that the vote was therefore illegal, the constitutional referendum, held two weeks later, approved the Assembly's draft, and Upper Volta by that action ended any connection with the Mali Federation.

Upper Volta's geographic position and the weakness and division of its political structures made the country susceptible to whatever groups could bring the most effective pressures to bear on the political leaders. The pressures that Houphouet-Boigny and France brought to bear were not simply verbal arguments, but effective, if implied, threats of eliminating a specific group or leader from participation in Voltaic political life. With no comparable means of bringing direct pressure to bear, the federalists in Dakar and Bamako had no effective counter. Dakar offered a chance at unspecified long-term gains; Abidjan (and Paris) guaranteed continued existence. For Upper Volta's politicians, the latter was the better offer.

The situation in Dahomey offered many of the same possibilities for maneuver that were evident in Upper Volta. The Dahomeyan economy, too, was dependent on outside aid, and no strong single political party dominated the scene. The issue of federation provided a chance for an ambitious leader like the Dahomeyan Premier, Sourou Migan Apithy, to build a more stable political base than that provided by the local ruling party. Since his opponents within his own party had been among the earliest federalists, and both were associated closely with Senghor, Apithy's strategy was to adopt an antifederalist stance, thereby making possible a rapprochement with the local RDA. Dahomey's peculiar economic and geographic position opened up even more interesting possibilities. Dahomey's economy was stagnating because the country lacked a good deep-water port. Extensive lobbying in Paris had brought a tentative French agreement in 1958 to build such a port at Cotonou, the Dahomeyan capital, as part of a general plan to reinforce trade links between Dahomey and its interior neighbor, Niger. This plan was of great interest to the northern Dahomeyan politicians whose hitherto isolated constituency would now be favored by a major commercial route.

After a quick trip to Paris, Apithy refused to join the Dahomeyan delegation to the Dakar Constituent Assembly and opened quiet talks with leaders of the Dahomeyan RDA and northern parties. At these talks he pointed out, as he later put it, "how necessary the good will of France was to us at this stage of our economic development."

The Dahomeyan Constituent Assembly met the following month, and in defiance of riots outside the building refused a motion to inscribe in the constitution "the intention of the Republic of Dahomey to bring about African unity." By accepting a new national constitution on February 14, 1959, Dahomey officially refused entry into the Mali Federation. The federalist leaders resigned from Apithy's cabinet; the total collapse of the federalist position was assured when they felt unable to present candidates at the April 2, 1959, elections, which were won by Apithy.

The Federation Survives

In neither Soudan nor Senegal, however, were the opponents of federation able to bring effective pressure to bear against the determined and committed leadership of the two territories' respective parties. The triumph of the federalist option in Soudan and Senegal was reinforced by the decisive victories of the Union Soudanaise and the UPS in the March 1959 elections for new territorial legislatures.

In waging their campaign, the Union Soudanaise leaders used the issue of federalism to split the opposition. The Union Soudanaise government had included two opposition members of the legislature in the Soudanese delegation to the Federal Constituent Assembly in Dakar. Being assured of continued jobs at the federal level, these two, and several of their followers, announced on February 14 that they would join the Union Soudanaise. The Socialist opposition was particularly vulnerable on the federalist issue, since it had formerly supported Senghor's and Lamine Guèye's attacks against the "Balkanizing RDA."

Nor did the Union Soudanaise neglect to use its absolute majority within the Soudanese government to decrease the opposition's freedom to maneuver. Since the referendum in September, most of the European district officers had been replaced by loyal Union Soudanaise men and numerous conservative chiefs had been deposed. The Union Soudanaise wrote an electoral law to its own specifications, and with these precautions it received 76 percent of the vote and all the seats. Soudan had thus voted, in effect, for federation. In the weeks following the election, the Socialist leaders, some under a certain amount of pressure, accepted the offer of the Union Soudanaise to dissolve their party and join the victor. Thus, the Union Soudanaise achieved its long-term goal of internal political unity at the same time that it was leading the way toward federal unity.

The situation in Senegal was more complicated, and the UPS federalists had a more difficult battle to wage than had their Soudanese colleagues. Once the UPS had firmly captured federalism as a campaign issue, the opposition party, the PRA-Sénégal, felt obliged to campaign on an anti-federalist platform. Since prior to the split the PRA-Sénégal leaders had been among the most ardent defenders of the West African primary federation, however, it was not difficult for the UPS to pin an opportunist label on their campaign. Because the PRA-Sénégal could count on help from neither Houphouet-Boigny nor the French, they were not by themselves much of a threat.

Much more serious was the opposition from Senegalese conservative interests, in particular the Muslim marabouts who had prospered and been accorded great honor under the French administration. Since Senegal is 80 percent Muslim, and since many of the Senegalese Muslims believe that their entry into paradise depends on following the wishes of their religious leaders, the great marabouts could wield considerable political power. The marabouts' attachment to France had been one of the major factors causing the UPS leaders to conclude that a negative vote in the referendum would be politically unwise; but by March the UPS was in a better position to handle this opposition.

Senghor had received support from many marabouts in his defeat of the Senegalese Socialists in 1951, and his government had to a large extent supplanted the French administration as the major prop for the marabouts' financial manipulations. Furthermore, the marabouts were divided among themselves by questions of personal prestige and by disputes over succession. Although the most politically and economically dissatisfied religious leaders formed a new political party, the Party of Senegalese Solidarity (PSS), to fight the March elections, and received some financial support from Senegal's French population and the Ivory Coast, it did not enjoy the backing of the French administration and was relatively ineffective.

Senghor, Mamadou Dia, and Lamine Guèye, in control of the government, wrote an electoral law like that of Soudan to maximize their party's chances. The UPS was even spared the opposition of the Senegalese RDA, which, since its leaders had chosen to back the Federation, integrated its candidates into the UPS lists. The final result gave the UPS 81 percent of the vote and all the seats in the new legislature. The PSS subsequently announced it would join the RDA, and then quietly disappeared.

Although credit for their victories must first go to the leaders of the UPS and the Union Soudanaise, it is apparent that things might not have gone so easily for them if the French had been truly determined to prevent the formation of the Mali Federation. But while neither the French government nor the administration in Senegal and Soudan can be said to have ardently supported the efforts of the federalists, they appear to have appreciated the costs of trying to unseat the mass parties of Senegal and Soudan. In neither country was there a convenient and effective indigenous force to manipulate.

The French business interests in Dakar, unlike the planters of the Ivory Coast, had no economic reasons to fear federation. Indeed, for those involved in Dakar's small manufacturing sector, close ties with other territories would assure continued access to a large African market. While there is no indication that the Dakar businessmen were especially enthusiastic supporters of the Mali Federation at this time, they at least did not actively oppose it. Finally, both Senegalese and Soudanese leaders went out of their way to offer public and private reassurances to France that they had no intention of leaving the Community.

Mali Is Ready to Go. . . .

With the elections out of the way, the leaders of Senegal and Soudan met in Dakar to pick up the pieces of their federation. Putting the best face possible on what had happened, Modibo Keita told the Mali Federal Assembly in a meeting on April 6, 1959,

> Mali is ready to go; it has thrown its excess baggage overboard. This lightening of the load brings Mali back to the limits of Senegal and Soudan in which our consecrated political unity and the action of our Governments will permit an acceleration of the process of evolution of our

> Federation towards the affirmation of its personality and its national sovereignty.

In a few hurried meetings in early April, Mali's leaders modified the structure of their government to compensate for the defections of Upper Volta and Dahomey but retained the basic principle of strict territorial parity that had been the dominant feature of the earlier constitution. The federal Council of Ministers consisted of an equal number of Senegalese and Soudanese, with responsibilities as carefully balanced as possible. Thus, Modibo Keita was named Premier, but Mamadou Dia was made Vice-Premier and in addition was given responsibility for defense. To maintain this approximate equalization of powers, the previous ineligibility of territorial ministers was dropped. (Mamadou Dia was also Premier of Senegal.) This change made the federal government more dependent on the will of the territorial governments than it had been previously when the federal executive could contain no members of territorial executive bodies. A second change, requiring all decrees of the federal government to be countersigned by both the federal premier and the minister responsible, could also restrict the ability of the premier to act unilaterally.

While such an emphasis on representational parity could go far to allay fears of either side's being systematically exploited by the other, it could also decrease the federal government's flexibility of action. In particular, it could lead to a series of permanent stalemates with both sides refusing to budge. Equally serious, if a repeated pattern of unilateral defection from territorial solidarity developed, one side could enjoy a permanent majority on all issues. While a defection of this sort was unlikely to occur in the ranks of the Soudanese, it was always possible for the less regimented Senegalese.

Parallel to the government, and in theory superior to it, was the new federalist interterritorial party, the African Federation Party (PFA). This new party, whose existence was made necessary by the fact "that the former political parties of Black Africa . . . no longer reflect the present political situation," took as its goal "the realization of African Unity in the form of a Federal Republic, of which the Mali Federation represents the first step." By providing also that "only one section of the Party can exist in each State," the PFA was designed to be the logical culmination of the realignment of political forces that had begun at the time of the referendum and continued at the Bamako and Dakar conferences. Although the principle was not formally inscribed in the PFA's statutes, the same principle of parity that characterized the institutions of the federal government was present in the federal party. Senghor became the PFA's president, and Modibo Keita was named secretary-general; similarly, too, an equal number of Senegalese and Soudanese held positions on the party's political bureau. There was one main difference with the Federation's governmental institutions, however; the PFA, faithful to Mali's open and expansionist ideals, included representatives from federalist parties in other territories. Among them were the PFA's two vice-presidents, Djibo Bakary of Niger and Emile Zinsou of Dahomey. These outside representatives constituted a third force, capable of breaking a deadlock between the Senegalese and Soudanese should the need arise, and introduced an element of flexibility lacking in the governmental structures.

Despite this flexible element, all of the formal institutions of the Mali Federation shared one principal handicap. Because they were controlled by the two territorial political parties, there was nothing to stop a quarrel started in one institutional setting from spilling over into all the others. Furthermore, because the decisions taken involved ultimately the policies of a very few political leaders, any dispute in any organizational setting would be forced up to the top for settlement. Since the settlement of any serious disputes at the summit directly involved the prestige and reputations of the top politicians, escalation of a minor dispute into a major interterritorial crisis was highly possible.

Ultimately, the success of any cooperative venture depends on the willingness and ability of each side to compromise. While there is no way of predicting how much the Senegalese and Soudanese would have been willing to compromise, we can identify certain objectives of crucial concern for each in which compromise would have been extremely difficult.

For the Senegalese leaders, maintenance of good relations with France was obviously an important point, as much for economic and political reasons as for sentimental ones. A second area of concern, particularly for Mamadou Dia, was Senegal's economic development plan. But for the Soudanese leaders formal independence was a primary goal and the only compromise possible was on timing. In addition, they felt that political considerations should dictate policy in other domains.

One overshadowing consideration—the need to retain domestic political power—was a condition of any political action for the leaders of both territories. For the Senegalese leaders, this meant maintaining a free hand to balance and control competing interests within the UPS. The problem of remaining in power was less acute for the Union Soudanaise leaders, but they too, in a longer perspective, had a definite interest in maintaining a sense of political momentum in federal affairs, in order to prevent a challenge from younger and more radical elements in the party.

Aside from these few crucial concerns, there were a multiplicity of issues the Federation would have to face on which compromise would be possible under the right conditions. Before people will compromise, however, they must first perceive a need to compromise. This involves an understanding not only of one's own deeper interests, but also of the other side's interests and likely reactions. Despite the many common goals and shared political experiences of the Senegalese and Soudanese leaders, their domestic political situations were quite different. It was primarily in regard to the Federation's effect on each territory's domestic situation that the requisite mutual understanding might be lacking.

Independence: A Conflict Resolved

The first great issue the new Mali Federation faced was independence, perhaps the most important issue on which the Senegalese and Soudanese leaders differed. The constitution of the Fifth Republic, which established the Community, granted sovereignty over internal matters to the constituent states, but left the domains of foreign affairs, defense, and monetary policy to the Community as a whole, that is to say, to France. This satisfied Senegal's desire for "independence in interdependence," but provided neither the formal recognition of complete national sovereignty nor the complete domestic political control that the Soudanese sought. The question of independence dominated the PFA's formal constituent congress, held in Dakar during the opening days of July, 1959. Senghor treated the delegates to a sixty-five page political report which brought in everyone from Marx to Teilhard de Chardin, but which studiously avoided the subject of independence. Senghor's report did not suit the mood of most delegates, and the smattering of applause he received came mainly from the Senegalese benches. The Soudanese, speaking through their Minister of the Interior, Madeira Keita, promptly defended the necessity of obtaining immediate independence. This position was rapidly supported by orators from the non-Mali territories, who felt it to be to their domestic political interest to promise independence while the regimes they opposed at home were enthusiastically cooperating with the French. Their speeches also received pointed applause from some of the Senegalese UPS youth movement delegates and quiet support from the PFA's organization secretary, Doudou Guèye, late of the Senegalese RDA.

The seriousness of the Senegalese-Soudanese dispute on this question was not diminished by the fact that some of the Senegalese seemed to sympathize with the Soudanese; were they and others like them to switch to the Soudanese side, Senghor and his associates would be put in an extremely delicate position within their own territorial party. Fortunately, the very fact that the non-Mali delegations took a pro-independence position blurred the fact that this was fundamentally a quarrel between Senegalese and Soudanese leaders and permitted the Senegalese to yield graciously to a majority, not of the Federation, but of the West African political party. The final compromise resolution, emphasizing that "along with *le fait national,* the other reality of the twentieth century is the *interdependence of Nations,"* and demanding the "transformation of the Community into a multinational Confederation," was a reasonable verbal formula for both sides and one in which neither side lost face.

France fortunately proved cooperative. When General de Gaulle visited the Mali Federal Assembly on December 13, 1959, he dramatically announced that France would cooperate in granting Mali its national sovereignty, and would furthermore continue to aid and assist the new nation. Negotiations for the transfer of powers lasted from January through March, and June 20, 1960, was set as independence day for the Mali Federation. Mali agreed to remain within the Community and the franc zone. As a sovereign nation, the Federation was to have its own army, but it agreed to allow French military bases on Mali's soil.

Unity Versus Federalism: The End of Cooperation

The question of independence was resolved peacefully and with a minimum of hard feelings in part because the world outside of the Federation proved accommodating. No such arrangement could solve the internal problems of the Federation. These quickly came to be cast in the familiar mold of a dispute over governmental centralization vs. states' rights. The Union Soudanaise leaders, faithful to their *mystique* of national unity, sought to concentrate supreme power in the hands of the federal government. The UPS leaders, attuned to the delicate functioning of the Senegalese political system, sought to guarantee, as Senghor phrased it "the autonomy of the Senegalese soul." This difference of orientation was epitomized by a dispute over the powers of the federal president. The Soudanese wanted to concentrate supreme political power in the hands of a single individual, by combining, once independence was proclaimed, the role of chief of state with the office of head of the government responsible for foreign affairs. This would definitely break the parity principle on which the Federation had been founded, since the next highest office, that of vice-president of the Council of Ministers responsible for defense, would not equal the presidency in either power or prestige. Furthermore, since under the April 1959 agreements Modibo Keita had been named president of the Council of Ministers responsible for foreign affairs, he would have a head start in the race for the supreme post.

The Senegalese argued strongly that the principle of parity must be upheld, i.e., executive functions must be divided between a chief of state and a head of government of different nationalities. This quarrel went on behind the scenes during the winter and spring of 1960. It was considered serious enough by the Senegalese that in April their two legal experts, Doudou Thiam and Gabriel d'Arboussier, secretly circulated a proposal that Mali be transformed into a loose confederation with the executive power restricted to an economic and technical coordinating role. Although Senghor agreed, as he later put it, that "things were not going well at all," he was reluctant to concede defeat in his quest for an African federation. A meeting of Mali's political leaders was called on April 14 to settle the differences.

The meeting, held behind closed doors, was a stormy affair at which each side accused the other of bad faith and of violating the original agreements. The meeting lasted three days, and although each side subsequently gave a different account of what took place, the following seems to have been agreed upon. First, the offices of chief of state and head of government would be separate, with the latter retaining control over foreign affairs, and secondly, a Senegalese "might be chosen" as chief of state. With further progress proving impossible, the details were left to a "conciliation mission" of the directing committee of the PFA, in which non-Mali members were included to break the deadlock.

The non-Mali members carried out their conciliation mission with dispatch. They arranged that a president of the Federation would be chosen by a congress made up of an even number of Senegalese and Soudanese Territorial and Federal Assembly members, which would meet before the opening of the fall's United Nations General Assembly, to which the independent Mali Federation expected to be admitted. This solution was accepted by a new meeting of the Mali leaders on May 21 and 22, and the crisis seemed ended.

The conflict between the Soudanese preference for a unitary political system and Senegalese desire for decentralized political control had its repercussions also on the level of the political party. The Soudanese emphasized the unifying function of the PFA, while the Senegalese sought to maintain control over internal Senegalese politics within the UPS. The immediate issue in dispute was whether a native of one territory residing in the other should join the section of the territorial party of his place of origin, or of his place of residence. The Senegalese were reluctant to include the new Soudanese arrivals in Dakar in the local committees of the UPS. Senghor and Dia were particularly concerned because of the tenuous nature of their hold over the loyalties of the federal (and Senegalese) capital, and because they rightly foresaw that inclusion of even a few of the dynamic and disciplined Soudanese political militants in Dakar local committees could greatly complicate their problem of maintaining control, especially if the Soudanese were to make an alliance with Lamine Guèye's supporters within the UPS. At the suggestion of the PFA conciliation mission, the Soudanese agreed not to press the issue, and it was left that those Soudanese who had already joined a local UPS committee would remain, while the others would stay out for the time being.

After the meetings in May, the Federation appeared to be back on the track. Whether this was the result of confidence reestablished between the Senegalese and Soudanese leaders or simply of the euphoria created by the proclamation of Mali's independence on June 20, 1960, all friction seemed a thing of the past. At the independence day celebrations, Modibo Keita brushed over any mention of differences between Senegalese and Soudanese, and pointedly emphasized some of the Senegalese leaders' favorite ideas, notably the importance of economic considerations now that formal political independence had been won. Senghor went even further. In his political report to the UPS congress on July 2, he went out of his way to praise the "brilliant" Soudanese leaders and to "deplore a certain campaign against our Soudanese brothers."

All through the difficulties of the previous few months, and despite the fact that the original Soudanese demands had jeopardized his claim to the presidency of the Federation, Senghor had shown himself most conciliatory toward the Soudanese "brothers." In large part his attitude reflected the peculiar political position in which he found himself. For so long had he been identified with the cause of federation that Mali's failure would have reflected adversely on his whole political career. Nor could Senghor easily accept a transformation of Mali into a loose confederation, for this would mean, most simply, that Houphouet-Boigny, the antifederalist, had been right all along.

Finally, Mali's failure would put Senghor in a very difficult domestic position which Lamine Guèye or perhaps a younger and more radical politician might be able to turn to his profit. The fact that Lamine Guèye and some of his close political associates had been noticeably reluctant to support Senghor in some of the backstage bargaining with the Soudanese did not reassure Senghor as to the former Socialists' intentions. On the other hand, following his understanding of the compromise decided on in April and May, 1960, Senghor had had himself invested as the Senegalese nominee for the Federation's presidency at a secret meeting of the UPS executive committee the day after independence was declared. He calculated that, once he had assumed this office, his prestige and influence in African affairs and his control over the UPS would be assured. Everything, thus, led him to support the Federation and to quiet the voices of dissent within his own party.

The position of the Union Soudanaise leaders was equally complex. Part of Mali's attractiveness to them had been its avant-garde standing in French-speaking West African politics. The Soudanese realized the danger to the Federation of pushing the Senegalese leaders too hard in the April-May controversy, and so compromised. This very compromise, however, constrained them to push for rapid advance on other fronts, notably to reinforce the Federation's political unity and the federal party's political control over the federal and the territorial governments. In addition, individual Soudanese leaders did not hide their impatience with what many of them considered to be the Senegalese leaders' truckling to the French on issues like the Algerian war and the Saharan atom bomb tests; and, although the subject was never broached directly, there was considerable pressure from within the Union Soudanaise to demand a revision of the Franco-Malian agreements at the earliest opportunity.

The first public indication of the Soudanese leaders' new resolve to press forward in consolidating political control came at the July UPS congress, to which their "fraternal delegation" had so warmly been welcomed by Senghor. The issue the Soudanese chose to champion at this time was the "Africanization" of all governmental and administrative posts within the Federation. The Senegalese leaders had always emphasized the need for technical expertise, as we have said, and employed many Europeans, particularly in the finance and planning ministries. Africanization had always been a sore point in Senghor's and Dia's relations with the UPS youth movement, and at the July 1960 congress they were obliged to spend most of an evening getting the younger delegates to approve a party platform that did not include a commitment to rapid and total Africanization. As the meeting was drawing to an end, Senghor asked Modibo Keita, as head of the visiting Soudanese delegation, to say a few closing words. Instead of confining himself to the usual perfunctionary expressions of solidarity, Modibo Keita invoked his role as PFA secretary general and Premier of the Federation to declare that he was not at all in agreement with "Comrade Senghor" on the Africanization question. This threw the meeting into uproar, and it required the better part of the night for Senghor and Dia, who were loudly hooted by some of the youth delegates, to reestablish control and get their resolution reapproved.

While the Soudanese leader probably did not foresee the effect his intervention would have, Senghor, and particularly Dia, were thoroughly outraged. They saw this demand simply as an attempt on the part of the Soudanese to create a faction within the UPS and particularly within the UPS youth movement that would be subservient to orders from Bamako. Whether or not this was the Soudanese intent, the whole experience of Senghor and Dia with Senegalese politics made them extremely sensitive to this sort of maneuver.

At about this time the Soudanese leaders learned that Senghor had had the UPS secretly approve his candidacy for president of the Federation. While the Senegalese subsequently defended the action on the grounds that according to the federal constitution and in keeping with previous practice, "it is always the [party] section of the State involved that approves candidates for a political position in Mali," the Soudanese saw this action as an illegitimate and dishonest way of bypassing the federal political party which should control federal nominations as well as policies. At this point, as one of the Soudanese leaders said afterward in an interview, "We decided that whoever became president, it would not be Senghor."

Relations between Senghor and Dia, on the one hand, and the Soudanese leaders, on the other, deteriorated rapidly after independence, and in this atmosphere actions that might otherwise have passed unnoticed or have been easily explained took on sinister implications in the minds of the other side. Soudanese hints that a revision of the Franco-Malian agreements would be desirable were magnified out of all proportion by the Senegalese. Modibo Keita's suggestion that "the establishment of an African monetary zone" might further the cause of a larger African regrouping was taken as an indication that the Soudanese wanted to take Mali out of the franc zone. This possibility was a matter of some concern not only to Mamadou Dia, who saw his development plan threatened, but to French commercial interests and the French government as well. Modibo Keita's avowal of the need to work with France to end the Algerian war was either not noticed or misinterpreted. However, off-the-record allusions by other Soudanese to the desirability of revising the military arrangements with France were interpreted by the French as an attempt to oust them from their important Dakar naval and air force headquarters and by the Senegalese Premier as a threat to the 40 million dollars that French military expenditures contributed annually to the Senegalese economy. In fact, however, it is highly likely that the Soudanese were concerned primarily with obtaining French evacuation of their base outside of Bamako.

If Mamadou Dia needed anything more to turn him against the Soudanese and the Mali Federation, the "affair of the colonels" did it. According to the Franco-Malian agreements, Mali was to have its own army, composed of Senegalese and Soudanese soldiers who had been serving in the French army. To command this new military force two colonels with distinguished military records, and separated by only a few days' seniority, were available. One, Colonel Fall, was a Senegalese, and the other, Colonel Soumaré, was a Soudanese, though he had spent considerable time in Senegal and indeed was distantly related to Lamine Guèye. Mamadou Dia, in his capacity of federal Minister of Defense, preferred the Senegalese. Modibo Keita, arguing his case on the rather tenuous grounds of seniority, chose the Soudanese Soumaré, and when Dia refused to countersign his nomination as chief of the general staff, Modibo Keita had it published anyway in the *Journal Officiel* on July 25. This definitively alienated Dia, who refused to receive Soumaré and cut off all communications with Modibo Keita.

When the following week a group of Dakar citizens closely associated with Lamine Guèye publicly congratulated Soumaré on his new job, it became apparent that Lamine had gone over to Modibo Keita's side. Here was what the UPS politicians most feared, a Senegalese who could serve as a front for Soudan's elimination of Dia, Senghor, and their followers.

Senghor, who had spent the second part of July at his summer home in Normandy, still had to be convinced of the need to end the Federation. The "affair of the marabouts" did this. It will be recalled how crucial a role the Muslim religious leaders played in Senegalese internal politics, and how much of Senghor's own political career had depended on the support he had received from these gentlemen whose piety was matched only by their sharp sense of economic and political realities.

In July, one of the younger and more fractious marabouts went to the Senegalese Premier and told him that he, along with several other religious leaders, had been approached by certain Soudanese who had suggested that Mali's evolution along Islamic lines might better be assured if a Muslim were to be president of the Federation instead of the Catholic Senghor. He, of course, had given no encouragement to such ideas, he declared, but he was not so sure that others, such as his uncle who had defeated him in a succession dispute three years earlier, had not succumbed to the Soudanese way of thinking.

Subsequent investigation revealed that emissaries of Modibo Keita had indeed repeated contact with the marabout and that Modibo Keita himself, in his capacity as federal Premier and acting chief of state, had sought to pay a formal call on Falilou M'Backé, the Grand Khalif of Senegal's most politically important Muslim sect and the man who had been the key to Senghor's defeat of Lamine Guèye's Socialists in the 1950s and his defeat of the PSS in 1959.

Whatever had been the Soudanese leader's motives in making contact with the Senegalese marabouts, Senghor and Dia interpreted this move as the most dangerous form of direct meddling in Senegal's internal affairs. Even putting the best possible face on it, Senghor concluded that he could not afford to have Senegal continue in the Federation so long as anyone else outranked him in the federal government's hierarchy. At the very least the Senegalese had to have a veto power, and that only the president of the Federation would have. In a meeting in Paris on August 8, Senghor, Dia, and d'Arboussier concluded that unless it were certain that Senghor would get the presidency and the Soudanese would, in d'Arboussier's words, "behave themselves," they would take Senegal out of the Federation. Even at this point, when most of his close advisers were decided on breaking with Soudan, Senghor clung to the hope that the Federation could be saved.

The Senegalese leaders returned to Dakar on August 12, and went immediately to the great festival of Falilou M'Backé's sect. There, Senghor and Dia clearly announced their position. As Dia said:

> I want Mali, but I want also Senegal. That is our motherland. Before setting up anything else, before consolidating anything else, before consolidating Mali, we must first think of Senegal. We must now watch out that after our liberation from the hands of the colonialists, there is no place for other colonizers. [*Marchés Tropicaux,* August 27, 1960 p. 1897.]

Lest the Mouride religious leaders misunderstand the situation, Senghor added, "The UPS will not forget the active support it has always received, not only from the great religious leaders of Islam, but also from the imams and their disciples." (*Paris-Dakar,* August 17, 1960.)

If this was intended to make the Soudanese back down, it had no apparent effect. On that same day the Soudanese federal Minister of Information insisted to the press that the president would be chosen without regard to his territorial origin. On August 14, it became known that the office of the PFA's organization secretary, Doudou Guèye, had been mysteriously burglarized, and the minutes of the April meeting at which the distribution of the top jobs had been decided had disappeared. This sleight-of-hand finally convinced Senghor that the Soudanese would never let him be elected. On August 15, Senghor, Dia, d'Arboussier, and three or four close associates decided that Senegal would break up the Federation.

The Breakup of the Mali Federation

Events now moved very swiftly, and in a pattern that suggests that neither side was entirely in control of what happened. The Senegalese leaders made repeated contacts with the French High Commissioner, and evidently explained at least some portion of the situation and of their plans. So far as one can tell, he sympathized with their side of the story and promised at least a benevolent neutrality. Although there is no indication that France actively sought the breakup of the Federation, once the breakup seemed inevitable there was no question as to which side it would choose. Certainly, a Federation without Senghor's strong moderating influence would not serve France's purposes. In the country outside Dakar the UPS political secretary took measures to assure that rural party members faithful to Senghor could be brought into the capital on short notice.

Whether by coincidence or from a partial realization of the extent of the Senegalese leaders' activities, Colonel Soumaré, on August 16, called into his office the French commander of the Mali gendarmerie, Lieutenant Colonel Pierre, and asked him how many gendarmerie platoons were in the vicinity of Dakar and ready to go into action should the need arise. Soumaré further asked Colonel Pierre to notify him of any requisition of the gendarmerie's services which did not come from his office. Colonel Pierre promptly notified Mamadou Dia, under whose ministry the gendarmerie was placed, and also, one may be sure, informed the French High Commissioner. Mamadou Dia, in his capacity of Minister of Defense, then promulgated an order on August 17, placing the gendarmerie under the exclusive command of the governments of the territories in which the units were stationed. That same afternoon, Mamadou Dia brought Senegal's regional governors together and informed them that they should be ready in case of trouble from the night of the nineteenth on. This date was presumably dictated by the fact that the conference of the Mali leaders, which was to attempt to decide on a single presidential candidate for presentation to the corps of electors meeting a week later, was to be held on the twentieth.

On the morning of August 19, without informing Soumaré, Dia addressed an order to Colonel Pierre asking him to have eight platoons of gendarmes ready to maintain order in Dakar starting at noon. This precaution and indeed the whole role of Colonel Pierre seem to have passed entirely unnoticed by the Soudanese. It was not until seven that evening, when someone reported seeing dozens of trucks and buses loaded with Senegalese peasants armed with flintlocks and bows and arrows on the way to Dakar, that the Soudanese became aware of how dangerous was their position.

Modibo Keita hastily called a meeting of the federal Council of Ministers, to which came only one Senegalese, Boubacar Guèye, the nephew and law partner of Lamine Guèye. The Council of Ministers formally revoked Mamadou Dia's functions as Defense Minister, transferred them to the federal premier, and decreed a national state of emergency. Modibo Keita then called in the French High Commissioner to inform him of the Council of Ministers' actions and received assurances that since this was a domestic matter, the French army of the Community would not intervene. Modibo Keita next broadcast a notice of his actions on Radio Mali and announced that the existence of Mali was in danger. He then ordered Colonel Soumaré to deploy the gendarmerie and the Mali army to safeguard public installations.

Modibo Keita's action evidently caught the Senegalese leaders by surprise. At the moment he was being deposed as federal Defense Minister, Mamadou Dia was out of Dakar, making sure that one of the marabouts was not going to side publicly with the Soudanese. Senghor was napping at the Federal Assembly building, which was already surrounded by troops. D'Arboussier, seeing the troops, roused Senghor and took him to Dia's house where they encountered, among others, Colonel Pierre and Colonel Fall (the Senegalese military attaché) who had been looking for Dia. Leaving d'Arboussier behind to alert the loyal Senegalese territorial assembly members, the others drove to the gendarmerie barracks. While Senghor whipped up the gendarmes' enthusiasm for their cause, Colonel Pierre telephoned Colonel Soumaré requesting him to come to the gendarmerie barracks on a matter of extreme urgency. Soumaré did so, and was promptly overpowered and put under arrest. With Soumaré out of the way, Colonel Fall, as the next highest ranking officer, ordered the Malian troops to yield their guard of public buildings to the gendarmerie. This they did, and the gendarmes then proceeded to surround the main administrative building, the radio station, and the residence of Modibo Keita.

Mamadou Dia, on his return to Dakar, called a midnight meeting of the Senegalese territorial assembly. Lamine Guèye and his supporters were absent, but the 67 members present voted to declare the independence of the Republic of Senegal from the Federation.

By this time, Modibo Keita was aware of what had happened, and he hurriedly called on the French High Commissioner to demand the intervention of French troops to safeguard Mali's integrity. The High Commissioner informed him that France still regarded this as an internal affair and saw no reason to modify what they "together" had decided earlier in the evening. By morning the streets were full of loyal UPS militants from the interior, all faithful to Senghor, while the Soudanese leaders and some of their Senegalese associates were under house arrest. The Soudanese were sent back home to Bamako by special sealed train on the morning of August 22.

The Senegalese party quickly purged its ranks of those seriously compromised by dealings with the Soudanese. With Senghor and Dia firmly in control, Senegal adopted a new constitution on September 26 and a week later elected Senghor its President. Lamine Guèye was allowed to retain his positions in the party and the government, but was kept very much on the sidelines for another two years. Although he obviously felt personal pain and some embarrassment at the failure of his long fight for federation, Senghor's control over the party and Senegal's political life remained unshaken. Many Dakar intellectuals denounced him for betraying the cause of African unity, but for most Senegalese the Federation's death, like its birth, was a matter of great indifference.

The Mali Federation lived a dwindling half-life in Bamako. The first reaction of the Soudanese leaders on returning home was to denounce the complicity of the "French colonialists" and "certain Senegalese traitors" in the events of Dakar and to proclaim that the Federation continued to exist with its government located provisionally in Bamako. *"Le Mali Continue"* was the slogan. In reprisal, the Soudanese cut the railroad with Dakar at the border and refused all Senegalese offers to establish diplomatic relations. But the logic of political events was too strong for the Soudanese leaders. On September 12, France, followed by most other nations, recognized the separate independence of Senegal and Soudan and offered to back their admissions to the United Nations. The Union Soudanaise called an Extraordinary Congress on September 22 which, under a banner proclaiming "Death Rather than Dishonor," formally took note of the Federation's breakup and announced that "Mali" would be continued by changing the name of Soudan to the Republic of Mali.

Although political facts were thus given their due, political passions took longer to subside. The Mali Republic maintained its blockade of communications and trade with Senegal at the price of painful economic dislocation for both countries, and for a time charges and countercharges of plots and espionage were hurled back and forth by the leaders of the two countries. It was not until September, 1963, that, under the influence of the newly formed Organization of African Unity, Senghor and Modibo Keita met at the Senegal-Mali border in an emotional embrace to reopen the railroad and usher in a new era of cooperation between the two independent states. Federation had failed, and its failure had passed into history.

The Problem of Political Union

This study has sought to answer two questions: Why was the Mali Federation founded? Why did it fail? Let us begin by looking at some tempting hypotheses that do *not* explain Mali's experience. First, there is no indication that Mali's founding was in any sense a "historical necessity." If, as many Africans have argued, Africa has a "federal destiny," if history points ineluctably to African political unity, this destiny is so veiled in mystery, and the workings of history take such an irregular course, that those who seek Africa's unity might better not rely on history to bring about their ends. Secondly, it cannot be shown that the Federation was dictated by any social, economic, geographic, cultural, linguistic, or other "natural" community, or that it was foredoomed to failure because of this lack. The most that one can say is that the situation was permissive, and that there were no serious nonpolitical obstacles. Thirdly, the Federation was neither created nor destroyed by any constellation of popular or interest-group pressures. The political leaders were able to maneuver with little reference to the immediate desires of the largely apathetic masses, and interest groups, where they existed, were either neutralized or subsumed within the political elites. Finally, the evidence does not support the contention that either the Federation's formation or its dissolution was dictated by any foreign power. France at various times and in various ways made life difficult for the Federation and at other times and in other ways helped the Federation. The initiative and responsibility for both its founding and destruction came from Africa.

Rather than seek the broad explanations of history, nature, or irresistible outside forces, we must find our answers to these political questions in the behavior of politicians. The Mali Federation came about through the actions of a few political leaders who sought what they assumed to be mutually compatible goals in uniting the territories under their control. When the implementation of these long-range goals of unity, development, and general prestige threatened their more immediate goals of retaining local political power, these same leaders withdrew their territories from the Federation.

Perhaps the prime lesson to be gained from Mali's experience is how intensely political leaders of new nations feel that they must retain firm control over their domestic political bases. Each defection from the Federation —of Upper Volta, Dahomey, and finally Senegal—was motivated by their leaders' fears that they would lose domestic power. Similarly, the initial enthusiasm for the Federation reflected the hope that by championing political unity political leaders would increase their local power, or at the very least that their domestic political strength would permit them the luxury of putting their ideals into practice.

In the characteristic African situation where little or no effective opposition is tolerated by the regime in power, and where virtually all status is dependent, directly or indirectly, on the government, the political and personal costs of losing office are too high for most politicians to risk. Accordingly, any successful politician who has painstakingly built himself a political base is likely to be particularly sensitive to any outside force that might disrupt it. The creation of a federation with a common central government inevitably increases the chances of some such outside interference, particularly if someone else occupies the chief post in the federal government. Only when a political leader feels absolutely secure in the domination of his home territory—a rare situation in a new nation—or where he feels so threatened that he must look to outside support to hold on—a questionable basis for political union—will a new federation appear a worthwhile gamble. Few African leaders today appear ready to take such a gamble.

Study Questions

1. Compare Mali's experience with the search for unity in Western Europe. What strategies have been adopted in each case? What difficulties were encountered?
2. The Organization of African Unity represents a different sort of attempt at bringing African states together. What strengths and weaknesses does it have that the Mali Federation lacked? Which of Mali's weaknesses are shared by the OAU?
3. Why is "African Unity" such a frequent slogan in African politics?
4. Senegal is often referred to as a "moderate" African state, while the Mali Republic (Soudan) is often called "radical." On the basis of what you know about these states, what, if any, meaning would you give to the words "moderate" and "radical"?
5. The argument is frequently made that the best chance for building viable political unions is to concentrate on building economic and communications links between states and to leave political union until much later. How useful would this approach have been in the case of the Mali Federation? What are its advantages and disadvantages as a policy for general African political integration?

Selected Bibliography

Ruth Schachter Morgenthau, *Political Parties in French-Speaking West Africa* (London: Oxford University Press, 1964) gives a detailed discussion of the French West African political background between 1945 and 1960, and includes chapters on Senegal, the Republic of Mali, Guinea, and the Ivory Coast.

Short studies of Senegalese politics are provided in Michael Crowder, *Senegal: A Study in French Assimilation Policy* (London: Oxford University Press, 1962), and in the chapter by William J. Foltz in James S. Coleman and Carl G. Rosberg, Jr., eds., *Political Parties and National Integration in Tropical Africa* (Berkeley: University of California Press, 1964).

Frank G. Snyder provides an interesting analysis of the Union Soudanaise in his *One-Party Government in Mali* (New Haven: Yale University Press, 1965), as do Thomas Hodgkin and Ruth Schachter Morgenthau in their joint chapter in the Coleman and Rosberg volume.

The official Senegalese version of the Federation's breakup is given in République du Sénégal, *Livre blanc sur le coup d'état manqué du 19 au 20 août 1960* (Dakar, 1960). The account is at some points more official than accurate, but the authenticity of the documents included in the report has not been seriously challenged.

Acknowledgments

This study is adapted from William J. Foltz, *From French West Africa to the Mali Federation* (New Haven: Yale University Press, 1965) with the kind permission of the Yale University Press. Additional background material and a fuller discussion of theoretical implications, as well as a detailed bibliography, can be found in that volume.

3

Government Versus the Unions

The Sekondi-Takoradi Strike, 1961

St. Clair Drake
Leslie Alexander Lacy

Sekondi-Takoradi, Ghana's major port and railway center, had been paralyzed for almost two weeks by a general strike. No trains had entered or left the city during that period and no buses moved within it. Bags of cocoa, Ghana's most valuable export, lay in the warehouses because dockers refused to load them. Mahogany logs floated beside the waiting ships and buckets hung motionless on the manganese conveyor belts. Essential services in the city were being neglected and the health of its 123,000 people was in jeopardy. All efforts by the government to end the strike had failed.

Then, on Saturday, September 16, 1961, the President of the state, Kwame Nkrumah, flew into Accra, the capital city, returning hastily from a prolonged overseas visit. Since the three-man Presidential Commission which he had appointed to run the country while he was away could not handle the crisis, it had urged him to come home.

On Sunday, Nkrumah spoke over the radio and asked the strikers to return to work. He gave his personal pledge as "Father of the Nation" that their grievances would be sympathetically considered. He lifted the curfew that had been imposed by the Presidential Commission, canceled the proclamation of a state of emergency, and ordered the release of the few persons who had been arrested in connection with the strike. He and the nation then waited anxiously for Sekondi-Takoradi's response to these conciliatory gestures.

On Monday morning, the strike leaders gave their answer. At a series of mass meetings in the port, speakers exhorted the strikers to stand firm until all their demands had been met. One excited orator warned against strike-breaking, shouting, "We shall cause the blood of anyone who chooses to play the role of stooge to flow like water." Another threatened that the cranes on the dockside would be "totally destroyed" if the workers who had returned to man them did not quit immediately. Some of the leaders of the influential Railway and Harbour Workers Union and of ten associated unions had decided to pit their power and prestige against that of the nation's President, whose devoted followers, a year before when Ghana became a republic, had bestowed upon him an ancient tribal title, *Osagyefo* (Warrior Chief Who Defeated the Enemy and Saved the Nation). The government now saw its very existence implicitly challenged: "If in the future, we win, we shall become the masters of this country." The *Osagyefo* had come home to meet this challenge.

Three days after the President's appeal the strike was still on, so Nkrumah addressed the nation again. The tone of his voice had changed. No government could allow itself to be coerced by one small section of the community, he said, and he ordered a return to work within two days, threatening to throw the whole weight of the nation's military and police power against the strikers if they held out. Two days later the strike was over.

During the next month the two cabinet members on the Presidential Commission were dismissed from office and suspended from membership in the ruling Convention People's Party (CPP). Several other cabinet members were also dismissed; a drastic governmental reorganization was carried out; and controls over the economy were tightened. The government then arrested a group of Sekondi-Takoradi trade unionists as well as several prominent officials of the opposition United Party (UP). Soon thereafter special courts were set up to try treason cases and were given power to hand down sentences of death. Never before had the government's reaction to an internal crisis been so intense. Its response to the Sekondi-Takoradi strike drastically altered the entire character of political activity in Ghana. How did the crisis arise and why was the reaction to it so extreme?

The incident that precipitated the strike was the deduction of 5 percent of the workers' wages from their August 1961 paychecks. The deduction was provided for in a "compulsory savings" scheme introduced in July as part of a new "austerity budget," which also included a property and a purchase tax. The government was seeking new sources of revenue to offset a decline in income from the export tax on cocoa, and was trying to shift some of the burden of taxation away from the cocoa farmers to wage and salary workers and businessmen. Prices had been rising for six months, partly because of increased taxes on imports, but wages had been frozen. The Industrial Relations Act of 1958 had made strikes virtually illegal,

Republic of Ghana, 1966

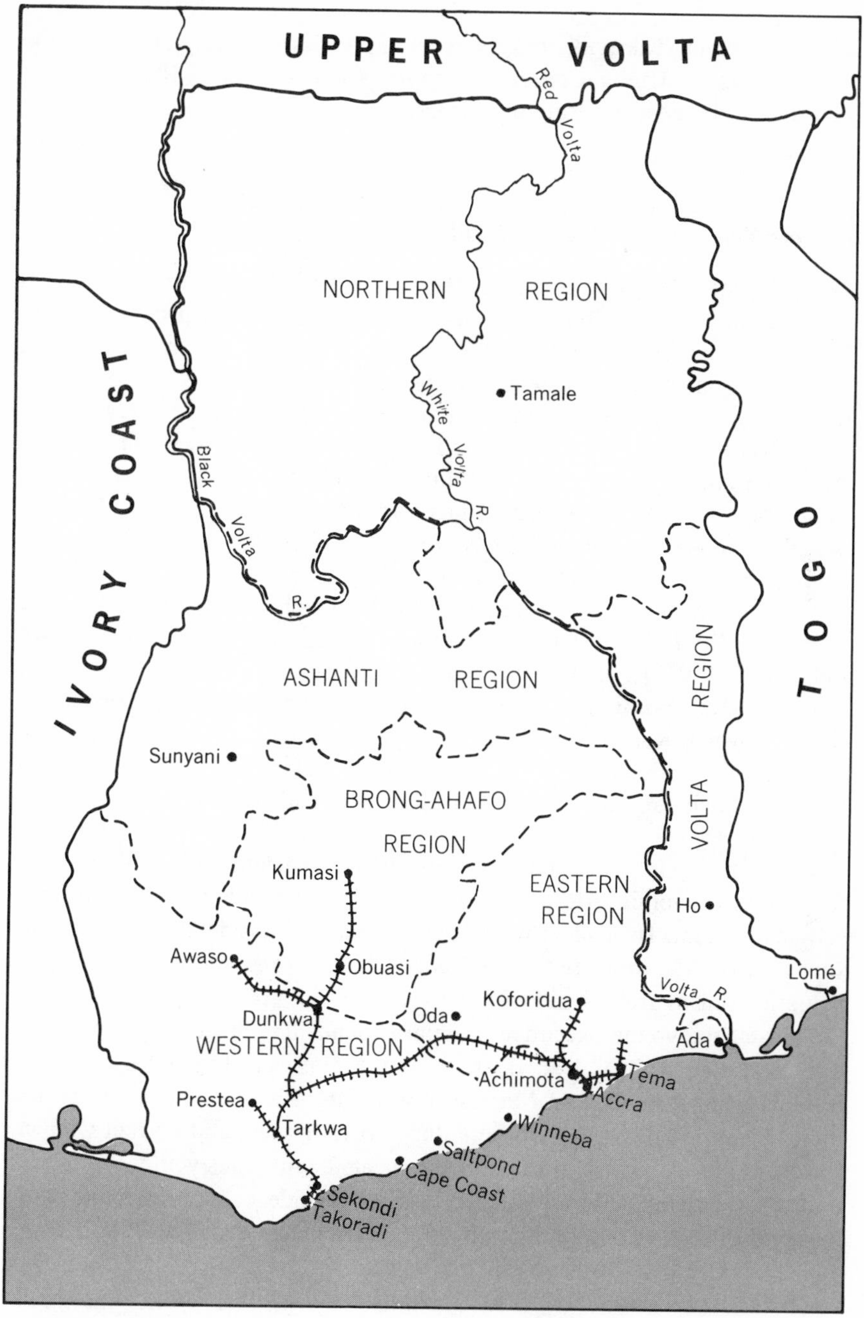

and the Sekondi-Takoradi strike was an expression of resentment over the national Trades Union Congress support of the Industrial Relations Act as well as over the new taxation schemes.

Kwame Nkrumah and the "Political Kingdom"

In 1961, when the strike occurred, the Convention People's Party had been in power in Ghana for ten years. Its Founder and Life Chairman, Kwame Nkrumah, had created it in 1949 as an instrument of struggle against British rule in the Gold Coast, and he had used it later as a mechanism for national mobilization after internal self-government was granted in 1951. Nkrumah had returned home in 1947 after twelve years of study in American and British universities, during which time he won a reputation as an able organizer of African student activities. He had also published a pamphlet, *Towards Colonial Freedom,* and had served as one of the organizers of the Fifth Pan-African Congress in Manchester, England, in 1945, along with the West Indian journalist, George Padmore (who later wrote *The Gold Coast Revolution*), the American Negro scholar and civil rights leader, W. E. B. Du Bois, and the Kenya nationalist leader, Jomo Kenyatta. He was invited home by the United Gold Coast Convention (UGCC) which wanted him to serve as its executive secretary, and the invitation was tendered by J. B. Danquah, a well-established Gold Coast lawyer, scholar, and newspaper publisher who had organized the Convention.

The United Gold Coast Convention had come into existence in 1947 to express economic grievances and to work gradually toward Ghanaian self-government. Its leaders were lawyers and businessmen, and it drew its support from the more prosperous cocoa farmers and successful entrepreneurs as well as from some of Ghana's chiefs, or traditional rulers. From the outset, the young executive secretary found himself at odds with Danquah and other UGCC leaders as to pace, timing, and principles of organization. Being a student of Marxist movements, Kwame Nkrumah insisted upon organizing the urban workers, the poorer farmers and market women, the unemployed, and the restless, half-educated, ambitious youth. A forceful orator and indefatigable traveler, he inspired confidence and attracted a following that bestowed upon him affectionate nicknames such as "Show Boy" and laudatory titles such as "Africa's Messiah" and "Man of Destiny"—words that symbolized the fact of his charisma.

Because the UGCC leaders preferred a less radical and more conventional movement, a clash between them and Nkrumah was inevitable. The issue that brought about the break was centered upon the decision of the British government to grant a new constitution to the Gold Coast, a constitution that broadened the franchise and increased African legislative representation but fell far short of granting self-government. Nkrumah dubbed it a "bogus and fraudulent constitution." A former divinity student, Nkrumah spoke a language the mission-trained literates understood when he exhorted, "Seek ye first the political kingdom and all other things shall be added unto it." The crowds roared back, "S.G. [self-government] now!" The UGCC leaders, on the other hand, vigorously defended the Coussey Constitution as a significant step in the quest for "self-government in the shortest possible time." Urged on by the youth groups active all over the Gold Coast and supported by various individuals and groups who felt they would profit from an all-African government, Nkrumah finally broke away from the more conservative leaders and formed the Convention People's Party in 1949. Danquah and the other older leaders never forgave him for what they considered an act of ingratitude. They denounced him as an irresponsible demagogue.

Early in 1950 the leader of the new party launched a Gandhi-style campaign of "non-violent positive action" with the goal of immediate independence. He found an ally in the Railway Workers Union of Sekondi-Takoradi and the Gold Coast Trades Union Congress (TUC), both of which called a general strike to support the CPP. The colonial government, which had already dubbed Nkrumah a Communist, arrested him and several of his lieutenants for sedition and proceeded with their plans for an election under the new constitution. The CPP decided to run in the election, even though it opposed the constitution.

With Nkrumah in jail, a loyal associate, Komla Gbedemah, an ex-school teacher and businessman, who had finished his own jail sentence and become what the nationalists proudly call a "P.G." (prison graduate), assumed the role of campaign manager and led the CPP to a landslide victory. The Governor immediately released Nkrumah and appointed him Leader of Government Business in the newly elected Parliament. In his hour of triumph, Nkrumah sought to clarify the ambiguity that surrounded his political orientation by announcing, "I am a Marxian socialist and an undenominational Christian. The places I know in Europe are London and Paris. I am no Communist and have never been one." (The London *Times*, February 14, 1951.)

For the next six years, Nkrumah seldom spoke of socialism, although the party newspaper referred to it frequently as the ultimate goal. The CPP structure included a small study group that diligently examined all varieties of socialism, but the party also had within its ranks a substantial number of small businessmen. Nkrumah devoted his major attention to negotiating for independence by means of what he called Tactical Action. Finally, on March 6, 1957, the Gold Coast Colony became the sovereign state of Ghana—named for an ancient African kingdom. Nkrumah was acclaimed throughout the world for having led his country to independence—the first colony in Africa south of the Sahara to make the breakthrough against colonial rule. He had won the keys to the "political kingdom."

In 1960, Ghana became a republic within the Commonwealth, and a presidential plebiscite was held. Running against Nkrumah, who boldly stated his intention to lay the foundations for a socialist society and who stressed the CPP's six-year-old record for erecting schools, roads, and hospitals and for achieving independence, was the elder statesman, J. B. Danquah, who pledged his party to a program of "the enlightened socialism of liberalism." Never before had the people of Ghana, other than in his own constituency, had a chance to vote for or against Nkrumah, since under the old constitution one could vote only for his own local member of Parliament. Nkrumah defeated Danquah, the man who launched his political career, by a 9 to 1 vote. He announced that the time had come for the second revolution to begin—*against* poverty and illiteracy and *for* social reconstruction. Nkrumah interpreted the victory as a mandate for himself and his party to proceed to build a "socialist society." But there were no means of production to be nationalized. Industrial development was given top priority in plans for the future.

Socialism and the All-Embracing Party

The vehicle for the realization of socialism in Ghana as conceived by Nkrumah was to be The Party, which every individual was expected to join, thus giving nominal allegiance to socialist goals. By 1961 a program of "socialist education" was underway to "raise the level of socialist consciousness" within and outside the party, and to give effect to the slogan, "We can't build socialism without socialists." Party branches were established in schools, offices, and workshops. The Vanguard Activists, dedicated and loyal, were to keep less zealous Ghanaians on their toes, while the Young Pioneer movement was to produce, out of the next generation, what the party called "Africa's New Man."

The term "Nkrumaism" came into vogue to designate "the ideology of the African revolution," and after much intra-party debate and discussion, Nkrumaism was defined as "a non-atheistic socialist philosophy which seeks to adapt the current socialist ideas to the solution of our problems. . . . It is basically Socialism adapted to suit the conditions and circumstances of Africa." (*The Party,* April, 1961.) During 1960–61, with CPP leaders in control of the key posts, the following organizations were defined as "integral wings" of the party: the United Ghana Farmers' Council, the National Cooperative Council, the National Council of Ghana Women, and the Ghana Trades Union Congress. Each organization was responsible for carrying out party policy in a strategic segment of the nation's life. Voluntary associations and churches were expected to cooperate with these groups and with the Young Pioneers in developing "socialist consciousness" and inculcating respect for the office and person of the *Osagyefo,* who was presented as leading the battle against neocolonialism and imperialism, and for a United States of Africa. Many existing unions, however, resisted incorporation into the framework of the all-embracing party, among them the Railway and Harbour Workers Union of Sekondi-Takoradi.

Projecting the African Personality

Ghana, with a population of about 7 million, had the highest per capita income of any African-controlled nation on the continent. Its small farms, owned by individuals and families, supplied over a third of the world's cocoa. By 1960 there was an increasing demand within Ghana for a wide range of consumer goods including radios, bicycles, automobiles, and imported foodstuffs, as well as for improved housing, education, and social services. The CPP promised a payoff through the socialist society of the future.

Although over three-fourths of Ghana's population was illiterate, the percentage of its people who could read and write and who had secured training above the secondary school level was high compared to other African states. The Ghanaians had developed a harmonious blend of African and European customs in religious and political activities, and the CPP symbols and organizational structure, combining African and Western forms, reflected the ethos of a society in which a literate elite supplied leadership for an illiterate mass, predominantly rural and folk but operating within a money economy.

Nkrumah and his party were determined to make Ghana a "show-piece" that would prove "the black man can govern himself." The government expended considerable money on Pan-African conferences between 1957 and 1960 and gave financial aid to nationalist movements throughout the continent, and its leaders lost no opportunity to "project the African Personality" on the world scene. That Ghana was able to play this role was due to the fact that it had built up a high level of invested financial reserves between 1940 and 1955 from the sale of cocoa on the world market.

The Austerity Budget of 1961

Ghana's First Development Plan was initiated in 1951. By 1959, the government had spent $329 million in laying down an economic infrastructure for industrialization (including the construction of a deep-water harbor), on improving agriculture, and for building roads, schools, and hospitals. From 1951 through 1955, annual revenue exceeded expenditure, and the surplus was added to the government's reserve funds invested in Britain. From 1955 onward, however, annual expenditure exceeded income at an accelerating rate (Figure 3, p. 77). The deficit was partially made up by borrowing from the Cocoa Marketing Board, a public corporation that had its own separate invested reserves built up by the monopoly it held on buying the entire cocoa crop each year from the producers at a fixed price and selling it on the world market. The Board was able to lend the government $74 million between 1951 and 1959. The government also drew upon its own reserves, which by 1961 had been reduced to about $120 million from $235 million in 1955. The use of both reserve funds for this purpose was defended on the grounds that the money was of more value to Ghana if used for capital investment than if merely drawing interest from the British securities that had been bought with it. So the securities were sold. None of these funds were used for meeting current expenses, annual revenues being large enough for that purpose.

After 1959, borrowing from the Cocoa Marketing Board and collecting sufficient revenue to meet current expenses were both made increasingly difficult by a decline in the price of cocoa on the world market. Until 1959 about 40 percent of the government's annual revenue was secured from taxes on exports (Figure 4, p. 77), and most of this income was derived from the tax on cocoa, which was set in relation to the world price. By 1960, however, less than one-fifth of the country's revenue was being secured from export taxes, but almost 60 percent of the $186 million collected from this source that year was from the cocoa tax alone.

The decline in revenue from export taxes was due mainly to the fact that the price for cocoa on the world market had been falling steadily since 1954, despite a slight upturn between 1956 and 1958. Near the end of 1960 it was approaching the lowest point in thirteen years (Figure 2, p. 76), although world production was at an all-time high (Figure 1, p. 76). Ghana's bumper crop of 1961 was expected to yield $4 million less than had a smaller crop the previous year. In 1960 the loan from the Cocoa Marketing Board was $8,960,000 less than had been expected because the Board had to pay out that sum to the farmers who had been guaranteed a fixed price over a four-year period, and the world price had tumbled below the agreed-upon figure. Thus, since 1959, the government had found it necessary to try to increase the proportion of revenue from sources other than export taxes and had been moderately successful (Figure 4, p. 77). The effort would have to be redoubled during the 1961–62 fiscal year to avoid the use of foreign loans for current expenses and the exhaustion of reserves and to prevent a slowing down of the pace of development.

A policy decision had been made in 1957 to diversify agriculture and to embark upon an ambitious program of industrialization and farm mechanization. A Second Development Plan, 1959–64 (replaced in 1962 by the Seven-Year Development Plan) was drawn up to provide for an expenditure of $980 million over a five-year period. As income from cocoa dwindled, some development experts suggested a drastic revision of the plan; others felt that in order to break dependence upon cocoa it was essential to implement the plan, using foreign loans where necessary. But they also suggested that individual and family consumption should be curtailed in order to conserve foreign exchange and prevent inflation, and that nonessential government expenditure be eliminated. They insisted that all ordinary current expenses be met from annual revenues and not from loans or by drawing upon reserves. The government decided not to abandon its development plans, but it was clear than an "austerity budget" was imperative.

The 1961 fiscal year would begin in July. The first stage of the budget-making process was well under way by the beginning of 1961—the preparation of estimates by various ministries and government departments of the amount each would like to spend, and for what, during the year. All government agencies had been asked to trim down requests for funds not directly related to development needs. However, since CPP power rested to a great extent upon its ability to maintain a high level of employment (and this partly through patronage), there was a limit to the cutbacks in personnel that could be made. The government also had extensive Pan-African commitments and a tradition of participation in international affairs that it wished to maintain. Expenditures were estimated at $358,500,000 for the 1961–62 fiscal year, of which about a third, $130,570,000 was to be allocated to development projects. At least $60 million more in revenue would be required than had been raised the previous year. New sources of income had to be found.

A plan had been introduced during the 1959–60 budget year to recoup some of the money paid to cocoa growers for price stabilization by the Marketing Board. The Ghana Farmers' Council leaders had assured the government that the majority of the cocoa farmers would be willing to have $1.68 withheld from the price paid by the Board for every sixty-pound load of cocoa (16 percent of the price paid to the farmer). The balance sheet for the year showed 8.8 percent of the revenue as coming from this and other "voluntary contributions," and 13.2 percent in the following year. There were also slight increases in revenue from import duties (Figure 4, p. 77). A decision was made to continue deducting this sum when cocoa was purchased during the 1961–62 season, and to ask each farmer, in addition, to accept a government bond, maturing in ten years, to cover 10 percent of the total sum owed for the crop. With cocoa farmers thus expected to contribute about one-fifth of their income, both prudence and justice demanded a widening of the base of taxation.

A budget was finally designed that estimated a possible $6 million in revenue to be obtained from a new purchase tax on durable consumer goods (such as cars and refrigerators), as well as $112 million from increased import duties on a wide range of commodities including textiles, kerosene, and some food products. Smaller sums were expected from increased export taxes on timber and a few other items, as well as from improved procedures for collecting income taxes from those earning over $1,344 a year and from

Economic Background of Sekondi-Takoradi Strike

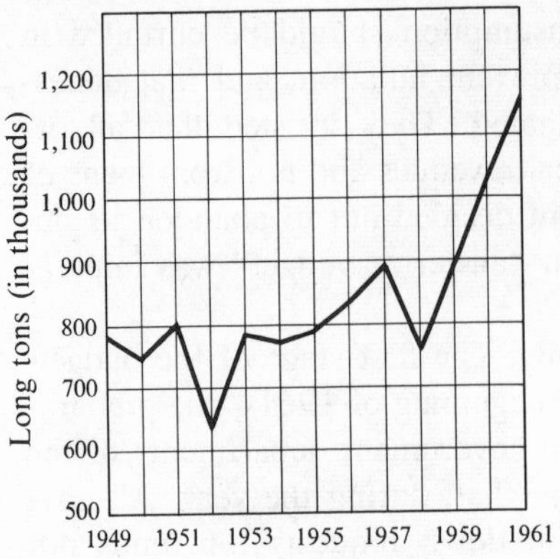

FIGURE 1. World Cocoa Production

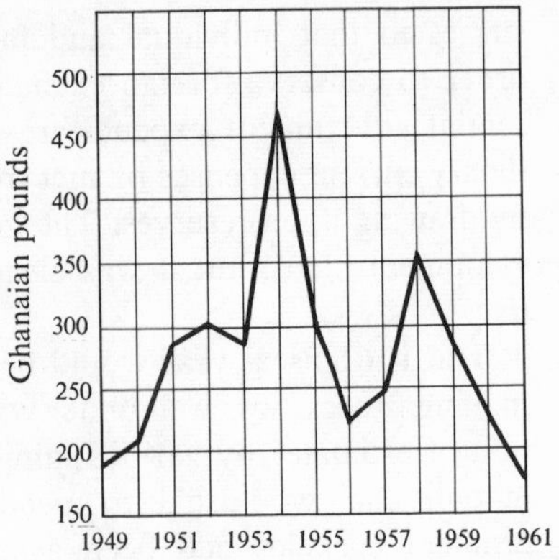

FIGURE 2. World Cocoa Price

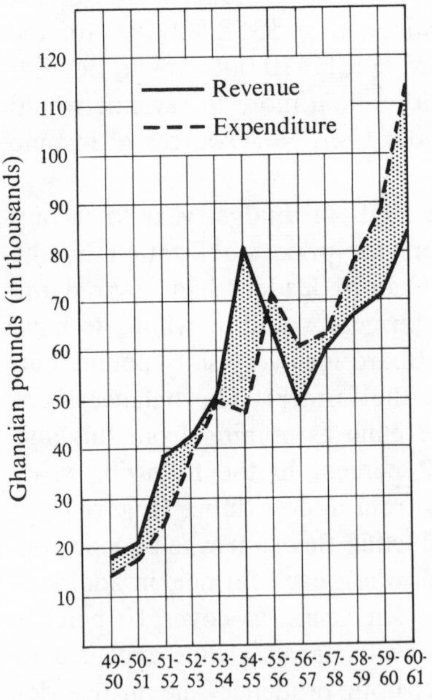

FIGURE 3. Rise of Expenditure in Relation to Revenue

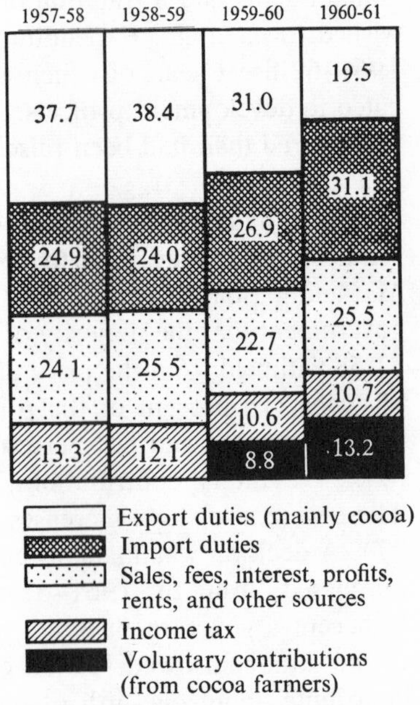

FIGURE 4. Sources of Revenue, 1957-58 through 1960-61.

SOURCE: *Economic Survey, 1961* (Accra: Central Bureau of Statistics, 1962).

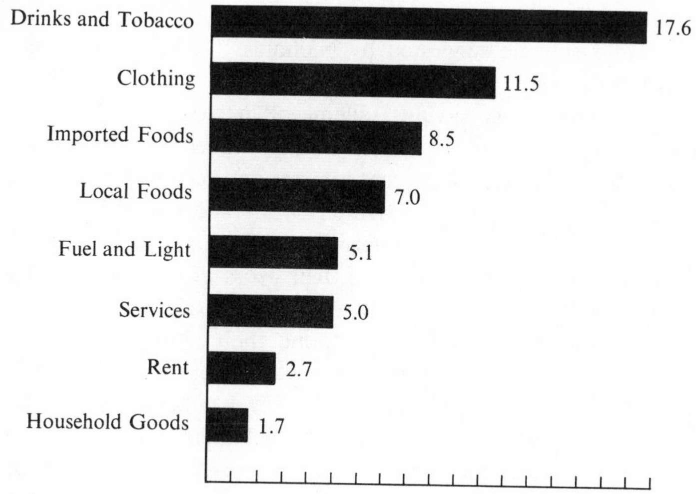

FIGURE 5. Percentage Increase in Prices from 1960 to 1961

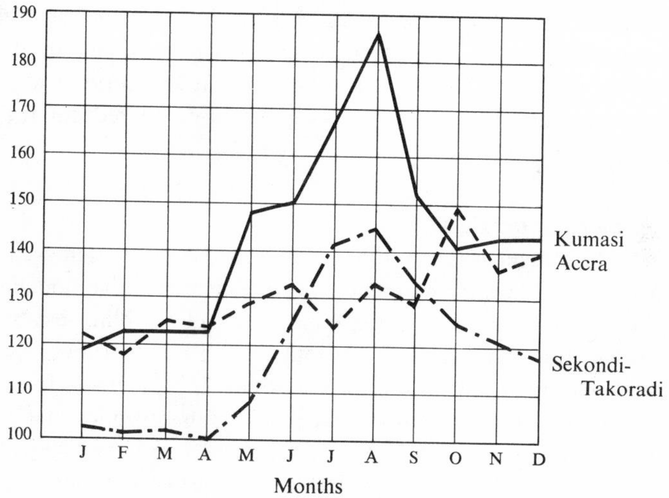

FIGURE 6. Price Index of Locally Grown Foods, 1961

business enterprises. An additional $31 million was hoped for from a compulsory savings scheme suggested by Nicholas Kaldor, an economist from Cambridge University.

Under the compulsory savings scheme all persons earning over $336 a year would have to accept 5 percent of their wages or salaries in National Investment Bonds drawing 4 percent interest and redeemable after 10 years. All employed persons who were neither farmers nor working for wages or salaries, as well as all business enterprises, were expected to buy National Investment Bonds with 10 percent of their gross income. Kaldor has stated that "the advantage of the scheme as against straightforward taxation is that people are merely asked to postpone their consumption and not to forego it altogether."[1] The people's acceptance of such a novel idea was bound to depend, in part, upon the current level of taxation as well as upon whether they believed they would actually get their money back. In 1961, the estimated per capita income for Ghana was $174. The budget proposals would impose about $42 a year, per capita, in direct and indirect taxes.

In line with British parliamentary practice, the details of the Ghana budget are always a secret until it is presented to Parliament. But rumors about its provisions had spread widely throughout the country before July, and there were rumblings of discontent over what many people considered too high a level of taxation. As to compulsory savings, there was much cynical comment indicating widespread disbelief in the promised future repayment. Confidence was not strengthened by suggestions in the CPP press, after the plan was announced, that it would be patriotic to give the deducted sum to the government without expecting to redeem the bonds later.

The Pilgrimage to the East

The austerity budget was coordinated with a drive for increased investment from abroad. The CPP had an official policy of positive nonalignment, which meant no commitments in the Cold War but a willingness to accept financial and technical assistance from both sides. Prior to 1960, Ghana had never sought a foreign loan except for a small line of credit from Israel, having financed development up to that point from revenues and reserves. A policy decision was made in 1960, however, to seek American financing for the Volta River hydroelectric project—the heart of the industrialization plan—and loans from the Eastern countries for a number of smaller industrial installations. When over $100 million for the Volta River project seemed assured, Nkrumah prepared to make his first trip to visit the USSR, the Communist nations of Eastern Europe, and the People's Republic of China. Accompanied by a large delegation, he left for a two-month trip

---

[1] Nicholas Kaldor, "Taxation for Economic Development," *The Journal of Modern African Studies* (March, 1963).

early in July, 1961, on what one newspaper called "a pilgrimage to the East." A three-man Presidential Commission was left in charge of the country. Komla Gbedemah represented the party's right wing and Kojo Botsio, the left wing (he was Director of Ideological Studies for the CPP), along with Chief Justice Arku Korsah. The situation seemed stable and secure.

The Debate on the Budget

Nkrumah presented his sessional address to Parliament on July 4 and left for the Soviet Union on the ninth. That same day the Minister of Finance presented the budget to Parliament. He defended it on the grounds that "any increases in burdens imposed by this budget will . . . be small in comparison with the increase in incomes and living standards which the people of this country have enjoyed since independence." He reminded the legislators of some remarks made by President Nkrumah in his sessional address when he had begun to prepare the public for the shock of the forthcoming budget: "As Osagyefo said in his speech, the increase in the total wage and salary payments since 1957 has been 49 percent. Last year we granted a general wage increase of approximately 22 percent." The Minister insisted that there was no basis for saying "the present budget could impose unbearable burdens," and announced "the firm determination of the government not to countenance any wage and salary increase," since, "if people were trying to react by trying to compensate for any increase in hardships which they suffer as a result of this budget by increasing their money income, our whole objective would be nullified, and we should have incurred all this sacrifice to no purpose."[2]

On July 10, the following day, a party newspaper, the *Evening News,* carried several significant headlines: "Kwame Calls for National Unity," "Beer and Cigarettes Will Cost More," and "Telegrams Back Budget." Almost simultaneously with Nkrumah's arrival in Moscow on the tenth a group of market women demonstrated over the rise of prices in the capital city of Accra, while another group of protestors demanded that the Presidential Commission reduce the price of bread and stabilize prices generally. Late in the afternoon of the same day during a scheduled parliamentary session, the new Minister of Finance moved "that this House approve the financial policy of the Government for the year ending 30th June, 1962." A CPP member of Parliament from Accra, whose constituency included many market women, drew the attention of the House to the demonstrations, charged that some goods were being sold at prices beyond the established standards, and asked the Finance Minister to institute regulations to stop these practices. The Minister replied that the market women were demonstrating against "exploitation" by wholesalers who were taking advantage

[2] *Economic Survey, 1961* (Accra: Central Bureau of Statistics, 1962), p. 80.

of uncertainty about the budget. His remarks drew shouts from Opposition benches, "They demonstrated against the Budget!" The Minister refused to accept this interpretation.

One of the significant features of this budget debate was the extent to which warning notes were sounded.[3] A leader of the opposition United Party, the very first speaker, Victor Owusu, from Ashanti, linked the budget with criticism of the general political situation, saying:

> Since independence, Sir, slowly but effectively and by means of threats, arrests, Preventive Detention, discrimination in disparaging [sic] patronage and other such agencies, the masses of this country have been cowed down into submission and have surrendered without a fight for their freedom of speech, freedom of association and freedom of conscience. It now seems that their last remaining freedom—that of a right to decent standard of living—is about to be taken away from them. *But let those who seek to do this remember the old Akan adage that there comes a time when a coward on the run beaten, threatened, humiliated, decides to make a stand and fight. And when he does this, he fights with the strength and ferocity of a wounded tiger.* [Italics added.]

A warning came also from the Northern Region, in this case from a loyal CPP backbencher, S. I. Iddrissu, who rose to say:

> I know from my own experience that the people in the rural areas are going to be victims of these tax proposals. I do not feel that we who are students of Nkrumaism based on Marxist Socialism should stand here and introduce these tax proposals which will only benefit the few and impose hardships on the majority. . . . I do not intend to go any further, but the note of warning which I should like to sound is this: *If you are pushing something on somebody and you think that he is a fool because when you always push the thing on him he merely says "Ah," a time will come when you take advantage of this and you try to push it on him, and then the result will be disastrous—it will affect you and it will affect him, too.* [Italics added.]

The second day of debate was dominated by the United Party's popular —and demagogic—parliamentarian from Ashanti, Joseph Appiah (who had created a sensation many years before, when he was a law student in London, by marrying the daughter of Sir Stafford Cripps). Appiah, known as "Joe" to CPP parliamentarians as well as to his own party colleagues, drew laughter with some of his remarks, and then launched a vigorous attack upon government fiscal policies, reminding the CPP parliamentarians that "the Government of this country belongs to all of us and those who sit or preside over the affairs of this country like birds of passage are here today

[3] The two speeches quoted below are from Ghana Legislative Assembly, *Debates*, July 10, 1961.

and gone tomorrow." He referred to what he called "devastating and crippling taxes" and taunted the front benches with the comment, "If the Government are truly sincere in their assertion that our economy is sound and that financially we are buoyant, then I challenge the Government to suspend this Budget for six months." This remained one of the main lines of the Opposition attack, the charge that an austerity budget had been concocted to prevent the economic collapse of the country and that the CPP was pulling the wool over the people's eyes by saying that the financial health of the nation was sound.

The budget debate took place against a background of rising prices caused by drought for locally produced foodstuffs, the cost of food reaching its peak in the port of Sekondi-Takoradi and the Ashanti capital, Kumasi, in August. In addition, the new budget became the focus of general concern about the rising cost of living. (See Figures 5 and 6, p. 77.)

Opposition to the Budget Grows

The press and the propaganda vans of the CPP had the job of trying to "sell" the budget to the people. The *Evening News* (a newspaper founded by Nkrumah and written in a style appealing mainly to those with less than a high school education) carried a front-page story as early as July 5 under the caption: "Compulsory Savings—Positive Action Budget Principles." The newspaper stressed the "equality of sacrifice" theme with the news that "Osagyefo Takes Lead in 'Tighten Belt' Movement—Kwame To Forego £2,500 Allowance."

But the next day some uneasiness over how "the masses" would take the budget was expressed in a columnist's comments on the seriousness of "the belt-tightening challenge." News items about telegrams and resolutions (from party branches, market women, groups of chiefs, and popular individuals) backing the budget appeared daily for the next two months in an attempt to create a bandwagon effect. Outside of official party circles, however, considerable scepticism was expressed over the spontaneity of the resolutions.

The opposite of the CPP press treatment of the budget was evident in an unsigned, mimeographed leaflet circulated widely throughout the country soon after the budget was announced. The title was "The Hour Has Struck." The government suspected that the United Party was behind the leaflet, since it also called for the abolition of the presidential system of government and a return to a Prime Minister to Her Majesty serving under a Governor General, a favorite UP idea. The leaflet ridiculed the recently appointed Minister of Finance who had replaced Gbedemah, the incumbent of the previous ten years:

> Call for the budget in its entirety to be scrapped! It is a total failure and a tyranny, oppressive, repressive, and suppressive, to borrow Kwame

> Nkrumah's own phraseology. With this bogus and fraudulent budget must go Judas Iscariot, the puppet minister responsible, fickle-minded F. D. K. Goka. He must be forced to resign and go back to his father's village.

Some people, however, did not oppose compulsory savings on principle, but felt that the ceiling was set too low and that the lowest paid workers should be entirely exempt.

The Sekondi-Takoradi Railway Workers Lead the Protest

The first organized protest against the budget came from the Sekondi-Takoradi branch of the Railway and Harbour Workers Union, which had appointed a working committee to plan a program of action. The opening move came in mid-July in the form of a letter from the general secretary-treasurer of the branch to John Tettegah, the general secretary of the Ghana Trades Union Congress (TUC). It referred to "a general upsurge of feelings" among union members and requested that the TUC ask the government to postpone payroll deductions "until such time as the effect of the whole budget proposals on workers' income has been studied." Copies of the letter were sent to the Western Regional Commissioner (the government representative in Takoradi), the general manager of the railways (government-owned), and the Western Regional secretary of the TUC. The resolutions of the working committee, which were enclosed, spoke of the "extreme hardship" imposed by a compulsory savings scheme that "strikes at the very root of the income of the workers."

In approaching the TUC, the Sekondi-Takoradi branch of the Railway Union was proceeding according to the provisions of the Industrial Relations Act of 1958. The officials, however, did not expect any vigorous action from the TUC; they were putting their legally designated bargaining agent "on the spot," and they backed up their action with a special letter to the Western Regional Commissioner which, in the African idiom, asked for his "fatherly sympathy with the financial plight of the workers." Having received no answers after a week, they appealed directly to a cabinet member, Krobo Edusei, the Minister of Transportation and Communications. They wrote a letter "begging" him to consider the proposals sent to the TUC—a letter that he did not answer. The letters had, however, set off serious discussions at top levels of government and TUC.

Deductions were scheduled to begin at the end of July, and the Sekondi-Takoradi branch held a mass meeting on July 30, at which the workers decided to go on strike during the first week in August. The top officials of the Railway and Harbour Workers Union immediately repudiated this rank-and-file action at the urging of the union's able and shrewd secretary-treasurer, I. E. Inkumsah (who was then accused by the pro-strike leaders of having favored the passage of the Industrial Relations Act, which they considered antilabor). The letters and the strike threat had some effect, however: There was no payroll deduction in July. The workers and their middle-level leaders, confident now of their strength, took a no-compromise position. Postponement was not enough for them; only a revision of the entire budget would suffice.

Two days after the initial mass meeting in Sekondi-Takoradi, a branch of the Railway Union in the inland city of Kumasi, center of the Ashanti cocoa-growing area, called its members together so that the branch secretary could explain why the government considered National Investment Bonds necessary. The workers were unmoved by what they interpreted as the secretary's defense of compulsory savings. They proceeded to adopt a resolution pledging to "solemnly and firmly support" the action being taken in Sekondi-Takoradi. The next day the Kumasi Permanent Waymen's Association wrote to the Sekondi-Takoradi branch promising "unflinching support of the actions of the Working Committee" and urging it to "fight on to get the bill withdrawn or suspended." Devotion to the national welfare was stressed as a sanction on the grounds that the 1961 budget would encourage less productivity and a lack of interest among the men. During the next week the Sekondi-Takoradi branch thanked the Kumasi workers for their support, but recorded its official "line" in a letter to them saying, "We are earnestly awaiting the Osagyefo's return to resume our struggle to be relieved of some of the hard budget exactions." The letter also contained a cryptic suggestion: "Meanwhile educate your men to understand precisely what we are about and to lend their unshakeable support."

Although the date of the payroll deduction had been postponed, the Presidential Commission informed the Railway Workers through TUC channels that no further action could be taken until Nkrumah's return. On August 8 a daily newspaper carried a report that employees earning less than £10 ($28.00) a month would be exempt from the compulsory savings scheme. This action, which had been urged by the TUC and the CPP "left," excited the anger of the Railway Union leaders in Sekondi-Takoradi, since very few of their members were in this low-income category. They decided to by-pass the TUC in a direct appeal to the Presidential Commission, and their letter implicitly charged bad faith on the part of the commissioners:

> Unfortunately our humble appeal for the suspension was not given deserving consideration due to the fact that Osagyefo, the President, was not in the country and in his absence you alleged no amendments could be made to such orders.
>
> It looks suspicious for us to read from the *Ghanaian Times* on August 8th, 1961, that employees of a certain wage level would be exempted from the Bond, for which we are grateful. But as a matter of fact this publication has put us leaders in great embarrassment to explain the situation, as we had thought any action by you would be known to us beforehand through the TUC, in order to reconcile your action with

> what we have been telling the rank and file. In this connection we humbly regret the action taken by you as it has rather aggravated resentment than cooling the feelings of the workers.

The Presidential Commission did not reply to this letter, but the Western Regional Commissioner who had been sent a copy summoned the Railway Union leaders. He told them that they should be patient and warned that if they were considering a strike, they should remember that it might lead to vigorous governmental counteraction. The union leaders then called a mass meeting, which passed a resolution to be sent to the Presidential Commission pointing out that "it has been obviously seen and understood that after all the Commission could do something to ease the situation."

The response to the Presidential Commission's action by the Kumasi union leaders was more extreme than that in Sekondi-Takoradi. They, too, called a mass meeting, six days after the one held in the port. They sent a resolution to the Presidential Commission, stating that "the economic condition of the country is rather growing from bad to worse," and they broadened their protest to include a demand for abolition of the purchase tax and property tax, arguing that these measures would "highly enslave the economic freedom of the workers." The unionists claimed to be "convinced that the introduction of the National Development Bonds tantamounts to the fact that the Government is rushing up developments, with the resultant cause that the workers are over-strained economically; so the Government must take up development step by step." They said they were perturbed over the Presidential Commission's insistence that nothing could be done without Nkrumah, commenting with thinly veiled sarcasm, "This is rather fantastic, since there is no country in this world that is governed by one man, except in dictatorial countries, which our beloved Ghana is not one." They proposed, further, that any deductions already made be refunded and that the purchase and property taxes be "amended to suit the ordinary worker," and then expressed their hostility to the TUC: "Whereas the TUC has definitely failed to express the true feelings of the working class; thus putting the worker in an unbearable position; we hereby resolve and do solemnly resolve that the National Union of Railway and Harbour Workers do secede from the TUC forthwith." A showdown was brewing, and it is necessary at this point to consider why the Railway Union rather than some other union took up the cudgel against the government, the party, and the TUC.

Why the Railway Union?

The railway men of Sekondi-Takoradi organized the first viable trade unions in the Gold Coast Colony, and have always been proud of their role as pioneers. In 1939, they organized the first large-scale strike in the Gold Coast. Two years before the United Gold Coast Convention came on the scene, the Railway Union had organized the unions of the country into a Trades Union Congress. The TUC put pressure on the Governor to release Danquah, Nkrumah, and their four associates after their arrest in 1948. This same organization gave Nkrumah the backing he needed to carry through the Positive Action campaign in 1950, for the general strike lent additional mass support to the CPP and reduced the appeal of Danquah and the conservative elites of the UGCC.

The TUC collapsed under colonial government pressure during the Positive Action struggle, but British labor officers and the unions which had not taken part in the general strike reorganized it and advised it to steer clear of politics. The CPP leaders, once they had formed a government in 1951, did not disapprove of this advice, for they were interested in consolidating their newly acquired political power and in building a mass party; it was clear to them that they could not immediately fulfill all their campaign promises. They had slowly to cross the gulf between national agitation and executive responsibility, and even though the governor and most of the civil servants were English, the CPP leaders were involved in the formation and execution of policy and were now being held accountable by their own people for what happened in the country. Any TUC focusing of the industrial unrest which was already rising could seriously weaken the fledgling government, just as it had weakened British colonial power.

Standing to the right of the CPP were the tribalists and "cocoa politicians," probing for every weakness. But forces that could embarrass the CPP government were also gathering on the left, and the man who led them was in the very bosom of the party, the popular E. C. Turkson Ocran, general secretary of the Railway Union of Sekondi-Takoradi (also parliamentary secretary, personal secretary to Nkrumah, member of the CPP executive committee, and general secretary of the reorganized TUC). Ocran drew followers from within the Railway Union and from among young radicals in the party. This group wanted changes in the existing wage structure, strongly criticized the type of courses being provided by the Extra-Mural Union (university extension) for workers, and urged the removal of the International Confederation of Free Trade Union (ICFTU) Centre for West Africa from Accra. They apparently wanted closer ties with the Communist-dominated World Federation of Trade Unions (WFTU), from which a group of American, British, and Belgian trade unions had withdrawn to form ICFTU.

Nkrumah and his close associates watched the growing popularity of Ocran with some apprehension. In the first place, although he considered himself a Marxist, Nkrumah opposed on principle any organic ties with the international Communist movement. In the second place, a strong "left" faction within the CPP would disrupt the unity that he insisted the party needed in the final phases of the struggle for independence. But an even more urgent consideration was the fact that the British government had suspended the constitution of British Guiana in 1953 on the grounds that the nationalist leader, Cheddi Jagan, was following the Communist line. Nkrumah was not inclined to give Great Britain any excuse for such action in Ghana. On October 23, 1953, the president of the TUC, a staunch supporter of Nkrumah, published a statement in the press saying that Turkson Ocran had been relieved of his duties as general secretary for being an alleged Communist. (Travel behind the Iron Curtain was soon banned, as was the importation of Communist literature.) By February, 1954, the Ghana TUC was in the International Confederation of Free Trade Unions. As one aspect of this shift away from the left, the young trade unionist and loyal CPP member, John Tettegah, was appointed as a full-time paid general secretary of the TUC, the Trade Union Ordinance having been amended to make this possible for the first time. In the meantime, the TUC headquarters had been moved from Sekondi-Takoradi to Accra.

The Railway Union resented these actions, not because its leaders were pro-Communist but because they considered the operations a takeover of the trade union movement by a political party. One study of trade unionism in Ghana notes, "at a meeting of the General Council [of the TUC] held at Accra on the 16th-17th of April, 1955, a section of the TUC made an attempt to overthrow the present leadership. Having failed, a rival Congress of Free Trade Unions was formed. . . ." The Railway Union played an active part in this abortive attempt to unseat Tettegah as secretary, but the maneuver was unsuccessful.

The New Structure

With the passage of the Industrial Relations Act in 1958, the entire trade union movement was formally brought under the control of the TUC. The act provided for sixteen national unions (the number was reduced to ten in May, 1965), a supreme congress, with elected representatives from each union and an executive board elected by the congress with a member from each union, and nine executive secretaries appointed by the executive board. The general secretary was to be elected biannually by the supreme congress. A cabinet minister made it clear, publicly, that all these posts were to be occupied by CPP militants. This organization was called the "new structure."

Although TUC officers are elected by the congress, the most influential posts must be filled by those who have CPP approval. Regional and local levels of trade union activity are controlled by the regional councils of the TUC, which are an integral part of the regional framework of the CPP and to a large extent dominated by it. Out of the total amount of dues collected from the workers in any one of the national unions, 40 percent goes to the national union, 22 percent to the TUC and 15 percent to the local union, with the remainder used for welfare benefits. The whole apparatus of collective bargaining and compulsory arbitration provides for representation through the TUC and not by the individual unions.

Ghana's new structure is a mixture of West German and Israeli trade union practices. At first glance these may seem strange labor models, given Ghana's Marxist orientation and the role assigned to labor in helping to build socialism. The foreign models had their origin in settings very different from Ghana, and some of the ideologies they incorporate are constantly under fire from Ghana TUC officials. However, the need for a more centralized labor organization and the relevance of the *form* it took in Israel and West Germany was decisive—not ideology. The TUC withdrew from the ICFTU and assumed leadership in the All-African Trades Union Federation (AATUF).

The new structure was questioned by many leaders of existing unions, who felt that their leadership was being challenged and the autonomy of the unions menaced. The most articulate and instransigent opposition came from within the ranks of the Railway Union of Sekondi-Takoradi. The union retained its registration certificates and demanded freedom to elect its own officers in accordance with its constitution. It warned the TUC not to interfere in the internal administration of its affairs. Only the personal plea of Nkrumah himself persuaded the Railway Union to try the new structure without putting up an open fight. Even so, a group of Sekondi-Takoradi unionists attempted to organize a Locomotive Electric Union in the hope of avoiding some of the provisions of the Industrial Relations Act. They had the sympathy and support of many workers in other unions, but their action had no chance to succeed.

Feeling against the TUC was intensified soon after the republic was established in 1960. President Nkrumah presented the Trade Union Congress with a $250,000 Hall of Labor as an acknowledgment of the workers' role in the nationalist struggle for independence. He stressed the need for labor discipline, high man-hour productivity, and restraint in wage-increase demands. The TUC pledged loyal support for these objectives. The Railway Union leaders, however, called the Hall of Labor a bribe to obligate top TUC officials to restrain workers from demanding wage increases. The railway workers were anxious for a chance to strike back at the TUC. The budget controversy gave them that chance.

The Sekondi-Takoradi Strike

On the Eve of the Crisis

Despite widespread grumbling and the actions of the Railway Union branches, Ghanaian life went on as usual during the fateful weekend before the strike broke out on Monday, September 4. In the Ashanti area, where resistance to unpopular measures had always been highly vocal and sometimes violent, the Kumasi sports stadium was jammed with soccer fans who came to see the Republikans play the Cornerstones in the national semifinals. Movie houses in Kumasi drew their usual large weekend crowds, this time to see *The Golden Horde, The Tank Commando, The Sword and the Rose,* and *Jail House Rock.* Beer and spirits flowed freely in Kumasi nightclubs, where a half-dozen bands played Western dance music and the West African "High Life" tunes. The *Ashanti Pioneer,* an Opposition daily, reported "the turnout of race fans and punters abundantly impressive" at the Kumasi Turf Club, as they placed their bets on Telephone, Jovial Judge, Admiral, Small Boy, Holas, and Rockefeller. The Kumasi churches were full on Sunday, and in the villages throughout the cocoa country the little "chop bars" (restaurants) and drinking bars catered as usual to customers clad in their Sunday best. The situation was essentially the same in Accra and in Sekondi-Takoradi. There was no sense of crisis in the air.

The CPP was winding up its campaign to "sell" the budget, an operation that had devoted special attention to Ashanti. A high-powered team of CPP leaders had been touring villages there during the week before the new budget provisions were to take effect. The team was led by the popular and flamboyant Minister Krobo Edusei (himself an Ashanti), and included the regional information officer, the regional secretary of the CPP, the Regional Commissioner, and the chairman of the Kumasi Municipal Council. The September 2 *Ashanti Pioneer* reported on their travels in detail, ("Krobo Edusei Explains Budget in Ashanti"), noting that Krobo Edusei's technique was to recount all the achievements of the CPP since 1951 and then to stress, "We obtained independence not to live in poverty but in happiness."

The Strike Begins

This atmosphere of normalcy masked much underlying resentment. The payroll deduction had been made on the last day of August, angering many workers. The Presidential Commission had made a few concessions, but in the absence of Nkrumah its members were reluctant to take further action. On Friday, September 1, the union officials in Sekondi-Takoradi appealed to the workers "to remain calm and await for Osagyefo's return," and on the following day the Regional Commissioner and the acting general manager of the railways (the manager was on leave in London) made personal appearances at the Railway Union headquarters and asked the men there to remain calm and carry out their duties while awaiting *Osagyefo*'s return. A similar appeal was scheduled for noon on Monday, September 4, but by 8:30 A.M. on that day all activities at the Sekondi Locomotive Works and at the Sekondi and Takoradi railroad stations had come to a complete standstill. Employees gathered in front of the administrative office of Ghana Railways while the delegates went in to complain about deductions from their salaries. All the crew members of the trains from Sekondi to Kumasi walked off and left the equipment unattended, as did all Ghanaians servicing ships in the harbor. Members of a large number of unions—the Transportation and Telecommunications Union, National Union of Railway and Harbour Workers, Public Utility Union, Maritime Dock Workers Union, Railway Engineman's Union (railway engine drivers who broke away from the mother union because of disputes over policy in 1949), Construction and General Workers Union, the Union of Catering Trades, Agricultural Workers Union, Timber and Wood Workers Union, Independent Commerce and General Workers Union, and the Municipal and Local Government Workers Union—had joined the railway strikers by noon. The Western Regional Commissioner, John Arthur, addressed an emergency meeting between the leaders of the unions and the representatives of management organized by the acting manager of the Railways and Harbour Administration. *The union officials denied any connection with the demonstration and consequently no agreement was reached.*

The railway employees in Kumasi struck simultaneously. Workers there went about "beating gong-gong" in order to attract crowds, and the Kumasi railroad station became the scene of a large mass meeting. The fact that no trains arrived that morning from Sekondi-Takoradi was cited as proof that the strike was solid. The irrepressible Krobo Edusei now turned his attention from the cocoa farmers to the urban workers, and in his role as Minister of Transportation and Communications rushed to the Kumasi station, where workers were shouting their disapproval of the budget. He asked them to go back to work and said he would head immediately for Accra to meet his cabinet colleagues, promising to report back to the Kumasi workers within a week. He was greeted with shouts and boos.

The Kumasi branch executive of the TUC then met, returning after a short conference to announce to the crowds that a six-man delegation had been appointed to confer with Minister Krobo Edusei. They agreed to tell him that since the strike was a nation-wide affair they could not give him any unilateral promises. They offered to dispatch emissaries to Sekondi and Accra immediately, however, to consult their fellow workers. Having thanked the Minister for his concern, the massed workers around the station then voted not to return to work until their delegation to Sekondi-Takoradi had come back. The *Ashanti Pioneer* reported on September 5, "In their grumbling the workers decried the government's measures and said it [the budget] was too much for them. It had worsened an already precarious financial situation and it was hard to make ends meet."

The strike took a different direction in the capital city of Accra. On Sunday, September 3, the secretary of the Railway Union branch there dispatched a letter by messenger to the Sekondi branch stating, "Information has reached us here that Sekondi as well as Kumasi are on strike; whether the news is true or not is yet to be confirmed." He stated the reason for sending the letter by messenger: "I have tried this morning to have a telephone conversation with you but failed. This failure is known to be government interception. The purpose of this letter is to know the position of this branch and what we are to do, if it is an official strike." Someone in the Sekondi office sent a message back for Accra to "go the anchor," a code phrase (meaning "strike") that had been coined by Pobee Biney, an early organizer of the Railway Union. As a result the Accra leaders held a special mass meeting on Tuesday, September 5, and sent a letter to the Presidential Commission saying that:

> We do not accept that the absence of the President could cripple the administration of the country. . . . Since we are part and parcel of the workers of Sekondi-Takoradi, Tarkwa and Kumasi, and since their slowing down is supported by us, it would be out of place if the workers of this region did not support the strike.

Thus the Accra workers went on strike. But they returned to work in two days. It is generally believed that they were persuaded to go back to work by the TUC, which had its headquarters in Accra and was urging all workers to return to their jobs.

On the second day of the strike the *Evening News,* which was encouraging workers to return to their jobs but was generally sympathetic to their grievances, printed a statement issued by the TUC:

> The Bureau noted with keen interest and concern matters variously raised by workers as regards the 1961–62 Budget Proposals, the Compulsory Savings Scheme of the Government and the rampant layoffs being instituted by Government departments and non-government employers —issues which have been the cause of dissatisfaction among workers of our national unions. *The TUC fully support these grievances, representations and demands.* [Italics added.]

The TUC appealed to the men to return to their jobs and to await the *Osagyefo's* return, promising to put their case before him. The *Evening News* admonished them to remember, "There is also adequate machinery under the Industrial Relations Act of 1958 for dealing with grievances of members of Unions."

Accra on the second day was quiet compared to other parts of Ghana. Trains remained at a standstill throughout the country and in Kumasi and Sekondi workers paraded in small bands and milled around listening to speeches by rank-and-file leaders who demanded an end to compulsory savings. The top leaders stayed in the background. In one city between Accra and Sekondi, a group of strikers attacked and beat up the drivers of a mail van and a government bus. A government White Paper, published some months after the strike, stated that the government had reliable evidence that, on the second day of the strike, a United Party member (a school teacher from Sekondi) was sent to Kumasi by a union leader to discuss possibilities of securing financial and moral support from United Party leaders. The Sekondi-Takoradi Railway Union officials deny this.

During the next two days, while Nkrumah was "projecting the African Personality" in the USSR, strikers in Sekondi-Takoradi were marching through the streets with signs protesting the budget. One of them read: A GOOD FATHER IS AT HOME WHEN HIS CHILDREN ARE SUFFERING. The *Evening News* brought out a special issue on September 6 calling for patience until Nkrumah returned with the loans for the factories which would "make a paradise of socialist Ghana." The front-page headlines read:

THE PARTY APPEALS TO THE ORGANISED WORKERS

* * * * *

LAYING-OFF ANTI-SOCIALIST:
IT WILL STOP
GO BACK TO WORK AND AWAIT OSAGYEFO
GOVERNMENT GIVING SERIOUS CONSIDERATION
TO GRIEVANCES

The general argument to the workers, presented in typical *Evening News* style, was as follows:

> On the Radio we have heard, and in the Press we have read, about Osagyefo's great, new pilgrimage to many countries in Europe and Asia. All of this is part of the planning for the new Ghana.
>
> . . .
>
> No one needs complain about the Budget. No one. It is a temporary means to an end. If we need money to speed up an industrialisation programme, it is better that we produce the necessary funds through the sweat of our own brow than through the grace of others.
>
> . . .
>
> Let us all wait for the great pilgrim's return, and while he is away, watch and pray for Ghana. He will come with his triumphs and spoils and put to shame the weak-hearted few who thrive on parasitic opportunism. The great day is not far when joy will stalk the streets with golden-shod feet. It is near! . . . WATCH.

The First Week: Thursday Confrontation

By midweek practically every activity in the port was closed down. Municipal bus drivers had joined the strike, as had the city employees who collected the sewage daily. Market women dispensed free food to the strikers at the municipal bus garages and other strategic points. Red headbands and armbands were in evidence everywhere; they were symbols worn in former days by Fanti tribal fighting men to mean, "We are ready for war." Ships were pulled away from the docks and anchored in the roadstead for fear of sabotage. There was an air of excitement and pride throughout the city over the fact that they, the people of Sekondi-Takoradi, had brought business to a standstill, had stopped train service to all of Ghana, and were displaying solidarity in the fight against the budget. Morale was high. The railway workers were heroes.

Thursday, September 7, was a critical day. In the early afternoon a crowd of over five thousand people gathered at the railway station in Sekondi-Takoradi in response to a rumor that Krobo Edusei and Gbedemah would be arriving soon to address the workers. The occasion was colorful and festive, with drumming and singing, and speeches that were fervent, passionate, and sometimes inflammatory. W. N. Grant, a prominent strike leader, told the crowd that if Parliament did not give way to the demands of the people, they would disband that body by force.

In midafternoon a motorcade arrived from Accra bringing Gbedemah and other government officials. Krobo Edusei arrived by helicopter. The delegation went into conference immediately with Railway Union officials at the Regional Commissioner's headquarters, and word spread quickly to the crowd at the railway station that the "big men from Accra" were in town. They roared with pleasure at the thought of confronting in person some of the ministers who had voted for the budget. But the ministers decided not to face the crowd. The people jeered and booed when informed that the ministers were on their way back to Accra. Speakers taunted them as cowards. The actual strike leaders had refused to attend the meeting and rejected an invitation to go to Accra for a conference. They suspected that an attempt was being made to arrest them. However, they sent a letter explaining why they had refused to go to the capital. It contained the statement, "Inasmuch as the Trade Union Congress of Ghana had earlier accused and painted the Railway Union as being troublemakers, their presence will not be conducive to peaceful negotiations in Accra." But the letter also put the Railway Union leaders on record as not being anti-government. "We reiterate that it is not the intention of the National Unions to flout your authority and therefore pray that you will sympathize with the request to come down for early and peaceful negotiations." The railway men were inviting the Presidential Commission to come to *them* in Sekondi-Takoradi! The officers of all eleven unions mentioned above signed the letter.

While these negotiations and mass demonstrations were going on in Sekondi-Takoradi, a group of market women were demonstrating in Kumasi, and a number of them were arrested. "Joe" Appiah was busy much of the day pleading for their release. There was some violence in towns along the railway line between Kumasi and Sekondi-Takoradi in an attempt to enforce a 100 percent shutdown. The Regional Commissioner in Ashanti spent much of the day conferring with union officials and strike leaders in Kumasi. The *Ashanti Pioneer* said little of these activities in its Friday, September 8, edition, but it did carry large and revealing headlines:

NKRUMAH CONTINUES HOLIDAY

FLASH: CABINET MEMBERS RUSH TO SEKONDI

RAILWAY EMPLOYEES STILL ON THEIR STAND

The government felt it had scored two successes that day despite the setback in Sekondi-Takoradi. In Accra, the Presidential Commission persuaded striking bus drivers to go back to work, and a pro-government rally which the CPP considered successful was held in the town of Saltpond, located on the coast between Sekondi-Takoradi and Accra.

Later, when the strike was nearing its end, one of the leaders told the cabinet that while the ministers were retreating from Sekondi-Takoradi a secondary school teacher, J. Kwesi Lamptey (later detained), had returned that day from Kumasi with a large sum of money supplied by United Party leader Victor Owusu (who had warned of trouble during the budget debate) to buy food so the market women could feed the demonstrators and pickets. If this actually happened, it interjected a potentially dangerous political element into the strike.

The Presidential Commission Acts

Negotiations on Thursday and Friday in all three cities resulted in some informal understanding as to changes the unions could expect in the budget when Nkrumah returned. After hearing the report from Gbedemah and Krobo Edusei of what was happening in Sekondi-Takoradi, the Presidential Commission and those cabinet members who were in the country decided to proclaim a state of emergency in the port and to institute a curfew. They believed that the majority of the workers were being kept from returning to their jobs only by fear of violence. The commission also decided to arrest several of the minor leaders and to have the army, police, and Builders Brigade stand by in case their services were needed to quell riots or to maintain sanitary services. The White Paper, discussing events between Friday and Sunday of the first week, states that the imposition of the curfew and the proclamation of a state of emergency "put the official union leadership of the Railway and Harbour Workers Union in an extremely difficult position." The government thus indirectly criticized the Presidential Commission, apparently assuming that the official union leaders had wanted to cooperate but that the rank and file would not let them, so great was their resentment over the curfew.

The Second Week: Pleas for Caution

In blending the old and new political structures, the Ghana constitution groups the chiefs or traditional rulers into five *regional* Houses of Chiefs (no counterpart to the House of Lords was tolerated at the national level). Chiefs often serve as "arbitrators" in traditional society; now a House of Chiefs carried the practice over into an industrial dispute and advised the unions to cooperate with the government. Their attempt is documented in a press release handed out during the second week by one of the unions involved in the strike:

> On Saturday morning the Standing Committee of the *Western Region House of Chiefs* offered to meet the Executive [of the Union]. This was arranged, and following the discussion held, and in order not to prejudice the case of the workers, we the National Union *strongly appeal to the workers* to return to work from midnight on Sunday 10th September 1961, to enable immediate negotiation to be carried out . . . We the National Officers would further wish it to be known that the *Railway Union as such has not officially declared a strike* but has sympathized with the workers in seeking redress for the hardship that the Budget had caused and [that we] were prepared to lead a delegation to negotiate.

What was the actual role of the union officials? Was it true that this was a "spontaneous" work-stoppage over which they had no control? Or were they protesting their innocence while surreptitiously managing the operation? No definitive answers can be given but interviews in Sekondi-Takoradi after the strike lend credence to the claim that top Railway Union leaders did try to persuade workers to return to their jobs during the first week of the strike. Lower-level leadership seemed defiant, however, near the end of the week, giving rise to rumors that the CPP's political opponents, the leaders of the United Party, were influencing the direction of the strike. The Railway Union denied the rumors and issued the following statement, again making a back-to-work appeal:

> To the best of our knowledge, however, any allegation of any sort of political influence is completely out of the question and if any individuals have made any statements to the effect they were personal views and the Union dissociates itself from those statements. . . . In the best interest of our renowned Union we once again appeal to our comrades to go back to work as from midnight of Sunday 10th September 1961. . . . UNITED WE STAND, DIVIDED WE FALL.

If the unions were actually trying to get their members to go back to work, who, then, was urging them to stay out? Early in the second week of the strike, the attitude of the CPP press towards the strikers changed. The sympathetic tone of the first week was gone: the *Evening News,* on September 9, called the strikers "counter-revolutionaries" and warned, "We know who you are. . . . Remember your wives and children. . . . They will suffer for your misdeeds." On this same day, Tawia Adamafio, Minister for Presidential Affairs, issued a statement blaming non-Ghanaians and not the union leaders for the strike. He charged that "foreign companies . . . were trying to exploit [the situation] by inciting their employees to stay away from work in order to embarrass the government." CPP leaders suspected that several groups were fishing in the troubled waters of budget discontent by urging the workers not to listen to any back-to-work pleas. Their reaction by the end of the second week was to warn *all* the suspects.

Strike or Insurrection?

When the first week of the strike ended, there was considerable optimism in government circles and at national TUC headquarters, where it was generally believed that the workers were not prepared to carry the contest any further. Despite demonstrations, there had been no mass uprising anywhere. Even on the railroads, one engine drivers' union had refused to join other unions on strike. The cocoa farmers were quiet. In Kumasi and Accra the situation had quickly returned to normal. Except in Sekondi-Takoradi and a few railroad towns nearby, the rank and file had answered the plea of the nation's leaders and drifted back to work, although some were physically attacked for doing so. It was thought that by Monday of the second week even the Sekondi-Takoradi strikers would be back on the job. But they did not return to work, and the White Paper insists that what began as a strike had now turned into an attempted insurrection: "Henceforward, the strike was confined to the Sekondi-Takoradi municipality and its control passed completely into the hands of the United Party. . . . The strikers had vowed to continue the strike until the overthrow of the Government was secured." The Railway Union leaders maintain, however, that United Party influence was minimal at this early stage of the strike, though they admit it became an important factor later.

The Presidential Commission was in a tight spot. Although some workers had returned, the trains were not running. The problem was to decide how much force should be used to break the resistance in Sekondi-Takoradi. Army and police were alerted. The Army Chief of Staff, Major General H. T. Alexander, an Englishman, was in Europe, but he sent a message (later printed in the White Paper) to Ghana on the eleventh saying, "On no account must impressions be caused that British officers will not take part in internal security if this is necessary. But it is obviously better that first troops committed should be all Ghanaian manned." No one wanted the blame for excessive use of force—neither Nkrumah, the British contingent in the army, nor the members of the Presidential Commission. But the actions of the strikers seemed to be such that drastic action would be taken eventually.

At the beginning of the second week some of the strikers attempted to sabotage the entire telephone system in Sekondi-Takoradi and essential workers in the electricity department were pressured into quitting work, endangering the water works as well as causing general inconvenience.

The Railway Union officials admitted that some acts of violence had occurred but disclaimed any responsibility for them. Now that a state of emergency had been declared, the union contended that a curfew would only make matters worse. The Kumasi leaders were particularly angry and unanimously adopted a resolution to be sent to the union in Sekondi-Takoradi. It asked that "the government be requested to lift the state of emergency imposed on Sekondi-Takoradi by Thursday 14th September, 1961, to enable workers to return to work. Will you please take the necessary action?" The same day, the standing committee of the Brong Ahafo House of Chiefs sent an appeal to the Sekondi-Takoradi union branch that ignored the union's contention that it had not called the strike and the fact that the leaders had made back-to-work appeals. The chiefs said, "in the interests of the nation . . . call off the strike . . . continued delay in strike action will jeopardize economy of the nation and eventually lead to untold hardships."

Violence continued, nonetheless, and on Wednesday of the second week the Sekondi-Kumasi train was derailed and sixteen persons injured. The same day three civil servants working for Ghana railways were beaten and their cars severely damaged. The next day the crew cleaning up the wreckage from the derailment was attacked by an angry crowd. Several arrests were made, but the Presidential Commission did not crack down, preferring to wait for *Osagyefo* to return and solve the problem.

The only action taken during the second week to lay the basis for an eventual settlement was a move by John Tettegah of the TUC. He sent a letter to all unions stating, "Following the recent events which have caused some measure of unrest in some quarters of the labour movement in the country, it has become absolutely necessary to review in detail all outstanding grievances in the different National Unions forming the Congress." He asked that "all outstanding grievances brought down from previous years and all other grievances" be forwarded to TUC headquarters without delay, "in order to seek avenues of redress and prompt actions." The TUC realized that even if the crisis over compulsory savings was resolved, other sources of potential trouble remained—that, in short, the strike was expressing more than opposition to compulsory savings.

The United Party Intervenes Openly

On Friday of the second week of the strike (September 15), the day before Nkrumah's return, J. B. Danquah, leader of the United Party, invited the press to his home to announce that his party was giving moral support to the Sekondi-Takoradi strikers. The government White Paper charged that on the next day, while the President was landing in Accra, emissaries of the strikers went to Kumasi to consult with "Joe" Appiah, and that it was agreed that Danquah should proceed to Sekondi-Takoradi to be available for consultation on action to be taken after Nkrumah's arrival. In addition, the Paper charged that three days before Danquah called his press conference the officials of the Railway and Harbour Workers Union had lost control over their members, and that on that day, "in order to establish a closer liaison between the leadership of the United Party and those who now had assumed control of the strike in Sekondi-Takoradi, a meeting was called by Dr. Danquah in Accra" at which all the important leaders of the United Party were present. It was alleged further that arrangements for financing the strike were left in the hands of Danquah and another prominent UP leader. All the persons mentioned were eventually arrested and detained for nine months. Although it is impossible, since they were not tried, to present their version of the role that the UP was playing at this stage, the open UP encouragement to continue the strike despite government pleas to end it is a matter of public record. But was such action subversive or seditious?

To understand why the UP intervened and why the government was so alarmed by its action, it is necessary to review briefly the history of opposition politics in Ghana. Between 1951 and 1954, Danquah and his colleagues in the United Gold Coast Convention constantly charged the CPP government with squandering the hard-earned money of the cocoa farmers and accused the party leaders of bribery, corruption, and nepotism. The first charge involved a difference of opinion as to how government expenditures should be allocated; the second had some basis in fact, as an investigating commission revealed in 1953.[4] The Opposition leaders also accused Nkrumah of being intent upon establishing a Communist state, despite the fact that he had expelled several members from his party in 1963 for alleged Communist connections. The CPP countered with charges that the Opposition was protecting the privileges of "feudal reactionary chiefs" (traditional rulers) and could not shed its "colonial mentality." The election of 1954 was fought on these issues. The CPP won 56 percent of the popular vote and 72 out of 104 seats in Parliament. This was the first election in the Gold Coast based on universal franchise, and the CPP took credit for forcing the British to institute the constitutional change that made it possible. It proceeded immediately to negotiate for full sovereignty.

A serious crisis erupted in the fall of 1954, soon after the elections, in the prosperous cocoa-producing region of Ashanti. A Cocoa Marketing Board had been established during World War II to buy the entire crop at a price lower than the world market price and to resell it at a profit; in 1954 it set the price at 72 shillings ($10.08) for a load of sixty pounds although the world market price was 140 shillings ($19.60). This action was coupled with a guarantee that the same price would be paid for four years even if the world price dropped below 72 shillings. Almost a half-billion dollars in invested reserves had been built up in the past from the margin between the world price and the price paid to farmers in Ghana. The new CPP government was determined to use both the reserves and a portion of the current profit from cocoa sales for financing the Five-Year Development Plan.

---

[4] *Report of Commission of Enquiry into Mr. Braimah's Resignation and Allegations Arising Therefrom* (Accra: Government Printer, 1954).

Many cocoa farmers felt, however, that the money should be used not for national purposes but only for the welfare of cocoa farmers and their families, and that certainly CPP politicians had no right to say how the farmers' money should be spent.

In 1954 all of these feelings crystallized around opposition to the price set for cocoa for the next four years. A National Liberation Movement (NLM) came into being in the Ashanti cocoa-growing area under the patronage of the paramount chief, the *Asantehene*. The leaders were sworn by oath to liberate Ghana from Nkrumah and the CPP. They insisted upon a federal rather than a unitary state after independence. The result was virtual civil war in Ashanti. Because of the tension and violence, the British government insisted that Parliament be dissolved and another election held before the date could be set for independence.

During the election campaign of 1956, an alliance was formed that included the NLM the Northern People's Party (representing the interests of the less highly developed Northern Territories); the Togoland Congress Party (espousing unification of the Ewe tribe); the Muslim Association Party; and a number of small splinter groups. In addition to playing what the CPP called "cocoa politics," the Opposition appealed to regional, religious, and tribal discontent in its attempt to unseat the party in power, but the popular vote remained about the same as it had been in 1954, and Nkrumah's party won 71 out of 104 seats. The British government accepted the results as the "reasonable majority" it had demanded as a prerequisite to independence. The Opposition pleaded with Britain not to grant independence unless a constitution was drawn up giving substantial regional autonomy. After a constitutional compromise had been worked out, sovereignty within the Commonwealth was attained in 1957. The Opposition was never reconciled to the outcome.

Tribalism was by no means dead. On Independence Day a group of Ewes in former British Togoland (joined to Ghana in 1956 after a UN plebiscite) mounted an insurrection that had to be put down by the army. Less than a month after independence another ethnic group, the Ga, who are dominant in the capital and surrounding areas, gave birth to an organization that created considerable disorder and was suppressed. The government then passed the Avoidance of Discrimination Act that made it illegal for any groups to organize parties based upon tribe, race, religion, or region. Six parties subsequently combined to form the United Party. Tribal politics went underground, and the main strategy of the UP became an attempt to find an issue that would split off enough CPP backbenchers to bring the government down with a vote of no confidence (a legitimate parliamentary objective). Corruption exposures became the main tactic, but they never achieved the desired end.

The UP was weakened soon after independence through the defection of a number of its Members of Parliament, who "crossed the floor" for the avowed purpose of getting more patronage for their constituencies. With UP power being eroded away and no elections scheduled until 1961, one segment of the party, including its executive secretary, began to consider plans for a coup d'état. The British police supplied information to the government on some of the activities of the executive secretary; the government's knowledge of his operations, none of which were clearly illegal under existing laws, was one factor in the decision to pass the Preventive Detention Act in August, 1958, which permitted the detention of a person for periods up to five years without trial and with no provision for court appeal.[5] In December, forty-eight individuals (mainly from the Ga tribe) were detained, some of them UP officials in the capital city of Accra and others members of the tough UP "action squads," who called themselves "Tokyo Joes."

Early in 1959, the government held hearings on an alleged plot to kidnap and assassinate Nkrumah. A three-man commission headed by a British judge came to the unanimous conclusion that the UP executive secretary and a Ewe associate had been planning some type of future revolutionary activity in Ghana, although one commissioner expressed some doubt about the assassination plot. Four men were held under the Preventive Detention Act, but the UP intellectual leadership, including "Joe" Appiah, Victor Owusu, and sociologist Kofi Busia, were exonerated. They dubbed the hearings a frame-up.

Once it became clear that one group of UP leaders was prepared to resort to a coup d'état and that the others, as Dennis Austin, an authority on Ghana politics, said in *Politics in Ghana,* "supported every group and cause that it thought might overthrow the state," the CPP government was no longer willing to consider the UP a legitimate and responsible opposition.

With open tribal politics tabooed, the essentially conservative United Party began to woo labor, and when Danquah ran against Nkrumah in the 1960 presidential campaign, he promised that "with the UP in power, workers throughout the country will have a fair deal." He appealed to resentment against the TUC "new structure," and told the workers, "You can remove the CPP to restore your lost liberty if you are determined to do so." Soon after Nkrumah was installed as President, an opportunity arose for the UP to continue its campaign for an alliance with labor. A group of workers protesting the high cost of living demonstrated against a foreign firm, booed and hooted Nkrumah's statue in front of Parliament House as well as Krobo Edusei in person, and demanded a minimum wage law. The *Pioneer* exploited the incident to the hilt between August 3 and August 24 with prominent headlines such as "Kumasi Workers Also Want To Demonstrate" and "Workers Demonstrate Against TUC Officials." The paper also ran a series of editorials needling the TUC leaders, especially execu-

[5] For a detailed account of this period, see Dennis Austin, *Politics in Ghana: 1946–1960* (London: Oxford University Press, 1964), pp. 380–82 and Appendix B.

tive secretary Tettegah. One of these, "A Chat With Workers," advised them to force the TUC leaders to end their "Siamese twin relationship to the CPP." One called on the workers to "take this simple positive process; speak plainly to the Nkrumah Socialist government," while another urged the TUC and the government to "stop this fooling of the workers." Editorial comment was caustic:

> Throughout the past ten years under the much trumpeted socialist policy of the CPP, there have been no measures to bring about any reduction in the cost of living in the country. Consequently the ordinary people, or the "masses" as the socialists choose to call them, have hitherto been suffering from hardships.

The government became so alarmed over the protests that it immediately announced its intention to set a minimum wage, but it also decided to punish the Ashanti *Pioneer* by allowing the TUC to install a censor at the elbow of its editor. (This marked the beginning of the end of the *Pioneer*.[6])

One reason for the government's prompt reaction to both the labor disturbances and the Ashanti *Pioneer* attacks on TUC leadership was that Ghana was deeply involved in the Congo crisis. A large number of police and soldiers had been sent to Léopoldville as a part of the United Nations contingent. Emphasis was being placed upon national unity and Pan-African solidarity. The *Pioneer* criticized this involvement as requiring wasteful expenditure while people in Ghana were suffering from a high level of taxation. From the CPP point of view such suggestions were seditious, although the editor considered them constructive criticism.

A year later, the 1961 budget offered the UP another opportunity to seek an alliance with labor when the Sekondi-Takoradi workers struck. By the end of the second week of the strike, the Railway Union officials were saying "Go back to work!" but the UP was telling the rank and file to hold fast and was cooperating with the lower-echelon strike leaders. The strike was turning into a contest between the CPP government and the UP.

The Osagyefo Comes Home

Nkrumah's plane arrived in the capital city of Accra around noon on Saturday, September 16, the day after Danquah's press conference. The CPP, sensitive to the challenge posed by the defiant workers and the UP, tried to make it the largest and most enthusiastic homecoming for the *Osagyefo* of the many that the Accra airport had witnessed. Busloads of the faithful came from all over Ghana; Young Pioneers, members of the Builders Brigade, chiefs in colorful attire, and market women singing traditional "praise names" to the chief were on hand. A fetish priest poured a liba-

---

[6] "In October, 1962, the government announced that it proposed to take over the paper and the Abura printing works." (Austin, p. 389.)

tion and performed the ritual slaughter of two sheep. After the *Osagyefo* had reviewed his honor guard and shaken hands with the assembled foreign ambassadors and the traditional rulers who graced the front line of the crowd, he went into conference with members of the CPP central committee, the heads of the party integral wings, and other advisers.

On Sunday morning the cabinet met, along with other concerned individuals. Opinion was polarized between the executive secretary of the TUC, who advised moderation, and the party secretary, Tawia Adamafio, who, with no trade union base to protect, referred to the strikers as "Western Rats" (a reference to Sekondi-Takoradi's location in the Western Region of Ghana), and favored a full show of punitive power. Nkrumah listened and then made up his mind. He went on the air Sunday and, as we have seen, announced that, having come home, he was canceling the state of emergency in Sekondi-Takoradi, lifting the curfew, and ordering the release of all persons who had been arrested in connection with the strike. He coupled these conciliatory moves with an appeal for the strikers to return to work immediately and promised that all grievances would be negotiated.

We Shall Not Be Moved

But some of the strikers would not be moved—even by the *Osagyefo's* persuasive voice and still effective charisma. On Monday morning many workers in Sekondi-Takoradi went back to work, but the railway workers' ranks remained solid. And the railway workers held the key to efficient transportation. At mass meetings in the streets, strikers were called upon to take care of the "blacklegs" ("scabs" in American terminology) who broke the front and went back to work.

It is likely that a split occurred within the ranks of Sekondi-Takoradi's labor elite on that fateful Monday morning, with some of the rank-and-file leaders taking an intransigent position. Those union officials who claimed to represent the "legitimate voice of unionism" maintained that the recalcitrant elements were acting without their official sanction. Three days after Nkrumah's Sunday appeal, the "legitimate" leadership in Sekondi-Takoradi answered a letter written to them a week before by the Kumasi branch and thereby put squarely on record where *they* stood:

> With reference to your letter . . . I am directed to inform you that the *Union* is not responsible, repeat *not,* for the strike action undertaken by its members.
>
> As you are aware, Osagyefo has taken immediate action since his arrival (by lifting the curfew) and the masses are not giving due respect to his authority.

W. N. Grant, the rank-and-file leader who later briefed the cabinet on the details of the strike, is reported to have said that on the day the Railway Union secretary wrote the above letter to Kumasi, Danquah arrived in

Sekondi-Takoradi. Grant reported to Danquah that he and another leader had persuaded the railway workers not to respond to Nkrumah's plea. Grant is reported in the White Paper as having told Danquah that he had assumed leadership of the strike and as having said that Danquah had urged the strikers to fight on despite anything the President might do and had assured them of the full support of the party. Grant is also said to have reported to Danquah that he sent telegrams to unions all over the world asking for support. He claimed that "Joe" Appiah drafted the telegrams and paid part of the cost of sending them. The return address was not that of any union, but rather the private post box of a UP leader in Sekondi-Takoradi. They were unsigned but bore the garbled name of the Railway and Harbour Workers Union. The government considered the text evidence of treasonable intent:

> Dockers and railway men on strike/stop/appeal financial moral support in struggle against government control of unions and for survival of parliamentary democracy/stop/reply urgently requested

Osagyefo Ends the Strike

The open support that the UP gave the strike, and the willingness of of some union leaders to accept it, convinced Nkrumah that the United Party had decided to try to find the base in labor that it had lost in tribalism and to use it to try to throw the country into chaos in the hope of precipitating an army coup. A railway strike not only crippled the economy but, if the defiance succeeded—especially since there was still opposition to the budget—it might set off renewed strikes elsewhere. He decided to get tough.

The *Osagyefo* went on the air again on Wednesday. This time his tone was firm. He pointed out not only that the strike was illegal under the Industrial Relations Act but that it had taken on insurrectionary overtones. He stated that no government could tolerate such coercion. He included a well-understood implied threat that maximum force would be used if necessary to get the trains moving and to restore the port to normal operation. He noted that the next day, Thursday, was a national holiday—his birthday—and he called upon the strikers to return to work on the day after, Friday. He warned that anyone who did not go back to work would be considered guilty of trying to overthrow the government.

There was, in fact, a general return to work on Friday. On that day, too, the Railway Workers Union mailed to the TUC, in answer to its request of the twelfth, a long list of grievances going back many years.

Now that the conflict was over, the traditional African custom of reconciliation (and face-saving) was in order. On the twenty-sixth, a modernized form of an ancient ritual began. Krobo Edusei invited all the union leaders to come to see him in Accra, which they did. Then, as part of the ritual, a letter to the *Osagyefo* was prepared and sent the next day through the Regional Commissioner and the general manager of the Ghana railroad system. The letter combined the tone of an approach to a chief with British formality:

> *Dear Osagyefo,*
>
> I have the honour to inform you that at a meeting held with our Minister Hon. Krobo Edusei in Accra on the 26th September 1961 he expressed his appreciation for honouring your advice to resume duty. He also mentioned with regret a cablegram sent by some of the strikers to some organizations outside Ghana for assistance.
>
> The union views this with all seriousness and graciously asks you grant the Executive Council members permission to meet you personally to have a fatherly chat on the situation as it is long since we met you in person.[7]
>
> I humbly hope you will give your personal attention to this request.
>
> I have the honour to be, sir,
> Your obedient servant,
>
> *General Secretary Treasurer*
> *of the Railway and Harbour*
> *Workers Union*

On the same day the union sent off a letter to the TUC adding one more grievance to the list, this time that of the lighthouse keepers against the harbour master. In addition, the union received a notice that no civil servants in Sekondi who had been on strike would lose their pay for the period when they had not worked. Most of the union officials were included.

Why after seventeen days did the men finally decide to return to work? Dennis Austin has suggested (in *Politics in Ghana*) that it was because their funds were exhausted. Other observers feel that the threat of massive violence intimidated the workers. Both factors were undoubtedly operative, but it seems likely, too, that the rank and file and their leaders had become aware by this time of the difference between a strike for limited objectives such as a wage increase, where collective bargaining is possible, and a political strike, which demands the reversal of legislative acts and basic changes in governmental policy. The most that could be asked for in the latter instance was a promise of future changes, and this the unions were given. By the seventeenth day, the strike had reached the point of diminishing returns and some of the rank-and-file leaders had taken the opportunity to dissociate themselves from it by pleading that they were now being "used" against their will by the United Party. The strikers had no choice but to return to work.

What, if anything, did the prestrike protest and the strike actually accomplish? It was not a total loss from the point of view of those who or-

[7] An invitation to a "fatherly chat" was not forthcoming.

ganized the action. The checkoff was delayed by a month, and when it came the lowest-paid workers were exempted. The TUC showed a renewed interest in settling outstanding grievances and the legislative assembly tightened up the price control laws. And after some months, the compulsory savings feature of the budget was actually abolished. But the leaders of the strike paid the price of nine months in detention for their defiance of the all-embracing party and its state apparatus.

Aftermath of the Strike

The Party Purge

The day after the strikers went back to work, President Nkrumah dismissed General Alexander, the English Chief of Staff, and assumed the post of Supreme Commander of the Army himself. Meanwhile a serious and acrimonious debate was going on within the central committee of the party as to responsibility for the prolongation of the strike, the manner in which the Presidential Commission had acted, whether concessions should be made on the budget, and whether the Sekondi-Takoradi union leaders should be punished.

The left-wing militants were insistent that certain reforms should be made within the party before any other action was carried out. Decisions taken over the weekend of September 23 had far-reaching repercussions. The *Evening News* on Monday, September 25, made it clear that the left wing of the party had won the argument. It presented the official party interpretations of the actions taken and its banner headline announced: "Socialist Revolution Begins." Two days later the paper printed the complete text of the Dawn Broadcast, a speech made by Nkrumah on April 8, 1961, in his role of *Osagyefo,* the chief speaking to his people of important matters as the sun rises. On that occasion the President promised to check excessive accumulation of property by party and government officials, rebuked leaders for arrogance and ostentatious display of their wealth, and intimated that a cleanup at the top was being demanded by those who were being asked to sacrifice for development goals. During the next six months, however, no vigorous attempt was made to implement the principles of the Dawn Broadcast. Suddenly, on September 29, three-quarters of the front page of the *Evening News* was devoted to pictures and stories of the beginning of a party purge:

OSAGYEFO'S IMPLEMENTATION OF "DAWN BROADCAST"

Six Ministers to Resign

Two cabinet ministers, one of them Krobo Edusei, and four other highly placed CPP officials were referred to under the caption: "They Are to Surrender Property." This action was received with enthusiastic approbation inside the party and out.

Both of the ministers who had served on the Presidential Commission were dropped from the cabinet: Kojo Botsio, who had accompanied Nkrumah home from England fourteen years before and was director of ideological studies for the party, and Komla Gbedemah, who had managed the CPP's first election campaign and had been a cabinet member ever since. Before another month had passed, both were suspended from party membership and thereby from Parliament. This news surprised the country and set off waves of speculation. Botsio was later restored to favor; Gbedemah left the country.

Punitive Measures

One month after the strike began, the full weight of CPP power fell upon those whom the government considered responsible for the crisis and for prolonging the strike. Regardless of their denial of complicity, and despite the attempted reconciliation ceremony, the official union leaders in Sekondi-Takoradi (except one who escaped to the Togo Republic) were picked up under the Preventive Detention Act. They were held for nine months. Active strike leaders, too, were arrested, as was one woman prominent in the Union of Catering Trades, who had organized the feeding of the strikers. The TUC then took over the executive management of the Sekondi-Takoradi railway union, thus effectively preventing a revival of strike action. One CPP leader was also detained, a former Minister who had vigorously opposed the "left" within his party. In all, some forty-seven persons were detained.

Most of the nonunionists detained were United Party leaders who were accused of both fomenting and prolonging the strike. Among them were Danquah and Appiah. Seventeen years before Danquah had been jailed by the British along with Nkrumah. Now, as has happened many times in revolutions elsewhere, one comrade had deemed it necessary to detain another. The justification of the action appeared in the White Paper published in December.

Socialist Institutionalization

By the end of 1960, Nkrumaism as an ideology had begun to take final form, and after various experiments the structure of the all-embracing Party had been worked out, but no basic alterations in governmental institutions had taken place. The Sekondi-Takoradi crisis provided an opportunity for introducing structural innovations that had been formulated at party conferences during the previous year at the same time the financial experts were developing the austerity budget. However, a clear victory for the left within the party was a prerequisite to implementation of these ideas.

Within a week after the strike ended, a State Control Commission was established under the chairmanship of Nkrumah with a nonparty civil servant as its executive secretary. A State Planning Commission was announced, to be headed by the deputy governor of the Bank of Ghana, whose ideological commitment to socialism was unquestioned (and who two years later became Minister of Finance). It was made very clear that the pace of socialist planning was to be stepped up and that opposition to it would not be tolerated. The National Farmers' Council and National Cooperative Council, both integral wings of the party, were given the monopoly in the buying of cocoa from farmers for resale to the Cocoa Marketing Board with the justification that this action eliminated brokers for foreign firms who had previously been middlemen in the operation.

The legislature authorized the establishment of a government-owned Ghana National Trading Company (GNTC), which proceeded to buy out a Greek firm that operated a large department store. The ultimate goal was to replace all foreign wholesale firms and to have "peoples' shops" serve as retail outlets for the GNTC. The Industrial Development Corporation and the Agricultural Development Corporation, both of which had made loans to entrepreneurs in the past and run some enterprises of their own, were abolished to make way for new planning and fiscal bodies deemed more consonant with a socialist system.

Concurrently, Nkrumah reaffirmed his assurance to private investors from abroad that a sector would be reserved for them in the manufacturing field within the "socialist" plan. A government-subsidized newspaper, the *Ghanaian Times,* carried a headline on January 14, 1962, calculated to reassure those who feared that the country was "going Communist": "Ghana's Socialism No Carbon Copy."

Parliamentary Postlude

In addition to the party "purge" and the punitive actions, the government decided to introduce a bill in Parliament to provide for special courts to try treason cases and with power to recommend the death penalty. When Parliament opened in October, no "Joe" Appiah was present to enliven the debate and only nine UP leaders were left, none of them men of eloquence or influence. On October 16 Gbedemah, now stripped of his cabinet post, led the opposition to the bill. The atmosphere in Parliament was tense as he brought his speech to a close with a warning:

> We may be pulled out of bed to face the firing squad after a summary trial and conviction. . . . Today we may think that all is well; it is not my turn, it is my brother's turn, but your turn will come sooner than later. [The Opposition members shouted "Hear," "Hear."]

The Deputy Minister of Defense expressed shock at Gbedemah's speech and referred to the strike:

> It is the duty of the Government to take measures to protect the Security of the State and the interest of the people of this country because whatever affects the government affects the individual or the common man in the street. . . . Recently about 47 persons who tried to coerce the Government to change their policy have been detained. . . . Those of us who were at Takoradi are aware of exactly what happened during those days and we know what was the intention behind the strike. Because the strike was confined only to Takoradi the people in other parts of this country did not grasp its implications. Ask the people in Takoradi and they will tell you what actually happened.

Later on, in closing, he referred to the episode again:

> The evidences of the Railway strike at Takoradi prove that there was something sinister behind it. No government will allow itself to be overthrown unlawfully. . . . Everyone knows that the recent strike was organized by people from within and outside this country. I support this Bill.

He was interrupted with a shout from a UP legislator, "It was the *Budget* which brought about the strike!"

The Bill passed, and within the four years five persons were sentenced, but all had their sentences commuted.

The Opposition Counterattack

While the new governmental structures were being introduced, the United Party in alliance with some of the disaffected CPP leaders decided to strike back. A bulletin, released in the neighboring Togo Republic on November 6, 1961, and circulated in Ghana, read in part as follows:

> COUNTRYMEN! THIS IS GHANA PATRIOTS CALLING
>
> The struggle for final liberation goes on. Keep away from Public Buildings; stay away from your offices. By day and night we will go on blasting the City and other places in increasing strength until Nkrumah's yoke is broken; until Nkrumah and his pack of villains run away and leave their shoes behind; until Nkrumah and his gang of ragmuffians who have strangled this country for 10 miserable years are thrown out of power.

(The reference was to Nkrumah's comment many years before that he would make the *chiefs* run and leave their sandals behind them.)

The leaflets came immediately after the bombing of Nkrumah's statue in front of the parliament building, the intent of that act being to discourage the Queen from making a planned visit to Ghana and to dissuade the U.S.A. from granting $160 million in loans to Ghana and the Kaiser Corporation for the Volta River hydroelectric and aluminum project. But the Queen came and the U.S.A. allocated the money for the dam and aluminum smelter nonetheless. Both events came at a moment when international support was most welcome, and they undoubtedly increased President Nkrumah's prestige and strength.

Toward the One-Party State

With the Queen's visit over, the Volta River funds in hand, and the strike leaders and UP officials in detention, there were no crises during the first three months of 1962. In fact, by the spring of that year, economic and political conditions seemed sufficiently stable to warrant some gestures of reconciliation by the government. Also, an international conference was pending on "The World Without the Bomb," and a conciliatory gesture would improve the nation's image. One hundred and fifty-two detainees were released on June 21, 1962, including all of the Sekondi-Takoradi trade unionists, Danquah, and Appiah. Another group was released soon afterwards.

The official reaction of the unions in Sekondi-Takoradi combined politics with the African courtesy extended to a chief who has granted a favor. A telegram was sent to President Nkrumah:

> Please accept our congratulations. Thanks. Your magnanimous sympathetic condescension releasing our detained men. We pledge unflinching support. Long live Osagyefo. Long live Ghana and African Unity.

The President replied through his secretary with unmistakable coolness:

> *Sir,*
>
> Osagyefo the President has asked me to acknowledge, on his behalf, your recent message of appreciation and loyalty.
>
> I am to state that Osagyefo has noted the sentiments expressed in the telegram, sent on behalf of your union.

The olive branch was held out to the UP detainees, but at the same time the CPP *Draft Programme for Work and Happiness* was circulating throughout the country, boldly proclaiming that the party, at a congress scheduled for July, was now determined to institute a one-party state. By the summer of 1962 the CPP press was appealing to all the former opposition leaders, including the released detainees, to get on the bandwagon by joining the CPP. The UP leaders spurned an appeal to close ranks and a segment of the Opposition living in exile in Togoland continued to call for the overthrow of Nkrumah and the CPP. By that time Gbedemah had gone abroad and joined forces with the Opposition-in-exile.

Opposition Reprisals

On August 2, 1962, Nkrumah was returning from a triumphant Pan-African journey to the Voltaic Republic, a neighboring nation to the north.

As he stopped to greet some school children in the town of Kulungugu just inside the Ghana border, a bomb exploded near him, killing twenty-two persons and injuring Nkrumah and several others. After the Kulungugu episode, Ako Adjei, who had originally recommended Nkrumah to Danquah as a prospective UGCC secretary, and Tawia Adamafio, a cabinet member from the Ga tribe who, as has been mentioned, once referred to the Sekondi-Takoradi strikers as "Western rats." A trainload of workers came to Accra to pledge loyalty to Nkrumah and to rejoice at Adamafio's downfall, bearing a sign that read: "From the Western Rats to the greatest rat of all."

During the next month a number of bombs were thrown into crowds in the capital city of Accra in an attempt to spread terror upon public occasions honoring Nkrumah. Several injuries and deaths resulted. This type of action was partially an expression of resentment by the Ga people over the detention of Adamafio and Ako Adjei. Three more attempts were made upon the life of Nkrumah, and several convictions were secured at the subsequent trials. That security measures were then progressively tightened was not unique to Ghana; similar assassination attempts had occurred in other African states with similar results. Danquah was detained again in 1964 after one of the attempts on Nkrumah's life, but no charges were preferred against him. He died in detention in 1965.

The "Revolution" Consolidated

Events in Ghana can only be understood as steps in an ongoing revolutionary process, first against the colonial power, and later against those sectors of the population that opposed socialist forms of development, the one-party state, or both. The steps taken after the Sekondi-Takoradi strike were irreversible, except by a violent overthrow of the government. By 1965, the country had embarked upon an ambitious Seven-Year Plan to achieve the goals set forth in *The Programme For Work and Happiness*. The Volta River project was well under way, the first factories were rising, new types of crops were being planted, and despite difficulties in servicing loans a vast expansion of physical facilities—hospitals, schools, hotels, TV station, new housing, and a new port—was taking place. The final step in bringing political institutions under the control of the all-embracing party was taken in June, 1965, when the Parliament was dissolved and the central committee of the party called upon to nominate candidates for a new election. Since only one candidate was nominated for each constituency, the formalities of an election were declared unnecessary. The 189 unopposed candidates took their seats and then elected the President as the constitution demands. Nkrumah was chosen. He picked his cabinet and sent it off immediately to the Kwame Nkrumah Ideological Institute for three weeks to study scientific socialism and to "meditate on the African Revolution." The second phase of revolution, which had begun with the inauguration of the Republic in 1960, had been consolidated. The next six years would test the adequacy of the new structures for meeting the demands of a period of mobilization for rapid industrial development.

The Significance of the Sekondi-Takoradi Crisis in Ghanaian Politics

Most adult Ghanaians are farmers and petty traders. No more than 600,000 of the 3 million employed persons work for wages or salaries, and of these only about 25,000 are in the fields of transportation and communication. About 8,000 were involved in the Sekondi-Takoradi strike. Ghanaians in other parts of the country did not respond to the call of the railway workers to "tie the country up" in protest against the budget, nor have there been any subsequent mass protests despite continued austerity measures. There may be some apathy and fear, but a guaranteed price for cocoa during a period of declining world prices has been a basic stabilizing factor. The gap between income and prices has not widened disastrously, nor have food shortages been critical. The people can see evidence of "progress," and channels of upward mobility for the youth are wide open. Cheerfulness in adversity, discipline under stress, a preference for letting politicians fight it out among themselves, and a tendency toward optimism are Ghanaian traits. Prospects of rebellion led by labor are remote.

The Sekondi-Takoradi strike was a dramatic reminder, however, that independent labor action in strategic sectors of the economy is always possible despite the disciplines imposed by the New Structure and the all-embracing party. The vigor and resourcefulness displayed by the railway workers at all levels revealed the continued viability of a tradition of conventional trade union practices, including strikes for economic and political ends, which neither the compulsory arbitration law nor appeals for "a new trade union mentality" had eliminated. Everyone was aware that what had happened once could happen again. Since rapid industrialization will continue to demand a higher level of direct and indirect taxation at the same time that wage increases are discouraged and some commodity prices are increasing, discontent among urban workers will probably manifest itself repeatedly in the future. The ethnically heterogeneous working class will increase in size in the next decade and will be organized by the New Structure. The main threat to national stability will no longer be tribalism, but the wildcat strike.

The Sekondi-Takoradi strike was not the first serious challenge to its power that the CPP government had faced during the ten-year period of its rule. It had weathered the National Liberation Movement's secessionist attempt in Ashanti in 1955 and stopped several tribalist thrusts from among the Ga in the capital city and the Ewe in Togoland. But never before had it been threatened by an alliance between an opposition party and a segment of organized labor. This time a group of workers allied itself with a conservative political party grasping desperately for a mass base. The government as well as the workers themselves considered it an unnatural alliance. But the pattern had implications for the future. A revolutionary left could arise within Ghana (influenced by various foreign Communist parties) making a proletarian appeal and attacking CPP socialism as revisionist and a betrayal of the workers. Such an alliance would have exceedingly dangerous implications. There are always dangers, too, that the Opposition-in-exile, encouraged by more conservative neighboring states and Western powers, will be tempted to exploit worker grievances during the future. From the CPP point of view the new pattern of opposition had to be stamped out at its birth.

The maintenance of what the CPP considered its mandate to rule, given by the people in the 1960 presidential election, was a primary consideration in the decision to break the strike and to punish those who had organized and sustained it. But it is clear, too, that the CPP leadership also decided to take advantage of the crisis to make certain structural changes in the government that were necessary if the party's socialist plans were to be implemented. The use of a crisis to introduce innovations already contemplated is a routine political practice everywhere. The downgrading and expulsion of antagonistic or lukewarm party members as a part of the process was consistent with Nkrumah's political style, which includes what he calls "Tactical Action" and has been influenced by Marxist-Leninist models.

The United Party leaders were convinced that the crisis was also used as an excuse for destroying their influence and imprisoning their most important leaders to further the establishment of a one-party state. They believed, too, that Nkrumah had planned to institute this form of political organization ever since the CPP first took power, but that he had had to maneuver toward his goal slowly and cautiously. Ghana's President, on the other hand, considered the UP action in Sekondi-Takoradi seditious and the punishment justified. Also, he has insisted in *Africa Must Unite* that he only gradually arrived at the decision to take drastic action toward the opposition after their "irresponsible" behavior made parliamentary democracy virtually unworkable by 1960.[8] CPP ideologists argue further that the concept of a permanent opposition is alien to the African way of life, and that a multiparty system plays into the hands of foreign interests who give financial—and even military—backing to parties opposing governments in power. Whatever the motives or rationalizations, the fact remains that the Sekondi-Takoradi strike gave the coup de grâce to the United Party.

Viewed functionally, the house cleaning within the CPP which followed

[8] See Austin, pp. 31–48, for an evaluation of the factors that led to the development of the one-party state. Cf. Kwame Nkrumah, *I Speak For Freedom* (New York: Praeger, 1961), pp. 113–14, and *Africa Must Unite* (New York: Praeger, 1963), Ch. 9, "Bringing Unity in Ghana."

the strike relieved some intraparty tensions and strengthened party unity. On the other hand, the punitive measures taken against the opposition reinforced tendencies toward clandestine violence that some individuals within the United Party had manifested since 1958.

Pan-African Implications

Resistance to the Restriction of Consumption

The major significance of the Sekondi-Takoradi case lies in its relevance to problems faced by all thirty-seven independent African-controlled states, which, with the exception of Liberia and Ethiopia, have only recently become free of foreign rule. Although these new nations differ greatly in colonial background and post-independence orientations and goals, all of them face certain common problems. Each is composed of diverse tribes that must be knit together into the fabric of a modern state. Each has, to a dangerous extent, a fragile economy based upon a single export commodity, or at most two, and each is at the mercy of uncontrollable price fluctuations in the world market. Illiteracy levels and disease rates are high. All of the new nations are trying to catch up rapidly with the developed countries.

In each, there has been a popular demand immediately after independence for the rapid expansion of educational and social services, but such expenditures cannot continue without a widening of the revenue-producing base and a diversification of the economy. Capital must be secured from foreign sources that demand fiscal restraints. Thus, a "moment of truth" is eventually reached when an austerity budget becomes an absolute necessity and when the call must be made for sacrifice, for restricted consumption, and for higher direct and indirect taxes. Because of the prosperity during and after World War II, their continuous exposure to advertising media, and their lack of experience with systematic taxation, citizens of the new African states are apt to express extreme dissatisfaction with economy measures imposed by their governments.

The nouveaux riches, including successful politicans, resist all attempts to limit their acquisitive activities, and the masses resent being asked to sacrifice if such accumulation at the top is not curbed. The governing parties must thus increase the financial burden upon lower income groups and at the same time try to discipline the emerging wealthy class and the embarrassingly wealthy in their own ranks. Their experts must devise effective means for collecting income and corporation taxes. The new governments are also inclined to force trade union leaders to keep to a minimum demands for wage increases by their members. The entire situation is complicated by the fact that political leaders out of power, dissident trade unionists, and extreme left-wingers are ready and willing to exploit the tensions for electoral advantage, to lead protests, and even to conspire to seize power. Occasional crises are inevitable.

Where illiteracy levels are high, tribal loyalties strong, and economic development just beginning, it would be unreasonable to expect carbon copies of Western political systems. A greater measure of authoritarian control than exists in older, more stable democracies (except in times of war) is almost inevitable. The one-party state is generally viewed with favor by African leaders, regardless of their ideological positions, as the type of organization most capable of coping with problems of rapid economic development and most effective for subordinating racial, religious, regional, and tribal loyalties to a strong central government. Some one-party states try to maintain a wide measure of competition and freedom within the party; others do not. Where intraparty democracy does exist, it allows for dissent and creative suggestions, but for those individuals who oppose the one-party state on principle, or who cannot accommodate themselves to it, extra-legal action is a tempting alternative. In Africa, where groups opposed to a one-party organization tend to be a small minority of the population, attempts to organize coups d'état occasionally occur but do not set off mass uprisings (Ethiopia, Algeria, Togo, Burundi, Dahomey, and Senegal are cases in point). The Ghana government interpreted the UP-worker alliance as an attempt to create chaos so that an army coup could restore order. It reacted as other states in Africa have in similar situations, but without the executions that have occurred in several other instances.

African Socialism

Of the thirty-seven African-controlled states, over half claim to be developing some type of socialism, and the term "African Socialism" is often used to emphasize their independence, ideological and structural, from the USSR, China, and Yugoslavia. Senghor's "humanistic socialism" in Senegal, Nyerere's "Umajaa" in Tanzania, Kenyatta and Mboya's "African Socialism" in Kenya, "Bourguibism" in Tunisia, "Arab Socialism" in the UAR, Ben Bella's "vertical socialism," Sékou Touré's "Communocracy," and "Nkrumaism" in Ghana—all are based upon the assumption that the welfare of the people and rapid economic development can best be attained by a degree of governmental intervention unneeded and often unwanted in the West. The leaders are just as insistent, however, that Communism—because of its atheism, its scorn for "primitive" cultures, and its tendency toward aggressive expansion—is un-African and unacceptable. Nevertheless, they seek financial and technical assistance from the East as well as from the West and resist the attempts to force them to take sides in the Cold War.

Of the three states that espouse a Marxist variety of socialism—Ghana, Guinea, and Mali—Ghana alone stresses the personality of the party leader as the symbol of national unity and attempts to utilize his charisma to endow socialist institutions with legitimacy, while at the same time developing a rationalistic neo-Marxian ideology. To the right of the official ideological position as stated in Nkrumah's book, *Consciencism,* is a small group of leaders who espouse a mystical doctrine that they call "arcane Nkrumaism"; and to the left is another small group with views close to those of the Chinese or Cuban Communists. The *Osagyefo* stays in the middle ideologically, though the Sekondi-Takoradi strike marked a significant leftward shift in the political center of gravity.

Dilemmas of Development and the One-Party State

There can be no African development without massive injections of capital. There is always the risk that grants and loans will lead to foreign domination (neocolonialism). Because Ghana hopes eventually to eliminate its dependence upon foreign capital, it makes heavy demands upon its domestic resources. In the short run, this means a shortage of some consumer goods, heavier taxation, and a limit upon wage increases. When measures such as these are taken, Ghanaian wage earners, like wage earners elsewhere, complain, protest, and eventually will attempt to strike if the wage level remains constant while living costs rise. Since Ghana is not likely to alter the structure of the wage level radically over the next decade, built-in tensions must be contained.

Ghana, like most African states, has advanced the same rationale for curbing personal consumption that classical economists in Britain and America did during the last half of the nineteenth century. Wages must be kept at relatively low levels until the economy is developed enough to warrant an increase. Given this rationale, no African government would have acceded to the full demands of the strikers at Sekondi-Takoradi. Tanzania and Kenya, when faced with similar problems, have also tried to discipline the unions. Dahomey, in 1965, was faced with a crisis in many respects like that which faced Ghana in 1961 (including resentment over a compulsory savings scheme). The response of the government was similar to Ghana's.

The Role of Labor in Developing Countries

There is a tendency for political leaders in all developing countries to try to curb what Nkrumah has called "militant unbridled trade unionism." One way to do this is to bind the trade union movement closely to the government. In those countries that profess to be following a socialist model of development, the main role allocated to trade unions—aside from maintaining grievance machinery in the hope of offsetting strike action—is that of attempting to indoctrinate workers in the official ideology. The unions must persuade them to accept some restriction of consumption in the present and to be satisfied with a wider range of social services in lieu of money in the pocket. To carry out such a role successfully requires from trade union leaders considerable knowledge of the dynamics of change in the national economy and the industrial complex as well as some psychological sophistication in the handling of their rank and file. They have the problem of interpreting to the workers the difficulties faced by a socialist government dependent upon the capitalist world. They must explain what seems like an inconsistency—the need for unity between capital and labor in the private sector of the economy if international commitments are to be honored or a unified economy, industrial peace, and labor efficiency achieved. Many leaders in such situations have not yet learned that their task cannot be carried out merely by reiterating political slogans such as "Sacrifice for the Future!"—"This is Your Socialist State!"—"Tomorrow You Will Be Happy!"

In trying to solve these problems Ghana developed a highly centralized government-controlled Trades Union Congress. By the time the Sekondi-Takoradi strike broke out it had not yet been fully accepted by workers, who were used to a more traditional system of union organization, nor had it developed techniques for dealing with the kinds of problems posed by a union such as that of the railway workers.

Trade Union Governments?

The railway workers of Sekondi-Takoradi did not raise any demands for a "government of the workers"; they did not pose a threat to the government from the left. They were interested rather in restoring traditional trade union privileges such as the right to bargain collectively and to withhold their labor if they could not secure what they wanted. They fought for a maximum amount of local union autonomy. They were unionists with an "economist" ideology. Most African unions are of this type (or would like to be), and they are held in check by political parties which, because their voting base is predominantly rural and their leaders are intellectuals, manage to strike a balance between urban and rural needs in their planning.

It is possible that, upon some future occasion and in specific African nations, unions with an economist ideology may be able to acquire the strength to form essentially trade union governments in alliance with the army and opposition political parties. The tendency would then be for the unions to force substantial wage increases for organized urban workers and to emphasize industrial development of immediate benefit to themselves at the expense of more balanced planning or agricultural interests. It is conceivable that, in the short run, the entire nation might benefit from such an emphasis, but the consequent heavy migration to cities would accentuate existing urban unemployment problems and could generate such a demand for imported foodstuffs and consumer goods generally as to create serious foreign exchange problems. The rise of a privileged working-class elite would eventually set off political opposition among farmers, who could retaliate by trying to starve out the cities or by supporting secessionist movements with appeals for foreign aid (as the Confederacy did in the American South during the Civil War). Problems could become so acute that only a military dictatorship would be able to contain the tensions.

The fact that no African government has, as yet, had to face this prospect does not make it a straw man. The large African unions in Zambia and Nigeria have shown their power upon several occasions in the past and could conceivably bring down a government and dictate the organization of one more to their liking. In 1964, the Nigerian unions tied up the railways and docks for two weeks and led a general strike of 800,000 workers. They won most of their demands. During the summer of 1963 the three organized trade union groups in the Congo (Brazzaville) overthrew the government of President Fulbert Youlou and presided over the installation of a new government in cooperation with the army. During the fall of the same year the unions of Dahomey played a preeminent role in the overthrow of President Hubert Maga, again in cooperation with the army. In these cases, while the unions did not insist upon a trade union government, they did dictate demands that were granted. The CPP government was taking no chances at Sekondi-Takoradi, and the subsequent events in Dahomey and the Congo (Brazzaville) confirmed them in their belief that the action was justified.

Study Questions

1. The Ghana Industrial Relations Act of 1958, which the Railway Workers Union opposed, provided for compulsory arbitration and virtually banned strikes. Are such laws ever justifiable? Under what condition?
2. Ghana and Guinea have taken the initiative in trying to organize an All-African Trades Union Federation (AATUF), unaffiliated with either the Communist-dominated World Federation of Trade Unions (WFTU) or the Western-based International Confederation of Free Trade Unions (ICFTU). The latter organization has vigorously opposed AATUF on the grounds that African labor unions need Western support in order to resist both domination by their own governments and Communist subversion. Is this position a wise one? Why, or why not?
3. Are African governments justified in their insistence that the wage level should remain low until productivity has been greatly increased, and that much of the national income should be diverted by tax measures to investment for development even at the cost of a lowered standard of living?
4. Most African governments contend that trade union leaders should not only curb excessive wage demands but should also actively support measures to raise man-hour productivity. From the point of view of American unions, such activity should not be a primary trade union function. In your opinion, which point of view is correct, and why?
5. Were the Ghana railway workers justified in using the strike to form an alliance with the Opposition which was mainly interested in preventing the drift toward a one-party state? Should foreign unions have given them the moral and financial support requested in their appeal?

Selected Bibliography

The following books and articles deal with the major problems discussed in this case:

Apter, David. *Ghana in Transition.* New York: Atheneum, 1963.

Austin, Dennis. *Politics in Ghana: 1946–1960.* London: Oxford University Press, 1964.

Berg, Elliott. "Trade Unions," in James S. Coleman and Carl G. Rosberg, Jr., eds., *Political Parties and National Integration in Tropical Africa.* Berkeley: University of California Press, 1964.

Carter, Gwendolen M., ed. *African One-Party States.* Ithaca, N.Y.: Cornell University Press, 1962.

Cowan, E. A. *Evolution of Trade Unionism in Ghana.* Accra: Ghana Trades Union Congress, *c.* 1963.

Cowan, L. Gray. *Dilemmas of African Independence.* New York: Walker, 1963.

Drake, St. Clair. "Prospects for Democracy in the Gold Coast," *Annals of the American Academy of Political and Social Science.* CCCVI (July, 1956), 78–87.

———. "Democracy on Trial in Africa," *Annals of the American Academy of Political and Social Science.* CCCLIV (July ,1964), 110–21.

Nkrumah, Kwame. *Ghana: The Autobiography of Kwame Nkrumah.* Edinburgh: Nelson, 1957.

———. *I Speak for Freedom.* New York: Praeger, 1961.

———. *Africa Must Unite.* New York: Praeger, 1963.

———. *Consciencism.* New York: Monthly Review Press, 1965.

———. *Neo-Colonialism: The Last Stage of Imperialism.* London: Nelson, 1965.

Rosberg, Carl G., Jr., and W. H. Friedland. *African Socialism.* Stanford: Stanford University Press, 1965.

Spark Editors. *Nkrumaism.* New York: International Publishers, 1965.

Tettegah, John. *Towards Nkrumaism: The Building of Socialist Ghana. The Role and Task of the Trade Unions.* Accra: Ghana Trades Union Congress, 1962.

Africa Report, published monthly by the African-American Institute, Washington, D.C., provides continuous documentation of strikes and political crises in African states as well as routine news, special articles, and book reviews. The issue for June, 1965, included five articles related to the theme "Paradoxes of African Trade Unionism: Organizational Chaos and Political Potential." W. H. Friedland analyzed the Brazzaville general strike of 1963, the Nigerian general strike of 1964, and the Dahomey coup of 1963. The May 1963 issue was devoted primarily to African Socialism.

Brief accounts of the Sekondi-Takoradi strike are presented in Dennis Austin (pp. 400–02) and in *Area Handbook for Ghana,* prepared by the Foreign Areas Studies Division of American University, Washington, 1962 (pp. 390, 508–09). The only published detailed analysis of the strike is the Ghana government's White Paper: *Statement by the Government on the Recent Conspiracy,* December 11,

1961. This official interpretation of the situation is one of a series of documents that are indispensable for an understanding of the severity of the punitive measures after the strike. The others are: Report of the Commission Appointed Under the Commissions Enquiry Ordinance, *Enquiry into the Matters Disclosed at the Trial of Captain Benjamin Awhaitey Before a Court Martial and the Surrounding Circumstances* (Accra: Government Printer, 1959); White Paper: *Statement by the Government on the Report of the Commission Appointed to Enquire into the Matters Disclosed at the Trial of Captain Awhaitey* (Accra: Government Printer, 1959); Blue Paper: *In Defence of Ghana: A Statement by the National Executive of the United Party* (Accra: United Party, 1959). An evaluation of the charges and counter-charges in these documents has been made in Dennis Austin (pp. 35–40).

The account of the day-by-day events during the strike is based upon critically selected data from the 1961 White Paper and news items in the *Ghanaian Times,* the *Evening News,* the *Ghana Graphic,* and the *Ashanti Pioneer,* supplemented by interviews.

The analysis of the role of the unions is based primarily upon correspondence, reports, minutes, and memoranda made available by officials of the National Railway and Harbour Workers Union for preparation of a master's thesis presented at the Institute of African Studies, University of Ghana, by Leslie A. Lacy, "The Railway Workers' Union of Sekondi-Takoradi." These documents are in the archives of the union's working committee. This primary and secondary source material has been supplemented by interviews with union leaders and members in Sekondi-Takoradi and government officials. One of the authors visited Sekondi-Takoradi during the first week of the strike, and the other lived in the city for six months in 1963.

Source material on economic and political conditions immediately preceding and following the strike may be found in Dennis Austin, *Ghana Handbook,* and in *Economic Survey, 1961,* and *Economic Survey, 1962* (Accra: Central Bureau of Statistics, 1962, 1963).

4

Nigerian Politics

The Ordeal of Chief Awolowo, 1960-65

Richard L. Sklar

The time is April 2, 1963; the place is the High Court of Lagos in the capital of the Federation of Nigeria. The eyes of the country are upon an accused person, Chief Obafemi Awolowo, as he begins his defense. Until recently, he has been Leader of the Opposition in Nigeria's federal Parliament. Now, he and twenty others are on trial for plotting to seize power by means of a coup d'état. Originally, thirty-one persons were accused; four of them are still at large outside Nigeria, four were discharged by the trial judge upon completion of the prosecution's case, and two have become witnesses for the Crown. (The British monarch is still Queen of Nigeria. On October 1, 1963, three years to the day after its attainment of independence within the Commonwealth of Nations, Nigeria will become a federal republic.) The specific offenses alleged in this case are treasonable felony, conspiracy to commit treasonable felony, and conspiracy to violate the Firearms Act. There is no jury, and the trial judge may impose a maximum sentence of life imprisonment. Chief Awolowo is a lawyer. He has decided to try his own case since the counsel of his choice, a Briton, has been denied entry into Nigeria. With quiet pride, he says, "By calling I am a politician."

Is this a "political trial"? The prosecution will deny that suggestion vehemently and refuse to admit of any concern beyond the particular points of alleged criminal conduct. Nonetheless, the political issues in this trial overshadow the criminal issues that will be determined in court. The principal defendant, one of Africa's best known and most experienced politicians, is notorious for his attempt to commit his party, the Action Group of Nigeria, to an increasingly radical and socialistic course. Deeply divided by this and related causes of controversy, his party has split and suffered a precipitous decline of strength. Awolowo himself is destined to be convicted and sentenced to imprisonment for ten years. Even so, he will retain his prominent position on the Nigerian political stage.

The Background

Who in that courtroom would not be aware that Chief Awolowo is one of the architects of modern Nigeria? Born in 1909, he completed one year of secondary school before going to work as a teacher in a primary school. Subsequently, he was employed as a stenographer, a college clerk, and a newspaper reporter. Having determined to study law in Britain, he undertook a succession of business ventures—moneylending, public letterwriting, taxi proprietorship, produce buying, and motor transport—all to little avail. Meanwhile he became an influential member of various forward-looking associations, including the nationalistic Nigerian Youth Movement. He earned a correspondence degree of Bachelor of Commerce from the University of London. During the Second World War he prospered as a food contractor for the army. By 1944, at the age of 35, his savings supplemented by loans were sufficient to pay for a journey to London where, two years later, he qualified as a member of the bar.

In London Awolowo also meditated on the course of Nigerian politics and published his thoughts in a small book which earned him a considerable reputation. In *Path to Nigerian Freedom,* published in London in 1947, he put forth the view that Nigeria was not properly speaking a nation, but "a geographical expression," including within its boundaries various cultural-linguistic nationalities, each of which consisted of tribes and clans. Furthermore, he maintained that each nationality group has its own indigenous constitution. Under alien rule, he argued, these African "constitutions" were abused and perverted to the detriment of public welfare and peaceful social progress.

Here it is germane to indicate some of the basic features of Nigeria's social background. Of all countries on the African continent, Nigeria, with a population of more than fifty million, is both the largest and the most obviously divided into linguistic and cultural sections. Though very many African languages are spoken in Nigeria, the three largest linguistic groups are the Hausa-speaking people of northern Nigeria, the Ibo-speaking people of southeastern Nigeria, and the Yoruba-speaking people of southwestern Nigeria. Each forms the largest population group in its section of the country, and these three sections made up the Federation of Nigeria that became independent of Great Britain in 1960. Forming this federation had required major skill and tolerance on the part of the leaders in adjusting and conciliating the interests of various groups, including both the dominant nationalities and the numerous minority groups within each region. The cohesion of the federation has depended upon high-level competence in the conduct of intergroup relations.

Federal Republic of Nigeria, 1966

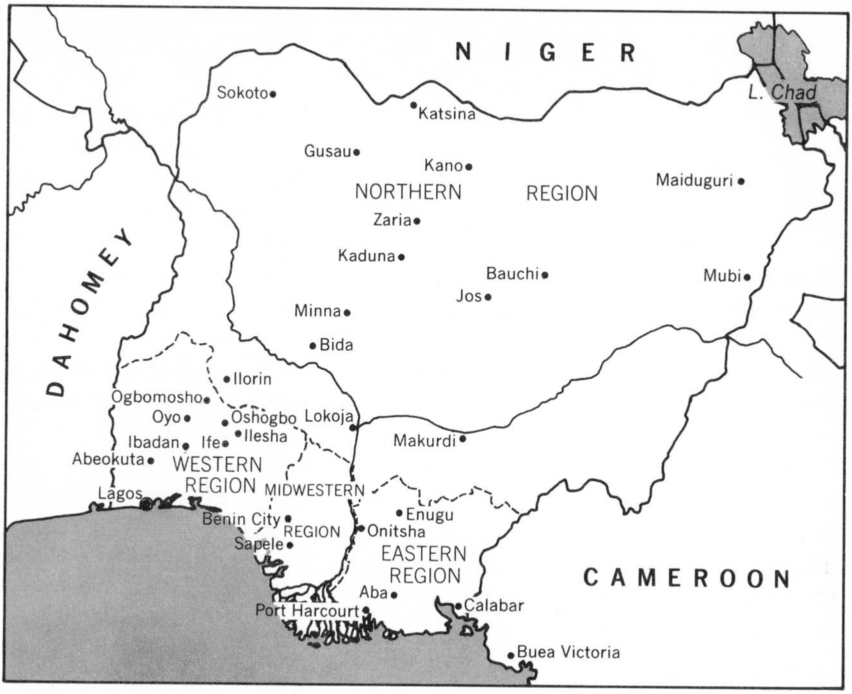

Main Ethnic Groups

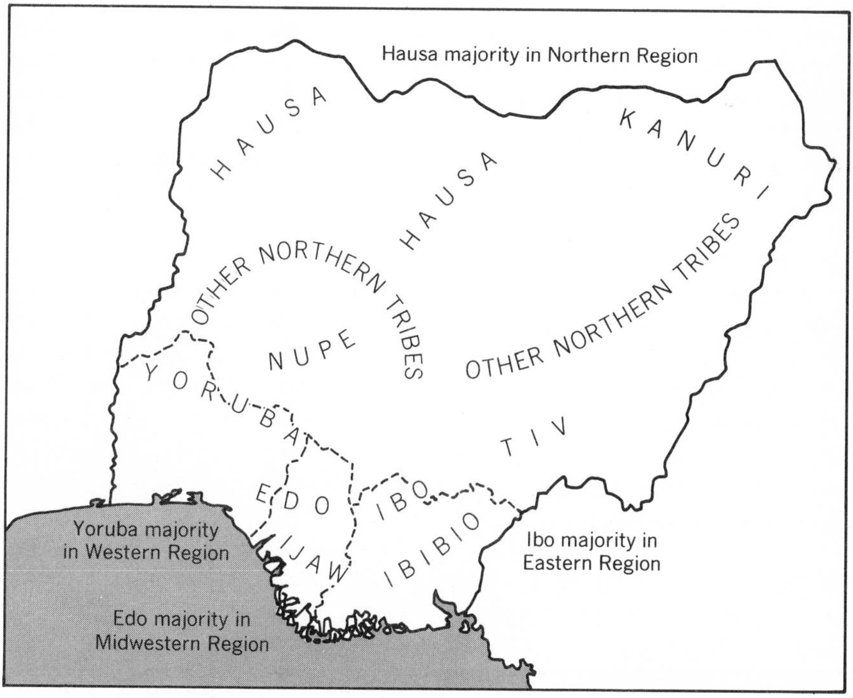

In Nigeria divisive cultural tendencies are accentuated by wide variations in the regional patterns and traditions of public administration. In northern Nigeria, most of the Hausa-speaking people inhabit the area of the classical emirates, where British administration was instituted on principles of "indirect rule," meaning government conducted through the medium of traditional authorities. This system of administration was ideally suited to the large-scale indigenous states of Hausaland. These states were ruled according to theocratic principles by Muslim emirs, all of whom owed allegiance to the Sultan of Sokoto. Each state had its nobility and its hierarchy of titled officials. Today the emirates form part of a system of local government in which traditional rule is modified by the practice of elected representation. However, the traditional authorities remain powerful, and traditional values still shape political developments in the northern part of Nigeria.

The British policy of indirect rule was much less successful in the southern part of Nigeria. As implemented by officials of the colonial government, that policy was entirely unsuited to the indigenous system of dispersed authority characteristic of the Ibo and other peoples of southeastern Nigeria. In southwestern Nigeria, where the dominant group is Yoruba-speaking, the people have long been organized into large and relatively centralized tribal states, each with its reigning *Oba,* or king. However, the king's traditional power is stringently limited by custom and by subordinate councils of chiefs representing the major constituent lineages of the state. In a real sense, the political tradition of the Yoruba people is constitutional as well as monarchical. This was not appreciated by British colonialists, who undertook to govern the Yoruba states along lines similar to their government of the Hausa states in northern Nigeria. As a result, they converted the constitutional kings into autocratic agents of the colonial administration and transformed the Yoruba states into untraditional despotisms. Inevitably, the movement against British rule involved a protest against the arbitrary rule of the puppet kings; it was expressed in a desire to regenerate the true Yoruba tradition by restoring the balance between kings, chiefs, and people.

As a Yoruba intellectual in postwar Nigeria, Awolowo was concerned both with reforming the structure of government in Yorubaland and with ending the regime of British colonial rule. In 1947 the most popular and aggressive section of the Nigerian nationalist movement was led by an American-educated journalist of Ibo-speaking extraction, Nnamdi Azikiwe. Besides being the proprietor of an influential daily newspaper in Lagos, the *West African Pilot,* Azikiwe, then 43, was president of a congress of nationalistic associations called the National Council of Nigeria and the Cameroons (NCNC). In Lagos, a great cosmopolitan seaport near the western end of the Nigerian coastline, Azikiwe's section of the nationalist movement was opposed by some of the most influential leaders of the social, economic, and intellectual life of the city, especially men of Yoruba descent. While the NCNC numbered many Yorubas in its ranks, Azikiwe's personal and political conflict with the social elite of Lagos was far-reaching in its effect and, in later years, proved to be deeply divisive of political opinion throughout Yorubaland.

In the immediate postwar period, many western Nigerian nationalists who were also antagonistic toward the NCNC joined the Nigerian Youth Movement. Before his residence in London, Awolowo had served the Youth Movement as its provincial secretary at Ibadan, the largest city in Yorubaland (and indeed the largest city of Africans on the continent), ninety miles inland from Lagos. Awolowo's thesis in *Path to Nigerian Freedom* found favor in Youth Movement circles and among other members of the Yoruba intelligentsia who were anxious to check the spread of the NCNC in the Western provinces. To the idea that every national group has its indigenous constitution that had been corrupted under colonial rule, Awolowo added the dictum that the constitution of each cultural nationality should be its own "domestic concern." Every such nationality is entitled and should be encouraged to develop its own political institutions within the framework of a Nigerian federation. Furthermore, he insisted, it is the "natural right" of the educated minority of each cultural group "to lead their fellow nationals into higher political development."

Awolowo's ideas, namely, political reform at the local level, political unity at the cultural level, a federal constitution at the national level, and the assumption of leadership within each cultural group by its educated minority, were to provide an intellectual program for political action by the Yorubaland opposition to Azikiwe. The first step had been taken by Awolowo and several other students in London in 1945, when they established a cultural society, dedicated to the unity and social progress of the Yoruba people, which they called the Society of the Descendants of Oduduwa—the mythical progenitor and culture hero of the Yoruba. In 1948 the society was inaugurated in western Nigeria with Awolowo as its general secretary. Although ostensibly a cultural organization, the society's political significance was unmistakable. It was joined by most of the luminaries of the Yoruba nation, among them many forward-looking *obas* and chiefs. These men saw that a "revolution from above" was inevitable and were anxious to ensure that it would be led by trusted sons of their communities who were sound in their appreciation of traditional values. It was anticipated that institutional reforms in western Nigeria would, of necessity, include the democratization of local government and related measures affecting the tenure and power of chiefs. Moreover, the constitutional development of Nigeria made it certain that such reforms would be instituted under the direction of elected leaders at the regional government level.

The Constitution of 1946 provided for the division of Nigeria into three governmental regions, namely, the Northern, Eastern, and Western Regions. Nigerian nationalists generally condemned this constitution for its failure to provide either democratic representation or responsible government with

Nigerians holding ministerial office. The NCNC also objected to regionalization, regarding it as an attempt by the British to perpetuate artificial divisions, which were inimical to the nationalist cause. Under pressure, the colonial government undertook to revise the constitution along more democratic lines. But the tri-regional framework was retained, as we have seen; indeed, it found favor with the dominant political groups in northern Nigeria and among leaders of the Nigerian Youth Movement and the Society of the Descendants of Oduduwa in western Nigeria. These latter perceived that, given the cooperation of the Yoruba chiefs, they could win a majority of seats in the Western House of Assembly that would soon be elected on a semi-democratic basis. To accomplish this objective, Awolowo and his associates in the Western Region organized a political party called the Action Group, which emerged from the election of 1951 with a majority in the Western Regional House of Assembly. Members of the Action Group were appointed to ministerial office; Awolowo himself became regional minister of Local Government and Leader of Government Business in the House of Assembly.

At the same time that the Action Group came to power in Western Nigeria, nearly all of the elected members of the Eastern House of Assembly declared for its opponent, the NCNC. In the Northern Region an overwhelming majority of the members of the House of Assembly declared for the Northern Peoples' Congress (NPC), a party of moderate nationalists dedicated to the preservation and gradual reform of traditional institutions in that region. Under the Constitution of 1951, each regional House of Assembly elected a specified number of its own members to a central House of Representatives. For reasons that are not directly pertinent to this account and that need not, therefore, be related here, the Constitution of 1951 proved unworkable and broke down during a political crisis in 1953. At that juncture, representatives of the several political parties met with colonial officials in London to frame a genuinely federal constitution that came into effect in 1954. Under the new constitution, the leader of the majority party in each regional legislature was appointed to the office of Regional Premier.

From 1954 to 1959 the destiny of Nigeria was guided by the "Big Three" Premiers: Dr. Nnamdi Azikiwe, Premier of the Eastern Region and national president of the NCNC; Alhaji Sir Ahmadu Bello, the Sardauna of Sokoto, Premier of the Northern Region and general president of the Northern Peoples' Congress; Chief Obafemi Awolowo, Premier of the Western Region and federal president of the Action Group of Nigeria. Their respective titles indicate their different paths to power and prestige. Azikiwe, who earned a master's degree in anthropology, holds honorary doctorates of law from three American universities. Ahmadu Bello is a lineal descendant of the founder of the Sokoto empire of the north. He is a devout Muslim and his title, "Alhaji," indicates that he has made a pilgrimage to Mecca. He has also been knighted by the Queen. Sardauna, a traditional title, identifies him as a councilor to the Sultan of Sokoto. In Awolowo's case, the title "Chief" does not signify a traditional ruler. Among the Yoruba, it is customary for honorary chieftaincy titles to be conferred upon eminent men in recognition of their personal achievements and services to their local communities. Awolowo holds several such "courtesy titles," which were conferred upon him by the traditional chiefs of various Yoruba communities after he became Premier.

The chronology of Nigerian political development from 1954 to 1960 may be outlined briefly. In 1954 federal elections were held for the first time. The constitution provided for the appointment of nine federal ministers—three from among the federal legislators elected in each region. It further stipulated that if no one party had a majority in the House of Representatives, federal ministers were to be appointed from among the majority party in the House from each region. Contrary to expectation, the NCNC won a majority of the seats in the West as well as in the East, giving it the right to designate six out of the nine federal ministers. The largest single block of representatives in the federal house, however, belonged to the Northern Peoples' Congress, owing to the fact that the Northern Region had some 54 percent of the Nigerian population. Consequently, the NCNC and the NPC formed a "government" (as yet no provision had been made for the office of Prime Minister of the Federation), while the Action Group provided the federal "opposition."

Each party then turned with alacrity to the task of consolidating its power in its region of primary strength. Two parties—the NCNC and the Action Group—sought to compete on a nation-wide basis: the NCNC had confirmed areas of strength in the Western Region and a strong ally, the radical Northern Elements Progressive Union (NEPU), in the Northern Region; the Action Group decided to exploit oppositional tendencies, first among non-Ibo groups in the Eastern Region, and subsequently among non-Hausa groups in the Northern Region.

In 1957 constitutional provision was made for a Prime Minister of the Federation, who would be empowered to choose his cabinet in the normal way without regard to regional representation. All parties agreed to the appointment of Alhaji Sir Abubakar Tafawa Balewa, vice-president of the Northern Peoples' Congress and leader of that party in the House of Representatives, as the first Prime Minister. Sir Abubakar then formed a national government, including ministers from the Action Group as well as the NPC and the NCNC. A second federal election, held in 1959, revealed the decisive supremacy of each regional government party in the majority group sector of each region. All told, the Northern Peoples' Congress emerged from the election with a strong plurality—142 seats out of a total of 312; the NCNC/NEPU alliance ran second with 89; the Action Group trailed with 73.

By this time, the relationship between the NPC and the Action Group had become bitterly antagonistic, mainly as a result of the Action Group's determined campaign for the creation of a new region in the main minority group area of the North and its simultaneous demand for a revision of the North-West boundary so as to transfer some 500,000 Northern Yorubas to the Western Region. In fact, the Action Group campaigned for the creation of a new state in each of the existing regions prior to independence. Meanwhile, the NCNC had established a notably cordial relationship with the NPC, notwithstanding its traditional alliance with the radical NEPU. After the election, the NPC and the NCNC formed a coalition government with Alhaji Sir Abubakar Tafawa Balewa as Prime Minister once again. Azikiwe, who had been elected to the House of Representatives, resigned his seat to assume the largely ceremonial office of President of the newly created Nigerian Senate; subsequently, he withdrew from active politics to become Governor-General of Nigeria, the titular head of state. Chief Awolowo became Leader of the federal Opposition, while the Sardauna of Sokoto, the only major leader who did not stand for the federal Parliament, remained in office as Premier of the North.

The Gathering Storm

In 1960 the Action Group presented a formidable front of opposition to the federal government coalition. Over half the Action Group members of the House of Representatives had been elected in minority group constituencies of the Northern and Eastern Regions by voters who responded to agitation for the creation of new states. Action Group operations in the Northern and Eastern Regions were financed liberally out of revenues raised in the relatively prosperous Western Region. For some dozen years, the economy of Western Nigeria had been relatively buoyant, owing to a postwar boom in the world price of that region's main export crop, cocoa. Upon this foundation of agricultural prosperity, a new class rapidly developed. Within its compass were many affluent businessmen, including merchants, produce traders, transport owners, building contractors, financiers, and incipient industrialists, most of whom supported the regional government party morally *and* with money. The party, in turn, fostered the creation of profitable opportunities for private enterprise. It used commercial patronage freely, including the allocation of loans, contracts, and trading licenses, to secure the support of businessmen and to guarantee a steady flow of funds into party coffers. For these and related reasons elaborated below, the Action Group had never been deficient in funds; it was, in fact, much better off financially than either of its major rivals, and it was reported to have spent no less than £1 million on the federal election of 1959, considerably more than the combined expenditures of all other parties. No effort was spared in creating vigorous units of the party in all parts of the Federation.

Within the party, supreme authority has been vested in an annual Congress, comprising two representatives of every federal parliamentary constituency, members of Parliament, and various other specified leaders. The principal executive body is the Federal Executive Council, which consists of more than one hundred members, including the federal officers, the several parliamentary leaders, and representatives of the several regions. Between meetings of the Federal Executive Council, control of the party is delegated to a much smaller working committee. In addition, the party's constitution provides for the formation of a parliamentary council in each legislature of the Federation. Each parliamentary leader is elected by a joint meeting of the parliamentary council concerned (comprising all members of the party in the legislature) and either the regional executive committee concerned or, in the case of the federal parliamentary leader, the Federal Executive Council. Provision is also made for the election of a supreme parliamentary leader, styled Leader of the Party, and a Deputy Leader of the Party, by a joint meeting of all parliamentary councils and the Federal Executive Council. Finally, these organizational arrangements are reinforced by periodic meetings of leaders, prominent members, and supporters of the party, which have been convened by the Leader of the Party.

In 1959 Chief Awolowo resigned as Premier of Western Nigeria to stand in the federal election. He was replaced by the Deputy Leader of the Party, Chief Samuel Ladoke Akintola, who had been the party's federal parliamentary leader and a federal minister in the national government of 1957–59. Like Awolowo, Akintola earned his political spurs in the Nigerian Youth Movement. Subsequently, he studied law in London and served as legal adviser to the pan-Yoruba cultural society—the aforementioned Society of the Descendants of Oduduwa. An early member of the Action Group, he was elected Deputy Leader of the Party in 1955. His several chieftaincy titles, like those of Awolowo, are "courtesy" titles conferred upon him by the traditional chiefs of Yoruba communities.

It has been alleged that Chief Awolowo was not altogether happy about the choice of Chief Akintola to succeed him as Premier of the Western Region. While there are no sure signs of serious deterioration in the political relationship of the two men prior to this time, Awolowo must have known that Akintola would be a forceful and self-reliant Premier. Akintola is only one year younger than Awolowo; his position in the old Nigerian Youth Movement as sometime editor of its official organ, the *Daily Service,* and as chairman of its Lagos branch in 1950 was somewhat more distinguished than that of Awolowo himself. If, as was later alleged, Awolowo meant to retain his personal control of the Western Regional government through intermediaries who were installed as directors of regional statutory corporations, he might have anticipated objections on the part of the new Premier. Nonetheless, Akintola was a logical choice, not only by virtue of his standing in the party but in view of his probable popularity with sections of the

Yoruba electorate which heretofore had lacked enthusiasm for the Action Group.

In point of fact, the Action Group under Awolowo had never been a popular party in Ibadan, the capital city of the Western Region. Ibadan and its environs contain the largest compact population group in Western Nigeria. Traditionally, the Ibadan community is part of the Oyo Yoruba kingdom. Although Akintola is not a son of Ibadan, he does hail from a town (Ogbomosho) with whose people the Ibadan people have a close traditional connection. They are all Oyo Yoruba. Awolowo, on the other hand, belongs to the Ijebu Yoruba with whom the Ibadan people have a long-standing rivalry. Specifically, the Ibadan have resented the economic and social ascendancy of Ijebu settlers in their city, which is, to be sure, the administrative and commercial center of the Western Region.

It is precisely this kind of divisive rivalry between traditional Yoruba groups that the Society of the Descendants of Oduduwa was designed to eliminate. Awolowo, who was secretary-general of the Society, established his law practice at Ibadan, but he was identified by the local people with Ijebu interests, and he failed to capture their hearts. Ibadan, therefore, was a stronghold of the NCNC in Yorubaland, and the Action Group hoped that the installation of an Oyo Yoruba, in the person of Akintola, as Premier of the West would sway the minds of the Ibadan people. This hope was partially realized in the regional election of 1960; the Action Group made substantial gains in Ibadan and was returned to power by the regional electorate as a whole, with a solid majority in the Western House of Assembly.

Firmly entrenched in the Western Region, Action Group leaders evaluated the strengths and weaknesses of their total situation. They agreed that under existing conditions their party on its own was unlikely to be voted into power in the federal government. Two schools of thought developed: one, looking toward the formation of a progressive alliance that would be able to dislodge the conservative regime in Northern Nigeria, favored a policy of collaboration with the NCNC; the other, concerned with preserving the political status quo in Western Nigeria and with securing for the Western Region full federal recognition in matters of national planning, opted for collaboration with the Northern Peoples' Congress within the framework of a national government that would include the ruling elements of all the regions.

These two rival schools of thought polarized opinion within the Action Group on other related issues. Those who favored closer cooperation with the NCNC hoped to revive that party's traditional spirit of antiregionalism in order to effect the division of Nigeria, especially Northern Nigeria, into more states. Those who leaned toward collaboration with the Northern Peoples' Congress reverted to the Action Group's earlier regionalist viewpoint as a dictate of political prudence. Logically, the antiregionalist position attracted those who would not greatly regret the passing of capitalistic and, in the case of the North, of quasi-feudalistic social systems based on established regional power. Antiregionalism, therefore, went hand in hand with equalitarian socialism, while the regionalist viewpoint appealed more strongly to members of the incumbent political class, defined to mean those persons who controlled the dominant institutions of society.

Within the Action Group, radical antiregionalism was championed by the Leader of the federal Opposition, Chief Awolowo. Some would attribute his seemingly sudden swing to the left mainly to motivations of a basically opportunistic sort. Undoubtedly, he did think and say that the Action Group would come to power only, if at all, as a party of popular protest against the existing social and political order. Others would interpret his ideological reorientation in a different vein as the outcome of his increasingly clear perception of the major faults in Nigeria's political economy. These explanations are not mutually exclusive. In any case, Awolowo rallied the radicals in his party, while the more conservative members gravitated to the leadership of the Western Regional Premier, Chief Akintola.

In mid-September, 1960, on the eve of national independence, Chief Awolowo presided over a lengthy meeting of the Federal Executive Council of the Action Group. Commenting on the political situation, he took note of rumors that once independence had been achieved the federal government would look for a pretext to dissolve the Western Regional Government and impose a caretaker regime in its place in order to destroy the institutional foundations of the Action Group. Some leaders of the party, he said, contemplated secession from the Federation in the event of "unconstitutional" action by the federal government. Awolowo did not favor the idea of secession nor did he believe the Action Group should join a new national government that would include all the regional government parties. In his view, "virile opposition" was essential to the well-being of Nigeria. "If there is any fear for the Action Group," he said, "it is not fear originating from without, but from within."

To deal effectively with these pressing problems, Awolowo proposed the creation of two special committees, one on ideology and one on tactics. With the agreement of the Federal Executive Council, Awolowo appointed four persons of known socialistic sympathies to serve with him on the ideological committee. The Federal Executive Council also agreed that Awolowo should be solely responsible for the functioning of the tactical committee, that its membership would be secret, and that it would not be required to submit reports to the Executive Council but would recommend specific courses of action as necessary.

In confirmation of the Action Group's turn leftward from liberalism, the party's annual congress adopted a manifesto which espoused the philosophy of "democratic socialism." The new party program envisaged the construction of a "mixed socialist economy," combining elements of public and private enterprise within the framework of a comprehensive national plan.

Awolowo then toured Nigeria to propagate the ideas of his party and to perfect its organization in various parts of the country. His public and parliamentary speeches throughout 1961 revealed the markedly leftward tendency of his thought. One recurrent theme was criticism of the growing domination of Nigeria's economy by imperialistic, capitalist interests. In June, 1961, Chief Awolowo went to Accra, Ghana, for discussions with President Kwame Nkrumah. Thereafter his criticisms of Nigerian foreign policy became increasingly explicit, and he seemed to align his party with the Ghanaian (and the radical Casablanca group's) persuasion in pan-African affairs.

Behind the scenes, Awolowo took steps to promote his grand design for the unity of "progressive" elements in opposition to the Northern Peoples' Congress. Central to his thought was the idea that Azikiwe, Governor General of the Federation, should be persuaded to return to active politics as the titular leader of the progressive movement. Tactfully, Awolowo pursued the goal of rapprochement with his former rival. He made a speech in Eastern Nigeria supporting the election of Azikiwe as the first President of a Nigerian republic. He discussed the question of political realignment with leading members of the NCNC, designated a few trusted associates to conduct negotiations in his behalf, and raised the matter personally in conversation with Azikiwe. All the while, he made preparations to intensify the propagation of Action Group ideas. In this connection, he solicited the aid of certain non-party intellectuals who were sympathetic to the creed of democratic socialism. He valued their intelligence and they, in turn, were ready with ideas to remedy the ills of Nigerian society.

In October, 1961, Awolowo formed a study group called the National Reconstruction Committee, which included about one dozen persons, among them university lecturers and professors, some of whom were not actually members of his party. The members of this committee produced several working papers on various topics, including the case for austerity measures in government, the implications of a commitment to the creed of democratic socialism, economic planning, and pan-African affairs. These papers were submitted to the Federal Executive Council in December, 1961. The paper on austerity measures, deploring the extravagant financial benefits extended at public expense to governmental ministers and civil servants, appears to have occasioned bitter debate; a few party leaders are reported to have alleged that Awolowo had fallen into the hands of "communists."

On February 2, 1962, Awolowo delivered a presidential address to the Action Group congress, assembled at Jos, in the Northern Region. In candor, he said, we must admit, "openly for once," the existence of "real and dangerous contradictions" within the party. He took note of "a growing disaffection between privileged and non-privileged classes (so-called) within the party." He also referred to several basic policy conflicts: on the question of sustaining the Action Group as an opposition party in the Northern and

Eastern Regions, on the issue of pressing for the creation of new states, on the desirability of joining the NPC-NCNC coalition to form a national government, and finally on the adoption of an explicitly socialistic program. Awolowo reaffirmed his advocacy of socialism, the creation of more states, and the maintenance of a vigorous opposition in the North, but he refrained from an explicit attack on Chief Akintola, and, in contrast to the recent editorial statements of newspapers under his control, spoke only in praise of the Western Regional government.

Debate on the address occupied two full days. After the first day, Chief Akintola, his close associate, Chief Ayotunde Rosiji, who was federal secretary of the party, and six of their supporters (including five ministers in the Western Regional government) withdrew from the congress and returned to Ibadan, ostensibly to greet the Northern Regional Premier, Alhaji Sir Ahmadu Bello, the Sardauna of Sokoto, upon the occasion of the latter's visit to the capital of the Western Region. In the absence of the federal secretary, the latter's report was debated by the Congress and rejected.

Chief Rosiji had drawn attention to the Action Group's electoral decline in the Eastern and Northern Regions during the previous year and had emphasized the consolidation of power by each major party in its regional stronghold. (In an election to the Northern House of Assembly in May, 1961, the Action Group won 9 seats to 156 for the Northern Peoples' Congress; the NEPU was held to a single seat. In the Eastern Regional election of November, 1961, the Action Group's percentage of the vote had declined sharply from 1959: the Action Group won 15 seats in the House of Assembly to 106 for the NCNC and 25 for other parties and independent candidates). In addition, chief Rosiji had circulated a memorandum containing personal proposals for the termination of party competition in Nigeria and for the merger of all political elements in a nonpartisan Nigerian Peoples United Front. Following the rejection of Rosiji's report, the Congress amended the constitution of the party to exclude regional ministers as such from membership in the Federal Executive Council and to provide for the removal of a parliamentary leader by the body which elected him.

The new version read:

> If in the opinion of the Federal Executive Council the Leader of the Party, the Deputy Leader of the Party, or any of the Parliamentary Leaders in the Legislatures has lost the confidence of the Party, the President of the Party shall summon a meeting of the appropriate body which elected him and require the meeting either to affirm their confidence in the person concerned or elect a successor.

Resolutions on matters of policy adopted by the congress confirmed the clear ascendancy of Awolowo's faction. Finally, supporters of Awolowo were elected to the key federal offices, in particular S. G. Ikoku, Leader of the Opposition in the Eastern House of Assembly and known for his left-wing socialist views, was elected to replace Chief Rosiji as federal secretary. Akintola's position in the Action Group was clearly imperiled.

Moments of Confrontation

When the Congress adjourned, Awolowo summoned a joint meeting of the Western Regional Executive Committee and the Western Parliamentary Council, apparently to implement the new constitutional clause and thereby to secure the removal of Akintola. His action was intercepted, however, by the intervention of party "elders" who summoned a peace meeting at Ibadan. The leading spirits of reconciliation were Akinola Maja, who held the personal honorary office of "Father of the Party," and the constitutional Governor of the Western Region, Sir Adesoji Aderemi II, the *Oni* of Ife. Once president of the Nigerian Youth Movement, Maja, a doctor of medicine, businessman, and financier of repute, was also president of the Society of Descendants of Oduduwa. The Governor, a preeminent *Oba* in Yorubaland (his title, *Oni,* is the distinctive title of the *Oba* or king of Ife), had long been associated with the journalistic and political ventures of Chief Awolowo. On February 9, 1962, he presided over a meeting attended by one hundred people, mainly members of the old ruling element of the Action Group—persons who were prominent in business and professional circles in addition to influential chiefs. Perhaps, they hoped, the antagonists could be persuaded to resolve their dispute, if for no other reason than to avert a political calamity in Yorubaland.

Akintola made the first complaint: he said that Awolowo's allusion in his presidential address to their dispute over the formation of a national government was contrary to their previous agreement not to air it publicly at the congress. In reply, Awolowo accused his deputy of having attempted to undermine his position as leader of the party in order to usurp it. He claimed to have been informed that Akintola had alleged to other members of the party that he, Awolowo, was then planning to overthrow the federal government by means of a coup d'état. Akintola and two other persons concerned, both ministers in the Western Regional government, denied this accusation vehemently, but an important party official (The Principal Organizing Secretary) corroborated Awolowo's story. In view of the gravity of this accusation, the Governor, in consultation with the other chiefs present, decided, contrary to the wishes of both Akintola and Awolowo, not to proceed with an inquiry then but to adjourn the meeting and refer the dispute to a more select body of "elders."

Ten days later, on February 19, the rival leaders met with twelve of the most important elders and chiefs associated with the Action Group. Awolowo alleged once more that Akintola connived at his political liquidation. Akintola replied to the effect that Awolowo had been adamant in his opposition to Action Group participation in a national government. At one point, Akintola was alleged to have said that there could be no peaceful alternative to positive political cooperation with elements then dominant in the federal government. Three witnesses, two of them supporting Akintola, were questioned inconclusively. Finally, Awolowo was asked to accept Akintola's denial of the specific allegation that he had spread any rumor concerning Awolowo's involvement in plans for a coup d'état.

After this meeting, Awolowo made an attempt to appear open-minded on the national government issue. He set up a committee under Akintola's chairmanship to consider what response the Action Group would make in the event of an invitation from the Prime Minister to join a national government. He even discussed this matter personally with the Prime Minister. However, he made it clear to his associates that, in the event of a national government, he would not be willing to accept office in it as a minister or even as the Deputy Prime Minister.

In March and April, an appearance of party unity at least at the parliamentary level was maintained. Following the example of Chief Awolowo's contingent in the House of Representatives, the Action Group majority in the Western House of Assembly declared its opposition to the creation of a Midwestern Region (as a new constituent unit of the Federation) unless certain specified areas, mainly Yoruba-speaking, were excised from it. (In Midwestern Nigeria, Edo-speaking groups constitute a majority of the population. There is also a large Ibo-speaking minority in addition to other linguistic groups). Moreover, the Action Group insisted that new regions should also be created in the North and the East. Obviously, this decision to reiterate its demand that five new states should be created in Northern territory conflicted with the notion of cooperation at the federal level with the Northern Peoples' Congress.

Under the surface, the struggle continued without abatement. The newly elected federal secretary, S. G. Ikoku, took steps to tighten central control of the secretariat cadres at local levels. Akintola countered this move by demoting, removing, or threatening to remove certain members of the boards of directors of regional statutory corporations who sided openly with Awolowo. Moreover, he was alleged to have instructed all officeholders, including legislators, from his home division of Oshun to donate their party tithes—the 10 percent of their salaries and emoluments which they had to contribute to the party—to a special "fighting fund."

In these bleak circumstances, the party elders made a last vain attempt to arrest the debacle. Another peace meeting, on May 16, 1962, actually produced a compromise agreement. But Chief Awolowo could not be dissuaded from his resolve to press for a decisive conclusion. On Saturday, May 19, he addressed a joint meeting of the Western and Midwestern executive committees, accusing Chief Akintola of "maladministration, anti-party activities, and indiscipline." Specifically, he alleged that the Regional Premier had squandered public funds through the allowances and expense accounts of regional ministers and legislators, that he had threatened and victimized loyal party men in the regional administration, that he had made major policy decisions with regard to taxation, school fees, and the level of price support for cocoa without consulting his party leader, that he opposed the party's ideology of democratic socialism, and that he advocated the cessation of Action Group efforts in the Northern and Eastern Regions.

Akintola's reply had little effect. A motion finding him guilty on all counts was passed by a unanimous vote. Reluctantly, upon the advice of certain influential friends, he tendered a full apology to the party. Nonetheless, a second resolution, demanding his immediate resignation as Premier of the West and Deputy Leader of the Party, was carried 81 votes to 29. On the following day, these resolutions were endorsed by a unanimous vote of the party's Federal Executive Council. Then the parliamentary councils of the Action Group, meeting jointly with the Federal Executive Council, deposed Chief Akintola from his office of Deputy Leader of the Party and, in view of his refusal to resign, called upon the Governor to remove him from the office of Premier.

Chief Akintola, in turn, asked the Governor to dissolve the Western House of Assembly. But the Action Group determined to force Akintola into the political wilderness without the benefit of a general election. For one thing, the party was short of funds; for another, Akintola was feared as a resourceful foe who might turn divisive tendencies, resulting from the recent radicalization of the party, to his advantage in an election. On Monday, May 21, sixty-five members of the House of Assembly (out of a total membership of 117) petitioned the Governor of Western Nigeria to remove Chief Akintola from his office on the constitutional ground that he no longer commanded the support of a majority of the assemblymen. The Governor agreed with the party; he refused Akintola's request for a dissolution and dismissed him from office. Alhaji D. S. Adegbenro, newly designated by the party as its parliamentary leader in the West, was then sworn in as Premier.

Akintola fought back. He asked the Ibadan High Court to invalidate the Governor's action, he petitioned the Prime Minister and the Queen to remove Sir Adesoji from his post as Governor of the Western Region, and, symbolically, he forced his way into the Premier's office, which had been locked. On May 25 the House of Assembly met at the request of Alhaji Adegbenro to debate a vote of confidence in the new government. Suddenly and without provocation, at the moment when a member rose to make a motion, some members supporting Chief Akintola, known to number ten in all, began to throw chairs and to commit other violent and disorderly acts in the chamber. Federal policemen, standing by, put an end to the commotion by releasing tear gas in the chamber.

Now the issue turned on the action of the police. As a result of constitutional provisions designed to safeguard the unity of the Nigerian Federation, control of the Nigerian police is vested in the federal government. Both Awolowo, who had witnessed the disturbance from the gallery of the House, and the new Premier-Designate, Adegbenro, telephoned the federal Prime Minister in Lagos, appealing to him for police protection within the Assembly chamber. The Akintola faction, however, warned the Prime Minister against permitting another meeting.

The Prime Minister then issued a statement acknowledging the right of the House to reassemble on that day. Although he would not provide police protection within the chamber, the police, he said, might be present if any party so insisted. However, he added, the federal government would not accept any decision reached in the course of a meeting so guarded. This ruling implied that the federal government would not recognize Adegbenro as Premier if policemen were in the chamber when he received a vote of confidence. Finally, in the event of a second outbreak of violence or disorder, Sir Abubakar instructed the police "to clear the Chamber and lock it up." Disorder did, in fact, take place again within a few hours of the Prime Minister's statement. Sir Abubakar then summoned the Federal Parliament to meet on May 29. A motion declaring the existence of a state of public emergency in the Western Region, made by the Prime Minister and supported by the NPC, the NCNC, and followers of Chief Akintola, was carried by a vote of 232 to 44. Various regulations based on a previously enacted Emergency Powers Act were also approved; these provided for the appointment of an Administrator who would govern the Region during the period of emergency. The Governor, Premier, ministers, and other officials were removed from office, and "commissioners" were appointed to discharge ministerial functions. Moreover, wide police powers of an exceptional nature, including censorship, curfew, search, detention, and restriction, were conferred upon the Administrator. To this office Sir Abubakar appointed his Minister of Health, Senator M. A. Majekodunmi, a distinguished gynecologist (and, incidentally, a Yoruba).

An academic observer, John P. Mackintosh, then senior lecturer at the University of Ibadan, has described the sequel in this way:

> As soon as he assumed power, the Administrator restricted all leading and many secondary politicians to places outside Ibadan, in some cases to extremely remote villages. By the end of two months virtually all the Akintola group and NCNC men were freed, but the officeholders and many of the principal organizers of the Action Group remained restricted. Pro-government newspapers declared that only evidence of penitence and the abandonment of all conduct likely to arouse political passions would be grounds for releasing these men. But such a criterion could be applied to any revival of normal political activities by the Action Group. . . . All public meetings and processions were banned for the month of June despite complete calm throughout the Region. Five weeks after the state of emergency had been

> declared, two leading AG journalists . . . were restricted to distant places in the Delta for what appeared to be normal journalistic criticism of the conduct of the Federal Government and Dr. Majekodunmi. On 9 August 1962 a further regulation under the Emergency Powers Act added two categories to the types of publications that could be prohibited and punished. Any person publishing matter likely to excite ill-will between sections of the community or to expose any part or member of the government to hatred, ridicule, or contempt "became liable to two years' imprisonment on summary convictions."[1]

This account suggests the increasingly obvious partiality of the Federal Emergency Administration for Akintola's side. Whatever hopes may have been entertained by the Awolowo faction steadily declined. Chief Awolowo was at first restricted to his home at Ikenne, midway between Lagos and Ibadan, where he was accessible to his supporters and the press. Subsequently, he was removed to a remote district, but he was brought back to Lagos in July and housed in his usual residence there so that he might be available to participate in the proceedings of a tribunal appointed by the federal government to investigate the administration and finances of the Western Region.

Battering the Action Group

To investigate the finances of the Western Regional government meant, first of all, to inquire into its relations with local banks. For several years prior to independence, the Western Regional government had given support to banking institutions owned by Nigerians who were associated with the Action Group. The one such bank of major importance was the National Bank of Nigeria Limited—the oldest and most successful of the private, Nigerian-owned banks then in existence—in which the Western Region Marketing Board had made an investment of £1 million. The political significance of the National Bank lies in the fact that it has provided loan facilities both to businessmen who support the Action Group and to the party itself. Furthermore, until 1960 the National Bank was the major shareholder in the Amalgamated Press of Nigeria Limited, the publisher of a national newspaper aligned with the Action Group. In addition, the bank provided generous loan assistance to yet another publishing company, Allied Newspapers Limited, which published an Action Group chain of sectional newspapers.

In 1961 the federal government prepared to launch an inquiry into the conduct of the National Bank. This maneuver ran afoul of the federal Supreme Court, which ruled certain sections of the pertinent act of Parlia-

[1] John P. Mackintosh, "Politics in Nigeria: The Action Group Crisis of 1962," *Political Studies* (June, 1963), pp. 145–46.

ment invalid under the constitution. (Thus far, this has been the only such exercise of power by the Supreme Court since independence.) Nonetheless, the bank was in serious trouble: a report by banking inspectors to the federal Minister of Finance revealed that its liquidity position, or ratio of deposits to reserves, had deteriorated to a financially precarious and legally questionable point. As a result, the Minister indicated that, in accordance with the Banking Ordinance, he might take action to revoke the National Bank's license to operate. In order to avert that danger, the Western Regional government, accepting a recommendation of the federal inspectors, took over the bank: the regional marketing board invested £2 million in the bank and converted its previous investment of £1 million from non-participating preference shares into ordinary equity shares.

Inevitably, the National Bank of Nigeria Limited was a prime target of the Commission of Inquiry appointed by the federal government in 1962 to examine the affairs of statutory corporations in the Western Region. The commission sat for ninety-two days, from July to November, under the chairmanship of Judge G. B. A. Coker of the Lagos High Court. It found that the National Bank had, in fact, made unsecured loans to the Action Group through the medium of fictitious accounts and that, on one occasion, it had concealed the party's actual indebtedness to the bank from a federal examiner. But disclosures of a far more damaging character were made with respect to yet another company, the National Investment and Properties Company Limited, which was owned in its entirety by four leading members of the Action Group who were also its directors. This company had been created in 1958, ostensibly to develop properties then owned by the National Bank. But its chief purpose, the commission found, for which allowance had in fact been made in the company's articles of association, was "to subscribe or guarantee money for charitable political objects." Three of the four owner-directors of the company were prominent businessmen holding high office in the Action Group; one of them was Akinola Maja, the "Father of the Party." The fourth owner, the personal political secretary to Chief Awolowo, was also the director of the Western Nigeria Development Corporation. It came to light that the shares held by all four owner-directors of the NIPC were purchased with funds diverted from the company itself.

The commission of inquiry also disclosed that this company had received loans in excess of £6 million from the Western Region Marketing Board. (In Nigeria, the regional marketing boards purchase export crops from farmers at stabilized prices for sale abroad. They are also empowered to supply capital to statutory corporations in furtherance of economic development.) Over £2 million more, allocated by the marketing board to the Western Nigeria Development Corporation, had also been diverted to the company, which realized close to another million pounds from the sale of property to the Western Regional government at inflated prices, and by other means of questionable legality. During this period, mainly between 1959 and 1961, the company contributed more than £4 million to the Action Group. It also settled the party's debt to the National Bank and, in 1960, it took over the National Bank's various commitments to publishing enterprises. The NIPC also entered into a fifty-fifty partnership with the Canadian publisher, Thomson International Limited, to inaugurate a new national daily newspaper aligned with the Action Group.

In the course of its investigation, the commission also revealed instances of grave maladministration and misappropriation of public funds for party political purposes. It found that a few individuals profited personally from such transactions, but this was a decidedly minor aspect of its report. The commission's primary impact was plainly political, and it came down hard against Chief Awolowo, who was alleged to have chosen all four owner-directors of the NIPC and to have had full knowledge of the surreptitious means whereby public funds had been diverted into the coffers of the Action Group. "His scheme," the commissioners wrote in their official report, "was to build around him with money an empire financially formidable both in Nigeria and abroad, an empire in which dominance would be maintained by him by the power of the money which he had given out."

Akintola was described politely as having been "a veritable deputy who all along the line had relied upon his leader." The commissioners were satisfied that he did not know that the NIPC had been formed to finance the Action Group, nor had he been aware that the company had borrowed large sums of money from the Western Regional government for that purpose. They observed that he did not even know about a loan of £2.2 million to the NIPC which he was alleged to have approved. Reference was made to Awolowo's indictment of Akintola at the joint meeting of the Action Group Western and Midwestern executive committees on May 19. Awolowo was alleged to have charged that the Western Premier had contrived to starve the party of funds by his refusal to hand back to the NIPC the titles to certain properties that had been deposited with the regional government as security for previous loans. Akintola's alleged obstinacy on this point was said to have denied the company a means whereby it might raise additional mortgage finance from other sources. The commission pointed out that Awolowo's indictment of his then deputy leader was made despite the fact that a compromise agreement had been negotiated at the informal "peace meeting" of May 16. Awolowo was alleged to have repudiated the terms of this agreement because they detracted from his virtually unlimited power to manage the finances of the party. Everything considered, the commissioners agreed to accept Akintola's version of the dispute and to "absolve him on all grounds."

The Coker Commission's report of December, 1962, set the stage for Chief Akintola's reinstatement as Premier of the Western Region. Earlier, in July, the federal Supreme Court had ruled that the ex-Governor of Western Nigeria had acted unconstitutionally in removing the Premier from office in the absence of an adverse vote on the floor of the House of Assembly. Although the constitutional provision under which the Governor acted did not specifically require a formal resolution by the House of Assembly, the court decided that it should be interpreted in the light of pertinent conventions of the British constitution. This holding was not unanimous and the respondent, Alhaji Adegbenro, was given leave to appeal to Nigeria's highest court of appeal, the Privy Council in London.

While the Coker Commission was in session Chief Awolowo appears to have tried to negotiate a settlement with the Prime Minister; they are reported to have met on two occasions in August. But a new and alarming turn of events came in September, when an arms plot involving members of the Action Group was uncovered by the police in Lagos. Awolowo was placed under house arrest in Lagos, his home in Ikenne was searched, and the Prime Minister spoke of the existence of a secret army organization. In November formal charges of treasonable felony were made against Chief Awolowo and thirty other persons. These charges included an alleged conspiracy to effect a coup d'état in Lagos in September on the occasion of a state visit there by Indian Prime Minister Nehru. Awolowo then declined to participate any further in the proceedings of the Coker Commission of Inquiry.

Four of the accused persons fled the country; one of them, S. G. Ikoku, the federal secretary, took a position at the Kwame Nkrumah Institute of Political Education in Ghana; another, Chief Anthony Enahoro, the second vice-president of the Action Group and Awolowo's principal deputy in Parliament, where he was the party's spokesman on foreign affairs, sought asylum in Britain. Under the Fugitive Offenders Act of 1881, the British government is bound to honor a request for extradition by another Commonwealth country unless it concludes that the accused person might not be given a fair trial. In other words, the Commonwealth citizen as a political-criminal exile, could not expect the protection that Britain would normally accord to an ordinary alien. After five months of wrangling, which was deeply resented in Nigeria as a slur on the reputation of the Nigerian judiciary, Chief Enahoro was extradited and put on trial separately.

In December, 1962, the Prime Minister announced that Chief Awolowo, whose followers in the House of Representatives had dwindled to twenty members, would no longer be recognized officially as Leader of the Opposition. When the emergency administration ended on January 1, 1963, Chief Akintola was reinstated as Premier of the Western Region, heading a coalition of his recently formed United People's Party (based mainly on his faction of the Action Group) and the NCNC, whose parliamentary leader in the West, Chief R. A. Fani-Kayode, became Deputy Premier. Of the 82 assemblymen who had been members of the Action Group in May, only 38 remained loyal to the party under Alhaji Adegbenro, now Leader of the Opposition. Eventually, in May, 1963, the Judicial Committee of the Privy

Council, reversing the Nigerian Supreme Court, ruled that the ex-Governor had not exceeded his constitutional authority in removing Chief Akintola from his premiership during the crisis. The Western Regional legislature then enacted a constitutional amendment (which the Federal Parliament endorsed) with retroactive effect to provide that the Premier could not be removed without an adverse vote in the House of Assembly. Subsequently, appeals from the Supreme Court of Nigeria to the Privy Council were abolished by constitutional amendment.

On Trial for Treason

The trial for treason of Awolowo and his codefendants took nearly eight months, from November, 1962 to June, 1963. Enahoro's trial, which commenced in mid-May, 1963, took two and one-half months. Both cases were tried by a single judge of the High Court of Lagos; both verdicts were announced in September. In this limited discussion of the issues involved, it is convenient to consider the two cases together and to distinguish three elements of the prosecution's argument: (1) the disputed activities of a special committee of the Action Group, called the tactical committee; (2) the alleged recruitment of persons for paramilitary employment, their training abroad, and their deployment in Nigeria; (3) the alleged arms plot.

The Tactical Committee

In September, 1960, the Federal Executive Council of the Action Group decided to establish a tactical committee to cope with anticipated moves by the federal government which might menace the Action Group's base of power in the Western Region. It was agreed that Awolowo would be solely responsible for this committee's membership, which would be known only by the members themselves. Awolowo testified that he appointed three other persons to the committee, namely, Chief Enahoro, who was a federal vice-president of the party and chairman of its "regional" organization in the Midwest, Chief Ayotunde Rosiji, the party's federal secretary, and Chief Akintola, the Deputy Leader of the party and Premier of the Western Region.

Awolowo further claimed to have outlined certain tasks for the committee at its first meeting, which were as follows: (1) to ensure that the party's field organization in the Western Region was maintained in a state of constant preparedness to deal with any attempt by the NCNC to provoke acts of lawlessness which might, in turn, serve as a pretext for federal intervention; (2) to conduct publicity in Nigeria and abroad so as to discredit any attempt by the federal government to seize control of the Western Regional government by other than electoral means; (3) to make overtures to the NCNC with a view toward cooperation on a nation-wide basis in order to enhance both the security of the Action Group in the Western Region and the likelihood of success by "progressive" elements in the next federal election; and (4) to intensify organizational efforts in the Northern and Eastern Regions so as to extend the Action Group's base of popular support and at the same time, to relieve the pressure on it in Western Nigeria. Chief Awolowo testified that meetings of the tactical committee were held irregularly, but he did not feel able to say under oath that all four members were always present. In March, 1962, some weeks after the meeting of party elders at which Awolowo had alleged that Akintola had been whispering it about that he (Awolowo) was planning a coup d'état, Awolowo had asked the Federal Executive Council to dissolve the tactical committee on the ground that its purposes had been misrepresented by Akintola with the result that members of the party appeared to have lost confidence in it. The committee was then dissolved by a vote of the executive council.

The chief prosecution witness with respect to the activities of the tactical committee was Sanya D. Onabamiro, a professor of zoology in the Western Regional University of Ife, who had been Minister of Education in the Akintola government. Onabamiro had been a reluctant signatory to the petition of May 21, 1962, by the Action Group Western Parliamentary Council, calling upon the Regional Governor to depose Premier Akintola. He decided to sign it, he explained, only because Akintola had been persuaded to apologize to the party at the fateful meeting of May 19. Acting upon an instruction from Chief Awolowo, Onabamiro had placed the name of Adegbenro in nomination to succeed Akintola as the western parliamentary leader. Subsequently, however, he resigned from the Action Group to join Akintola's United People's Party. He testified against Awolowo in December. On January 1, 1963, he was appointed Minister of Natural Resources and Agriculture upon the reinstatement of Akintola as Premier.

Onabamiro agreed that there had been four members of the tactical committee, but he testified that in addition to Awolowo and Enahoro the two other members were Ikoku and himself, rather than Akintola and Rosiji. He said that he only attended two meetings of the committee. At the first meeting in February or March, 1961, he told the court, Awolowo had said that the Action Group could never come to power through the ballot box because elections in the North would never be free and fair. In preparation for a coup d'état, Awolowo was alleged to have given each one of the other three members of the committee a special assignment. Ikoku was to reconnoiter military installations in Nigeria and make plans for their seizure or demolition; Enahoro was to recruit about two hundred youths from Action Group sympathizers for training in Ghana and elsewhere; and Onabamiro was to enlist the cooperation of a few senior officers in the Nigerian police force. Onabamiro said that he was "astounded by Chief Awolowo's revelation of the working of his inner mind and perplexed by the assignment given me. I decided to go home and think." After much thought and some reading on the subject of revolution, he concluded that irrespective of moral or political considerations, the project was ill-conceived and could not succeed. He decided that he would not carry out his assignment and would seek instead to withdraw from the committee.

Months later, he testified, in October or November of 1961, Onabamiro blundered into another meeting of the committee to which he had not been invited, owing to his failure to report on the progress of his assignment. On the spur of the moment he told the other members that he had been waiting for just such an opportunity to say that the plan was not feasible. Awolowo had spoken to them of a "bloodless" coup d'état. But, he said, that would require something that Awolowo lacked—the decisive support of the army—and he cited the cases of Nasser in Egypt, Abboud in Sudan, and Kassim in Iraq. Awolowo's plan actually implied guerrilla warfare, which might take years. In the conduct of guerrilla warfare, he told them, there were four prerequisites to success: guerrillas need hide-outs to which they can retreat; the leader of such an insurrection must have fanatical followers who would rather hang than betray his cause; the incumbent government must be unpopular; and the guerrilla forces must not be dependent upon an external source of arms. In support of his thesis, he cited the examples of Castro in Cuba, Grivas in Cyprus, and the Jews in Palestine. These conditions, he said, did not obtain in Nigeria; he told Awolowo that the government of Nigeria was popular and that no young man would agree to hang so that Awolowo might become Prime Minister. When Awolowo asked about the sources of his ideas, Onabamiro obtained permission to fetch a book from his house and returned to the meeting with a thin volume by S. E. Ayling entitled *Twelve Portraits of Power*. Awolowo asked to borrow the book and suggested that Onabamiro be given leave to withdraw from the committee. Onabamiro offered to swear an oath of secrecy, but, he said, Enahoro told him simply that the committee would know if he betrayed his trust. As noted above, the committee was dissolved formally in March, 1962. When, however, in September, 1962, an arms plot was uncovered in Lagos, Onabamiro inferred that the tactical committee had not actually ceased to exist. In view of his previous involvement with the committee and since Awolowo had not returned his copy of *Twelve Portraits of Power* (and another book on the Cyprus rebellion), he decided that he should make a statement to the police. The police then recovered *Twelve Portraits of Power* in Awolowo's voluminous personal library.

Awolowo replied simply by asserting that Onabamiro's story was a fabrication. A tactical committee set up to ensure the political security of the Western Region must, he said, of necessity have included the Premier. He mentioned two occasions on which Akintola supplied vital information to the Action Group. First, in December, 1961, Akintola reported that the advisability of introducing a preventive detention act in Parliament had been discussed at a meeting consisting of only the Prime Minister and the three regional premiers. The tactical committee referred Akintola's report to a larger ad-hoc committee of party leaders, but its substance was not divulged to the public until Chief Awolowo did so himself in June, 1962, after he had been restricted. Secondly, as Premier, Chief Akintola was entitled to receive police intelligence reports. In February, 1962, on the eve of the Jos congress, Akintola had produced a Special Branch report stating that leaders of the NCNC, in preparation for the forthcoming plebiscite in the Midwest on the creation of a separate state, had decided to send "about 2,000 thugs" into the area, with instructions to disrupt Action Group activities by violent means, including political assassination. This document was tendered in court and it became part of the trial record. It might have suggested an alternative purpose for the type of training the prosecution alleged was received by various persons in preparation for a coup d'état. Chief Awolowo's attempt to negotiate an alliance between his party and the NCNC had not resulted, in fact, in an abatement of political tensions in the Midwest region, where partisan conflict of an extremely bitter and frequently violent sort persisted.

Apart from the two defendants and the one prosecution witness who admitted membership in the tactical committee, no other witness could testify with any degree of certainty about its membership or activity. Both sides agreed that its membership, consisting of four persons, was secret. Ikoku, alleged by Onabamiro to have been a member, was in Ghana; neither Akintola nor Rosiji, alleged by the defendants to have been members, was called to testify. One witness testified that Onabamiro had asked him if he knew the identity of the members, but Onabamiro said that he had done so merely to demonstrate that neither that witness nor his sources of information were fully informed about the inner workings of the party. Other witnesses testified that on two occasions Awolowo had spoken of a possible resort to violence. One was in mid-1961 after the Northern Regional election, which the Action Group held to have been unfairly conducted; the other occasion was in February, 1962, during his crucial confrontation with Akintola, when Awolowo was alleged to have said in the presence of twelve party leaders that he had enough trained men to shake the federal government to its foundations if it overplayed its hand in the Western Region. Other witnesses rebutted these allegations, which do not, in themselves, prove anything conclusively about the tactical committee.

The Paramilitary Corps

The prosecution also alleged that at various times members of the Action Group went to Ghana for special training in the use of arms and explosives. Ten persons were alleged to have traveled to Ghana for that purpose in December, 1961—vainly so, however, since training facilities had not been adequately prepared. Six of these persons and three others were alleged to have gone to Ghana in June, 1962, for intensive paramilitary training. Another group, probably ten to fifteen in all, went in September, 1962. Eight men, all prosecution witnesses, confessed in court to having participated in this training, and nearly all of the others who were alleged to have been involved were shown to have traveled from Nigeria to Ghana at the material times. Some of them gave alibis, such as business reasons or attendance at various international conferences.

In his own defense, Chief Enahoro suggested that two crucial witnesses for the prosecution had been sent to Ghana purely for training in party organization. One of these, upon his return, told Enahoro that his training in Ghana included the use of firearms. Enahoro said that while he was surprised to hear about such training, he never supposed it to be for any purpose other than party defense. The other witness testified that the scheme of illegal action called for the training of one thousand recruits in the use of firearms. Most of them, he said, had in fact been trained in a bush area about twenty miles from Lagos, but he could only remember one name and no witness was produced by the prosecution to corroborate this testimony. Both witnesses testified that in July and/or August, 1962, they, along with eight other persons including seven of the defendants, were given specific assignments to prepare to destroy military and police installations and to seize control of the Lagos airport and electric powerhouse. Other witnesses gave evidence of subsequent acts by these persons which appeared to be related to their alleged assignments, e.g., one of the accused persons, a member of Parliament, gained admission to the airport control tower on the grounds that he wanted to learn from members of the staff whether they had any complaints that should be aired in Parliament.

The Arms Plot

On September 19, 1962, Chief Enahoro, M.P. (second vice-president of the Action Group and chairman of its Midwestern organization), eluded policemen at an immigration checkpoint leading to Dahomey and slipped across the border to make his way, eventually, to Accra, Ghana. From there he proceeded to London, and we have previously noted the celebrated case of his subsequent extradition to Nigeria. When Enahoro made his escape from Nigeria, he left behind a briefcase which contained a sheet of airline notepaper, alleged by the prosecution to outline various tasks to be performed in connection with the intended coup. Enahoro testified that these notes were written in Rome on August 21, 1962, to record his discussion of the previous day with another person, a discussion that he had decided to report to Chief Awolowo at their next meeting. The individual concerned was Oladipo Maja, a Lagos medical practitioner and son of Akinola Maja, president of the Society of the Descendants of Oduduwa, and an owner-director of the National Investment and Properties Company Limited.

Oladipo Maja was arrested in the Awolowo case but the charges against him were dropped when he turned state's evidence. He testified that in 1961, acting on his own initiative, he had offered money and arms to three important leaders of the Northern Regional wing of the Action Group, one of whom, J. S. Tarka (an M.P. and leader of a separate state movement in the southerly portion of the Northern Region called the Middle Belt), was a defendant in Awolowo's case, while the other two gave evidence for the prosecution. The latter two, Alhaji Ibrahim Imam (first vice-president of the Action Group and Leader of the Opposition in the Northern House of Assembly) and Patrick Dokotri (another leader in the Middle Belt state movement), testified that Maja wanted them to precipitate a disturbance in the North in order to divert the army, while a group of insurgents with which he was associated would take over the government in Lagos. Dokotri reported the younger Maja's proposals to Awolowo, who in turn asked the elder Maja to restrain his son from embarking on wild schemes that were bound to reflect adversely on the Action Group, if only because of his name. Father and son, however, were not on speaking terms. Awolowo claimed to have personally admonished the younger Maja on three occasions in 1961 to desist from his attempts to suborn the Northern leaders of the Action Group, who had taken money but not arms from him. Ibrahim Imam testified that in mid-1961 Awolowo had warned him to steer clear of Maja, since the Action Group had a similar plan and Maja was an unreliable person who might turn out to be a police spy.

For his part, Maja claimed to have obtained £7,000 from Ghana government sources, some of which he gave to the Northern Action Group leaders. He said he had arranged in June, 1961, for Awolowo to meet with President Nkrumah in Ghana. Furthermore, he testified, on May 29, 1962, immediately after the declaration of the emergency in Western Nigeria, he had been summoned by Awolowo, who expressed the view that other ethnic groups in Nigeria would never tolerate the kind of treatment that was being meted out to the Yoruba. On the following day, he said, Awolowo had sent him £2,000 for the purchase of arms and ammunition in Ghana. He had turned over £1,100 to S. G. Ikoku, the party's fugitive federal secretary, in Ghana and had returned to Nigeria with £900. He claimed to have spent most of that amount to purchase explosives in Nigeria. The trial judge concluded that he probably used part of the amount, as he had used money previously obtained from Ghanaian sources, to meet personal expenses in connection with the construction of a "luxurious surgery" in Lagos.

Awolowo denied having relied upon Maja to establish contact with Nkrumah, whom he had known since 1945. He also denied having spoken with Maja at the time of his restriction in May, 1962. He did say, however, that he had sent for Maja in September, 1962, to inquire about a sum of £2,300, which had been given to him for transmission to Ikoku.

An explanation for Maja's role as an Action Group courier was provided by one of the accused persons, V. O. Onabanjo, the editor of the party's national daily newspaper published by the Amalgamated Press Limited. Onabanjo explained that on May 30—after restriction orders had been served on Awolowo, Enahoro, and others—party leaders, including Awolowo, decided to send £2,500 to the federal secretary, Ikoku, who had slipped out of the country the previous evening in order to project the Action Group image from Ghana. Awolowo had written a check on the Action Group Trust Fund (countersigned by the officer in charge of party finance) for £2,500 payable to the Amalgamated Press. He had instructed Onabanjo to deduct £200 for local expenses and to send the balance to Ikoku. Onabanjo, however, had been informed of certain difficulties by his chief accountant at the press. While the Amalgamated Press had a branch office in Accra, it had been unable to open a current account there, so that Ikoku could not be paid by a check drawn on a bank in Ghana. A telegraphic transfer of the money, he said, involved other complications and would take a few days to accomplish. Feeling the need for haste in a situation of many uncertainties, Onabanjo had turned for help to his old acquaintance Maja, knowing that Maja frequently traveled to Ghana for business purposes. He cashed the check and gave £2,300 to Maja, who was, fortuitously, about to go to Ghana. Twelve days later, Awolowo received a letter from Ikoku that did not indicate one way or the other whether the money had been received.

Maja therefore testified as a confessed accomplice, and there is no doubt about his intention to commit a violation of the law. The question is whether or not he acted independently or as an agent of Chief Awolowo. Both Awolowo and Enahoro claimed to have been apprehensive that the Action Group would willy-nilly be implicated by Maja's activities. The incriminating notepaper recovered by the police from Enahoro's abandoned briefcase now becomes relevant. Enahoro explained that prior to his departure from Lagos for London via Rome (where he was to meet Ikoku) on August 20, Maja had come to see him to solicit his cooperation in his (Maja's) plan for a coup d'état. Maja, Enahoro said, told him that Ibrahim Imam and Dokotri, who were prepared to cooperate, were anxious to recruit Enahoro. In court Enahoro claimed to have warned Maja on the spot that his plan was not feasible, that it might endanger the Action Group, and that he would have to report their conversation to Awolowo. For that purpose, he said, he made notes of his recollection of Maja's plan when he arrived in Rome. There he received a telegraphic message from Accra that Ikoku could not travel on account of illness. So Enahoro flew to Accra on August 23.

The prosecution asserted, and Enahoro denied, that en route to Accra he stopped briefly in Lagos. Although this assertion could not be verified by any entry in Enahoro's passport, an immigration official testified that at the time in question the passports of Nigerian citizens were not being stamped either upon their arrival or departure. Ibrahim Imam testified for the prosecution that on August 23, the day of Enahoro's arrival in Accra, the two of them (first and second vice-president of the Action Group respectively) had met briefly in Lagos. According to Imam, Enahoro told him that the Action Group had decided to team up with certain elements in the country then preparing to launch a coup, since the party would be nowhere if the coup succeeded without its participation and could hardly escape blame by implication if it failed. Furthermore, he testified, Enahoro said that the coup would be bloodless and entirely successful since it would be supported by the army. Imam said that Enahoro wanted him to provide some sort of "cover" for twenty trained men who would be sent to the North in preparation for the coup. He claimed to have told Enahoro that the plan was ill-conceived and could not work.

Enahoro testified that this alleged meeting never took place. His own version was to the effect that he met Imam upon his return to Lagos from London on September 18, the day that reports of an arms plot first appeared in the Lagos press. Enahoro claims to have expressed his shock to Imam concerning the latter's association with Maja, saying that his involvement in Maja's scheme was bound to hurt the Action Group. His resort to such a desperate plan was doubly deplorable in view of Action Group negotiations with the NCNC that would soon alter the political situation in the country. On the following day, said Enahoro, he reported his discussion of August 20 with Maja to Chief Awolowo, who told him that he had known about Maja's activities for some time, had given stern warnings to all concerned, and did not want to hear any more details from Enahoro at that moment since he had been through it all before.

The prosecution observed that Awolowo, at his own trial, had not given evidence about Enahoro's report of his discussion with Maja, nor had he cross-examined Maja about Enahoro's report. Therefore, asserted the prosecution, Awolowo, who appeared as a defense witness in Enahoro's case, warned the latter not to say that he had reported any details of his conversation with Maja. Enahoro wanted the court to believe that he waited a month (from August 20 to September 19) before reporting Maja's scheme to Awolowo; that Awolowo did not want to hear any details; that he (Enahoro) did not inquire if Awolowo had information of Maja's most recent activity in addition to that in the past. The council for the prosecution observed wryly that Enahoro had complained of gastric trouble and requested an adjournment of the court, which was granted soon after the commencement of his testimony about this incident.

Moreover, the prosecution drew attention to marginal jottings on the airline notepaper written with a different ink than had been used to write the original notes. These jottings were alleged to have been made in Ghana. For example, next to item one, which reads "Training camp flooded," is the jotting in different ink, "emergency site in one week." Enahoro said that all of these jottings were made in Rome but he could not recall the significance of some of them.

In Awolowo's case, Ibrahim Imam testified that on September 1 he and

Tarka went to see Awolowo, who told them that certain people were urging him to give his blessing to a coup d'état, but he would not do so unless he could count on their support. Imam claimed to have told Tarka that he, personally, would not take part in a coup. Patrick Dokotri testified that on September 4 Awolowo had spoken to him and Tarka about an impending coup that would be both bloodless and 100 percent successful. Both Dokotri and Imam testified that subsequently, on about September 10, Awolowo summoned them and Tarka to his residence to accuse both Dokotri and Imam of disloyalty. Awolowo denied this, alleging that the two witnesses had been suborned to save their own skins and that Imam, in particular, had conspired with Maja to import arms in connection with Maja's own plot.

Arms and ammunition were discovered in Lagos by the police on September 15. Arrests were made and another search was conducted in Awolowo's home at Ikenne, where it was alleged that the arms had been shared among the conspirators. Two gas pistol bullets and some charred particles, alleged to have been the burnt remains of materials in which the contraband had been wrapped, were discovered there. More arms were found in another town and large quantities of explosives were discovered in two other places. Forty-eight special (Mares) torchlights, alleged by the prosecution to have been purchased by Enahoro in Rome for use during the coup and said by Enahoro to have been purchased for the use of Action Group defense units in the Midwest, were also discovered.

A year later in September, 1963, Enahoro was convicted in the High Court of Lagos and sentenced to fifteen years imprisonment. A few days later, a verdict of guilty was also returned by the judge in Awolowo's case. Awolowo was sentenced to ten years imprisonment and seventeen of his codefendants were sentenced to prison terms varying from two to seven years, while three were acquitted. The convictions were appealed to the Supreme Court of Nigeria. On July 1, 1964, the sentences of Awolowo and nine of his coappellants were confirmed by the Chief Justice and four of his colleagues. The Chief Justice of Eastern Nigeria, acting as a Justice of the Supreme Court in this case, held that Onabamiro's evidence about the tactical committee was dubious per se, uncorroborated save by accomplices, and inadequate, therefore, to sustain a conviction. He based his concurring opinion on that portion of the evidence which related to the importation and unlawful possession of arms, ammunition, and explosives. In May, 1965, the Supreme Court also sustained Enahoro's conviction but reduced his sentence to seven years.

The Party System in Transition

For a decade, from 1952 to 1962, government in Nigeria rested upon a tripartite balance of power. The overthrow of Action Group rule in the Western Region and its replacement by a coalition beholden to the federal government was bound to effect the stability of the Federation as a whole. How the fall of the Action Group set the stage for a major national crisis is the subject of this section.

During the first session of the Independence Parliament in November 1960, the federal Attorney General, an NCNC nominee, stated in response to a query that the constitution did empower the federal government to dissolve a regional legislature and appoint a caretaker government. Moreover, he declared, the federal government could not permit a state of disorder to prevail in any part of the Federation. In rebuttal, Chief Awolowo (Leader of the Opposition) said that no such power had been granted by the Constitution (Section 65), nor was it even implied. This debate might have seemed to confirm the fear that Awolowo had expressed in September, when he asked his party's Federal Executive Council to authorize the formation of a secret "tactical committee."

Despite Awolowo's growing cordiality with the likeminded leaders of the NCNC in consequence of his continuing efforts to build a "progressive" alliance in opposition to the NPC, he could not depend upon the NCNC, as a party, to support him in a crisis in which his own political future and that of the Action Group might be at stake. For one thing, his party was bitterly opposed by many NCNC leaders in the Western Region who thirsted for power after ten lean years of opposition. In the Midwest, an NCNC stronghold, hostility to the Action Group mounted daily as the campaign for creation of a separate region neared its conclusion. Surely, if the Action Group could be crushed, there were many old line NCNC members in various parts of the Federation who would not scruple to settle old scores. For them, the crisis of 1962 presented too strong a temptation to resist, however well aware they may have been that the overthrow of the Action Group in Western Nigeria would not be an unmixed blessing.

On the eve of the Western crisis, a few top NCNC leaders affirmed on principle that in cases of conflict between party leadership and parliamentary leadership, party leadership must prevail, a principle that had been vindicated in the NCNC ten years earlier. On May 22, M. I. Okpara, national president of the NCNC and Premier of Eastern Nigeria, suggested that Premier Akintola should resign honorably rather than flout the authority of his party. Three days later, however, after the fracas in the Western House of Assembly which had been precipitated by Akintola's stout minority of ten, Premier Okpara observed that law and order had broken down in the Western Region and called upon the federal government to assume control. On May 28, a joint meeting of the NCNC's National Executive Committee and Federal Parliamentary Party voted to back the federal government fully. The following day, all members of the NCNC parliamentary delegation voted in favor of a declaration of public emergency in Western Nigeria. When the emergency period ended on January 1, 1963, the Western NCNC entered a coalition government under the reinstated Premier, Chief Akintola, now leader of the United People's Party.

Nonetheless, radical elements within the NCNC had been won over to Awolowo's idea of a "progressive" alliance. During the Western emergency a few prominent members of the NCNC had pressed for unity with the Action Group and the NCNC even extended some financial assistance to help the Action Group meet its political expenses. Thereafter, various developments strengthened the hand of the NCNC faction that favored a fundamental realignment of the parties. In October, 1962, the Action Group demonstrated its vitality in Yorubaland by winning decisive control of the Lagos City Council in a straight fight with the NCNC. This was widely interpreted to signify Yoruba solidarity with the beleagured Awolowo. In token of its desire to collaborate with the NCNC, the Action Group offered to retain the NCNC national secretary in his office as chairman of the Lagos City Council. While this offer was appreciatively declined, the NCNC accepted a generous allocation of committee assignments, including chairmanships.

In July, 1963, Midwestern Nigeria took the decisive constitutional step in its evolution as a separate region when an overwhelming majority of its electorate voted in a plebiscite in favor of regionhood. This action eliminated an old bone of contention between the Action Group and the NCNC, especially in view of the fact that many of the old line Action Group leaders in the Midwest declared for Akintola's United People's Party, then in coalition with the Western wing of the NCNC. With the Action Group unable and unwilling to provide serious competition to the NCNC in the new region, anti-NCNC elements there were receptive to offers of support from the NPC. In October, 1963, a candidate of the NPC-supported Midwestern People's Congress defeated his NCNC opponent in a by-election for a vacant parliamentary seat. Immediately thereafter, the Midwestern People's Congress merged with the Midwestern branch of the United People's Party and other anti-NCNC groups to form a new party, the Midwestern Democratic Front, which allied with the NPC. In February, 1964, elections were held for the new Midwestern House of Assembly. The NCNC won 53 seats to 11 for the MDF; the Action Group, having all but disappeared from the Midwest, polled less than 2 percent of the vote and did not win a single seat. Henceforth, certain Midwestern NCNC leaders remained implacably hostile to the Action Group on principle (or for reasons of a personal or overall political nature) rather than in consequence of electoral necessity.

In Western Nigeria, representatives of various shades of Yoruba opinion were deeply disturbed by the predicament of their leaders and concerned to explore the possibilities of reconciliation. Inconclusive negotiations involving the three major factions—Action Group, UPP, and NCNC—were reported in July, 1963. Subsequently, influential Yoruba personalities who were sympathetic to Chief Akintola formed a cultural organization, called the Society of the Descendants of the Yoruba. Early in 1964 this society merged with a conciliatory wing of the Society of the Descendants of Oduduwa to form the Society of the Descendants of Olofin (said by its sponsors to be the proper name of the legendary ancestor of the Yoruba, Oduduwa). Among the founders of the new organization were Senator Majekodunmi, Federal Minister of Health, former Administrator of the West and president of the Society of the Descendants of the Yoruba; Akinola Maja, president of the Society of the Descendants of Oduduwa; Sir Adetokunboh Ademola, the Chief Justice of Nigeria; several other eminent jurists; Premier Akintola; Sir Adesoji Aderemi II, the former Regional Governor; his successor, Chief J. O. Fadahunsi; and most of the leading *obas* of Yorubaland. However, the Action Group and Action Group-inclined Oduduwans denounced the new organization as a partisan maneuver and criticized the participation of members of the judiciary on that ground.

Meanwhile, a serious conflict erupted between the NPC and the NCNC over the results of the decennial census. Population statistics are politically crucial in Nigeria because the constitution provides for apportionment (and reapportionment) of parliamentary seats among the regions according to the principle of proportionality of population. (Universal adult suffrage obtains in southern Nigeria. In the Northern Region, however, the franchise is restricted to adult males in accordance with an NPC interpretation of Islamic custom, but women are included for the purpose of delimiting constituencies.) Unofficial reports of a census conducted in 1962 indicated a redistribution of population in favor of the southern regions. But this count was rejected as being unreliable by a meeting of the Prime Minister and the Regional Premiers, who decided upon a recount in 1963. In February, 1964, the federal government released preliminary statistics: 55.7 million people were enumerated, distributed thus: Northern Nigeria 29.7 million; Eastern Nigeria 12.3 million; Western Nigeria 10.2 million; Midwestern Nigeria 2.5 million; the Federal Territory of Lagos 675,000. The NCNC-controlled governments of the Eastern and Midwestern Regions immediately challenged the accuracy of these figures, which preserved the Northern Region's population edge over the rest of the country. The Northern and Western Regional governments accepted them. At this juncture, all but two of the eleven NCNC Western Regional ministers bolted their party and rallied to Premier Akintola's standard in the formation of a new regional party, named the Nigerian National Democratic Party, to which their supporters in Lagos adhered. Thereupon, NCNC loyalists in the Western Region formed an alliance with the Action Group, which still appeared to be the most popular party in the Region, despite the decline of its contingent in the House of Assembly to a hard core of 27 (out of 90). Previously, opposition parties in Northern Nigeria, principally the Nigerian (formerly Northern) Elements Progressive Union (an ally of the NCNC) and the

United Middle Belt Congress (formally an ally of the Action Group), had combined to form a Northern Progressive Front. Only die-hard opponents of the Action Group, mainly in the Midwestern Region, still held out against the formation of a nation-wide "progressive" alliance.

As a result of the disputed census (challenged unsuccessfully in the Supreme Court by the Eastern Regional government), the North was allotted 167 parliamentary seats (a reduction of 7) out of a total of 312; the East was allotted 70 (a reduction of 3); the West received 57 (an increase of 10); the Midwest 14 (a reduction of 1); and Lagos 4 (an increase of 1). In August, 1964, the NPC, in alliance with the NNDP, the MDF, and the separatist Niger Delta Congress of Eastern Nigeria, inaugurated the Nigerian National Alliance, to which other small parties in the Eastern Region, notably the Dynamic Party (a self-described "totalitarian" party of social protest) and the new Republican Party (a dissident Ibo group) also adhered. In accordance with the terms of the alliance, Sir Abubakar invited two NNDP members of Parliament (including Chief Rosiji) to join the federal cabinet. Soon thereafter the NCNC-Action Group-Northern Progressive Front Alliance was launched formally as the United Progressive Grand Alliance. Now the stage was set for a two-party battle on election day.[2]

The ensuing campaign was marked by propaganda of a bitterly tribalistic sort, emanating largely from the NNDP. The positive side of that party's *raison d'être* is Yoruba unity. Its negative corollary is the allegation that the NCNC and, perforce, the UPGA are Ibo-dominated organizations which necessarily and perniciously serve Ibo interests at the expense of other ethnic groups. Thus an NNDP publication alleged that the federal government was dominated by an "Ibocracy"—a network which secured for Ibos a disaproportionate share of jobs, commercial opportunities, federal scholarships, etc.

In Northern Nigeria, too, Ibophobic tendencies were strengthened by the new political alignment. To begin with, acrimony between the large, cohesive, and prosperous communities of Ibo settlers in the Northern towns and the indigenous townsmen is an old source of social tension, to which religious disparity between the Muslim northerner and non-Muslim southerner often contributes. In the charged atmosphere of heated political controversy, defamatory propaganda and threats both to the property of Ibo settlers and the means whereby they earn their livelihood were not uncommon. Under these circumstances, many Ibo householders in the Northern towns decided to send their families "home" for safety to the Eastern Region.

As the election drew near, reports of political thuggery in all parts of the Federal Republic became increasingly common. In late October, the major

[2] For information on the major Nigerian political parties and the party composition of the Nigerian legislatures, 1960–65, see charts on pp. 159–61.

party leaders met to issue an appeal for a free and peaceful election campaign; they also agreed to integrate the various local government police forces with the Nigeria police force, under the control of the inspector general of police, for the duration of the campaign. This notwithstanding, frequent complaints of mass arrest, malicious prosecution, and harassment (including maltreatment of lawyers) were voiced by partisans, mainly UPGA spokesmen in the Northern Region. On December 10, the President of the Republic, Nnamdi Azikiwe, broadcast a dramatic warning of the threat to national unity which had been engendered by "calculated" violations of the constitutional rights of citizens in connection with the election campaign. If, he said, the politicians have decided to dismember the Federal Republic, they should summon a conference to divide the "national assets" peaceably; otherwise he predicted, Nigeria might suffer a tragedy of such proportion that the recent experience of the Democratic Republic of the Congo would be "child's play" by comparison. His tabulation of specified kinds of infringement of constitutional rights seemed to reflect on the Northern Region mainly. Sir Ahmadu Bello, Premier of the North, replied immediately, observing that secessionist utterances with regard to the Eastern Region had been made by members of the NCNC; he warned that the Nigerian constitution makes no provision for secession or disintegration.

Before the election, UPGA leaders calculated that they would have to win some 20 to 30 seats out of 167 in Northern Nigeria in order to win an overall majority of the 312 parliamentary seats at stake. Their hopes were shattered when 68 NPC candidates were returned unopposed when nominations closed on December 20. A few days later, however, the chairman of the Federal Election Commission announced that some candidates appeared to have been returned unopposed improperly and that elections would be ordered in such cases. UPGA now demanded a postponement of the election; in the absence of clarification on the disputed "unopposed" returns, UPGA, professing to despair of a free and fair election, decided upon a boycott.

President Azikiwe now urged the Prime Minister to postpone the election for six months (suggesting also that the United Nations be asked to assist in its conduct). Sir Abubakar rejected the idea of postponement and the election was held on December 30 in the face of an UPGA boycott that was supported by the resignations of three members of the Federal Elections Commission, representing the Eastern and Western Regions and the Federal Territory of Lagos. In accordance with the instruction of Okpara, no voting took place in the seventy Eastern constituencies, although NCNC candidates were returned unopposed in nineteen of them, which were in any case safe for that party. In the Midwestern Region, leaders of the NCNC disagreed and vacillated with the result that voting there was light as the NCNC won all 14 seats. In the Western Region, NNDP candidates were declared elected in 36 constituencies to UPGA's 18 (13 Action Group and 5

NCNC). In the Federal Territory of Lagos, an independent candidate who received less than 600 votes was declared elected in the one constituency (out of four) where any voting took place. The Northern Region, true to form, gave the NPC 162 out of 167 seats, boosting the NNA total to the comfortable figure of 198. All told, only 4 million voters went to the polls, compared with more than 7 million in 1959. The percentage of the eligible electorate actually voting dropped from nearly 80 percent in 1959 to something on the order of 20 percent in 1964. It has been reported that over 20 million people were eligible to vote, compared with some 9 million in 1959. (It should be noted, however, that the official registers of electors were compiled from the controversial census reports.) It was alleged that voting percentages in Lagos, the West, and the Midwest would have been appreciably higher but for the intimidatory acts (including the destruction of polling booths) of irregular UPGA bands seeking to enforce the boycott. On the other hand, certain returns in the Western Region were alleged to have been flagrantly inflated. Official statistics indicated a turnout of some 23 percent in the Western Region.

For six days the unity of the nation appeared to hang in the balance while intensive negotiations were conducted involving the President, the Prime Minister, leaders of the regional governments, and other influential personalities. Both the President and the Prime Minister appear to have consulted leaders of the armed forces. On New Year's Day, President Azikiwe informed the Prime Minister (and the nation) that he would rather resign than perform his mandatory constitutional duty to appoint a new Prime Minister as a result of the election. But three days later, a settlement, based on a compromise formula prepared by two senior members of the Nigerian judiciary, was announced. The President then invited Sir Abubakar to form a government, declaring, "I have his permission to say that he intends to form a broad-based national government." In his own statement, the Prime Minister confirmed that he would form "a broadly-based government." Following consultations with his party leader, Sir Ahmadu Bello, the Premier of Northern Nigeria, in Kaduna, Sir Abubakar submitted a list of seventeen cabinet members for appointment by the President. Nearly all of them were northerners belonging to the NPC, but it was understood that additional members from the Eastern and Western Regions would be added after the early conduct of elections in the boycotted constituencies of Lagos and the Eastern Region. In the end, UPGA leaders salvaged a promise of early arrangements to review the constitution and the machinery for elections. It was also understood that elections for the Western House of Assembly, due in 1965, would not be postponed. On the major issue, UPGA had to accept the validity of the election, subject to the relatively insignificant proviso that particular results could be challenged by aggrieved persons in the courts.

Deeply disappointed, UPGA militants blamed President Azikiwe for his "capitulation." At best, they said, the compromise was premature. But Nigeria had come to the brink of confusion if not disintegration. In his personal account of the crisis, which he entitled "State House Diary" and released to the press for publication in Lagos, President Azikiwe reported a preelection threat of secession by the Eastern Region. His account has been disputed, although respectfully and with restraint, by the Eastern Premier. In any case, it seems more probable that some sort of military action would have been the upshot of a prolonged failure to reach a compromise agreement. One week before the election, Okpara had proposed military supervision of the election to ensure its fairness. The compromise avoided a test of the army's reaction and cohesion in the event of political deadlock. Azikiwe's maneuver for a settlement tarnished his reputation in the UPGA camp, but it also spared Okpara and his associates the experience of having to choose between a showdown and a humiliating retreat. Okpara defended UPGA's boycott gamely as a stroke in the continuing fight for free elections in Nigeria.

As the crisis fever subsided, it was apparent that fundamental issues remain unresolved. Nor could either side derive much satisfaction from the state of affairs. While the NNA had nominal control of the federal government, that government's authority and legitimacy were gravely impaired. In "defeat," UPGA was buoyed by a new sense of intergroup solidarity because the Easterners were not thought to have betrayed their partners in the West. UPGA leaders agreed to give the compromise "a fair trial," while numerous, mainly futile, petitions challenging the validity of the election results were made to the courts.

In the "little election" of March, 1965, UPGA won 50 out of 52 seats at stake in Eastern Nigeria and all 3 in Lagos. The Prime Minister then enlarged his cabinet to include seven members of the NCNC and seven from the NNDP in addition to fifteen NPC and three of no party status. Then the focal point of Nigerian politics shifted once more to the Western Region. In May, 1965, Sir Ahmadu Bello, Premier of the North and president of the NNA, said publicly that Chief Awolowo would be released from prison if the UPGA won the forthcoming general election to the Western House of Assembly. Of course, the NNDP was determined to retain power in the West. But its popularity was problematical. Perhaps the Northern Premier was anxious to avert an outright north-south showdown in the event of an irrepressible electoral surge for Awolowo's party.[3]

[3] The Western Regional election was held on October 11, 1965. The regional government banned public meetings and processions for eight weeks, including the entire three-week campaign period and five post-election weeks, allegedly to prevent violence. But the election was misconducted and violence ensued despite precautions. With 94 seats in the House of Assembly to be contested, 16 NNDP candidates were returned unopposed, including Akintola, whose opponent withdrew before election day. The UPGA alleged that its candidates in most of the uncontested constituencies were eliminated fraudulently. On election day, police-

Conclusion

In Africa, as elsewhere in the "third world," anticolonial revolutions pave the way for social revolutions. The leader of an anticolonial movement who seeks also to effect a fundamental change in the structure of his society may expect to face severe trials of strength and conscience. Awolowo's ordeal may be interpreted in this light.

In the 1950s Awolowo had been the principal political spokesman for an emergent and nationalistic class that came to power in Western Nigeria. His party, the Action Group, was, in fact, the political instrument of that class. However, the fortunes of political warfare made him Leader of the Opposition in Nigeria's Independence Parliament. In that capacity, congenial to his radical bent, he became the voice of social and political protest. His party then threatened to undermine the security of the regional power groups that control Nigeria's federal government.

Inevitably, the more conservative members of his party, who formed the nucleus of a power group in the Western Region, were alienated by Awolowo's increasingly radical posture of defiance to the moderate federal government. Many of them were deeply pained by their party's split and their estrangement from Awolowo. But they accepted the principle of regional security, which he rejected. In the main, therefore, they cast their lots with his rival, Premier Akintola, who promised to collaborate with the federal government and its virtual master, the power group of the Northern Region.

Strategies of the Regional Power Groups

While this study has not been concerned with the internal politics of the Northern, Eastern, and Midwestern Region, it has considered the actions of each regional government party in relation to the Western Regional conflict. Two sets of observations concerning these parties may be recapitulated in summary form.

(1) *The Northern Peoples' Congress.* The statements and actions of Northern leaders for over a decade confirm that they regard regional political security as a condition for the successful operation of federal government in Nigeria. While they have not tried to eliminate party competition per se in the Northern Region, they have been unalterably opposed to penetration of the north by political parties based in the south, that is, or-

---

men discovered many thousands of ballot papers in the illegal possession of electoral officers who were appointed by the regional government. In addition, there were many reports of "stuffed" ballot boxes. Official election results, giving the NNDP a 3-to-1 victory, were disputed by UPGA spokesmen, who claimed victory for their side. The Action Group Leader, Adegbenro, and several of his associates were arrested and charged with attempting to set up an illegal government; subsequently, they were discharged by the High Court of Western Nigeria when the government decided not to prosecute them. Furthermore, local authorities in the Eastern and Western Regions have banned newspapers that oppose the positions of their respective regional government parties. Thus, the long national crisis has entered another critical phase.

ganized, led, and financed by southerners. This doctrine has worked effectively to eliminate opposition elements in the Northern Region from serious contention, at least for the time being.

The obduracy of Northern resistance to "southern penetration" may be explained in terms of the Northern Region's delayed awakening to modern developments. In comparison with southern Nigeria, the educational level of the North is low and the region is deficient in highly trained professional and technical manpower. To be sure, the Northern leaders do not lack zeal for economic, social, and political development. Nonetheless, they aim to preserve their historic systems of traditional authority—in particular, the uniquely Northern system of Islamic emirate rule—as a counterpoise to the introduction of far-reaching political and legal reforms. In the South, Islam is a personal and family religion (there are few Muslims in the Eastern and Midwestern Regions, but some 50 percent of the Yoruba people are Muslims); in the north, Islam is a civilization—a system of authority and a fount of the law. In that circumstance, under conditions of political stress, religious precepts tend to clash with various democratic assumptions that are strongly held in the south. Cultural division, then, may pose a serious impediment to the operation of parliamentary democracy in Nigeria.

At one time, Northerners feared the "threat" of "southern domination" after the withdrawal of British power. This fear was largely alleviated by the allocation of most of the seats in the federal House of Representatives to Northern members in accordance with the principle of population. Since 1962, the NPC contingent in Parliament has been sufficiently numerous for that party to control the federal government by virtue of its hold on a single region. In this anomalous situation, many southerners perceive a clear case for partition of the North, so that one unit of the federation will not dominate all of the rest of it.

For their part, the northerners disavow any desire to dominate southern Nigeria. Claiming to want nothing more than political security for their own institutions, they have encouraged the formation of regional political organizations in the south. Thus they have given consistent support to Premier Akintola—initially to his faction of the Action Group, subsequently to his United People's Party and its successor, the Nigerian National Democratic Party. But they have also indicated that they would treat any move to reconcile the antagonistic parties in Western Nigeria as a purely domestic question for the Yorubas in which they would not meddle.

(2) *The National Convention of Nigerian Citizens.*[4] The NCNC, which controls the Eastern and Midwestern governments, shifted its support from Akintola to Awolowo after the latter's imprisonment and conviction, largely in consequence of its own conflict with the NPC. In so doing, the NCNC

[4] Previously, National Council of Nigeria and the Cameroons. The NCNC adopted its new name in 1961 after the Southern Cameroons separated from Nigeria to join the Cameroun Republic.

lost the major part of its Western Regional wing, which had been instrumental in the overthrow of the Action Group Regional government. When it came to a choice between loyalty to their party and loyalty to their regional power group, most of the western leaders of the NCNC opted for the power group. Shorn of its Western wing, the NCNC assumed the mantle of protector of the Action Group. After the election crisis, Okpara added a member of the Action Group to his cabinet in the Eastern Region. What is more, it was widely believed that the NCNC was prepared to accept Awolowo as leader of the United Progressive Grand Alliance upon his release from prison.

However, in Midwestern Nigeria a powerful faction of the NCNC has remained firmly opposed to its party's alliance with the Action Group and strongly in favor of collaboration with the Northern Peoples' Congress. Since the principal ethnic tension in Midwestern politics is between the Ibo-speaking and non-Ibo-speaking (mainly Edo-speaking) groups, it is significant that opposition to the NCNC's Awolowan tendency is centered in the non-Ibo group. The NCNC is wary of the latent danger that non-Ibo elements may bolt the party in sufficient strength to jeopardize its control of the regional government. That danger would become more probable in the event of a showdown between the NCNC and the NPC. Therefore, the Midwestern wing of the NCNC has tried to conciliate disputes between the Eastern and Northern Regional governments.

Strains on the Federal System

Within the regions powerful forces operate to minimize if not to exclude party competition. The whole "machinery of government," including the power of patronage and control of local law enforcement and taxation, is brought to bear against organized opposition to the regional government party. As a result, by mid-1965, three of the four regions were, for practical (i.e., electoral) purposes, all but one-party states. In the fourth, the Western Region, two rival parties vied in deadly earnest to determine which one of them would bury the other. To the victor would belong not merely the spoils of office, but potentially permanent, i.e., indefinite, control over the most significant means of acquiring wealth and social prestige in the region.

As a result of this one-party tendency in the regions, effective competition at the federal level means that at least one whole region, and maybe more than one, will appear to be in "opposition" to the federal government. This means that a whole "people" or nationality group may come to feel itself at odds with the regime, as the Yoruba people have tended to feel for several years and the Ibo people appeared to feel after the election crisis of 1964–65. Unallayed, regional disaffection may grow until it culminates in secession.

One remedy, advocated by Akintola, Balewa, and the Sardauna, requires the participation of all regionally dominant parties in a national gov-

Figure 1. Major Nigerian Political Parties (with dates and leaders)

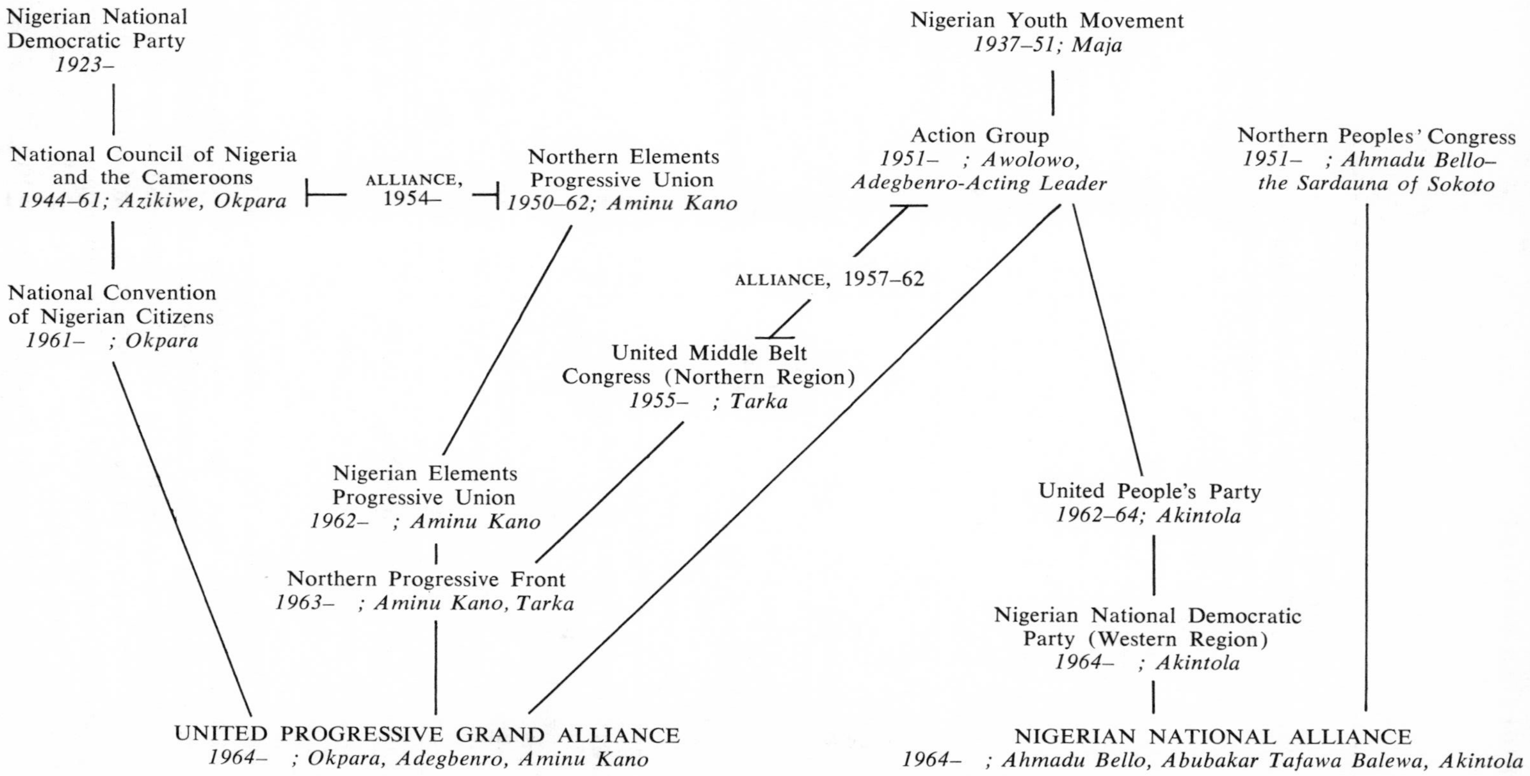

Figure 2. Party Composition of the Nigerian Legislatures, 1960–65

	Federal House of Representatives	*Northern Regional House of Assembly*
1960	NPC and allies 148* NCNC/NEPU Alliance 89 (NPC and allies + NCNC/NEPU Alliance: Govt. bloc) Action Group 75 Oppos. Others 16	
1961		NPC 156* Govt. Action Group/UMBC 9 Oppos. NEPU/NCNC 1
1963		
1964	NNA bloc: NPC and allies 176; NNDP 26 UPGA bloc: NCNC/NEPU 83; Action Group/ UMBC 19 (176, 26, 83: Govt. bloc)	
1965	NNA bloc: NPC 162*; NNDP 36 UPGA bloc: NCNC 84; Action Group 21; Northern Progressive Front 4 (162, 36, 84: Govt. bloc) Others 5	

* Result of an immediately preceding election.

ernment. This solution, effected in 1965, is intended to stabilize the political status quo and has been widely deprecated on that account. An alternative remedy, advocated by Awolowo, Azikiwe, and Okpara, calls for the division of existing regions, especially the North, into smaller states. Many southerners favor this idea on the assumption that it would entail the dispersion of political power in Northern Nigeria. It is also supported by radicals generally, including Northern radicals, who seek to break up all existing aggregations of regional power. This, as Awolowo saw with increasing clarity, is the key to revolutionary social change in Nigeria.

Eastern Regional House of Assembly	*Western Regional House of Assembly*	*Midwestern Regional House of Assembly*
* NCNC 106 Govt. Action Group 15 Oppos. Others 25	* Action Group 79 Govt. NCNC 33 Oppos. Others 10	
	NCNC 43 } Govt. bloc United People's Party 40 Action Group 38 Oppos.	
	NNDP 58 Govt. Action Group 27 } Oppos. bloc NCNC 5	* NCNC 53 Govt. Midwestern Dem. Front 11 Oppos.
		NCNC 63 Govt. MDF 1

The Constitution and the Courts

Ruling out partition of the North, to which the NPC is so adamantly opposed at the present time, southern Nigerians count upon constitutional revision to both alleviate their grievances and safeguard the unity of the federation. One proposal to countervail Northern control of the House of Representatives would raise the federal Senate, which gives equality of regional representation, to the status of a coordinate legislative chamber. (Currently, the Senate has coordinate powers only for constitutional amendments and a few other specific legislative acts.) It has also been suggested that certain executive functions should be vested in the President of the Republic, who is now but a formal head of state, elected by a joint meeting of the Houses of Parliament. Specific recommendations of this nature have been made with respect to recruitment into the federal public service, administration of the decennial census, the conduct of elections, and employment of the armed forces and police for internal security purposes.

Other proposals for reform within the present political framework envisage stricter constitutional protection for the fundamental rights of citizens. President Azikiwe, for one, has called for the elimination of provisos and exceptions that hedge the declaration of fundamental rights in Nigeria's constitution and render them legally ineffectual. Libertarians also place great store by the politically independent judiciary. For this reason, the participation of leading members of the judiciary in such quasi-political exploits as the formation of the Society of the Descendants of Olofin has given rise to concern in libertarian circles. It is, however, less than realistic to expect men of eminence on the bench in a developing country to remain politically chaste for the sake of their judicial reputations. They can hardly fail to heed the call to political colors. For example, both the Chief Justice of Nigeria and his colleague, the Chief Justice of the Eastern Region, were instrumental in settling the election crisis of 1964–65. Nigerian judges, like American judges, are in politics; inevitably, the courts are used to achieve political ends. Whether or not such ends will be compatible with libertarian means may well turn upon the viability of the constitution. The question, simply, is this: Will the government be so organized as to give the powerful forces of change their way?

Study Questions

1. Why did Awolowo turn to the "left"? Were his policies after independence consistent with his previously avowed social and political principles?
2. What is a "progressive" in the Nigerian setting? a "conservative"? Who are the "progressives"? the "conservatives"? How meaningful are these ideological labels?
3. What is meant by the principle of regional security in Nigerian politics? Is it compatible with the development of democracy?
4. Is it realistic to hope for the existence of a loyal and constructive parliamentary opposition in today's Nigeria?
5. Describe the Nigerian system of political patronage. How does it compare with political patronage in Ghana? in Britain? in the United States?

Selected Bibliography

I regard this case study as an addendum to my book, *Nigerian Political Parties: Power in an Emergent African Nation* (Princeton, N.J.: Princeton University

Press, 1963). In that work, I was concerned to examine the mechanics of the movement for Nigerian independence during the final decade of British colonial rule. Through an account of party competition and intraparty conflict, I attempted "to reveal the interplay of three converging social forces, namely, the thrust of nationalism, the persistence of cultural particularism, and the crystallization of emergent class interests." The major political parties of that period were the National Council of Nigeria and the Cameroons, the Action Group of Nigeria, and the Northern Peoples' Congress. In the case of the Action Group of Nigeria, I feel that the discussion in my book lacks logical completeness because the seeds of conflict within that party did not ripen until some sixteen months after independence. While the present study is intended to stand by itself, it is also intended to supplement the account and the argument in my book. Given the nature of this essay, I could not marshal my supporting evidence in the form of footnoted documentation, but the main sources are listed below.

Background to this study

AWOLOWO, OBAFEMI. *Path to Nigerian Freedom*. London: Faber, 1947.

———. *Awo: The Autobiography of Chief Obafemi Awolowo*. Cambridge, Eng.: Cambridge University Press, 1960.

COLEMAN, JAMES S. *Nigeria: Background to Nationalism*. Berkeley: University of California Press, 1958.

SKLAR, RICHARD L. *Nigerian Political Parties: Power in an Emergent African Nation*. Princeton, N.J.: Princeton University Press, 1963.

General works on Nigerian government and politics

AWA, EME O. *Federal Government in Nigeria*. Berkeley: University of California Press, 1964.

BRETTON, HENRY L. *Power and Stability in Nigeria*. New York: Praeger, 1962.

EZERA, KALU. *Constitutional Developments in Nigeria*, rev. ed. Cambridge, Eng.: Cambridge University Press, 1964.

NWABUEZE, B. O. *Constitutional Law of the Nigerian Republic*. London: Butterworth, 1964.

ODUMOSU, OLUWOLE I. *The Nigerian Constitution: History and Development*. London: Sweet and Maxwell, 1963.

POST, K. W. J. *The Nigerian Federal Election of 1959*. London: Oxford University Press, 1963.

SKLAR, RICHARD L., and C. S. WHITAKER, JR. "Nigeria," in James S. Coleman and Carl G. Rosberg, Jr., eds., *Political Parties and National Integration in Tropical Africa*. Berkeley: University of California Press, 1964.

———. "The Federal Republic of Nigeria," in Gwendolen M. Carter, ed., *National Unity and Regionalism in Eight African States*. Ithaca, N.Y.: Cornell University Press, 1966.

Published works of direct relevance to aspects of this study

ABERNETHY, DAVID B. "Nigeria Creates a New Region," *Africa Report*, IX, 3 (March, 1964), 8–10.

ANGLIN, DOUGLAS G. "Brinksmanship in Nigeria," *International Journal*, XX, 2 (Spring, 1965), 173–88.

AZIKIWE, NNAMDI. "Essentials for Nigerian Survival," *Foreign Affairs,* XLIII, 3 (April, 1965), 447–61.

BROWN, CHARLES V. *Government and Banking in Western Nigeria.* Ibadan: Oxford University Press, 1964.

DIAMOND, STANLEY. "The Trial of Awolowo: A Nigerian Tragedy," *Africa Today,* X, 9 (November, 1963), 22–28.

ENAHORO, CHIEF ANTHONY. *Fugitive Offender: The Story of a Political Prisoner.* London: Cassell, 1965.

HARRIS, RICHARD L. "Nigeria: Crisis and Compromise," *Africa Report,* X, 3 (March, 1965), 23–31.

MACKINTOSH, JOHN P. "Electoral Trends and the Tendency to a One Party System in Nigeria," *Journal of Commonwealth Political Studies,* I (November, 1962), 194–210.

———. "Politics in Nigeria: The Action Group Crisis of 1962," *Political Studies,* XI, 2 (June, 1963), 126–55.

SKLAR, RICHARD L. "Contradictions in the Nigerian Political System," *The Journal of Modern African Studies,* III, 2 (August, 1965), 201–13.

UWANAKA, CHARLES U. *Awolowo and Akintola in Political Storm.* Yaba, Lagos, 1964.

WHITAKER, C. S., JR. "Three Perspectives on Hierarchy: Political Thought and Leadership in Northern Nigeria," *Journal of Commonwealth Political Studies,* III, 1 (March, 1965), 1–19.

Action Group publications

Constitution of the Action Group of Nigeria (as amended by the 8th Congress of the Party held at Jos From February 2nd to 7th, 1962). Lagos: Amalgamated Press Limited, 1962.

Report of the Eighth Congress of the Action Group of Nigeria held at . . . Jos, Northern Nigeria, February 2–7 1962, with Appendices A–I. Mimeographed.

Policy papers prepared under the auspices of the National Reconstruction Committee. Mimeographed.

Democratic Socialism. Being the Manifesto of the Action Group of Nigeria for an Independent Nigeria. Lagos, 1960.

African Unity. Being the text of Chief Obafemi Awolowo's press conference statement on June 28, 1961. Lagos, 1961.

Government publications

Western Nigeria. *White Paper on the New Political Alignment in Western Nigeria* containing serious charges against the NCNC as an enemy of Western Nigeria by some of the leading members of the Party. Western Nigeria Official Document No. 1, 1964.

Western Nigeria. *House of Assembly Debates, Official Report.* Tenth Session, 1961 to 1962.

Federation of Nigeria. *Parliamentary Debates, First Parliament . . .* House of Representatives, especially November 29, 1960, and May, 1962.

Federation of Nigeria. Report of *Coker Commission of Inquiry into the Affairs of Certain Statutory Corporations in Western Nigeria,* 1962. 4 vols. Lagos, 1962.

Federation of Nigeria. *Comments of the Federal Government on the Report of Coker Commission of Inquiry into the Affairs of Certain Statutory Corporations in Western Nigeria.* Sessional Paper No. 4, 1962.

Federal Republic of Nigeria. *The Constitution of the Federal Republic of Nigeria.* Lagos, 1963.

Cases and court records

DOHERTY V. BALEWA (1961) 1 all N.L.R. 604

ADEGBENRO V. AKINTOLA F.S.C. 187/1962

ADEGBENRO V. AKINTOLA (1963) All E.R. 544

THE QUEEN and MAJA and 30 OTHERS, in re OMISADE. Record of Appeal from the High Court of Lagos to the Federal Supreme Court. Index of Reference and 11 volumes.

THE QUEEN V. OMISADE and 17 OTHERS. F.S.C. 404/63

THE QUEEN V. ENAHORO. Record of Appeal from the High Court of Lagos to the Supreme Court of Nigeria. 8 volumes.

Magazines and newspapers (Political orientation in parenthesis)

The Nation. A monthly magazine (NCNC)

Nigerian Opinion. A monthly journal of the Nigerian Current Affairs Society

The Service. A weekly magazine 1960–62 (Action Group)

Daily Express (Action Group; subsequently independent)

Daily Sketch (NNDP)

Daily Telegraph (NCNC)

Daily Times (Independent)

Morning Post (Federal Government)

Nigerian Citizen (NPC)

Nigerian Outlook (NCNC)

Nigerian Tribune (Action Group)

West African Pilot (NCNC)

5

The Politics of Separatism

Katanga, 1960-63

Crawford Young

On July 11, 1960, Moise Tshombe, freshly elected President of Katanga Province, solemnly declared Katanga a sovereign and independent state. "We appeal," he said, "to the whole free world, and ask all to recognize in us the right of every people to self-determination."

On January 14, 1963, the Katanga ministers informed Belgian Foreign Secretary Paul-Henri Spaak that they were "prepared to proclaim to the world that the Katanga secession was ended."

In the thirty months that lay between the two declarations, Katanga had suddenly become a vortex of world political conflict. A few short years before, few nonspecialists could have situated this provincial backwater on a map. Those who held stocks in copper companies were perhaps aware of the incredible concentration of mineral deposits in the Copperbelt shared by Katanga and Northern Rhodesia (now Zambia). But nothing ever "happened" there of any consequence to the world.

During the two and one-half years of its "independence," however, Katanga became a household word around the world. United Nations Secretary-General Dag Hammarskjöld lost his life when the aircraft transporting him to a rendezvous with Tshombe crashed near Ndola airport, Northern Rhodesia. United Nations troops from Indonesia, India, Mali, Ethiopia, Ireland, and Sweden found themselves on garrison duty—and in combat—in Katanga. An international network of Katanga lobbies was established in a half-dozen key Western capitals. Katanga emissaries offered to pay Costa Rica $2,500,000 for diplomatic recognition—but this and other efforts to win international acceptance were to no avail.

To justify its withdrawal from the Republic of the Congo, the secessionist state invoked the right of self-determination. Conservatives, formerly unmoved by such "woolly idealism," suddenly found this doctrine morally binding. Liberals, who had hailed self-determination as a necessary dimension of freedom, discovered limitations to its applicability, at least in Katanga. Disgruntled French army officers who had fought two demoralizing, seven-year wars in Indochina and Algeria to maintain French sovereignty embraced a new cause in Katanga "independence." European settler groups in the Rhodesias and white South African authorities, who were resisting African political advance at home, found African rule in Katanga a valuable dike against the tide of African nationalism further to the north. For utterly different reasons, the United States and the Soviet Union found themselves in agreement that the unity of the Congo must be restored.

The Katanga secession thus brought about an unusual intersection of the political currents and dilemmas of postcolonial African politics: the limits of self-determination, the problem of separatism in new states, the political role of European settlers and expatriate enterprise, the uses of the United Nations, to name but a few.

In this case, we will explore the tangled pathway which led to Katanga's effort to "go it alone" in 1960 and follow the fortunes of the secessionist state until its collapse before United Nations forces in January, 1963.

The European Stake in Katanga: Companies and Settlers

"The whole world knows," Ghana President Kwame Nkrumah cabled Tshombe on August 8, 1960, "that your pretended state has been set up with the support of foreign interests . . . . Your whole administration depends on Belgian officials who are fundamentally opposed to African independence, and who are merely using you as their tool." Nkrumah spoke for most of Africa and for a large part of the outside world in voicing his conviction that Katanga secession was at bottom a plot hatched by Europeans and merely carried out by African hirelings to serve European interests.

Nkrumah was right in suggesting that immense foreign economic interests were involved in the struggle for Katanga. Belgian geologists had labeled the copper deposits, running 250 miles east to west in southern Katanga, a "geological scandal" because of the high copper content of the ore, its accessible location near the surface, and the magnitude of the deposits. Geologic good fortune comes in abundance; the Copperbelt is also the world's largest producer of cobalt. The uranium that built the first atomic bomb was from Katanga. Zinc, germanium, cadmium, and tin are also mined, while numerous other precious metals are mingled in the rich

Republic of the Congo, 1960

Areas of Electoral Strength in Katanga, 1960

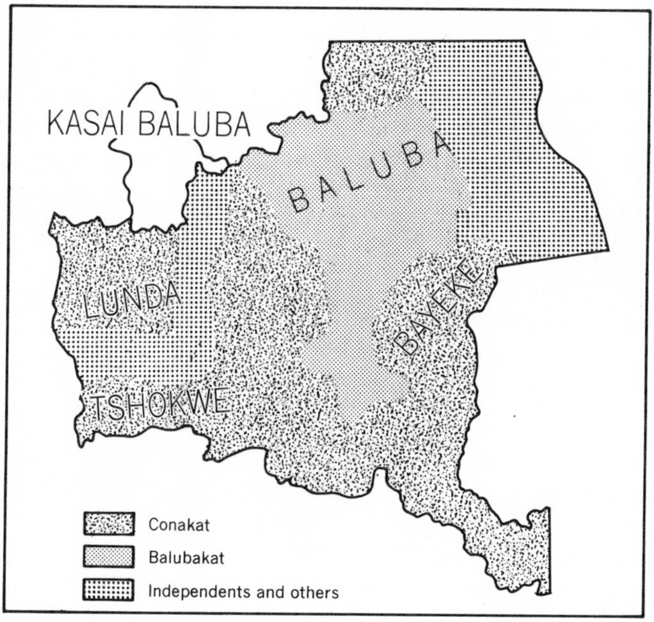

lodes. About 45 percent of Congo state revenues came from Katanga, and more than half the foreign exchange earnings.

The giant corporation built upon Katanga copper, Union Minière du Haut-Katanga (UMHK), produced annually $150 million worth of copper and is the world's third largest copper mining enterprise. UMHK is linked in turn to a giant Belgian holding company, the Société Générale de Belgique, whose various subsidiaries accounted for approximately 70 percent of the Congo's total output in 1959. In Katanga, a whole complex of industries had grown up, many of them affiliates of UMHK, founded upon the servicing of the mining enterprise. UMHK was also connected through a complex pattern of interlocking directorates and ownership with the mining companies of the Rhodesian Copperbelt and South Africa. The corporate stake in Katanga stability was thus enormous, and involved not only Belgian but also British and South African interests. Union Minière was inevitably a major actor in the secession drama.

The copper complex—and the temperate climate of the mile-high Katanga plateau—had attracted a sizable European population. At the beginning of 1960, there were 31,887 whites living in Katanga, about 2 percent of its population.

The white community, supported by a clamorous local press, had for long years wielded an influence out of all proportion to its numbers. The absence until 1958 of any effective means of expression for the African population created a political echo chamber, in which the tiny settler voice reverberated with extravagant demands for massive European immigration and for the establishment of a settler-dominated government in Katanga to supplant the colonial administration. The Katanga white community considered itself quite distinct from the European population in the rest of the Belgian Congo. It constituted nearly a third of the total number of Europeans resident in the colony and saw itself as being much more rooted in Katanga than were the administrators, missionaries, and plantation operators in other parts of the Congo.

Separatist aspirations among the settlers had a long history. As early as 1920, the leading company managers and Catholic mission leaders issued a manifesto demanding complete separation of Katanga from the rest of the colony. In 1931 a European newspaper spoke of the possibility of "independence" for Katanga and published a list of "ministers" for the first Katanga government—all settlers, needless to say. But despite the strident demands of the Katanga whites, a trend toward administrative centralization in Leopoldville had been growing over the years of colonial rule. To the indignation of the Katanga settlers, the proliferating colonial bureaucracy in Leopoldville was largely financed by revenues from the mining complex in Katanga.

In the postwar years, settler groups became more organized and were increasingly attracted by the Rhodesian pattern of a white-dominated autonomous state to the south. Many felt that the political goal should be the accession of Katanga to dominion status under settler leadership. Others were willing to concede some continuing links with the rest of the Congo, but only in a loose, "federal" form. If the important powers were seated in Elisabethville, even with African participation, the mining lobby and settler groups felt reasonably confident of being able to defend their interests. But if power came into the hands of radical nationalist leaders in Leopoldville, the Katanga European community feared that it would be unable to protect its privileged position. Separation was a tempting answer to this danger.

Birth of a Nation? Katanga's Africans

President Tshombe, speaking at ceremonies in Elisabethville marking the second anniversary of the declaration of Katanga "independence," suggested that, far from being a bastion of European privilege, Katanga was an African nation ordained by history and born of common resistance to European imperialism:

> To serve certain political designs, people have pretended that Katanga did not exist, that it was a construction of the colonizers. This is to deny that, when the first white explorers discovered the part of Africa called Katanga, they found three monarchies which were not only bound by family, economic and social links, but, and this is by far the most important, their historic destiny had been linked for centuries . . . . These monarchies constituted in the heart of Africa an entity apart, matured slowly over a long historic period, with July 11, 1960, only the manifestation of an awakening self-consciousness . . . .
>
> When the Belgians and the English . . . tried to lay their hands on Katanga, the Baluba, Lunda, and Bayeke chiefs were united in the face of the new danger which threatened their sovereignty . . . . It was for the first time the common resistance to a foreign effort to impose its will on Katanga.

Although Katanga itself was not created until the Belgians gave this title to the southeastern province of their sprawling colony, it is true that precolonial history in this part of Central Africa was largely the tale of three kingdoms. Beginning in the sixteenth century, a powerful Baluba state emerged in the northwest of what is now Katanga. A century later in the southwestern corner of the province, the Lunda empire extended its control over a wide area, spilling over into Northern Rhodesia and Angola. In the middle of the nineteenth century, a band of warrior-traders from Tanganyika expanded its commercial beachhead into a political kingdom headed by the cunning empire-builder Msiri.

Despite the extensive traditional political systems created, Katanga was not densely populated. The soil was thin and poor, and the dry season of six months left a long period without food crops to harvest. Even on the eve of Congo independence, the Katanga population was only 1,654,000 (about the size of Detroit), in an area of 191,666 square miles (roughly equivalent to Michigan, Wisconsin, and Minnesota combined). Earlier the population was a great deal smaller.

"Strangers" in Town

When mining began in earnest in the 1920's, the sparse Katanga population could not fill the vast manpower demands, and Union Minière recruiters began moving into the more densely inhabited zones to the north and east of Katanga, especially neighboring Kasai province.

The new mining towns, Elisabethville, Jadotville, Kolwezi, and others, began filling up with "strangers," or immigrants from other provinces. The largest single bloc of strangers were Kasai Baluba, an ethnic group that, from the first days of colonial contact, had shown unusual receptivity to European influences and social change. They flocked to the new mission schools and readily accepted wage employment at the European posts, plantations, and mining centers. In both trade and white-collar occupations in Katanga towns, Kasaiens were markedly more numerous than the sons of the Copperbelt.

The term "stranger" is full of ambiguities. Logically, all Africans in the new towns were strangers, as almost none of them came from the very sparsely inhabited areas immediately surrounding the city sites. But social labels are often not very logical; the African townsmen in Elisabethville, Jadotville, and Kolwezi who came from within Katanga's borders were firmly convinced that those from other provinces of the Congo were strangers. The confusion in this label is compounded by the fact that members of the Baluba ethnic group were to be found in both Katanga and the adjoining Kasai province. Those in Katanga had all at one time belonged to the Baluba empire, although the kingdom had fallen on evil days in the decades before colonial conquest and exercised its authority only in the northwestern part of Katanga when the Belgians arrived. The Kasai Baluba, although conscious of their cultural relationship to Katanga Baluba, had always been separate from the old empire. In the copper towns, Kasai Baluba were considered strangers, while Katanga Baluba qualified as native sons of Katanga.

"Authentic Katangans" and the Origins of African Separatism

The pedigree of Katanga authenticity was claimed with particular fervor by the various peoples situated, roughly speaking, in the southern half of the province. From the perspective of these southern Katanga groups, the limited number of privileged places open to Africans in the new colonial urban society were occupied by strangers who were suspected of conspiring with the colonizer to protect their social advance. Among the most militant in asserting the rights of "authentic Katangans" were the Lunda and the Bayeke descendents of Msiri's empire.

In the postwar years, awareness of the social disparity between strangers and authentic Katangans began to grow. In 1957, copper prices broke on the world market and dropped by 50 percent. For the first time since the war unemployment existed on the Copperbelt, the repercussions of which were most sharply felt by the lowest strata of workers, mainly authentic Katangans. At the same time, the first elections in Congo history were held in three cities to choose municipal councils; two of the cities, Elisabethville and Jadotville, were in Katanga. The elections resulted in a clear triumph for the strangers, largely because of ethnic cohesion in their ranks. The four African boroughs in Elisabethville designated burgomasters from outside Katanga, two being Kasai Baluba. Suspicion of favoritism towards Kasaiens by the new burgomasters was widespread in such matters as allocation of public housing and of residence permits; the fear grew among authentic Katangans that unless vigorous action were taken immediately, the social hegemony of Kasai Baluba, reinforced by political leadership, would result in a permanent caste system with themselves frozen at the bottom.

In October, 1958, authentic Katangans organized themselves into the Confédération des Associations Tribales du Katanga, popularly abbreviated as Conakat. Its first president was Godefroid Munongo, a keenly intelligent civil servant, educated to be a priest, already feared for a ruthless streak, and, coincidentally, the grandson of the Bayeke chief, Msiri. The reasons for formation of the Conakat propounded by another leader, Evariste Kimba, future Katanga Finance Minister, are instructive:

> To show the settlers that Katanga was not a desert before the arrival of the Europeans and that this province could not serve as an outlet to certain settlers who have dreamed of making the region a zone of massive European settlement . . . .
>
> To combat the policy of the companies who have recruited a large part of their labor force from outside the province. This policy has handicapped Katanga tribes in their material and intellectual development, owing to the fact that most good schools are found only in the industrial centers . . . .
>
> To avoid any repetition of the results of the municipal elections of 1957.

Conakat President Munongo soon made it clear that his organization intended to demand priority for Katangans in employment opportunity. During 1958, 758 unemployed families, for the most part authentic Katangans, had been forcibly repatriated to their villages by the administration. Munongo wrote a sharply worded letter to the Katanga Governor on February 13, 1959:

> The Katangans of birth wonder with good reason whether the authorities are not deliberately granting permanent residential permission to the people from Kasai in our towns so that the natives of that province can, thanks to their ever growing number, crush those from Katanga. This fact could well cause violence in the near future between the inhabitants of the two provinces. We would respectfully point out to you that very numerous are the native sons of Katanga who would like to work in the great cities of their province; mercilessly, they are told that there is a decree forbidding access to the towns. And yet they are the ones who should have priority.

In January, 1959, Belgian King Baudouin pledged that the Congo would become independent, although he gave no promise on the date. This statement set in motion the formation of political groups up and down the country, and made it urgent for the Conakat to define its views as to the political future. In May, 1959, the Conakat gave its first public indication of parochial ambitions, demanding "an autonomous and federated state" with political control firmly exercised by authentic Katangans.

Union of Separatists: The Conakat-Settler Alliance

The open commitment of the Conakat to federalism paved the way for the fusion of European and African autonomy aspirations. Fate makes strange bedfellows; the Conakat-settler alliance was hardly based on any deep-seated mutual esteem. The Conakat leaders could remember the 1950 testimony of the settler association opposing lowered segregation barriers for educated Africans: "The European community is too much aware of the excellence of Western civilization to let it run the slightest risk of being submerged under the flood of a hybrid combination of civilization and barbary." The settlers for their part were aware of the antisettler current just below the surface in the Conakat. But by 1959 settler hopes for dominating an independent state had vanished; only through an African alliance could their interests be protected. For the Conakat, support from the European community could bring valuable assistance in money and organization. In July, 1959, the settler movement, Union Katangaise, was admitted to membership in the Conakat.

The intertwining of the two threads of autonomy thought brought an absorption of traditional European arguments into Conakat thinking. The economic considerations, crucial to Katanga Europeans, had until then never been of much consequence to the Conakat. The real issue had simply been a reaction to stranger sociopolitical pre-eminence; political perspectives did not extend beyond the Katanga. Few of the Conakat leaders had ever visited Leopoldville before 1959; they had almost no contacts with the emerging leadership in the national capital or in other provincial centers. Until 1959 the only really significant political movement in Leopoldville was the Bakongo ethnic association, Abako, which was equally parochial in orientation. But in April, 1959, the first national political congress was called in Luluabourg; the dominant figure was a rising star in the nationalist firmament, Patrice Lumumba. The unitarian nationalism preached by Lumumba began to be recognized by the Conakat as a new threat to authentic Katanga aspirations for leadership on the Copperbelt. The age-old European complaints about centralizing, revenue-devouring Leopoldville now began to find their African echo.

The Conakat thus developed a political program tinged with separatism and adopted an alliance tainted with what seemed to other political groups to be the perpetuation of European domination under a new guise. The strangers reacted to the growing xenophobia of the Conakat by an increasing interest in the Lumumbist unitary theses; as one journalist put it, "for people considered as strangers in a region, the only chance to be able to remain where they were was to see the triumph of a unitary Congo."[1]

In mid-1959 Munongo was forced to resign as Conakat president by the Belgian administration because as a civil servant he was not permitted to engage in "political activity." The new president was Moise Tshombe, a forty-year-old businessman whose father had been one of the rare Africans to accumulate modest wealth through commercial success. Tshombe was educated in American Methodist mission schools and had an affable personality, which contrasted sharply with the rigidly determined style of Munongo. Tshombe's wife was the daughter of the Mwata Yamvo, paramount chief of the Lunda.

The Round Table: United Front for Independence

As 1959 drew to a close, the colonial administration had lost all control over the pace of decolonization. The militant nationalist parties were demanding independence for 1960; the Belgian pleas for a four to five-year period of transitional apprenticeship fell on deaf ears. In a last effort to break out of the political impasse, Belgium summoned all Congolese political movements to a Round Table Conference in Brussels, beginning January 20, 1960, to seek a final settlement in the Congo with representatives of the three major Belgian political parties. On the eve of the Round Table a spectacular surprise occurred: the fragmented Congolese political parties established a "united front" to demand with a single voice "immediate independence and national unity." The most surprising member of all in the "united front" was Moise Tshombe.

Indeed, no group was more startled by this development than the Conakat executive committee remaining behind in Elisabethville. A hurried meeting

---

[1] Pierre Davister, *Katanga enjeu du monde* (Brussels: Editions Europe-Afrique, 1960), p. 78.

was called simultaneously with the formal opening session in Brussels. The minutes of the meeting record the mood of the Conakat:

> "What will we do after the Round Table if we don't obtain satisfaction [on autonomy for Katanga]," asked one executive committee member. "Will we carry out a coup d'état or will we accept the unitarian regime for all the Congo?"
>
> The members present opted for the first solution . . . . Better to risk a coup d'état and fail than to remain, arms crossed, and accept like a woman a regime which will bring nothing to Katanga. Sékou Touré [Guinea] seized power; it is not impossible that we can do the same. Let us prepare the mass.

Meanwhile, in Brussels, Tshombe found himself isolated and suspect at the Round Table. He had brought along a former president of the Katanga settler association as his adviser, which seemed to other delegations to be dramatic confirmation of their worst fears concerning the Conakat. He was not alone in wanting a federal structure; several major parties in other parts of the Congo also opposed continuation of the tightly centralized colonial pattern, but for rather different reasons than Tshombe. The image of the Conakat as a thinly disguised tool of European mining and settler interests made Tshombe's support a veritable kiss of death for other "federalist" parties and strengthened the hand of the unitarian parties led by Lumumba, which were convinced that only a strong, centralized state could achieve rapid progress.

On January 25, 1960, agreement was reached on independence for the Congo five months later, on June 30, 1960. The conference went on to discuss the broad outlines of a provisional constitution.[2] The other federalist parties greatly reduced the scope of their federal demands from their pre-Round Table position. Tshombe found himself too isolated to push the sweeping proposals for a loose federation which the Conakat executive committee had given him a mandate to present. The only heated public arguments between the Conakat delegation and other parties took place over the issue of whether authority to grant mining concessions and receive the royalties should be a provincial or central function. Another grandson of the Bayeke empire-builder Msiri, Paramount Chief Antoine Mwende-Munongo, declared, "If we attribute this power to the central government, the inhabitants of the provinces will be left in misery and ignorance, and by this very fact in a condition of servitude." Another Conakat delegate added, "The Katanga is good for providing money . . . . What our Congolese brothers are interested in is above all our money."

The final resolutions adopted by the Round Table did call for a framework of government less centralized than that of the colonial administration. Above all the Round Table provided for the creation of a representative

[2] For a complete account of the Round Table proceedings, see G.-H. Dumont, *La Table Ronde Belgo-Congolaise* (Paris: Editions Universitaires, 1961).

government at the provincial and the national level. Provincial governments were to be elected by and responsible to elected provincial assemblies. A specified list of powers was to be exercised by the provincial government. Although the term "federal" was eschewed, in many respects the transitional constitution sketched out by the Round Table was in fact federal. Although the degree of decentralization fell short of Conakat demands, at the close of the Round Table Tshombe declared himself fully satisfied with the results; "The independent Congo of tomorrow will now escape the breakup with which it was threatened," he said flatly.

The Certainty of Independence and Its Uncertainties

The elections for national and provincial assemblies were scheduled for May, and the political campaign got under way immediately. The psychological climate of early 1960 had an air of unreality, of mingled euphoria and fear, of joy at the painless achievement of almost immediate independence and yet of uncertainty as to just what the morrow would bring. Only two years before, few really believed independence would come within a decade; it was too remote to be tangible. A year earlier, some said five years, but many others felt that this forecast was visionary. But at the close of the Round Table independence was suddenly less than five months away. The European owned-and-operated colony had somehow to be converted into an independent African state.

What would it be like? No one could really know. The proliferation of parties and the absence of any meaningful measure of their potential strength outside the urban areas made the impending elections totally unpredictable. Although it was possible—though only barely—to create African legislatures and designate African ministers, it was quite impossible in this brief period to take any meaningful steps toward Africanization of the wholly European senior civil service posts and army and police commissioned ranks. Was it really conceivable that a European civil service, bred in the authoritarian ways of a highly efficient colonial system, could suddenly become the docile instrument of a militant African nationalist regime? Conversely, would not an African government feel that its program could only be implemented by an abrupt and radical Africanization of bureaucracy and army? An ethnic pattern of politics had already emerged in municipal elections; could minority ethnic groups be sure that the winners in May would not then establish a caste system with ethnic chauvinism restricting the fruits of independence to chosen groups? Few Africans in early 1960 mourned the demise of the colonial system, yet many had vague anxieties about what exactly would take its place. Insecurity lay close to the surface on all sides and could easily explode into violence in the heated polemic of an election campaign.

Elections in Katanga

A subtle but crucial change had occurred in the nature of political rivalry among Katanga Africans. Although the Conakat continued to make clear its hostility to strangers, the major competition in the May 1960 elections was not from the Kasai Baluba but rather from the Baluba of northern Katanga. Led by Jason Sendwe, a Protestant pastor, the Katanga Baluba had formed their own political party, the Association des Baluba du Katanga, better known as the Balubakat. The Balubakat was founded primarily because of fears of ethnic chauvinism on the part of southern Katanga's Conakat leaders and suspicion of the settler and company influences behind the Conakat. Thus, as elections approached, Katanga politics were dominated by a bitter contest between the Conakat, primarily representing southern Katanga, and the Balubakat, representing northern Katanga and the immigrants from the north in the southern Katanga cities.

The north-south polarity was not quite complete; each had an ally behind enemy lines. The Conakat had committed itself to reinforcing the powers and prerogatives of traditional chiefs. This enabled it to win support from several important Baluba traditional chiefs in the north, which in turn brought some electoral support for Conakat in Baluba zones. The Balubakat, for its part, found a militant ally in the Association des Tshokwe du Congo, de l'Angola, et de la Rhodésie (ATCAR), grouping the Tshokwe of the urban centers and those scattered in pockets in Lunda country. Tshokwe and Lunda ethnic communities lived interspersed in southwestern Katanga; both retained a vivid recollection of bitter wars between them at the end of the nineteenth century. Tshokwe feared the Lunda aristocracy would use independence to reconquer and impose their rule on the Tshokwe, ending the administrative autonomy that had been permitted under the colonial regime. Lunda believed the Tshokwe to be an alien and subversive element on their lands; some advocated a massive repatriation of Tshokwe to Angola, reputed to be their original homeland.

The Kasai "strangers" were now placed in a peculiarly difficult position. Fedeka (Fédération des Associations des Ressortissants de la Province de Kasai), their political wing, initially supported the Balubakat, as dictated by ethnic logic and Conakat hostility to Kasai Baluba. However, a new element entered the picture. Back in Kasai, Lumumba chose to ally his party, MNC-Lumumba, with aggressively anti-Baluba political movements whose major objective was the expulsion of Kasai Baluba from many parts of Kasai to which they had migrated during the colonial period. Meanwhile, in Katanga, the Balubakat had entered into a cautious alliance with Lumumba. The strangers found themselves with no place to turn; the Balubakat alliance in Katanga by extension meant association with Lumumba, whose Kasai allies were assuming a position even more menacing to the Kasai Baluba than that of the Conakat.

As the electoral contest sharpened, the whole Katanga community, European as well as African, was drawn into its vortex. The settler group was solidly aligned with the Conakat. Union Minière had too large a stake in the future course of events to remain aloof; the company personnel in Katanga leaned strongly toward the Conakat, despite the fact that the majority of their working force and the great majority of their African clerical staff were strangers. At UMHK headquarters in Brussels, a more prudent attitude was adopted; subsidies were given to both the Conakat and the Balubakat, as it was not clear which would triumph. Complete identification with a possible loser was too great a risk. Although the Catholic missions as such did not play an overt role, the Catholic milieux generally favored the Conakat.

The Balubakat also had its European collaborators. Professor Arthur Doucy, director of the Institut de Sociologie Solvay and an eminent socialist intellectual, helped the Balubakat establish a Brussels office and served as Balubakat leader Sendwe's juridicial adviser during the Round Table Conference. The Solvay Institute, part of the Free University of Brussels ("free" meaning laic, secular, and non-Catholic), also had a team of research assistants at a social center in Elisabethville; several of these researchers became deeply involved with the Balubakat. Some members of the academic staff of the State University of Elisabethville also lent moral and organizational assistance to the Balubakat.

"Nowhere," declared André Schoeller, last colonial Governor of Katanga, "are Europeans so intimately linked to the activity of Congolese political parties [as in Katanga]. I have no doubt as to the sincerity of their intentions, but I really fear that they are making a mistake, that they are serving neither their own cause, nor that of the parties they support." The type of European support was very different in the two cases. For the Conakat, the backing was that of the great majority of the established European community in the Copperbelt towns. For the Balubakat, the support came in large part from outside, i.e., from Belgian sources. This latter backing derived from two classic themes in the psychology of the Belgian left: anticlericalism and hostility to the giant corporations of Katanga. As the Conakat seemed to have both company and Catholic support, the left instinctively associated itself with the Balubakat. Conversely, the visible support for the Balubakat from Belgian socialist and anticlerical elements gave to Sendwe and his followers by association the appearance of anticlerical and anticompany attitudes, which they did not really possess.

At stake in the May 1960 elections were 16 seats in the national Parliament and 60 provincial assembly slots. All adult African males were eligible to vote. The results were extraordinarily close; in the national elections, the Conakat took 8 seats, the Balubakat 6, and its Atcar (Tshokwe ethnic party) ally one, with one independent. For the provincial assembly, the Conakat won 25 seats, the Balubakat alliance 22, with 13 seats going to independents. The popular vote was as follows:

National

Conakat	104,871	32.07%		
Balubakat	80,434	24.60%	Balubakat alliance: 110,091	33.67%
Atcar	29,657	9.07%		

	CONAKAT		BALUBAKAT & ALLIES	
Provincial District	*Seats*	*Votes*	*Seats*	*Votes*
Elisabethville	3	8,617	2	8,610
Jadotville	1	4,970	2	8,079
Tanganika	3	11,342	6	26,898
Haut-Katanga	9	23,323	(no Balubakat candidates)	
Lualaba	6	28,716	3	23,991
Haut-Lomami*	3	17,470	6	27,285
	25	94,438	19	94,863

* In one territory, Malemba-Nkulu, the Balubakat Cartel ticket of three candidates was unopposed, and no election was held; this brings the Balubakat alliance up to 22 seats, and would have added approximately 10,000 votes to the Balubakat column.

The Balubakat was convinced that the election had been stolen. The method of seat calculation happened to work out to their disadvantage; if we exclude districts where there was no direct competition, we find that the average Conakat seat was won with 4,445 votes, while the average Balubakat seat took 4,992 votes to win. The Balubakat appealed the results, charging numerous irregularities and voter intimidation; the Belgian magistrates charged with supervising the elections rejected the appeals. Thus it was in an atmosphere of mutual distrust that the provincial assembly came together in June, 1960, to elect the first Katanga government.

Balubakat indignation mounted when it was discovered that all thirteen of the independent deputies had been enticed to support the Conakat, giving Tshombe's party a 38–22 majority as the provincial assembly convened on June 1. The Conakat majority produced a solidly Conakat provincial government, presided over by Moise Tshombe. Thus the Balubakat found that insult had been added to injury; not only had all of their protests of electoral irregularities been rejected, but they were entirely excluded from the provincial government.

Tshombe and Lumumba: The Lines Harden

Meanwhile, in Leopoldville, feverish consultations were being held for the formation of the first national government. The largest single party, MNC-Lumumba, had only 33 out of 137 seats in the directly elected Chamber of Deputies, or 41 if one counted direct allies. The next largest party, the "moderate," administration-supported PNP, had only 15. A total of fifteen different parties were represented, mostly of a regional and/or ethnic character; the task of constructing a clear majority out of the competing welter of personal ambitions and regional jealousies was almost overwhelming. Only two had a chance: Lumumba and Abako leader, Joseph Kasavubu. Tshombe actively negotiated with both. His price: Conakat designees for the ministries of Defense and Finance and a "federalist" for Interior (controlling the security police and relations with the provinces).

Lumumba, by agreeing to support Kasavubu as chief of state, finally succeeded in constituting a government on June 23. There were two Conakat members in the giant cabinet, which included twenty-eight ministers and ten state secretaries—an inflation necessary to gain even a narrow majority for confirmation. However, both the Conakat ministers received relatively insignificant positions. Further, archrival Sendwe was nominated as central government High Commissioner for Katanga (although he never assumed his functions), a post of ill-defined but potentially considerable powers. Tshombe was livid and declared immediately, "It is with outrage that I learn by radio the final composition of the central government." The Conakat had been duped and considered itself free of any obligation to support a government "in the hands of extremists."

Two days later Belgian authorities learned that a plot was afoot to declare the independence of Katanga on June 28. A former agent of the colonial security police was seized and found in possession of an air ticket routed to Brussels, New York, and Washington, and fresh credentials as "Special Ambassador of the State of Katanga." Under interrogation, the agent admitted to Belgian officials that the plan called for a proclamation of independence, followed by a plea for recognition first by Belgium and the United States, then by Portugal and Great Britain. According to their special ambassador, Conakat leaders were persuaded that the Belgian administration would not stop them if they acted before the Lumumba government became fully sovereign on June 30.

Belgian authorities were quick to inform Tshombe that on the contrary they would take all measures necessary to squelch any such scheme. Tshombe and his colleagues thereupon solemnly swore that they would drop the secession scheme, provided their ambassador was released.

Thus, as the gold and blue flag of the new Congo Republic was raised on June 30 in Leopoldville and Elisabethville, the chasm of mistrust between the Congo Prime Minister and the Katanga President could scarcely have been wider.

Katanga Walks Out

The opportunity to carry out the aborted operation of June 28 came sooner than anyone could have expected. On July 5 discontent with harsh conditions and absence of promotion opportunities led to a mutiny in the ranks of the Congo Army in Leopoldville against the entirely European officer corps. The mutiny spread rapidly to other units; three days later the first symptoms of indiscipline appeared among troops stationed in Katanga. On July 9 Europeans began a panic flight toward the Rhodesian border and five, including the Italian vice-consul, were shot down by the mutineers in a machine-gun ambush in Elisabethville. That same night, on the urgent plea of remaining Belgian officials and Tshombe, Belgian military units were sent on their way to restore order in the Katanga cities.

On July 10 an emergency session of the Katanga cabinet decided that the moment had come for a declaration of independence, coupled with an appeal to Belgium and other "friendly countries" for military and technical assistance. Belgian Foreign Minister Pierre Wigny advised caution and warned that Belgium would not recognize an independent Katanga; however, Wigny's directives were not heeded by Belgian military commanders in Katanga, who openly encouraged secession. On July 11 Tshombe formally declared Katanga an independent state and appealed to Belgium for technical, financial, and military help.

Later that same night a plane on which President Kasavubu and Prime Minister Lumumba were traveling tried to land at Elisabethville airport. Godefroid Munongo, who was now Katanga Interior Minister and who saw in Lumumba a mortal enemy, was running the control tower himself. "Landing permission is refused," he curtly informed the Belgian pilot. When the plane tried to land anyway, Munongo ordered the runway lights extinguished, and the plane had to turn back. Kasavubu and Lumumba, once back in safe territory, immediately cabled the UN and requested military aid to repel what they felt to be Belgian aggression. "We accuse Belgian government of carefully preparing Katanga secession to retain control over our country," the cable concluded.

Belgian Reaction: Help but No Recognition

"Entire ethnic groups headed by men of honesty and worth . . . ask us to help them construct their independence," King Baudouin declared ten days after the secession. "It is our duty to respond favorably."

Belgium did respond favorably, but with one major qualification: Formal recognition was refused, and NATO allies were requested to follow suit. Belgium had interests in all parts of the Congo and was not prepared to sacrifice everything in the interest of Katanga. Also, Belgium suddenly found itself pilloried before the world; hasty recognition would have seemed to much of the world conclusive proof that the Katanga secession was indeed a plot masterminded by Brussels to break up the Congo. On the other hand, the government was subjected to formidable and domestic pressures. The first Belgian refugees, bitter and terrorized, arrived back at Brussels airport. Hair-raising and lurid accounts of rape and atrocity by the mutineers filled the newspapers. With Lumumba accusing Belgium of aggression and sabotage, the public clamored for support for Tshombe, Belgium's "last friend" in the Congo.

The legal fiction adopted was that technical assistance would be offered to any province requesting it, where peace and order reigned. However, what was given to the Katanga went far beyond mere "technical assistance." Belgian army officers oversaw the disarmament and expulsion of all Congolese troops stationed in Katanga except a handful from ethnic groups loyal to the Conakat; these latter formed the embryo of the Katanga gendarmerie, placed under the command of a regular Belgian army officer, Major Crevecoeur. The commander of Belgian troops in Katanga, General Charles Cumont, announced on July 13 that his forces were placed at the disposition of President Tshombe. Belgian civil servants were ordered to remain at their posts in Katanga; elsewhere in the Congo, they were told that their security would no longer be assured and that they were free to return to Belgium, where places in the metropolitan public service were promised (a promise later withdrawn). Thus Katanga appeared to the world as an oasis of order in a country of turmoil.

On July 14 the Congolese government announced that it was rupturing diplomatic relations with Belgium because of the Belgian role in supporting the Katanga secession.

Enter the United Nations

United Nations prestige stood at a peak in 1960. The shrewd and capable personal diplomacy of Secretary-General Dag Hammarskjöld had brought a string of triumphs in de-fusing crises. The Congo provided an opportunity for the world organization to demonstrate that it had come of age, that it was capable of providing politically acceptable guidance for the infant republic during its first faltering steps.

The UN was not prepared, however, to cope with a crisis of the magnitude it quickly faced. An emergency session of the Security Council was called July 13 to consider the Congolese appeal for immediate military assistance. From this first meeting, the beginnings of a fundamental misunderstanding as to the nature of the UN role were clear. The Congolese government believed the intervention was designed to restore the Leopoldville authority throughout the country. Hammarskjöld's object on the other hand, was "to maintain order in the country and protect human lives." The resolution adopted called for the withdrawal of Belgian troops and authorized the Secretary-General to furnish military assistance to the Congolese government "until the time when national security forces . . . are fully able to fulfill their task." The Congolese government felt that UN troops should operate under Congolese orders; Hammarskjöld believed that UN forces were subject only to orders from New York and responsible solely to the Security Council, although acting in consultation with Congolese authorities.

Belgium quickly agreed to withdraw its troops progressively from other parts of the Congo as soon as they were replaced by UN forces. Four days after passage of the resolution, the UN already had 3,500 men, from four countries, on duty in the Congo. The crucial test was soon to follow in Katanga.

Hammarskjöld Hesitates

A race against time was in progress in Katanga. The drive was to create a Katanga armed force at top speed before the Lumumba government could regain control over enough troops to invade Katanga or before the UN moved in on his behalf. Belgian forces were required to prop up the secessionist state as long as it was diplomatically possible to maintain them in Katanga. Brussels, accordingly, argued that as order reigned in Katanga, UN troops did not need to be dispatched there.

On July 21 the Security Council was called back into session, in the face of Belgian reluctance to withdraw troops from Katanga. On the one hand Hammarskjöld argued that UN troops could not take part "in any internal conflict;" at the same time he insisted that Katanga was covered by the resolution. A Security Council resolution voted July 22 made more explicit its demand that Belgian troops be withdrawn from all of the Congo, including Katanga, and invited all states to abstain from any action that might compromise the reestablishment of public order or sap the territorial integrity and political independence of the Congo.

Hammarskjöld arrived in Leopoldville on July 28 to complete arrangements for the movement of the first UN detachments to Elisabethville. He found that Lumumba's impatience with UN hesitation to act in Katanga was growing rapidly. Plans were laid to move the first UN troops to Elisabethville on August 6, with UN Undersecretary Ralph Bunche sent as an advance party the day before.

Elisabethville airport on Bunche's arrival was decked out with the new red and green Katanga flag. The still embryonic Katanga gendarmerie was skillfully transported about to lend the illusion of omnipresence. Tshombe and his European councilors told Bunche that Katanga would fight to the death to resist Lumumbist rule. The Undersecretary learned of an armed European volunteer corps, and was told that thousands of villagers would rise with spears and poisoned arrows at the given signal to annihilate any UN intruders. Munongo added that the airfields could all be rendered unserviceable by covering the runways with empty oil drums. Bunche cabled back to Leopoldville to postpone the arrival of UN troops because of the "fanatic opposition" likely to be encountered, and because rather different plans would be required if the UN units did in fact encounter armed resistance.

Was this simply a gigantic bluff? Probably. The Belgian forces could hardly have opened fire on the UN troops; the Katanga gendarmerie was as yet a tiny force, and the village warriors whose poisoned arrows were so frequently invoked were a transparent fraud. Only one real armed force then existed which could have opposed the UN: the volunteer corps of the Katanga European community, a special force which had been in training for years. Although the small advance party that the UN had initially planned could have been repulsed by such a group, it is doubtful whether a determined show of force by the UN would have met prolonged resistance. All this, however, was far from clear in August, 1960. Moreover, the increasingly erratic behavior of Lumumba and the fragmentation of his government caused growing disenchantment among UN officials, in Western and even in many Afro-Asian capitals. Hammarskjöld hesitated to risk serious bloodshed involving UN forces in Katanga, a new exodus of Katanga Europeans, and a shutdown of the Katanga economy. "Mr. H" (as Hammarskjöld was popularly known) called off the UN entry into Katanga and went back to the Security Council for a new mandate.

Katanga Wins the Race

The Security Council meeting on August 8 explicitly demanded that Belgian troops be promptly withdrawn from Katanga, but reaffirmed the policy of noninterference in internal conflict, "constitutional or other." Armed with this new mandate, Hammarskjöld went to Elisabethville himself on August 12. Tshombe, smiling and affable, assured Mr. H that he had no objection to the removal of Belgian troops and garrisoning of UN forces in Katanga—if nine conditions were met, amounting to a pledge not to interfere with the operation of the Tshombe regime. The UN could not, of course, accept an ultimatum from a provincial government—but Hammarskjöld's pledge that his mandate would not influence the outcome of any constitutional disputes meant that the UN would not enforce Lumumba's fiat on the Copperbelt.

The race against time now began in earnest. Belgian officers hastily trained the new recruits. A large part of the equipment of the colonial army, the Force Publique, had been quietly transferred to Katanga, and the Belgian forces apparently "forgot" to take all of their equipment back to Belgium. The Belgian contingent included eighty-nine former Force Publique officers and noncoms, 326 from the regular army who volunteered for detached service in Katanga and seventy officers and noncoms from the

Belgian gendarmerie. On September 7, a Belgian Airline DC-7 landed at Elisabethville with nine tons of small arms and ammunition; a spokesman for the Katanga Interior Ministry declared that this was a part of a continual airlift from Belgium.

On August 13 the first UN units arrived in Katanga. By the beginning of September the withdrawal of metropolitan Belgian army units (but not all military personnel) was complete. But this was far from meaning that the UN was in control of Katanga.

The end of August was a decisive period. Relations between the UN and Lumumba had virtually been broken off, and the Prime Minister had decided to invade the Katanga himself, with whatever troops he could muster and whatever direct external assistance he could obtain. In Lumumba's view, not only had the UN failed to act against the Katanga secession, but the presence of UN troops made it difficult for him to act on his own. At this juncture, only one country had both the logistical capability and the political desire to give armed support to the volatile Lumumba—the Soviet Union.

From the Russian standpoint the Congo crisis seemed a remarkable opportunity to prove what Moscow had maintained for years. The Western powers, allied with the mining corporations, would never permit "true" independence in any area where their economic interests were at stake. The United Nations, the Soviets had long argued, was controlled by the imperialist powers. The only true friends of new nations seeking genuine independence were in the "camp of socialism." At the end of August, an airlift of Soviet bloc personnel began. Twelve Ilyuchins with Soviet crews were put at Lumumba's disposal, and an initial shipment of trucks arrived at Leopoldville airport. A Congolese invasion force was collected in Luluabourg (midway between Leopoldville and Elisabethville), and the Armée Nationale Congolaise (ANC), reinforced by the Soviet equipment, set out to conquer the Katanga.

However, en route to Katanga, the ill-disciplined ANC troops responded with savage brutality to some minor acts of provocation by the civil population. An estimated three thousand men, women, and children were massacred by the troops, giving some indication of what an "invasion" in Katanga carried out at this point by the ANC would most likely be. The overt and unilateral Soviet intervention galvanized the heterogeneous opposition elements in Leopoldville. More important, it assured them of the sympathy and support of Western powers, which now concluded that Lumumba was definitely committed to the Soviet camp, and, to a lesser degree, of much of the UN staff and a number of Afro-Asian states that deplored great-power intervention outside the UN framework. On September 5 President Kasavubu suddenly announced over the Leopoldville radio that, acting on a somewhat ambiguous power in the provisional constitution, he was dismissing the Prime Minister and his followers. On the

Copperbelt, Tshombe, his Conakat followers, and the European community breathed a loud sigh of relief. The Katanga "miracle" had succeeded; the race against time had been won, and secession appeared secure.

"Independent" Katanga: Bastion of Democracy or Fortress of Imperialism?

What was the profile of power in the now secure Katanga state? We may discern a complex of forces, internal and external, overt and clandestine, in response to the classic political question: Who governs?

At the apex of the pyramid was Tshombe himself—a master (some would say prisoner) of ambiguity, flexible (some would say slippery), susceptible to diverse influences. He was an elusive negotiator, adept at giving the appearance of agreement with his interlocutors—agreements which always seemed to evaporate almost as soon as achieved. Beneath Tshombe were two very different political figures: Interior Minister Munongo and Finance Minister Jean-Baptiste Kibwe. The Munongo-Kibwe diumverate was far more ruthless and extreme than the Katanga President; they were determined to brook no compromise and to defend secession to the end. They were also particularly susceptible to influences from extremist elements in the local European community, and later from the coterie of disgruntled French "ultra" plotters, who saw in Katanga the last stand of Western civilization against "communism," broadly defined by them to include not only the Sino-Soviet system but Afro-Asian nationalism as well.

Munongo and Kibwe were not identical personalities, however. Munongo felt he was merely using European support for African ends. As he told Conor Cruise O'Brien, UN special representative in Elisabethville, "Outsiders are completely wrong in imagining that Katanga was run by Belgians. Personally, [I] hate the Belgians. Belgians had murdered [my] grandfather; [my] father died in a Belgian jail."[3] His dream was the reconstitution of a traditional state in Katanga—the one that his grandfather Msiri had begun; his own son was named Msiri.

In Kibwe's case, intransigence was liberally dosed with a reputation for exceptional corruption. The usually docile Katanga assembly three times voted censure motions against his conduct as Finance Minister, the last two times by unanimous vote, and finally declared the office vacant—without, however, succeeding in dislodging Kibwe from his highly profitable position.

The Chiefs

The rural support for the Tshombe regime came from the traditional rulers, who were granted extensive new privileges by the Conakat. In par-

[3] Conor Cruise O'Brien, *To Katanga and Back* (London: Hutchison, 1962), p. 105.

ticular, the three most prominent paramount chiefs—Kasongo Nyembo (Baluba), Mwata Yamvo (Lunda), and Mwende-Munongo (Bayeke)—were given arms and money to equip their own private militias.

The Councilors

Each Katanga minister had his own entourage of European councilors, who collectively formed an intricate political subsystem of their own. Often the direction of the political wind was indicated by whichever faction of councilors was enjoying best access to the key ministers. Initially, several of the most important European figures, such as Major Guy Weber and Major Crevecoeur (Belgian army officers) and Count Harold d'Aspremont-Lynden (of the personal staff of Belgian Prime Minister Gaston Eyskens), were officially connected with the Belgian technical assistance mission. After the fall of Lumumba and renewal of friendlier Belgian relations with Leopoldville, the Belgian official role sharply diminished. Katanga resentment at the failure of Belgium to accord recognition also intensified, and other European influences emerged. Although many of the settlers who had played significant roles in colonial politics disappeared from the scene, some continued to play an advisory part. Some Union Minière executives had close personal ties within the Katanga cabinet. Other Belgian advisers were associated with the University of Liège, which took charge of reorganizing the University of Elizabethville and purging the academic staff; prominent among these was Professor of Law René Clemens, author of the Katanga constitution. Beginning at the end of 1960, right-wing French influences also became visible, as a counterpoise to the Belgians. Although the councilors had different access points to the Katanga government and were divided into "moderate" and "ultra" wings, they had in common a place in the European political spectrum ranging from moderate conservatism to extreme right-wing viewpoints.

In the early phases the inexperienced Katanga ministers relied almost entirely on their European councilors. As time wore on, the abler could pick and choose among advisers, and learned to play one clique of European councilors against another; the councilors became accessories rather than star actors in the drama.

The Mercenaries

Beginning in late 1960, to compensate for the inexperience of the Katanga soldiery, centers of recruitment were established in Belgium, France, Rhodesia, and South Africa for the enlistment of "mercenaries." About five hundred adventurers signed on, half Belgian, and the rest mostly Rhodesian, South African, or British. The English-speaking mercenaries were organized into an "international company" that undertook various commando missions; the Belgians were integrated into the gendarmerie units as commanders. The *affreux,* as they became known, joined for diverse reasons—greed, adventure, the struggle against "communism." They contributed to the military potential of the gendarmerie, but whether this compensated for the public relations liability is an open question.

The Fatal Flaws

In the long run, two critical weaknesses led to the downfall of the Katanga regime: international nonrecognition and irreducible Balubakat opposition in the north.

Nonrecognition

Tshombe, and even more his European advisers, was aware from the outset that no matter how rich the Copperbelt, the landlocked Katanga state could not survive in international isolation. True, Sir Roy Welensky, head of the Federation of Rhodesia and Nyasaland, was an open supporter of Tshombe; South Africa was well disposed towards such a "reasonable" African state, and Portugal facilitated shipment of the mineral exports over Angolan rail lines (for cash payment in hard currency). But this kind of support was not enough.

Belgium was really the key; the Belgian decision in July, 1960, to limit support for Katanga to material aid, and to withhold recognition, was crucial. Support for Katanga separation in Belgian governmental circles steadily weakened after Lumumba's overthrow, and especially after April, 1961, when a new Socialist-Christian Democratic coalition government took office in Belgium, with former NATO secretary and moderate socialist Paul-Henri Spaak as Foreign Minister. Thereafter, Belgium disengaged itself from the Katanga adventure and by 1962 exerted increasing pressure in favor of reconciliation with Leopoldville.

Katanga delegations combed Africa, Europe, and the Americas in late 1960 in pursuit of the elusive recognition. Tshombe's major African bridgehead was in Brazzaville, capital of the former French Congo, which became a veritable staging point for diverse clandestine operations. Its President, Abbé Fulbert Youlou (overthrown in August, 1963), had some sympathy for Tshombe's "moderate" ideology and even more for the notion of reducing the importance of Leopoldville, directly across the Congo river from Brazzaville. Youlou also demanded and got an electoral campaign contribution and a pledge of Katanga financial support for his projected giant dam at Kouilou. But although Youlou paid what amounted to a state visit to Elisabethville in February, 1961, the recognition never came.

In Great Britain the Katanga cause enjoyed the support of the right wing of the Tory party. Captain Charles Waterhouse, the leading spokesman for the "Suez Tories" for several years, became a member of the board of directors of Union Minière during the Katanga secession period. In France the Katanga likewise enjoyed some conservative sympathies, mingled with a desire to add Katanga to the French sphere of interest.

In the United States a Katanga Information Service headed by Michael Struelens set up an office in Manhattan. According to *Newsweek,* Struelens spent \$140,000 in "operational expenses" in Capitol corridors in six months—a report that he vigorously denied. He did win some friends; an American Committee for Aid to Katanga Freedom Fighters was established in November, 1961, and published full page ads in the New York *Times* and seventeen other important dailies under the heading: "Katanga is the Hungary of 1961." In March, 1962, the group organized a Katanga rally in Madison Square Garden featuring Senator Barry Goldwater, which netted \$80,000 in collections for the Katanga cause. Senator Thomas J. Dodd (D-Conn.) was also won over and became an indefatigable, one-man crusader for Katanga, but to little avail. From September, 1960, the State Department was heavily committed to supporting reunification of the Congo. Katanga was obviously a losing proposition, tainted by its associations with Welensky, South Africa, and Portugal; support for Katanga would have compromised relations not only with Leopoldville, but with most other African states.

Thus Katanga's efforts to secure international recognition for its act of secession were a total failure. Even Belgium, despite initial sympathy and support from Brussels, was not willing to go so far. A few other countries, like Congo-Brazzaville, gave unofficial backing, but not a single state officially recognized Katanga's "independence." The great majority of Afro-Asian states were bitterly hostile to the Katanga secession, seen as a maneuver by imperialist powers and mining interests. UN officials, stung by accusations by radical African states and the Soviet bloc that their passivity in August, 1960, had permitted the secession to consolidate itself, believed that perpetuation of Katanga "independence" would permanently discredit the world body in the eyes of the developing nations. The secessionist state faced a hostile world.

The North in Revolt

In the days following the secession, urgent efforts were made to secure the support of all or part of the Balubakat Cartel. Of the ten ministers in the Conakat government, two were of Baluba origin (Evariste Kimba, Foreign Affairs; Valentin Ilunga, Justice), but of Conakat political persuasion. If the Katanga government could have been enlarged and made fully representative of the province as a whole, the case for secession would have been immeasurably strengthened.

Tshombe offered the Balubakat five ministries. For a short period the Balubakat hesitated; on July 21 Sendwe representatives submitted to Tshombe a list of their proposed ministerial candidates, but without specifying whether they thereby accepted the secession. Six days later the

Balubakat denounced the secession and announced it had refused the Conakat's offers. By August the first reports of dissidence in Balubakat zones of North Katanga began to appear; in September, with the Lumumba threat removed, the young Katanga gendarmerie launched its first "pacification" sorties against what was by then a wide-spread revolt.

In January, 1961, Balubakat leaders in Stanleyville proclaimed that a separate province was created in the north, loyal to the idea of a united Congo. "Given the illegality of the proclamation of Katanga independence without a popular referendum . . . . Given that Tshombe and his acolytes embark with joyous heart upon the collective massacre of the Tshokwe and Baluba, majoritarian and convinced nationalists . . . . We officially proclaim [our own Baluba-Tshokwe province]." Sporadic fighting continued in North Katanga throughout the secession period; Tshombe never succeeded in regaining control over large parts of the Balubakat zones.

The Conakat self-determination argument was greatly weakened by the Baluba-Tshokwe dissidence, and particularly by the Balubakat "secession" from Katanga to form a new province, loyal to the Congo. Tshombe resisted this initiative in precisely the same way that Lumumba had reacted to the original Conakat secession—attempting to crush it by force, even at the cost of bloody massacres. The principle of self-determination had its limits for the Conakat, too.

Katanga at Flood Tide

The period from Lumumba's downfall in September, 1960, until March, 1961, represented the high-water mark of the secession. In September, 1960, it seemed certain that neither Leopoldville nor the UN could or would force Katanga to its knees. During this period of prosperity, when order and stability in Katanga (if we avert our eyes from the carnage in the Baluba zones) seemed to contrast starkly with the disorder and demoralization in Leopoldville, two fundamental options appeared to exist for Katanga leadership:

(1) To seek actively reunification of the Congo on Katanga terms, that is, a loose confederation.

(2) To take advantage of the respite to consolidate the secession on all fronts and make independence permanent.

Historians will long debate which of these policies was in fact pursued; an uncertain vector of ambiguity enters because the first option was both policy and propaganda. With international recognition impossible to achieve, the pressures from the outside world for reunification could only be warded off by appearing to accept the principle of reentry into the Congo—always providing that a somewhat elastic string of conditions were met. On July 18, 1960, Tshombe first spoke of the desirability of a new confederal Congo, constructed from Elisabethville; Belgian Foreign Minister Wigny immediately responded favorably, cabling the chief of the Belgian technical assistance mission, "All rallying of other Congo provinces to Katanga is to be encouraged, although obviously with discretion." Once Lumumba had been ousted from power in Leopoldville, a formula for reunification was certainly desired by the Belgian government; the top executives in corporate home offices in Brussels likewise appeared to favor some such plan. On the other hand, the intransigent wing of the Katanga government (Munongo-Kibwe) and the "ultras" in the European community opposed any dilution of Katanga "independence."

Meanwhile, the problem of "reunification" had been complicated by the emergence of a rival "central government" in Stanleyville. Neither Lumumba nor his backers had ever accepted the legality of his removal from office. The moderate coalition that succeeded him in Leopoldville had placed Lumumba under arrest, but in November, 1960, his supporters proclaimed the establishment of a Lumumbist government in Stanleyville. The deposed Prime Minister proved a most difficult prisoner; twice he nearly escaped his captors. Leopoldville authorities searched desperately for a safe repository; on January 17, 1961, he was placed aboard a plane bound for Elisabethville with two of his close collaborators. Shortly after their arrival, the three were assassinated, with Interior Minister Munongo, by all accounts, playing a central role. The deaths were concealed for nearly four weeks, then a story was concocted that the prisoners had escaped and been recognized and slain by indignant villagers. Munongo, announcing the official version at a press conference, hardly seemed to expect anyone to believe it:

> I would be lying if I said that the decease of Lumumba saddens me. You know my sentiments towards him; he is a common criminal, responsible for the deaths of thousands in Katanga, tens of thousands in Kasai, without counting the persecutions and exterminations in Orientale and Kivu . . . .
>
> We will be accused of having assassinated them. I reply: Prove it!
>
> . . . I will recall here the cases of Sacco and Vannetti [sic], Julius and Ethel Rosenberg, even Caryl Chessman in the United States. I don't want to compare them to Lumumba and his accomplices, nor judge their guilt or innocence. I intend simply to recall that, in these celebrated cases, public opinion throughout the world . . . persistently demanded a pardon for the condemned. In vain. The United States acted anyway, feeling that the matter was uniquely within its jurisdiction.

The confirmation of Lumumba's death provoked a massive shock wave of indignation throughout Africa—and of manipulated indignation in the Soviet bloc. Under the backlash of this event, the UN Security Council met on February 21 and adopted a new policy which in the long run, gradually expanded by implementation, was to prove the end of Katanga "independence." Its key passages read:

> [The Security Council]
>
> Urges that the United Nations take immediately all appropriate measures to prevent the occurrence of civil war in the Congo, including arrangements for cease-fires, the halting of all military operations, the prevention of clashes and the *use of force, if necessary, in the last resort.* [Italics added.]
>
> Urges that measures be taken for the immediate withdrawal and evacuation from the Congo of all Belgian and other foreign military and para-military personnel and political advisers not under United Nations command, and mercenaries.

The resolution, which now specifically authorized the use of force and as a corollary the forcible removal of the European councilors, initially caused greater panic in Leopoldville than Elisabethville, as it was accompanied by news that Stanleyville troops were making spectacular advances toward Leopoldville. The Leopoldville coalition now seemed disposed to pay whatever price was necessary for a Katanga alliance against Stanleyville. The Leopoldville leaders accordingly agreed to attend a Round Table Conference to be organized in Tananarive, Madagascar, at the beginning of March, 1961, to establish a confederal Congo on Katanga terms. Stanleyville, although invited, refused to attend the Tananarive sessions.

Tananarive was Tshombe's supreme triumph. The demoralized Leopoldville delegation unanimously accepted the Conakat blueprint for a "confederation" whose central organs would have limited powers in the field of foreign affairs and external trade, whose decisions would all require unanimity, and whose budget would be met by voluntary provincial contributions. Tshombe returned to a tumultuous Elisabethville welcome; Katanga was indeed at high water-mark, and "victory" had never seemed so close. Under this plan, Katanga autonomy would be almost complete. Plans were laid for a follow-up conference to fill in the details of the Tananarive accords.

Triumph to Isolation: The Road to Lovanium

The victory celebrations were hardly over when several of the Leopoldville delegates repudiated the accords. The patent absurdity of trying to govern tropical Africa's largest state by such emasculated central institutions dawned on many. The Stanleyville offensive toward Leopoldville proved to have been largely a mirage; relations between UN officials and Leopoldville took a turn for the better. When the succeeding Round Table was convened at Coquilhatville (a river town three hundred miles upstream from Leopoldville) on April 23, the atmosphere was totally transformed. Leopoldville no longer felt under an immediate threat. The Tananarive accords were quickly abandoned as a basis for discussion; when Tshombe tried to walk out in protest, he was arrested in an improvised coup by the local Congo army detachment. After some hesitation, Leopoldville decided to keep Tshombe in its grasp and transferred him to the capital.

For the first time since September, 1960, Katanga began to sense itself in a weakened position; the noose of isolation was slowly closing. Tshombe, after two months of champagne confinement in a comfortable and abundantly supplied villa in Leopoldville, was released on June 22 after signing an eleven-point agreement with the central government, which represented an across-the-board capitulation to Leopoldville positions. Safely back in Elisabethville, he quickly let it be known that the agreements were simply to be submitted for discussion to his cabinet, not considered as binding.

But while Tshombe evaded these accords, another decisive development placed Katanga in total isolation. The Congolese Parliament was reconvened, sequestered in the imposing new buildings of Lovanium University outside Leopoldville; a tight UN guard sealed off the hilltop premises to protect the deputies against any external influence or intimidation. Tshombe reneged on his promise to send the Conakat deputies, so the Leopoldville and Stanleyville groups met alone. On August 2 a new national government, headed by Cyrille Adoula, received a unanimous vote of confidence. The United Nations and a reunited central government, supported by all parts of the country except southern Katanga, now turned their attention to the runaway province.

The UN Strikes: Operation Rumpunch

Section A (2) of the February 21 Security Council resolution had called for removal of mercenaries and political advisers; elsewhere, the resolution had authorized the "use of force, if necessary, in the last resort." The next step, UN authorities decided, was to bring Conakat leaders to reason by removing the apparent source of unreasonable views; let but the evil councilors surrounding the Conakat be purged, and all would be well.

But what is a "political adviser"? Skin pigmentation was an inadequate criterion; it could not be assumed that every European was an occult adviser. On the other hand, many of the most influential non-Africans did not hold formal titles in the Katanga government; they ran local businesses, were doctors and lawyers, or, in some cases, Union Minière executives. Not all Europeans employed by the Katanga government were really advisers; in fact, 750 Belgians (not counting teachers) served as Katanga functionaries —incidentally, a higher number than had been employed by the colonial province. Also, not all advice was "evil"; some councilors were preaching reconciliation. Finally the UN's capacity to detect the presence of political advisers was limited. The UN had no secret service capable of ferreting out the clandestine operators. Also, there was no UN staff in the important towns of Jadotville and Kolwezi. Even if advisers were expelled from Elisabethville, dozens of tracks led across the Rhodesian frontier back into Katanga.

The Belgian government was prepared to cooperate in a purge, provided that it was a single swoop and did not have the character of a witch hunt. Over the summer months of 1961 a little list was drawn up in consultation with Brussels, Léopoldville, and Katanga authorities. In charge of the Katanga list was Albert Nyembo, secretary of state for the Civil Service in the Conakat government. To the astonishment of UN authorities, the longest expulsion list of all was produced by—Albert Nyembo. UN representative O'Brien records in his unusually candid—and indiscreet—autobiographical account, *To Katanga and Back* (p. 182), their negotiations:

> On the first day we produced our list, mainly *chefs de cabinet* of the principal Ministers . . . . On the second day M. Nyembo and his colleagues agreed, with little demur, to these names. Then M. Nyembo asked whether they, the Katangese, had a right to suggest names? . . . We read them paragraph A.2—immediate withdrawal and evacuation of all foreign and political advisors, Belgian or other. M. Nyembo and his friends seemed, from their smiles, to think paragraph A.2 rather well drafted. M. Nyembo himself favored an inclusive interpretation of this paragraph. "All Belgians," he said with simplicity, "are political advisors." His colleagues, the nominal heads of the various civil departments, eagerly corroborated this; each had his own list of Belgians who, they said, gave them political advice . . . . M. Nyembo went to the door and satisfied himself that there was no one in the outer office. "Add," he said as he came back, "my *chef de cabinet,* M. B[rodur]."

On August 4, as a first step, eleven political advisers, mainly *chefs de cabinet* in the ministries, were expelled; a piecemeal removal of a handful of turbulent Elisabethville white residents, such as Albert Decoster, editor of the *Echo du Katanga,* followed. The next target: 443 "mercenaries" and European officers serving with the Katanga gendarmerie. This step, mooted for several weeks, seemed likely to provoke sharper resistance from Katanga authorities, as paralysis of the Katanga armed forces could only lead to the quick collapse of the secession. Accordingly, plans for Operation Rumpunch were prepared by Indian General Raja, commander of UN forces in Katanga. The plan was to occupy before dawn the radio and post office, in order to block any appeals for popular resistance and to interrupt telephonic communications, and temporarily arrest Munongo, the leader most likely to resist decisively.

Rumpunch was smoothly executed. Before dawn on August 28, the post office, radio, and Munongo were in UN hands. The catch was 338 mercenaries and European officers. By midafternoon, on the basis of pledges by the Belgian consul that he himself would see to the completion of the operation as far as the Belgians were concerned, the operation was halted. However, this promise was later "clarified" as only applicable to regular

Belgian army officers seconded to the gendarmerie, not the 175 Belgian mercenaries. On September 8, 105 were still missing, including most of the irreconcilables. And, of course, expulsion merely meant being placed on a plane for Europe; the UN had no means of preventing the expellees from filtering back into Katanga along one of the numerous mercenary trails via Rhodesia.

Mercenary Revenge: Operation Morthor

Tension mounted rapidly. Animosity toward the UN sharpened; the Katanga radio, now returned by the UN to Katanga authorities, maintained that Indian UN troops were raping and pillaging or, alternatively, scheming to evict the Europeans and supplant them as settlers. UN troops and the American consulate were stoned by Conakat "youth." On September 10 O'Brien's top aide, Michel Tombelaine, was arrested, presumably to be held as a hostage.

The next day Mahmoud Khiari, chief of UN Civil Operations in the Congo, arrived in Elisabethville. In his briefcase was an invitation for Tshombe to come to Leopoldville for a meeting with Hammarskjöld, who was arriving from New York on September 13. Tshombe invited Mr. H to come to Elisabethville instead. Khiari, meeting alone later with O'Brien and his staff, produced another document from his briefcase:

REPUBLIC OF THE CONGO

PRO JUSTITIA

Warrant for Arrest

. . . . In view of the proceedings instituted against: Tshombe, Moise; Munongo, Godefroid; Kimba, Evariste; Kibwe, Jean; Mutaka-wa-Dilomba [President of Katanga assembly]; charged with: Sedition, Murder, Arbitrary Arrests and Bodily Torture, crimes envisaged in and punishable under Articles 43, 44, 45, 67, 180, 189, 192, 193 of the Penal Code;

Pursuant to the ministerial decrees of 6 September 1961;

Pursuant to the Parliamentary Resolutions of 8 and 9 September 1961;

As there exists against the aforesaid grave evidence of guilt and as there is reason to fear that they may attempt to evade arrest;

Request and require that the aforesaid be arrested and produced before us;

Requests all commanders of the armed forces to assist in the carrying out of the present warrant.

Leopoldville, September 9, 1961
For the Ministry of Justice[4]

[4] O'Brien, p. 248.

This remarkable document highlights the UN dilemma in coping with Katanga. UN operators in the field, especially O'Brien and his staff in Elisabethville, were intensely frustrated by their inability to coax or cajole Tshombe back into the national fold and irritated by the open hostility of most of the white community in Elisabethville and by the arrogance of the mercenaries. Meanwhile, in New York the UN Secretariat was subjected to enormous and conflicting pressures. The Soviet bloc had bitterly attacked Hammarskjöld and the Secretariat in the 1960 session of the General Assembly, and he had only been saved by support from the smaller states. Yet many of the Afro-Asian powers were losing patience with the apparent inability of the UN to put Tshombe in his place as a provincial leader, not head of an "independent" state. The 1961 session of the General Assembly was scheduled to open in late September, and stormy debates were in prospect unless the Katanga problem were eliminated by that time. And yet Mr. H was sharply limited by his mandate, which authorized force only to remove mercenaries and advisers or to prevent civil war. The Western powers, especially Britain, Belgium, and France, were equally opposed to offensive action against Katanga without clear authorization by the Security Council.

To execute the arrest warrant issued by the central government against the top Katanga leadership seemed a way out to some—but apparently not to all—of the UN field staff in the Congo and Katanga. If by a sudden coup Katanga resistance could be ended, the legal problems of interpreting the mandate would become academic; in any case, the move was likely to be approved by an overwhelming majority of the UN General Assembly. As O'Brien suggests in his account of the September drama, it would have been embarrassing to have the coup occur after Hammarskjöld arrived in the Congo for the purpose of negotiating. Accordingly, plans for Operation Morthor were laid to go into effect at dawn September 13, while the plane carrying Mr. H from New York was in the air. Basically the plan was the same as Rumpunch, but the real object—to liquidate the secession—was much broader. Tshombe's residence was to be surrounded, but he was not to be arrested at first. The others whose names were on the arrest warrant were to be seized, if possible. The radio and post office again were to be occupied, and the security police and Information Ministry offices raided, with the files seized.

Morthor, however, had some flaws:

(1) *In planning:* Success depended absolutely on the capacity to secure the key points and persons quickly and without resistance. While Rumpunch was a complete surprise, the imminence of Morthor had been widely rumored. No plans were made beyond the occupation of Elisabethville; except for a lone Irish company in Jadotville, there were no UN troops in southern Katanga. Unless the leaders were seized and agreed to surrender, the operation was bound to fail.

(2) *In execution:* The key to Morthor was confining Tshombe to his

residence, convincing him that the game was over, and persuading him to broadcast an appeal for his gendarmerie not to resist and a proclamation of the end of the secession. Yet, inexplicably, Tshombe's palace was left unguarded for four hours at the beginning of the operation—which enabled him to disappear.

(3) *In Secretariat authorization:* Hammarskjöld, scheduled to arrive in Leopoldville later in the day of September 13, had not been informed about Morthor. Further, Sture Linner, supreme UN commander in the Congo, although having approved one version of Morthor, had been unaware that his assistant Khiari had delivered the arrest warrants to O'Brien.

(4) *In Security Council authorization:* The February 21 resolution clearly covered Rumpunch and the removal of mercenaries. But Morthor had a different objective: to terminate the secession by force. The only possible justification was the mandate "to prevent the occurrence of civil war," and a novel and extended interpretation of Security Council intent was required to explain why the UN was now doing what it had refused to undertake for Lumumba in 1960—a refusal for which it had won a vote of confidence.

Of the five leaders cited in the warrant, only Kibwe was arrested. Units of the Katanga gendarmerie, to everyone's surprise, put up stiff resistance at the radio and post office. UN troops were then subjected to sniping attacks from mercenaries and gendarmes; a lone Katanga jet strafed and harassed UN units. A stray UN mortar shell hit a hospital; other accidents of house-to-house city warfare quickly stirred up worldwide indignation. When the Irish company at Jadotville was forced to surrender, it was clear that Morthor was a disastrous defeat.

Making matters worse was a highly inaccurate "explanation" of Morthor put out by the UN in Leopoldville on September 14, after Hammarskjöld's arrival. United Nations document S/4940, paragraph 15, provided the following account of the genesis of Morthor:

> In the early hours of September 13th, the UN forces therefore took security precautions similar to those applied on August 28th, and deemed necessary to prevent inflammatory broadcasts or other threats to the maintenance of law and order, while the UN resumed carrying out its task of apprehending and evacuating foreign military and paramilitary personnel.
> At this point, an alert was set since arson was discovered at the UN garage. As the UN troops were proceeding toward the garage premises, fire was opened on them from the building where a number of foreign officers are known to be staying. UN troops were subsequently also resisted and fired at as they were deploying toward key points or while they were guarding installations in the city.

This tale had several defects: There was neither a UN garage as such in Elisabethville nor any known fire in any other garage early on September

13. More important, the real purpose of the operation, in the mind of its executors, was to bring the secession to an end; an effort to use the cover story that the purposes were the same as Rumpunch strained the truth too far for credibility. O'Brien's premature announcement the morning of September 13 that "the secession is over" did not make the Leopoldville statement any more plausible.

Hammarskjöld's last days were spent under enormous pressure. In Leopoldville, the British Ambassador informed him that unless the fighting was stopped forthwith and an adequate explanation provided, Her Majesty's government would remove all support from the UN Congo operation and, by implication, from the Secretary-General. With France and the Soviet Union already opposed to him, he could hardly afford the loss of support of a third permanent member of the Security Council. At 5 P.M. on September 17 he boarded a UN aircraft bound for a Rhodesian rendezvous with Tshombe to make peace—and to abandon Morthor's objective of forcing Tshombe to capitulate. Near midnight, the plane established radio contact with the Ndola tower, just over the Rhodesian border. A few minutes later the plane crashed into a wooded hill a few miles from town, and all those aboard were killed.

Round Two: UN Versus Katanga

Katanga had another moment of euphoria. After Hammarskjöld's death, the UN negotiated a cease-fire with Tshombe, and secession had a new reprieve. But pressures soon began mounting again. On November 24 the Security Council passed a tougher resolution on Katanga, reaffirming its authorization of force for removal of mercenaries and deploring the prolongation of the secession—but without explicitly broadening the authorization for the use of force. On November 28 two senior UN functionaries were kidnapped and beaten by Katanga gendarmes—while en route to a reception by the American consulate in honor of Senator Dodd, the voice of Katanga in the United States Senate. On December 2 fighting broke out between Indian UN troops and the gendarmes at Elisabethville airport. Katanga forces set up roadblocks at several key passages; when they refused to remove the roadblocks, Swedish and Indian troops eliminated them by force. Sporadic fighting took place in Elisabethville until December 19. This time the UN did not seem to have deliberately planned the hostilities, but rather to have reacted in self-defense to a Katanga effort to limit what had come to be considered an established UN right: freedom of movement for its troops in Elisabethville.

But now there was no effort to seize the Katanga leaders. The official explanations, although placed under a cloud by the equivocations of September, this time were closer to the truth. And this time the Katanga was not to win an easy psychological victory; UN forces succeeded in taking the key points in Elisabethville and in regaining their freedom of movement. On December 15 Tshombe cabled President Kennedy indicating that he wanted to negotiate various outstanding problems with Adoula. A meeting at Kitona, near the mouth of the Congo River, was quickly arranged for December 20; the UN agreed to cease fire from the moment that Tshombe's plane was en route toward the conference.

Kitona Accords: Another Mirage

With American Ambassador to Leopoldville, Edmond Gullion, playing a key mediating role, Tshombe and Adoula signed an eight-point agreement after two days of intensive discussions. Now it was Leopoldville's turn for short-lived euphoria; the agreement seemed to be a clear pledge by Katanga to rejoin the Congo as a province, on the basis of the provisional constitution. But, back in Elisabethville, Tshombe announced that the Katanga Council of Ministers had decided to submit the Kitona accords to the Katanga assembly for "further consideration."

It was not until February 15 that this consideration was completed. A resolution was adopted indicating that the Kitona agreements "could serve as a basis for discussion" and authorizing the government to carry out further discussions. Tshombe, after obtaining broad guarantees as to his personal security from the UN, left for Leopoldville on March 15.

Dance of the Cranes: The Tshombe-Adoula Talks

Between March 18 and June 26, 1962, arduous negotiations were carried forward between Adoula and Tshombe on the constitutional basis for a reunification. The Katanga proposals adhered closely to the "spirit of Tananarive," which conceded only a limited and probably unworkable confederal link. For Tshombe, Katanga was a sovereign state preparing to abandon a portion of its authority; for Adoula, Katanga was a province that had left the national community and had to rejoin as if there had never been an "independent" Katanga. The provisional constitution bequeathed by Belgium had to be the starting point for any solution, although Adoula was prepared to make concessions toward provincial autonomy.

The UN exerted strong pressures on both participants throughout the talks and actively played a mediating role. The cost of the Congo operation was becoming a serious financial burden and threatened literally to bankrupt the organization. The same sense of urgency was shared by the United States, Belgium, and Britain—the principal influential parties at this juncture. International pressure was exerted in favor of any solution that could be politically feasible for the Adoula government.

However, the gap between the two positions proved too great to overcome. Although headway had been made on some points, on June 26 the negotiations totally collapsed; the two parties could not even agree on a final press communiqué announcing failure.

Toward the Climax: The U Thant Plan

Pressures were rapidly growing. All hopes for any solution negotiated directly between the participants now vanished. The United States, deeply committed to support of the Adoula government and covering most of the $100 million annual UN bill, feared that the moderate coalition headed by Adoula could not survive without an early end to the Katanga crisis, and that the alternative would be a radical, probably militantly anti-Western regime. The UN Secretariat felt that it could not continue to be bogged down in a ruinous stalemate; either a humiliating failure would have to be conceded, and the Congo left to its own devices, or more vigorous action taken. Belgium likewise wanted a solution which would permit resumption of close relations with Leopoldville without damaging the economic machine in Katanga; continuation of the secession was a cul-de-sac. Britain was more reserved. The Rhodesia lobby was influential in the right wing of the ruling Conservative Party; however, the British government was reaching the conclusion that the Federation of Rhodesia and Nyasaland was not viable in its existing form, and the Katanga buffer was of less interest than it had been in 1960.

Thus was born the "U Thant Plan," published August 10. This provided for the preparation of a draft constitution by UN experts on the basis of the Tshombe-Adoula discussions, an equitable division of tax revenues, integration of all armed forces, a general amnesty, and participation of Conakat representatives in the Adoula government.

The pattern of earlier Tshombe "agreements" seemed to be repeated; on September 3 Tshombe "accepted" the plan and noted "with enthusiasm the decision to provide the Congo with a federal constitution." Mixed Katanga-Leopoldville commissions resumed work on the thorny questions of military, foreign exchange, and fiscal policy. Again, these quickly bogged down. U Thant tried one final time to relaunch the negotiations at the beginning of November, but without success.

By December, 1962, the state of tension in Katanga again reached an apogee. Both sides expected round three between the gendarmerie and the UN to begin at any moment. On Christmas Eve the igniting spark fell: the UN accused the gendarmes of shooting down a UN helicopter, killing an Indian officer. Katanga maintained that the helicopter had fired on their positions. Road barriers were again set up by the gendarmerie; again the UN removed them by force. On December 28 Tshombe made an incendiary speech, calling on the whole population to rise up against the UN, using "traps, poison, spears, and poisoned arrows"; at the same time, he threatened to blow up Katanga's dams and processing plants.

This time the UN was ready, and it was determined to pursue the operation to a conclusive finish. For the first time UN troops went beyond the mere occupation of key points in Elisabethville; on December 29 Irish and Ethiopian troops moved towards Kipushi on the Rhodesian frontier; Swedish fighter planes destroyed the Katanga "air force" on the ground. In a radio appeal to the population, UN spokesmen declared: "The cause for which Tshombe has armed you is that of foreign interests, which maintain the secession to profit from your natural wealth."

On December 31 a UN column headed for Jadotville, where mercenaries and gendarmes had regrouped after fleeing from Elisabethville. U Thant announced that "the operation which began on the afternoon of December 28, destined to remove all the road blocks of the Katanga gendarmerie in the Elisabethville area, is now terminated." He gave Katanga fifteen days to move forward with the application of the U Thant Plan "before envisaging other measures."

Again, the course of Katanga history was changed by what almost certainly was a local initiative of UN authorities on the spot, not specifically ordered from New York. The principal actors have not joined O'Brien in producing their autobiographic accounts, so the details remain more obscure; nonetheless, it is clear that the day after the U Thant statement indicating that the operation was for the time being terminated, the UN column resumed its march towards Jadotville. A subsequent UN report referred to "grave inadequacies in communication and coordination between the UN Secretariat in New York, the headquarters in Leopoldville, and the military detachments in the field."

The fact remains that Jadotville was taken without serious resistance on January 3.

The Credibility of a Deterrent

The promised guerrilla warfare by village warriors did not materialize. But would Tshombe—or Munongo—carry out the threatened scorched earth policy? The two great hydroelectric dams, holding back billions of gallons of water, were known to be mined, although no one was certain whether the demolition preparations were thorough enough to completely destroy the dams. To blow them up would not only have caused hundreds of millions of dollars in damage to the dam and turbines, but would have sent a wall of water surging downstream, which would have destroyed many villages and caused serious flooding far downstream. And the highly automated, multimillion dollar Union Minière copper processing installations at

Katanga's third largest city, Kolwezi, were also vulnerable to sabotage. The sabotage threat had been frequently invoked by Katanga authorities and had been one of the major factors causing the UN to fear a final showdown of force. Would the Katanga leadership, in a final desperate act, commit economic suicide and destroy the livelihood of their own populations? This was hardly a rational deterrent, but who could calculate the rationality of Munongo? Who could be certain one of the "ultras" in the European community might not find this last melodramatic gesture profitable?

The UN halted at Jadotville, and the world waited. On January 14, 1963, at 9 A.M., Tshombe and his ministers announced at Kolwezi that they "were prepared to declare before the world that the secession was terminated."

Conclusions: The Politics of Separatism

Katanga was removed from the agenda of world crisis. What lessons can be drawn from the Katanga secession, now that the intense emotional reactions that it generated have begun to wane?

In the first place, the enormity of the task of nation-building in the larger tropical African states is clearly shown. In the Congo, national integration started virtually from scratch in 1960; the emergent African leadership in Elisabethville had never met their counterparts in Leopoldville or Stanleyville. Mutual suspicion was strong; Katanga leaders felt little stake in the Congo. Within Katanga itself, the sudden introduction of political competition, beginning in 1957, rapidly produced deep divisions within the African community, with relatively prosperous "strangers" resented by "authentic Katangans," and Baluba from northern Katanga suspicious of the settler-mining company associations of the southern Katangans. An important part of the pressure for secession was quite independent of European interests and simply reflected the fragility of most new African states. Indeed, one reason many African leaders felt so strongly on the Katanga issue was that many other states have potential Katangas—regions poorly integrated into the new nation or relatively well endowed with natural resources compared to the rest of the country. In the last decade, threats of secession have been openly made by groups or regions in Ivory Coast, Chad, Nigeria, Ethiopia, Uganda, Kenya, and Sudan; it is small wonder that there is keen sensitivity to the threat of separatism.

Secondly, the problems of transition to independence in Katanga were compounded by the presence of a numerically small but economically and politically important white community, and the powerful mining giant, Union Minière. Both the settlers and the corporation were accustomed to having their privileges protected by a compliant colonial regime. The sudden prospect of independence for the Congo produced acute uncertainty; how could the future be secured? The advent to power of a radical nationalist government in Leopoldville appeared to confirm the worst fears of Katanga Europeans. Enthusiastic support for secessionist tendencies in the new Katanga government was hardly surprising, and it was of decisive importance in aiding the secession to consolidate itself in the early days. Katanga autonomy, after all, was an old European dream—although the assumption in the past had always been that an autonomous Katanga would be directly ruled by its white community, rather than by Katanga Africans. But once "independence" had been achieved, the settlers and even Union Minière found themselves contending with international forces they were not in a position to influence. As long as the future of the Congo was merely debated in Belgian colonial circles, companies and settlers had a large voice. But once Katanga became the arena for the competing interests of the Soviet bloc, Afro-Asian states, the United States, and the United Nations, Union Minière became only one of a large number of actors.

Thirdly, the limitations to the doctrine of self-determination were thrown into sharp relief. Although few would today dispute the proposition that African peoples should have the right to rule themselves, the unspoken corollary is that self-rule must be within the framework of the existing territorial divisions—divisions imposed arbitrarily by the colonial powers during the partition of Africa in the late nineteenth century. Once the principle of self-determination for every region or ethnic group is admitted, there is virtually no end to the potential for fragmentation. Katanga seceded from the Congo; northern Katanga in turn seceded from Katanga. The small scale of many African states already constitutes a major obstacle to the rapid economic development so earnestly desired by Africa's new elites; were there to be a further proliferation of microstates, the possibility of progress would virtually evaporate. However unsatisfactory and artificial present boundaries may be, nearly all African leaders agree that there is no alternative to their maintenance (Somalia, with irredentist claims to parts of Kenya, Ethiopia, and French Somaliland is the major exception). Further, boundary reshuffling or separation of portions of states almost inevitably means an international crisis—and any crisis in today's world draws into its vortex the great powers and their global competition.

Thus, neither the world community nor African states can accept the extension of the principle of self-determination to regions or ethnic groups. The Katanga case showed that a state only becomes a state if it is able to secure recognition of its independence from the world at large. The failure to obtain recognition by any country was a crucial factor in the eventual downfall of the secessionist regime. The world at large, through the United Nations, finally acted to coerce Katanga back into the Congolese framework.

If self-determination for regions is to be excluded, can an adequate substitute be found in large states like the Congo through a federal constitution, which provides for some satisfaction for localist impulses through loose institutional structures? Many African nationalists feel that such compromises merely provide an opportunity for fragmenting forces to strengthen themselves at the expense of nation-building. And yet, in states like Nigeria and the Congo, some compromise with regionalism appears the only way to hold the country together at all.

Finally, the Katanga experience raises a host of perplexing questions about the possible role of the United Nations in mediating conflicting aims and objectives in an African crisis. Radical African states considered Tshombe a mortal danger for African independence everywhere. He was seen, rightly or wrongly, as the servile instrument of European mining and settler interests and, subsequently, as the assassin of Patrice Lumumba, the symbol of radical African nationalism. If Tshombe were permitted to succeed, they felt, no independent African state would be secure against the machinations of neocolonialist and imperialist interests. Considerable bitterness developed among these states over the hesitations and subtle legalisms of the UN in its dealings with Katanga; the cause of African freedom would have been greatly advanced, in this view, had the decisive action of January, 1963, been taken in August, 1960.

The Soviet bloc and Western powers also placed strong pressures on the UN Secretariat on its Katanga policy. In September, 1960, Soviet Premier Khrushchev himself opened a full-scale assault on Hammarskjöld for his Congo policy generally. Although the Soviets were unsuccessful in trying to force Hammarskjöld out of office or to achieve major structural changes in the UN, the Secretariat was necessarily keenly aware of the barrage of criticism from the Soviet side. On the Western side, there were some divergences between American, British, and Belgian views, but all shared a strong reluctance to see the UN embark upon a policy of force until all possibilities of ending the Katanga secession by negotiations had been exhausted. In 1960 suspicions of the volatile Lumumba seemed to the West to dictate a cautious outlook toward coercing Katanga back under the control of the Lumumba government.

The great disparity in viewpoints among UN member nations toward coping with the Katanga secession resulted in compromise resolutions which uusally contained a good deal of vagueness and were open to differing interpretations. This made even more difficult the task of the Secretariat in choosing an interpretation which was acceptable to as broad a spectrum of UN members as possible. The conflicting pressures and divergent viewpoints were inevitably reflected within the UN staff itself. These strains were compounded by the complexity of the task of maintaining adequate controls and responsibility in an international civil service and a multinational peacekeeping force. Important initiatives were taken by field representatives without full clearance from the Secretary-General, both in Operation Morthor and in the final advance on Jadotville in January, 1963. Although the great majority of UN members no doubt approved these moves, they constitute disturbing precedents. If the UN mechanism is to play a key role in international crisis situations, the world cannot afford any uncertainty as to where the critical decisions will be made, or whether field commanders of peace-keeping forces can be fully controlled.

And yet, despite these shortcomings, the UN was the decisive factor in restoring unity to the Congo. The UN did cushion the impact of great power rivalries upon the Katanga crisis. The UN did ensure that the vital economic infrastructure of the Copperbelt remained intact, preserving for the Congo at least the possibility of progress.

Postscript: Tshombe's Revenge?

Moise Tshombe was a thoroughly defeated man in January, 1963. In June of that year he went into exile, fearing that his arrest was imminent; his political influence even in Katanga was at a low ebb. But in July, 1964, in one of history's most spectacular comebacks, Tshombe was designated Prime Minister of the Congo. Like the Jeffersonians in the early days of the American Republic, the states' righters in opposition became centralizers once in power. In the first six months of his stewardship in Leopoldville, Tshombe, with Munongo again his right hand man as central Minister of Interior, moved to consolidate central authority and put down a rebellion which swept the northeastern quadrant of the country. The memory elsewhere in Africa of his role in the Katanga secession and in Lumumba's death embittered the Congo's relations with other African states; for many African leaders, Tshombe was still the man of Union Minière. The violent antipathy toward Tshombe in many quarters was never overcome; but Tshombe may yet go down in history as a man whose final contribution was to help build a Congolese nation rather than to help destroy it before it was born.

Study Questions

1. Was the Katanga secession inevitable? What steps might have been taken to avoid its occurrence?

2. Was the secession in any sense legitimate? Are there circumstances in which it might have been considered a proper exercise of the right of self-determination? What are the limits of self-determination in Africa?

3. What role can and should expatriate minorities play in independent African states?

4. Assume that you are a member of the Board of Directors of Union Minierè in 1960. How would you have balanced your obligations to company shareholders on the one hand and to the country in which the company conducted its operations on the other? Are there any circumstances in which

foreign-owned companies are justified in trying to influence political outcomes?

5. What is the balance sheet on the UN role in the Katanga crisis? Discuss the positive contributions and the liabilities of the UN as a mechanism for resolving crisis situations in Africa. Might there have been a more appropriate way to seal off the Congo from great-power competition and to assist in mediating the conflict?

Selected Bibliography

The abundant documentation produced by the United Nations has been conveniently collected and published in three volumes by the Belgian foreign affairs journal, *Chronique de Politique Etrangère,* as "La Crise Congolaise" (XIII, 4–6, July–Nov., 1960); "Evolution de la Crise Congolaise" (XIV, 5–6 Sept.–Nov., 1961); and "L'O.N.U. et le Congo" (XV, 4–6, July–Nov., 1962). U.N. documents cited in this case study may be found in these volumes.

The outstanding work on the subject is J. Gérard-Libois, *Sécession au Katanga* (Brussels: CRISP, 1963). The various other documentary studies of the Congo published by CRISP constitute an invaluable and highly trustworthy guide; these include *Congo 1959, Congo 1960* (3 vols.), *Congo 1961,* and *Congo 1962*. Belgian and Congolese documents and official statements, except as otherwise cited, may be found in the CRISP collections. The occasional publication, *Courrier Africain,* and the monthly of its sister organization in the Congo, Institut National d'Etudes Politiques, *Etudes Congolaises,* have valuable current material.

The memoirs of former UN chief in Elisabethville, Conor Cruise O'Brien, *To Katanga and Back* (London: Hutchison, 1962), provide an extraordinarily candid, although somewhat controversial, account of events in 1961, especially Rumpunch and Morthor, and the workings of the UN mechanism. On the UN, see also the useful books by Arthur Gavshon, *The Mysterious Death of Dag Hammarskjöld* (New York: Walker, 1962); Joseph P. Lash, *Dag Hammarskjöld* (London: Cassell, 1962); and Arthur Lee Burns and Nina Heathcote, *Peace-keeping by UN Forces from Suez to the Congo* (New York: Praeger, 1963).

Several journalists have published reports; these include Pierre Davister, *Kantanga enjeu du monde* (Brussels: Editions Europe-Afrique, 1960); Davister and Philippe Toussaint, *Croisettes et casques bleus* (Paris: Editions Actuelles, 1962); and Smith Hempstone, *Rebels, Mercenaries, and Dividends: The Katanga Story* (New York: Praeger, 1962), although the last work is marred by many factual errors and doubtful interpretations. Various "mercenaries" have produced their own, obviously highly colored accounts; see Christian Lanciney, *Les Héros sont affreux* (Brussels: Editions Charles Dessart, 1962); Michel Borri, *Nous—ces affreux* (Paris: Editions Galic, 1962); Roger Trinquier *et al., Notre guerre au Katanga* (Paris: Editions de la Pensée Moderne, 1963).

To disentangle the web of ownership on the Copperbelt, see *Morphologie des groupes financiers* (Brussels: CRISP, 1962) and a useful volume by two officials of the Belgian Communist Party, which is accurate in most of its factual information, if tendentious in interpretation, Pierre Joye and Rosine Lewin, *Les Trusts au Congo* (Brussels: Société Populaire d'Editions, 1961). Useful biographical information on Katanga political figures is contained in Pierre Artigue, *Qui sont les leaders congolais?* 2nd ed. (Brussels: Editions Europe-Afrique, 1961).

For an excellent short article dealing with one major aspect of the Katanga problem, see René Lemarchand, "The Limits of Self-Determination: Katanga," *American Political Science Review,* LVI, 2 (June, 1962), 404–16.

For background on the Congo generally, several books are now available. On the emergence of nationalism and the growth of political movements, René Lemarchand, *Political Awakening in the Belgian Congo* (Berkeley: University of California Press, 1964) is excellent. On postindependence developments, see Catherine Hoskyns, *The Congo Since Independence: 1960–1961* (London: Oxford University Press, 1965), and Crawford Young, *Politics in the Congo: Decolonization and Independence* (Princeton, N.J.: Princeton University Press, 1965). For a more compressed but lucid analysis of the Congo as a political system, Edouard Bustin's chapter on the Congo in Gwendolen M. Carter, ed., *Five African States* (Ithaca, N.Y.: Cornell University Press, 1963) is valuable. Colin Legum's description of the 1960 crisis, *Congo Disaster* (Baltimore: Penguin Books, 1961), is also useful.

For a more extensive bibliography, see Catherine Hoskyns, "Sources for a Study of the Congo Since Independence," *Journal of Modern African Studies,* I, 3 (Sept., 1963), 373–82; in addition to the bibliographies in the Bustin chapter and the Young volume.

6

A Hope Deferred

East African Federation, 1963-64

Donald Rothchild

On Wednesday, June 5, 1963, East Africa's "Big Three"—President Julius Nyerere of Tanganyika, Prime Minister A. Milton Obote of Uganda, and Prime Minister Jomo Kenyatta of Kenya—issued a joint communiqué pledging themselves "to the political Federation of East Africa." "We believe," they declared, "that the day of decision has come and to all our people we say there is no more room for slogans and words. This is our day of action." The announcement spread excitement through Africa, for it portended not only the most important scheme of formal union yet proposed by African leaders but also the creation of a significant new force in African affairs.

Uganda, Kenya, and Tanganyika (now Tanzania) cover a contiguous area of 680,000 square miles, an area almost as large as Mexico. All three countries touch on the shores of Lake Victoria, a great inland body of water and a source of fisheries and electric power. They have long had close relations, but up to 1963 their African leaders had resisted a formal union.

Uganda, which gained its independence from British colonial status in October, 1962, is the smallest of the three countries in area and population (7,016,000). Its high altitude provides a largely temperate climate, and its most important cash crops are cotton and coffee. It has developed power resources through the Owen Falls hydroelectric project, opened in 1954, and its major industries include textiles, cement, and copper.

Kenya gained its independence from Britain in December, 1963. It is more than twice Uganda's size and has a population of 8,595,000. Partly because of its long-established white resident population, its industrialization is much greater than that of the other two and includes the production of various consumer goods and the processing of foods. Kenya has a fertile area for raising livestock, dairy herds, wheat, coffee, tea, and pyrethrum in its cool highlands, while sisal and cotton are grown at the medium altitudes. Kenya also possesses one of the two major ports in the East African area, Mombasa.

Tanganyika, once German administered, became a British mandate under the League of Nations after World War I and gained full sovereignty in December, 1961. It is the largest of the three countries in size and population (9,607,000), but the population is densest on the outer perimeter; the vast underdeveloped areas in the center are infested by the tsetse fly or lacking in good soil or adequate rainfall. Tanganyika's main cash crops are sisal, coffee, and cotton, and diamonds provide a steady source of revenue. Industrialization has only recently become a significant factor. Tanganyika possesses East Africa's other main port on the Indian Ocean, Dar es Salaam.

The majority of the people in these three countries are small farmers, but in each country there is a small core of highly trained professional men and women. Their governments also hire foreign experts as a temporary expedient until more of their own nationals have received training. At present a comparatively low percentage of the people are literate by Western standards, but the literacy rate is increasing rapidly as more educational opportunities are offered. Communications from village to village are carried on by radio, newspapers, and word-of-mouth.

The implications of the projected East African federation were chiefly administrative and political, for the basis of a common market already existed. Yet naturally enough it was in the political sphere that most problems could be expected. Each of the three territories had its own political structure and faced its own distinctive political problems.

Uganda's Prime Minister A. Milton Obote, the leader of the nationalist and pan-Africanist Uganda People's Congress (UPC), heads the central government in a quasi-federal system. This political system was agreed upon prior to independence primarily to accommodate the powerful kingdom of Buganda within a country containing many ethnic groups and kingdoms with varying degrees of influence. The other two parties were the largely Catholic Democratic Party (DP) and the party dedicated to maintaining the identity and interests of the Baganda, Kabaka Yekka (KY). Obote, a northerner from Lango, showed his political skill in coming to power through a coalition of UPC and KY, a union dissolved later when KY's unity was broken and Obote felt strong enough to rule on the basis of UPC support alone.

Jomo Kenyatta has for decades been the symbol of indigenous Kenya's struggle for independence. Because his name is known throughout the continent in connection with African independence and Pan-Africanist aims, he was commonly considered the most likely first president of any East African federation. Kenyatta became independent Kenya's first Prime Minister in 1963 through the majority position of his Kenya African National Union (KANU) based primarily on the Kikuyu and Luo tribes. The main opposi-

East Africa, 1966

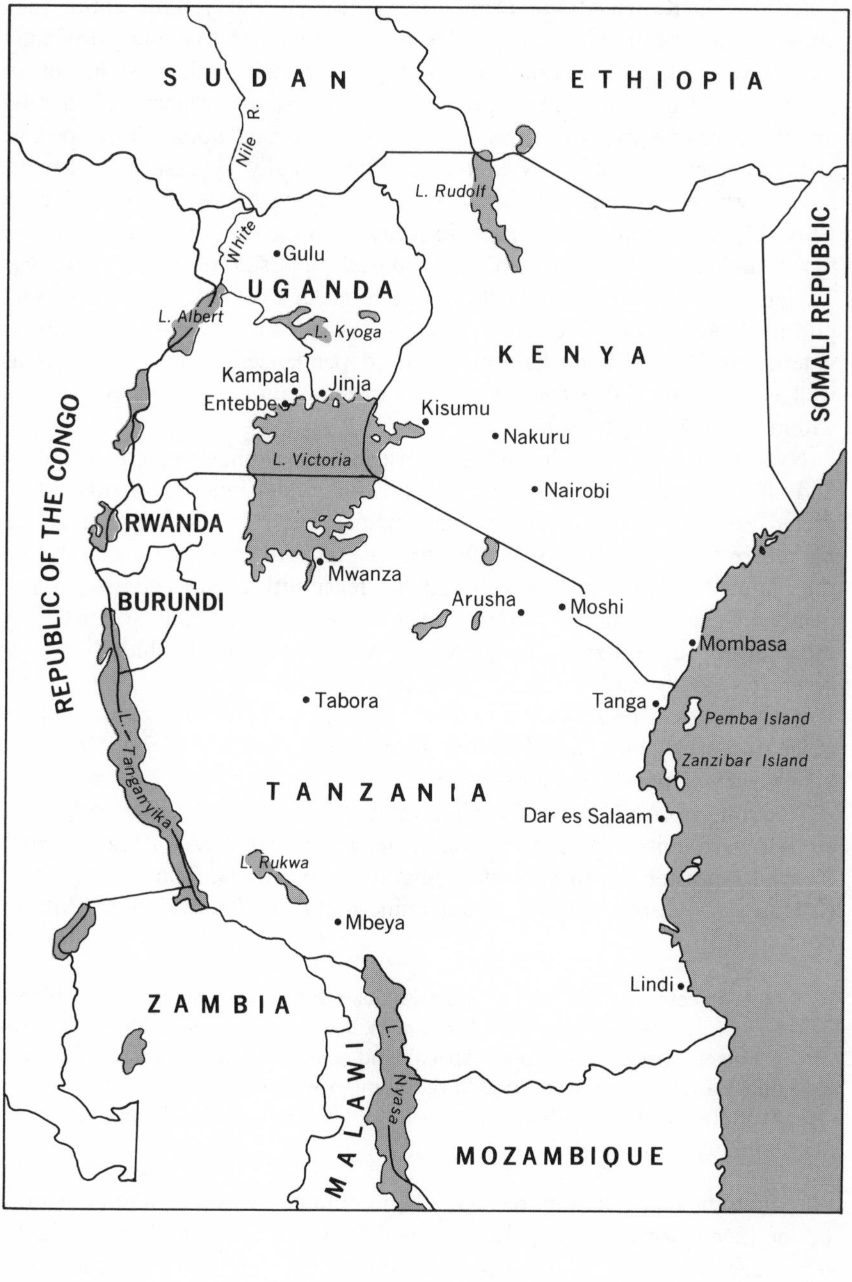

tion party, the Kenya African Democratic Union (KADU), representing such ethnic groups as the Masai, the Kalenjin, and the coastal peoples, originally insisted on a regional or quasi-federal type of constitutional system but, in 1964, it yielded to the general pressure for a one-party system and thereby undercut the effectiveness of regionalism as a restraint upon central power.

In Tanganyika, Julius Nyerere, an intellectually sophisticated leader, heads both government and party—the Tanganyika African National Union (TANU). Unlike his counterparts in Kenya and Uganda, Nyerere has never faced difficulties with an ethnically based opposition, in part because Tanganyika has a broad diversity of ethnic groups rather than one or more powerful ones. Consequently, Nyerere's TANU won a nearly unanimous vote in the 1960 election held prior to independence. Nyerere, a liberal as well as a militant Pan-Africanist, strives to maintain democratic procedures within the single-party system.

Nyerere had long sought an East African federation, so much so that he had offered in 1960 to postpone Tanganyika's independence so that a federated East Africa could emerge from British overrule as a single unit. On his return from the Nairobi "little summit" talks in 1963, he declared that the planned federation demonstrated the feasibility of surrendering sovereignty to achieve greater African unity. "We are not going to waste any more time," he asserted. Tanganyika's Vice-President, Rashidi Kawawa, Nyerere's young and dynamic associate, declared on June 8, 1963, that federation would preserve the region's dignity, give East Africans a bigger voice in world affairs, and "remove foreign powers from Africa." Tanganyikans seemed united in their support.

Kenyatta's KANU, fresh from an election victory in May, welcomed the steps toward unity. "What this country needs, and what East Africa needs," Kenya's Minister for Justice and Constitutional Affairs, Tom Mboya, told its House of Representatives, "is a genuine unity, an effective unity." Mboya continued,

> Our objective is not just an East African Federation alone, but a higher aim . . . . As genuine Pan-Africanists, we intend to move ahead towards a bigger Africa, a stronger Africa, and an Africa in which the Western and Eastern powers will not have room to manoeuvre and intrigue in the exploitation of everything that we have been talking of, dreaming of and thinking about.

Although the Opposition party, KADU, maintained that federation must not be the means for destroying Kenya's regionalism, its leader, Ronald Ngala, introduced a motion in the Kenya legislature on June 27 welcoming East African federal union in 1963.

In Uganda, the dominant forces at the center readily accepted the need for federation. John Kakonge, then secretary-general of the UPC and the leader of the radical faction of the party, said his country fully supported federation, and Minister of Justice Grace Ibingira, a more moderate force within UPC, urged all leaders to give the federation idea their unqualified support "irrespective of our internal political leanings." On July 6, 1963, the Opposition Leader in the National Assembly, Basil Bataringaya, declared, "We must act now . . . . Let us be forward looking and broad minded. . . . Let there be no fears that someone is going to lose his head in trying to form an East African Federation."

The most problematic group was that of the various federal states in Uganda. At the time the leaders issued their communiqué, the governments of the kingdoms of Buganda, Bunyoro, and Toro reserved comment. Nevertheless, they seemed cautious, not intransigent. M. T. Katuramu, the *Katikkiro* (Prime Minister) of Bunyoro, soon issued a statement congratulating the East African leaders for setting up a planning committee to work out a federal constitution. "Let the draft constitution be written, give the people time to study it and opportunity to suggest amendments," he advised. In due course authorities in Ankole and Toro fell into line with Bunyoro. On July 11 the *katikkiros* and ministers of these three western kingdoms, after a two-day conference in Kampala, announced their acceptance in principle of the Nairobi declaration "pending the publication of the draft constitution." Even though the territory of Busoga reserved comment until its *Lukiiko* (Parliament) received the draft constitution, it was clear that the smaller federal states presented little obstacle to the building of an East African federation.

Buganda was the greatest cause for concern, as Baganda suspicions of federation had a long history. During the 1920s the attempt of the Kenya white settlers, supported by the British government, to unite East Africa and thus to spread their control had brought a bitter reaction from the Baganda, who wished to preserve their kingdom's distinctive status. This intense feeling had been revived as recently as 1953, when British officials again showed interest in federation. Yet after the African leaders issued their call for federation in 1963, a secret session of the Buganda *Lukiiko* reportedly gave the *Kabaka's* (King's) government a mandate to open talks on federation. Moreover, on June 13, members of the working party on federation held a ninety-minute meeting with the Kabaka at Mengo. Although nothing conclusive was decided upon, the conferees left the palace in a jovial mood. "It is quite obvious," conferee Mboya stated in summary, "that everyone wants unity."

Nevertheless, to bring pressure to bear on Buganda, a "unity rally" in which Kenyatta, Mboya, Kakonge, and Obote participated was held on June 29 in Kampala, Uganda. The audience, which included a sizable Baganda element, heard the speakers repeatedly condemn tribalism as an obstacle to Pan-Africanism and East African federation. Kenyatta and Obote, however, also pointedly assured Uganda's kings and hereditary rulers that their fears over African unity were groundless. Obote reiterated on several occasions that "unless we are prepared to venture into the unknown world, we shall never progress."

Baganda leaders were not prepared to oppose East African unity openly; at the same time, they were not willing to sanction a drift toward federation through lack of leadership on their part. The signal for a change of tactics came on July 1 when the *Kabaka* of Buganda failed to attend a meeting at the parliament building with East Africa's "Big Three." He pleaded short notice, but his failure to appear was inevitably interpreted, and almost certainly intended, as a snub. Within days Baganda spokesmen used the platforms afforded by parliament and the press to insist that the kingdom's monarchy, customs, and traditions must be safeguarded in an East African federation. As Abu Mayanja, then Minister of Education in the *Kabaka's* government, stated in an open letter to the three heads of government, Buganda would only like to enter a federation that would permit it to retain its identity, institutions, and culture. But, while members of the Buganda power elite such as *Katikkiro* Michael Kintu remained unenthusiastic at the prospect of federation, they were, at least in theory, prepared to accept the inevitable.

In sum, then, the communiqué received widespread, though not unanimous, support throughout East Africa. A public-opinion poll conducted by Marco Surveys near the end of 1963 indicated widespread approval of federation. The response outside was equally encouraging. Such neighboring states as Zanzibar (a small island country of 315,000 people off the coast of East Africa that was joined to Tanganyika in 1964 to form the United Republic of Tanzania), Somalia, Burundi, and Rwanda indicated, either immediately or in a few months time, that they were keenly interested in the possibility of joining the projected union. Moreover, the decision to form a federation was praised by the United States, India, Chile, and Iraq at the United Nations Special Committee on Colonialism. The British Secretary of Commonwealth Relations, Duncan Sandys, pledged his government's fullest support and cooperation. The basis was laid for action.

The "Big Three" approached the task of drafting a federal constitution with extraordinary dispatch. The June 5 communiqué had been explicit as to the timetable. A working party was to prepare a framework of a draft constitution for the new federation and report back to a conference of East African governments. Then, in the third week of August, a full-scale conference would be convened to examine the proposals.

All started according to plan. The working party met in Dar es Salaam, Tanganyika, on June 9. Although the public learned little about what actually happened at these meetings, what it did learn sustained its confidence in the prospects of a speedy move toward federation. Immediately after the conference completed its sessions, the chairman, Mboya, issued a press statement announcing that during the meetings the working party examined fully all the points relating to the Federal constitution, reached agreement on every issue, and accordingly gave instructions to the lawyers to enable them to start with the drafting of the Constitution at once.

The next conference met as scheduled in Kampala in late June. At the meetings the "Big Three" received and discussed the plan for the federal system outlined by the Dar es Salaam working party. As far as the public knew all went well. The prospects for federation seemed bright, and a sense of destiny filled the air.

The Predisposing Conditions

In 1963 many observers considered that a federation of the East African states would be the easiest of all African federations to organize. Their optimism was based in part at least upon the favorable objective conditions for union in that area.

A common historical background provided a base for wider cooperation. In centuries past, ethnic groups had ranged far and wide across the region, leaving behind a pattern of shared experience, traditions, and language which paid little heed to modern territorial lines. Coastal traders set up stations across eastern and central Africa, treating it as a unit for commercial purposes. In more recent times, a common British overrule had meant the establishment of similar political institutions and legal systems, a common official language, and a joint transportation and communications structure.

The region is a geographical unity and its varied types of climate, soil, and agriculture overlap political divisions. Rational plans for economic development must treat as a unit such geographical areas as the Lake Victoria basin, which is heavily populated by all three countries. The natural transport routes for exports from Tanganyika's Lake and West Lake provinces lie by way of Lake Victoria and the Kenya railroad. Moreover, Uganda exports its goods to the world market from the port of Mombasa, Kenya, and any threat to its right to use this port would involve serious repercussions. On its part, Kenya depends upon imports of Uganda electric power as well as upon Uganda's markets for its exports. In addition, the distribution of the peoples of East Africa emphasizes the artificiality of present national boundaries. The Masai live on both sides of the Kenya-Tanganyika border; the Abaluyha are split by the boundary running between Kenya and Uganda.

Another predisposing condition is the growth of a sense of an East African community. A web of social relationships is developing on an East African rather than a strictly territorial basis. Students from the three territories have built lasting friendships at Makerere University College in Kampala, and often these students continue to meet at seminars on administrative problems or at technical conferences. The business community, largely dominated by Asians and Europeans, tends to be East African rather than territorial in its outlook. And African political leaders have built a close working relationship through their participation in the East Africa High Commission, now the East African Common Services Organization (EACSO), that administers ports, railroads, mail and telegraphs, and so forth, on behalf of all three; through the pre-independence Pan-African Freedom Movement of East and Central Africa (PAFMECA); and at international trade, labor, and educational conferences.

Finally, the spirit of Pan-Africanism acts as a force for cohesion. The parties in power in all three countries, and also opposition parties and other groups, shared a common Pan-Africanist ideology. The existence of this fraternal sense of ideological oneness was an important spur to unity.

Earlier Administrative Cooperation

In the prewar period, plans for union had foundered on the fear that they would lead to the consolidation of white power in East Africa. Interterritorial planning and cooperation had developed during World War II, however, and in 1945 the East Africa High Commission and Central Legislative Assembly were established. This decision also drew some hostility from the indigenous population, because, in practice if not in law, the resulting organization reflected substantial European representation among the legislative members and administrators. Nevertheless, as African governments approached independence in East Africa, initial African fears were allayed. The organization gradually became an accepted feature of the East African scene.

As Tanganyika moved toward full statehood in 1961, representatives of the High Commission and of the governments of Kenya, Uganda, Tanganyika, and the United Kingdom decided at a London conference to maintain the interterritorial organization and to transform the High Commission into the East African Common Services Organization (EACSO). The East Africans now became the creators of EACSO as well as its administrators. Moreover, this decision, like the June 5, 1963, declaration, had as one of its objects the speeding up of Kenya's advance to independence.

EACSO

The East African Common Services Organization differs from its predecessor, the East Africa High Commission, in a few essential respects. Its executive body, composed initially of the President of Tanganyika and the Prime Ministers of Kenya and Uganda, took over executive control from the High Commission. The chairmanship of the executive body now rotates among its members. Four ministerial committees, or triumvirates, each made up of one minister from each territory, assist the executive. The triumvirates exercise jurisdiction in the fields of communications, finance, commercial and industrial coordination, and social and research services. The new Central Legislative Assembly reflects an emphasis on local participation. It now consists of a Speaker, two official members (the secretary-general and the legal secretary), twelve ministerial members (the members of the triumvirates), and twenty-seven members chosen by the elected members of the territorial legislature, nine from each of the three territories.

EACSO controls a wide range of East African activities. For fiscal purposes, it distinguishes between "self-contained" services, which attempt to cover costs through charges made to the consumers, and "nonself-contained" services, which are paid for from the EACSO general fund. The first category includes East African Railways and Harbours, East African Posts and Telecommunications, and, for all practical purposes, East African Airways.[1] In the second category, the more costly nonself-contained services in the 1963–64 budget included revenue collection and financial control, health, education, agriculture and forestry, meteorology, and civil aviation.

Though EACSO is significant in the economic life of East Africa, it plays an essentially nonpolitical role. Like its predecessor, EACSO is primarily concerned with technical rather than political coordination. Thus it involves only a limited commitment on the part of member states. The three governments retain the right to terminate membership after a year's notice. Moreover, at every level of the organization's operations—the Central Legislative Assembly, the authority, the triumvirates—each state has an equal voice. On matters of policy, decisions of the triumvirates must be unanimous. In the event differences arise, the issue is appealed to the authority, where any member's objection terminates discussion.

Common Market

In a genuine common market, there are no restrictions on the movement of goods, capital, and labor within the area and a common tariff exists on imports from outside the area. According to this description, East Africa is an imperfect common market; Kenya and Uganda have had a free trade and customs arrangement since 1917. Tanganyika joined the market later, and by stages. Nevertheless, governments have placed restrictions on the free

[1] To indicate how substantial these enterprises are, it seems sufficient to note that in 1962 East African Railways and Harbours had total revenues of £25,549,000 and expenditures of £26,931,000; East African Posts and Telecommunications had revenues of £7,126,000 and expenditures of £7,464,000. East African Airways, one of the few profitable airlines in the world, showed net earnings of £461,000 in 1963 on total operating revenues of £7,623,000. By comparison, the approved 1962–63 estimates for recurrent and non-recurrent expenditures of the Uganda government were £34,300,000. EastAfrican Common Services Organization, *Economic and Statistical Review* (Nairobi: Government Printer; December, 1963), pp. 100, 101; *East African Standard* (Nairobi), May 8, 1964, p. 15; and Uganda Government, *Background to the Budget 1963–64* (Entebbe: Ministry of Finance, 1963), pp. 35, 36.

flow of interterritorial trade, particularly in the case of agricultural commodities. In 1961 the Uganda Ministry of Commerce refused maize export licenses, causing Kenya officials to look elsewhere for food supplies. The next year, when the Uganda government reversed its policy, Kenya and Tanganyika authorities had made other commitments and prohibited maize imports from Uganda. Unofficial restrictions on Kenya workers in Uganda have been reported. Furthermore, in 1963 Ugandans criticized the decision of a Uganda sugar company to invest in a Kenya sugar venture. Failure to invest in Kenya might have meant the loss of the valuable Kenya sugar market to the producer; at the same time the pressures themselves represented an artificial interference with the movement of capital.

Moreover, bilateral interterritorial agreements and the activities of marketing boards and government development agencies (such as the Uganda Development Corporation) have tended to interfere with the free play of market forces. An interterritorial agreement between Kenya and Uganda assured Uganda sugar producers a market in Kenya and Kenya wheat producers preference in Uganda. But as Kenya becomes self-sufficient in sugar, Ugandans may begin to purchase lower-priced wheat from abroad. In addition, Ugandans and Tanganyikans contend that Kenya marketing boards have sold them wheat flour, beef, bacon, ham, butter, and cheese at higher prices than those charged on world markets.

Despite the common market's long history in East Africa, interterritorial trade became important only in the postwar period, in which it has absorbed a steadily increasing proportion of total East African exports. However, the rate of growth of Kenya's exports within the common market has tended to be more rapid than Uganda's and Tanganyika's,[2] and trade between Tanganyika and Uganda remains relatively stagnant.

Consequently less-industrialized Tanganyika seems to be the least dependent upon the common market and to gain the least advantage from it. Kenya, in contrast, shows an increasing dependence on the benefits of the common market. Not only does Kenya sell a substantial proportion of its wheat, pigs, and dairy products to its neighbors, but Kenya's program of industrialization relies heavily on the common market. The Economic and Financial Commission (Raisman) Report of 1961 estimated that about a quarter of Kenya's manufactured goods are sold in Tanganyika and Uganda. These countries purchase large amounts of Kenya-produced clothing, beer, cigarettes, footwear, insecticides, iron and steel coated plates and sheets, paper, and bicycle tires and tubes. The result is to increase East African prosperity as a whole, to save foreign exchange, and to make the region less dependent on the outside world.

---

[2] Whereas Kenya's exports to her partners rose to £17.2 million in 1962, Uganda's and Tanganyika's exports to Kenya amounted to £5.4 million and £2.0 million respectively during that period. Uganda Government, *Background to the Budget 1963–64* (Entebbe: Ministry of Finance, 1963), p. 30.

Related Forms of Association

In the related field of common currencies, taxes, and external tariffs, and particularly in the first two, European countries can find much to envy in East Africa's accomplishments. A common money system facilitates interterritorial transactions;[3] parallel taxing policies reduce complications in the running of EACSO and the common market; and common tariff policies bring revenue and protect industries. Nevertheless, coordinated policies in these areas depend largely upon continuing negotiations between governments. Thus the three finance ministers negotiate common rates among themselves but are not committed to maintaining a common tariff. Indeed Tanganyika's refusal in the past to follow Kenya's and Uganda's lead in increasing tariffs on enameled ware has caused tension between the territories.

Arrangements exist to compensate for the market's uneven distrubtion of benefits. This unevenness results from the effects of custom duties upon government revenues, the pattern of interterritorial trade, the location of industries, and the share of "invisible" exports (insurance, stock transactions, accounting, advertising). The Raisman commission recommended fiscal compensations for Tanganyika and Uganda in order to establish some balance in territorial advantage from the market's operations. Under the distributable pool set up in 1961 after these recommendations, each territory contributes 40 percent of its receipts from the company income tax on profits from manufacturing and finance, and 6 percent of customs and excise duties. EACSO distributes the pool, after deducting for costs of administration, by allocating 50 percent to meet the cost of EACSO's nonself-contained services and 50 percent on an equal basis among the three countries. Indirect redistribution results from the smaller proportions Uganda and Tanganyika pay for the operation of the general fund services; direct redistribution results as these two countries receive back considerably more than they contribute. Thus while Kenya's net loss from the arrangement in the 1962–63 period was £737,000, Tanganyika and Uganda showed gains of £312,000 and £288,000 respectively.

Major Advantages of Federation

In view of what already existed, why did East African leaders propose to share power in an enduring union? In particular, because it would provide a wider guaranteed market, administrative economies, better coordination of planning, and a more important international position.

[3] An indication of the fragility of these links was the June 10, 1965, announcements by the finance ministers of all three countries that their territories were withdrawing from the common currency arrangement and were establishing their own national currencies.

Economies of Scale

For economic development, national self-sufficiency is impractical within East Africa today. The separate markets of Kenya, Tanganyika, and Uganda are insufficient in size and purchasing power for the establishment of such capital-intensive industries as steel, paper, and chemicals, but collectively the three states can provide prospective manufacturers—domestic or foreign —with a broader and potentially more profitable market. Manufacturers are likely to consider a wider market as offering brighter prospects for efficient operations, as an industry's average costs ordinarily decline as a consequence of enlarging the size of the market. In this respect, two United Nations commissions to North and West Africa have maintained that it is imperative to establish integrated steel industries on a supraregional basis to achieve economies of scale.

Economies of Scale in Administration

Few have questioned the substantial savings, in capital outlays, equipment, and personnel, of the joint administration of the EACSO services. Duplication of research activities is wasteful and funds are desperately needed for economic development. To establish customs posts at the Uganda-Kenya border when customs collection can be done efficiently and easily at the port of Mombasa is carrying national autarchy to absurd lengths. In addition, significant economies result from the standardization of equipment, bulk purchasing, joint training, common maintenance and control, and the interchange of equipment and personnel to meet seasonal demands. To extend this principle to the establishment of a federal external affairs ministry could avoid duplication in embassies and staffing abroad as well as secure greater representation for East Africa as a whole at current levels of expenditure.

Central Bank

Although the East African Currency Board had proved useful in facilitating commercial and financial interunit transactions, many African leaders felt that the time had come to establish a more effective banking system. A central bank, accountable to a federal government, could inject vigor into the economic development of the area, assist economic planning, mobilize savings, and increase public influence over commercial banking activities. It might also be able to raise external loans on more attractive terms than can national banks acting separately, as well as effect economies on joint reserve requirements.

Coordination of Agricultural Marketing Arrangements

Federation could also facilitate the setting up of joint agricultural marketing boards. National marketing boards seek to stabilize prices as well as to raise the quality of commodities and to ensure the best possible terms of trade. Joint marketing boards for coffee, tea, sisal, and pyrethrum might facilitate price reductions to meet the challenge of substitutes and permit the sale of a maximum amount of high quality commodities (for example, *arabica* rather than *robusta* coffee) into quota markets. Within East Africa itself, marketing boards for sugar and maize could encourage interterritorial trade by helping to end restrictions and price differentials, prevent foreign dumping, and economize on transportation costs.

Increased Diversification

A further advantage of more coordinated planning and action would be to encourage the diversification of exports. Of Uganda's £37.6 million exports outside East Africa in 1962, two commodities—coffee and cotton—made up 76 percent of the total. Efforts are therefore being made within Uganda to raise tea, cocoa, sisal, and sugar. But a broader-based diversification encompassing much of eastern Africa would permit Ugandans to reduce their vulnerability by making it possible to share the incomes from such exports as pyrethrum and diamonds. The resulting stability of incomes would greatly facilitate the task of development planners. So would the stimulation of regional specialization in the course of industrial development.

Coordinated Planning

Many East Africans have felt that the greatest advantage of federation might be to assure coordinated planning that would provide uniform fiscal policies, use scarce factors of production most effectively, and foster social and economic opportunities in the less developed parts of the area. In the past, the existence of a common British hegemony and a common market had assured generally parallel policies regarding customs and taxation as well as in other fiscal policies. But post-independence budgets reflected diverging state interests. Moreover, the adoption of separate comprehensive economic plans raised the possibility of even greater differences of approach in the future. So far the three planning staffs had made no effort to coordinate their policies. And without the underpinning of federation, these separate plans could well come to stress competing objectives on such issues as balance of payments, inflation, and quota restrictions.

Such competition would be the more serious because of the scarcity of important factors of production in the area: skilled technicians and administrators as well as capital. Overlapping facilities in the cement industry, for example, have led to a situation where plants in all three countries are operating at less than 50 percent of capacity. Provided the planning agency could act from an East African point of view, coordinated planning could avoid much unnecessary duplication in other industries, particularly at this early stage of economic development. Planning would thereby make a more effective mobilization of available resources possible in East Africa as a whole.

International Leverage

East African leaders were agreed on the need for international leverage. Thus Prime Minister Kenyatta told a BBC broadcasting audience in October, 1963, that the formation of a federation would mean that "the world would have to reckon with us." He explained, "Instead of speaking for 8,000,000 people in Kenya and 12,000,000 in Tanganyika or another number in Zanzibar, we would be speaking as a solid bloc." Indeed, federation would put East Africans in a better position to bargain with Western or Communist bloc nations. East Africa's position in negotiating with the European Common Market was surely stronger because the area's leaders presented a united front at the bargaining table. Similarly, East Africa's negotiating position at the United Nations, in the Commonwealth, and with other African states is more formidable when the territories act in unison than when they move along separate paths. In the meantime competition for capital and markets is growing among partners and might have the effect of weakening East Africa's common front—unless cooperation were buttressed by a more formal political framework than presently exists.

Enhanced Military Capability

The desire for greater military capability, an important inducement in such federations as Australia, Malaysia, and the United States, was also evident on the East African scene. In the spring of 1963 the Defense Ministers of Uganda and Tanganyika declared jointly that any military attack on one East African country would be regarded as an attack on all three. Following the Kenya elections, the June 5 communiqué listed a common defense program among the subjects for further joint action, and the Defense Ministers of Tanganyika, Uganda, and Kenya considered military coordination in the context of the working party deliberations on federation. These efforts at military coordination were given a new impetus by the January, 1964, army mutinies over pay and the rate of Africanization within each of the three countries.

Increased Aid Appeal

From the external viewpoint a federated East Africa, by becoming a powerful force on the African continent, would show itself to potential donors as an effective unit that could make efficient use of funds. In particular, aid-givers would probably be attracted to broad-based, multinational projects such as dams, power systems, and irrigation schemes. At a time when competition for all kinds of assistance is intense, those countries that are able to attract potential donors have a considerable advantage. East Africa experienced this phenomenon in October, 1963, when the East African governments held negotiations with American and West European donor agencies in Italy on means of financing the University of East Africa's current deficits and long-term capital needs. The conference report was explicit on the fundamental importance of maintaining a federal university in East Africa. Many members pointedly "stressed the extent to which their interests in the university stemmed from the success with which the East African countries had established an international university to achieve the planned and co-ordinated development of higher education in their three countries."

The Danger of Retrogression

Not only were there obvious advantages to be gained from federation; it could also be feared that without it gains already made might slip away. As Tom Mboya told the 1963 Nairobi conference on federation, East Africans must decide after Kenya's independence "whether they wish to continue the present piecemeal uncoordinated drift." Further delay might give free play to centrifugal forces.

An outstanding example of divisive tendencies was at hand in the general ineffectiveness of the industrial licensing system. In 1948 identical ordinances in the three territories had set up an East Africa Industrial Council with power to grant licenses to local producers of certain goods. Industrial licensing sought to accomplish two objectives: to locate the industries on a scheduled list in an advantageous place for their successful operations, and to assure these industries an adequate, protected market for a reasonable period of time. But the licensing system never proved a great success. At the start it was assumed that a detailed development plan would determine the location of industries, yet such a plan was never forthcoming. Moreover, from the outset few major industries were included on the scheduled list. The council's authority extended to textiles, glassware, enamel hollowware, metal windows, door frames, and steel drums, but not to a host of other industries. All attempts after 1955 to broaden the list proved fruitless, as the Tanganyikans, in particular, feared new limitations upon their industrialization.

Discussions over the granting of licenses also became a source of friction between the partners. Kenyans and Tanganyikans resented the council's decision in 1949 to give an exclusive five-year license to Nytil Textiles of Uganda for the manufacture of cotton yarn and piece goods. After the five-year period expired, the council issued other licenses to manufacture cotton piece goods, but it was careful to protect Nytil Textiles against uneconomic competition, a measure which represented one of Uganda's chief benefits from the common market arrangement. As Uganda began to lose this advantage in the 1960s, its political spokesmen became increasingly resentful of what they described as an unequal arrangement. Ugandans charged that the licensing system involved "a lot of injustice": not only had it failed to protect such scheduled industries as textiles, but industries such as cement, in which Uganda had had an initial advantage, were not within its scope. In brief, by failing to operate within a coordinated development plan, industrial licensing led to the emergence of new tensions between the East African partners. By the 1960s, the industrial licensing system had reached such a low point that the Raisman Commission and all three World Bank missions to East Africa recommended abandoning the scheme. Here was a classic case of failing to run fast enough to stay in the same place.

Centrifugal Tendencies Within EACSO

EACSO itself had been affected by the emphasis on national, as compared to interterritorial, activities. Tanganyika had barely become independent in 1961 before Nyerere's government decided to withdraw from both the Marine Fisheries Research Organization and the East African Navy. Though his government changed its position on participation in the former when outside funds were forthcoming, the decision on the latter remained unaltered, thereby breaking up the only defense force operated as a common service. At the time of the breakup the navy consisted of only two minesweepers and a patrol boat. However, the reasons behind Tanganyika's withdrawal went deeper than mere ineffectiveness. The fact that Kenya's Mombasa served as the navy's main base of operations irritated Tanganyikan sensitivities and also raised questions of cost and advantage. Moreover, Tanganyikans criticized an arrangement which tied their country to a Kenya still at that time under colonial status. By withdrawing from the navy, Tanganyikans seemed to cleave to such tenets of the traditional state system as national sovereignty and national interest; the precedent it set for others to follow was prejudicial to unity.

Another example of centrifugal tendencies occurred in February, 1963, when Uganda severed links with the quasi-official East African Tourist Travel Association (EATTA). Adoko Nekyon explained that Uganda paid substantial contributions to EATTA without receiving a proper return. In the Central Legislative Assembly at its May 8, 1963, session, R. S. Alexander of Kenya admitted that Uganda contributed 25.1 percent of the subvention to EATTA but received only 9.5 percent of East Africa's revenues from tourism, and that Kenya, in contrast, contributed 52.7 percent of the subventions and earned 69 percent of the gross revenues. He maintained, however, that inequalities of benefit did not justify withdrawal (though perhaps a reorganization of the association was in order), and he urged the Ugandans to reconsider their action. Another Kenyan member, Sheikh M. A. Alamoody, noted that in 1961 a Tanganyika ports deficit of £91,773 had been covered by the net surplus of £289,028 earned in Mombasa. "This is an example," he observed, "to prove that we have to have interterritorial balancing if we are to have common services." The Ugandans refused, however, to reverse their decision.

First Signs of Hesitation

Though many East Africans urgently wanted to unite the territories, others became increasingly reluctant. The euphoric atmosphere over federation lasted only briefly, and the first signs of hesitations appeared soon after the June 5 communiqué.

Political Interests

First to express dissatisfaction were the Ugandans. Had doubts been confined to the Baganda, they would have occasioned little notice. It soon became apparent, though, that the Uganda government itself had reasons for being vague and indecisive. An early and seemingly harmless indication was a proposal on July 12, 1963, to amend a motion which approved the declaration on federation by adding the words "of intention" after the word "declaration." The Opposition, suspecting a change of policy, asked for a fuller explanation. The government never answered the question fully, but Adoko Nekyon, leader of Uganda's delegation to the working party, told parliament a number of times that the three nations were not "committed" to East African federation.

By mid-August Tanganyika and Kenya ministers pointed openly at Uganda as the cause of delays on federation and pressed it to fix the date and place for a further meeting of the heads of state. Nekyon responded swiftly and dramatically. On August 20, 1963, he dismissed the statements of the Kenya and Tanganyika ministers as "interesting" and said that he saw no need to hurry the negotiations. More important was his insistence on specific guarantees. "I am not prepared," he warned, "just to throw my nation into darkness, so I must know exactly where we are going and to whom we are surrendering our powers. And, as a small state, Uganda needs certain guarantees for her future within a larger unit."

Nekyon's statement was the signal for Ugandans critical of federation to air their fears openly. The Buganda Minister of Education at that time, Abu Mayanja, urging that Buganda join federation as a constituent state, declared on the following day that the kingdom did not want East African unity if it were to be at any cost. Two days later, Ali Kisekka, the secretary of the Buganda-based Kabaka Yekka (KY) Parliamentary Group, urged Prime Minister Obote to "think twice before taking any further steps towards this Federation." Federation at that time, Ali Kisekka predicted, would reduce Uganda to a permanent third-place position. Though East Africans generally remained confident over the eventual achievement of federation, they were now jarred into discovering, as European integrationists had, that federation would not be born without a long period of negotiation and compromise.

Further signs of Uganda hesitations followed. Some people attributed Prime Minister Obote's failure to attend the Nairobi summit talks in mid-September to irresolution on East African unity. Regardless of Obote's reasons, the effect was to put off further high-level talks on federation until after Kenya had become an independent country. Moreover, Obote dispelled any lingering doubts that Nekyon might not have been giving a true picture of government policy when he told the press on October 7, 1963, that "all the aspects of the design of the Federation must be sorted out and put into writing before the Federation comes into being."

Ugandans, then, searched for safeguards for their political and economic interests vis-à-vis the two larger states, not necessarily for a way to end the negotiations. They contended that an enduring union was worth the price of frustration and delay. Furthermore, they emphatically denied charges emanating from Kenya and Tanganyika that the Ugandans were an obstructive element in the negotiations on federation. Nekyon told the National Assembly on September 27, 1963, that Ugandans had "specific and genuine demands to put forward" and that although Ugandans wanted "to ask for certain guarantees as a smaller nation," they had not brought anything into the talks in order deliberately to frustrate the achievement of federation.

Nevertheless, the Kenyan and Tanganyikan leaders exhibited a certain amount of restlessness over the pace of federation and a skepticism toward Uganda's assurances. Thus on October 24, 1963, Joseph Murumbi, Kenya Minister of State in the Prime Minister's Office, suggested in an informal speech to the Nairobi Rotary Club that Kenya and Tanganyika might go ahead and form a federation on their own, with Uganda joining at a later stage. "I feel," Murumbi said, "that in Uganda, we have this difficulty of the leadership there fearing they will be absorbed into an East African Federation. Some of the Uganda leaders feel they might become nonentities overnight."

Obote reacted swiftly. He rejected accusations that Uganda's leaders feared a loss of stature and demanded to know from Kenyatta whether Murumbi's remarks on forming a two-unit federation were official Kenya government policy. "It does no harm to Uganda if she joins now or later," he said, "and if they want to go ahead let them do it." Kenyatta subsequently dissociated his government from Murumbi's remarks, which he described as the latter's "own personal views." The incident was then closed officially, but not before it had disclosed tensions between the negotiators.

At the same time, Obote also made public the existence of substantial differences within the working party. He pointed out that the working party had not yet resolved such questions as citizenship, interstate movements, finance and borrowing powers, responsibility for agriculture and animal industry, policies on foreign affairs, higher education, and the civil service. On foreign policy, Obote contended that the working party could not act until a sovereign Kenya was in a position to set its own course. By late October, then, it had become evident that the existence of fundamental differences precluded the achievement of federation in 1963. Could it still be achieved in the foreseeable future?

Strains on the "Federal" University

The one field in which the tendencies had been strongly toward closer relations was university education. The establishment of the University of East Africa as a "federal" institution, bringing together Makerere University

College in Kampala, Uganda, the University College, Dar es Salaam, Tanganyika, and the University College, Nairobi, Kenya, had distinct advantages in aid appeal, administration, and world recognition. Yet as we have seen, considerable pressures soon became evident within the university over the allocation of funds, faculty, and students. Because Makerere is the oldest and most entrenched of the three university colleges, Ugandans see the least advantage in grouping them together. The development of the two newer university colleges has meant a sharing of EACSO higher education appropriation estimated in 1963–64 at £404,250. At the same time Makerere's own position for attracting new capital was not enhanced by the arrangement. Whereas the University College, Nairobi asked for £1,483,-000 in capital funds at the Lake Como Conference of the University of East Africa in October, 1963, and the University College, Dar es Salaam indicated needs amounting to £2,040,000, Makerere requested a mere £315,300. In large part this difference could be attributed to Makerere's past building program, but some Ugandans feel it can also be attributed to restrictions that the federal institution places upon Makerere's assumption of new activities. Thus Prime Minister Obote, in commenting on October 26, 1963, upon quarrels within the university structure, said that the move for closer East African unity had been responsible for Makerere's marking time while the other university colleges caught up. He cited the recommendation of the Needs and Priorities Committee Report to stop construction of a Makerere residence hall in its final stages in order to divert the funds to university facilities elsewhere in East Africa. Though the Uganda government went ahead in any case with building the residence hall, there was hard feeling over the recommendation.

Ugandans are also highly critical of any suggestions of tampering with the student selection process and of what they fear to be a breakdown in university college specialization. For example, they protested strongly against Dar es Salaam's decision to start a school of medicine since Makerere's medical center is already firmly established. At the Central Legislative Assembly on May 2, 1963, Semei Nyanzi, a Ugandan and lecturer in economics at Makerere, specifically questioned the diversification of faculties at Nairobi and Dar es Salaam. He pleaded for specialization and warned: "If we find that [specialization] is, in fact, impossible because of the desires or wishes within territorial countries, then in that case . . . I do not see how we can tie this in with the idea that we want the University Council to continue in being." From the opposite side, Tanganyika's Chief A. S. Fundikira answered, "this is not duplication because the needs of East Africa with regard to these basic faculties could not be met by Makerere alone."

Fears of Preference Within EASCO

Resentment of alleged Kenya domination of EACSO activities also finds expression from time to time. Kenyans do in fact predominate on EACSO's staff; this is partly because most EACSO headquarters are situated in Nairobi, and therefore it is not easy to attract qualified people in large numbers from Tanganyika and Uganda. This situation of inequality of staff among the partner countries seems likely to continue, for as top EACSO positions are Africanized, university-trained people will fill these positions. Of the East African students in the United States in 1963, 210 were Tanganyikans, 160 Ugandans, 25 Zanzibaris, and 1,015 Kenyans. In Britain students from these countries are more evenly distributed. Yet despite Kenya's head start, Tanganyika and Uganda spokesmen use every opportunity to close the gap. They watch staff assignments closely and at every turn question the ministers to uncover preferential treatment.

Alleged Outside Pressures

Allegations of outside pressure were made so frequently that they became symptomatic of the air of uncertainty surrounding the federation issue in many quarters. Some East Africans seemed to suspect the intentions of such Western countries as Britain and the United States that quickly endorsed federation. "It is really strange," P. Muwanga told Uganda's National Assembly on July 12, 1963, "that countries like Great Britain and America . . . should have so keen an interest in an East African Federation." These suspicions became more pronounced upon Britain's appointment of a High Commissioner-Designate to the East African federation. Prime Minister Obote described himself as "seriously disturbed" by this action, implying that it represented an interference with Uganda's sovereignty.

Of greater significance were the widespread suspicions of Ghanaian intervention to oppose East African moves toward unity. Although President Kwame Nkrumah in January, 1961, had cabled Mboya his support for the "noble ideal" of East African federation, he had reversed his position sometime during the next year and had come to regard regional federations as a hindrance to the broader goal of continental unity. Ghanaian newspapers quickly followed his lead. *The Spark,* a semi-official paper published in Accra, Ghana, ran frequent articles describing East African federation as a neocolonialist effort to maintain control in that area. An editorial in *Spark* warned on December 6, 1963, for example, that East African federation was the "meeting point and vehicle" of various neocolonialist policies. But did Ghana's antipathy to federation stop with denunciations? A spate of rumors circulated in Kampala after June, 1963, to the effect that the Ghanaian Embassy was working actively against federation. The rumors were never proved or disproved; yet it is important to note that the Ghanaian High Commissioner to Uganda, D. Busumtwi-Sam, placed a two-column advertisement in the *Uganda Argus* on October 28, 1963, which in effect denounced regional federations in Africa. Certainly the persistence of such rumors acted as a drag on the efforts to build up widespread support for federation.

Extended State of Expectancy

From October, 1963, when the Obote-Murumbi exchange took place, until January, 1964, when the Zanzibar coup d'état occurred and the problem of the army mutinies engulfed East Africa, hope for and some doubts about the achievement of federation existed side by side. It was a period of expectancy. Leaders in the three countries gave repeated assurances of progress at the bargaining table. However they revealed little information on the actual state of the negotiations, which led to a spate of rumors and speculations.

Leaders in Tanganyika, Kenya, and Uganda continued to espouse the cause of East African unity, but with varying degrees of enthusiasm. For President Nyerere, the failure to establish a federation in 1963 was the biggest disappointment of the year. Kenyans spoke of federation with undisguised zeal. Home Affairs Minister Oginga Odinga, in his opening speech to the United Nations, asserted that when the time came, Kenyans would "gladly surrender their territorial sovereignty for the good of East Africa as a whole." Ugandans, however, remained reticent. Although the Uganda government, through the media of President Sir Edward Mutesa's opening speech to the National Assembly on November 4, 1963, indicated that it could see "political and economic reasons behind the intention and the urge to set up a federal government in East Africa," the Prime Minister seemed less than enthusiastic. On December 2, for example, he dismissed a reporter's question on East African federation with the following reply: "Whether we federate or not, I think the main issue will still be how to decolonize Africa." Even so, in January, 1964, Obote joined Nyerere and Kenyatta in reaffirming his backing for federation at a high-level Nairobi conference.

The University of East Africa Conference

During this interim period in late November, 1963, the University of East Africa sponsored an unofficial conference at Nairobi on federation which was important for three principal reasons. It gave leaders from the three countries an opportunity to pledge their support for federation anew; it enlightened the East African public on the range of issues in dispute; and it provided an unofficial forum for an interchange of ideas.

Spokesmen for all three delegations endorsed federation. Kenya's Tom Mboya pointed to the necessity for "a bold move towards political federation." Tanganyika's Amir Jamal stressed that "It is impossible to overestimate either the practical or the idealistic importance of a United East Africa." And Uganda's Grace Ibingira spoke of the "great need" for East Africa to follow the lead of the United States and the Soviet Union in forming a powerful federal union. The Ugandans' approach was positive but cautious. Ibingira emphasized the need to accommodate state diversity within the federation and to safeguard the interests of smaller states, and

Uganda's Opposition leader Bataringaya urged that careful attention be paid to the division of powers.

The Nairobi conference threw light on the broad lines of policy differences between the countries. Criticism of excessive secrecy about working party deliberations had become increasingly persistent, and the differences of emphasis among the national delegations became exposed during the conference discussions. Whereas the Tanganyikans and Kenyans talked of creating a strong, tightly constructed federation, the Ugandans sought to restrict the authority of the new federal government by delegating extensive powers to the constituent units. The Kenyans accented the need for freedom of movement throughout East Africa; the Ugandans called for territorial control over interunit movement of peoples. And much controversy occurred over the site of the federal capital. Nairobi, Arusha (Tanganyika), and Entebbe (Uganda) all had their strong advocates.

The Nairobi conference also provided a useful forum for an unofficial exchange of ideas. Thus the study group on machinery of government and administration recognized that a smaller state such as Uganda was apprehensive about a strong, tightly constructed federation and sought to deal practically with these feelings. Among a number of possible approaches, the study group suggested departing from orthodox formulas for dividing powers between the states and the federal government by providing for a brief list of exclusive federal subjects (for example, foreign affairs and defense), a confederal list requiring unanimous territorial consent prior to federal action, and a provision leaving the residual powers to the states. Another alternative was to transfer powers to the central government by phases. Such a phased approach would ensure federation in the future, while giving the territorial governments an opportunity to prepare for the transfer in a more gradual and leisurely manner. Other alternatives included provisions for a second chamber, a plural executive, indirect elections, territorial ratification of crucial constitutional amendments, and constitutional limitations on federal use of emergency powers. The ideas were there. What use would be made of them?

Growing Impatience

The period of expectancy after the initial excitement over federation had worn off had also been a period of growing impatience. As the months of negotiations went by, Tanganyikans in particular began to show signs of increasing restlessness. They pointed proudly to their contributions to East African unity—their willingness to delay Tanganyika's *uhuru* (independence) so that all the East African territories might gain independence at the same time, their pursuance of common currency, taxation, and customs policies even when short-term interests might have dictated a separate approach, and their readiness to join an independent Tanganyika to a largely British-run EASCO. In other important ways as well Nyerere's government had acted to maintain a politically fluid situation.

Nyerere had recognized that substantial constitutional divergencies among the countries would complicate the task of region-building, and he made a conscious effort to preserve a similarity of institutions after independence. This meant a temporary halting of efforts to set up a legally sanctioned Tanganyikan one-party state which could have meant that TANU would be in a position in a federal East Africa to compete in elections in Kenya and Uganda (either through alliances or on its own), while restricting participation by Ugandan and Kenyan parties in Tanganyika's politics.

As the prospects for transition to an East African federation dimmed, however, Tanganyikans began to give serious consideration to revising their stand on the question. On December 3, 1963, John Nzunda, the parliamentary secretary to the Vice-President's Office, told the National Assembly that since it seemed that federation would not materialize as soon as it was once thought likely, President Nyerere would appoint a committee to inquire into the setting up of a constitution for a one-party state. Tanganyikan officials were clearly thinking of returning to their former plans in the event that the proposed federation did not come into being.

The Letdown

Both the Zanzibar coup d'état (in which the largely African Afro-Shirazi party seized power from a predominantly Arab government) and the armed mutinies in Tanganyika, Uganda, and Kenya in January, 1964, helped jolt East Africans into coming to grips with the federation question. Military turbulence engulfed all the countries simultaneously, demonstrating to observers the oneness of both the area and its problems. Zanzibar's uprising helped to set off the mutiny in Dar es Salaam by drawing police away from that city at a critical time. The mutiny by the soldiers left behind in Dar es Salaam soon led to mutinies elsewhere. The mutineers of Tanganyika, Uganda, and Kenya compelled their governments to concede major pay increases and to promise to expedite the Africanization of all ranks. These three countries, moreover, all called for British military assistance to bring about a return to normalcy. It had become apparent throughout the area that countervailing forces were lacking and that governments were fragile.

Thus on the surface it seemed that the existence of parallel and overlapping defense problems and a general feeling of insecurity over the future role of the army might well cause East African leaders to speed federation as a means of stabilizing the situation. Similar factors had influenced the decision to federate in the United States, in Australia, and in Malaysia. For once, the fear of the consequences of not uniting might seem to outweigh the disintegrating effects of local fears and jealousies. But would East Africa's leaders be willing, in the last analysis, to commit themselves to an effective coordination of military activities by sharing power in such a crucial field of responsibility?

What actually emerged was a strange mixture of Pan-Africanism, regionalism, and unilateral action. In practice all these factors combined to constitute a major setback to the cause of federation. On January 27, 1964, at the height of the army crisis, President Nyerere sent a message to all heads of independent African states warning that the situation in East Africa was critical and a grave danger to the whole continent. He appealed to them to dispatch their Ministers of Foreign Affairs and Defense to an emergency meeting of the Organization of African Unity (OAU). This hastily summoned meeting assembled in Dar es Salaam two weeks later. Nyerere asked the OAU for African troops to replace the British forces called in to maintain security in his country. The OAU agreed to sanction his requests. Thus Pan-African solidarity had served a useful purpose by rescuing Nyerere from his embarrassment over the use of British troops. It did little, however, to further continental unity. The Ghanaians were disappointed by the failure to agree on their proposed African armed force which could be rushed into trouble spots on quick notice, and Dr. Obote asserted pointedly on February 14, 1964, that it was "disappointing that the resolutions [dealt] with matters which the Government of Tanganyika could have decided even without calling a conference."

The aftermath of the mutinies also came to represent a backward step for East African supraregionalism. In early March, 1964, Duncan Sandys held a series of talks on defense matters with the East African heads of government. His negotiations started well. The Kenya government, concerned over the possibility of serious fighting with Somalia over the northeastern region, agreed to have Britain help expand and reequip Kenya's army and to give flight training to Kenya pilots as well as to establish a small navy for coastal defense. Moreover, Kenya accorded the Royal Air Force overflying and staging facilities. In making such a broad commitment, Kenyatta placed a higher priority on Kenya's immediate national interests than upon any doctrinal rejection of close military ties with a former colonial power and NATO member.

Any hope of developing an East African federal force disappeared, however, with Sandys' talks several days later with President Nyerere. Since the British government considered separate air-training facilities in Tanganyika to be uneconomical and inefficient, it offered to include Tanganyikan pilots and ground crews in the air-training scheme being established at Nairobi. Nyerere rejected such an approach and insisted that Tanganyika's air personnel be trained in that country. Ugandans took to a middle course by agreeing to air force training in Kenya but limiting the British military presence in Uganda to a few British officers attached for training purposes. These widely differing approaches not only exposed East Africa's unreadiness for defense coordination but had the adverse effect of bringing new centrifugal forces into play. Henceforth national forces would acquire different training, organizational patterns, equipment, and traditions.

Centralization of Power in Tanganyika

In the wake of the mutinies, Nyerere acted to tighten governmental control over various elements in his society. One of his first actions was to establish a single trade union, the National Union of Tanganyika Workers, for all of Tanganyika under the control of a government minister. This action was hotly criticized in some East African quarters, and H. M. Luande, a UPC member of parliament and president of the Uganda Trades Union Congress, proposed in late May that Tanganyika be left out of an East African federation unless its restrictions on the labor movement were repealed.

Nyerere, believing that the two-party system was too expensive a luxury in a state in the early stages of economic development as well as a possible source of disunity in an ethnically pluralistic society, now took the long-mooted step of suggesting the establishment of a legally sanctioned single-party system. On January 28, 1964, he announced the appointment of a thirteen-member presidential commission to consider the constitutional changes necessary to put a "democratic" one-party state into effect. The decision to establish a one-party state was final; the commission's task was limited to designing a political system where the equality of citizens, the rule of law, the independence of the judiciary, and maximum citizen participation in governmental affairs and in the choosing of representatives would take place within the one-party structure. By accentuating the constitutional differences between the partners, this decision greatly reduced the flexibility of the East African political situation.

Crisis over the Common Market

Tanganyikan impatience with delays over federation also brought on a crisis over the common market. At a secret Entebbe conference on March 17, 1964, on the coordination of economic planning, Nsilo Swai startled the participants by announcing that Tanganyika considered leaving the common market and setting up a separate currency. Since it was unlikely that the federation would materialize in the near future, Nyerere had concluded that the time had come "to equalise the disadvantages of indefinite talking about federation." He therefore proposed to modify the common market arrangement by putting a tariff and import quotas on various products imported from the common market, primarily from Kenya. In this way Nyerere and his colleagues hoped and expected that Tanganyika's growing trade deficits with its common market partners could be corrected without undermining either EACSO or Kenya's economy.

In the face of Tanganyika's insistence upon modifying the common market, hurried efforts were made to recover as much lost ground as possible.

Mboya held talks with Nyerere in Dar es Salaam on various aspects of the crisis during early April, and on April 10, 1964, crucial negotiations opened in Nairobi. East Africa's "Big Three" plus Zanzibar's new Vice-President, Kassim Hanga, and Minister for External Affairs and Trade, Sheikh Abdulrahman Mohamed (Babu), led large delegations to the meeting. The questions faced were twofold: Could the conference satisfy Tanganyika's demands for an equalizing of disadvantages within the context of the existing common market arrangement, and could it thereby encourage new moves toward federation?

The communiqué issued at the close of the official Nairobi conference of East African leaders declared that it had "examined thoroughly and in a brotherly spirit several issues affecting East Africa such as the East African federation, East African common market, trade relations within East African countries, and industrial development." It went a long way toward solving the immediate problem. The Tanganyikans gave assurances that they had no intention of withdrawing from the common market; at the same time, the conference agreed to set up an emergency committee to examine East African trade relations and Tanganyika's proposals for correcting its trade imbalances with Kenya and Uganda as well as for establishing a separate currency. As for East African federation, the conference gave instructions to the working parties to continue with their labors.

The reactions to the talks were varied. Mboya told reporters in London on April 13 that the East African leaders had made progress toward the goal of unity at the conference; in spite of difficulties ahead, there was still a good hope of bringing about an East African federation. Obote was less sanguine about the chances of federation. Upon his arrival in Uganda on April 12, he told newsmen that he and his delegation had objected to discussing the issue of East African unity under a threat from Tanganyika to disrupt the present trade arrangement. Oscar Kambona, Tanganyika's influential Minister of External Affairs, responded by denying that his country had resorted to economic threats in order to achieve political unity in East Africa. He asserted that Tanganyika was "feeling the pinch" of existing trade relationships and merely sought Kenyan and Ugandan cooperation in finding ways to solve the problem.

The KANU Parliamentary Group had held its own meeting before the Nairobi conference on trade relations to urge swifter action on federation and had marched in this cause outside the prime minister's office; now KADU as well as KANU expressed sharp criticism of the results of the talks. On April 13, a KANU Parliamentary Group working committee denounced the communiqué as vague and equivocal on federation. It regretted "that instead of going ahead boldly to effect political federation of East Africa immediately, a new committee to examine trade relations in East Africa has been established . . . because it will only conjure up new problems which will make it difficult for us to federate." It urged an immediate federation of Tanganyika and Kenya and proposed to convene a joint meeting of East African Parliamentary Groups to hold discussions on East African unity. The followers were attempting to lead the leaders, a dangerous formula.

Two significant events occurred at this time that had a bearing on the federation discussions. First, after comparatively little negotiation, President Nyerere of Tanganyika and Abeid Karume of Zanzibar exchanged instruments of ratification on April 27, merging their two countries under Nyerere's leadership into the new United Republic of Tanganyika and Zanzibar, to be known subsequently as Tanzania. The new union was important to a possible East African federation in that it enlarged Tanganyika by 300,000 people, gave some substantiation to Nyerere's earlier stress upon the necessity to unite countries while the situation still remained fluid, and demonstrated the feasibility of moves toward African unity. Nyerere expressed hopes that the Tanganyika-Zanzibar union would act as an inspiration both to East African federation and to a wider African unity. And in the Tanganyika National Assembly debate on the ratification of the merger agreement on April 25, 1964, Bibi Titi Mohamed asked: "If a country with a population of about 300,000 does not fear union with a country of 10,000,000 people, how can two countries with populations of 7,000,000 and 5,000,000 respectively fear us?"

Second, President Nyerere presented the £246 million five-year development plan to Tanganyika's National Assembly on May 12, 1964. The plan called for a significant expansion of agricultural output as well as massive investment in manufacturing industries. How would this affect the common market? Nyerere reminded the Assembly that in the past Nairobi had produced manufactured goods for the Tanganyika market. If Kenya and Uganda had not agreed to remedy this situation of industrial imbalance, Nyerere explained that Tanganyika would have had little alternative but to break the common market arrangement. "This," Nyerere asserted, "we were reluctant to do." He revealed that through the cooperation of Kenya and Uganda, however, a solution to this problem had been found.

A few days later it became clearer just what this cooperation entailed. Upon receipt of the Ministerial Emergency Committee's report, the three heads of government assembled in Nairobi on May 15, 1964, to agree on the following three means of redressing Tanganyika's trade imbalances. First, they accepted the Emergency Committee's recommendations for the introduction of a temporary quota system. Voluntary restrictions would be placed upon certain items of interterritorial trade such as beer, cigarettes, and shoes in order to give Tanzania and to a lesser extent Uganda an opportunity to build up their "infant" industries and to give Tanzania in particular a chance to balance its trade.

Second, East Africa's "Big Three" agreed to the allocation of a number of manufacturing activities so as to bring about an equitable sharing of those large-scale industries that require the entire East African market for profitable operations. Details of the division showed that the industries allocated to Tanzania included car, truck, and radio manufacture and assembly and the manufacture of motor vehicle tires and tubes. Allocations to Uganda consisted of bicycle assembly and manufacture and the manufacture of nitrogenous fertilizers; Kenya was allotted the manufacture of incandescent and fluorescent lamps.

Third, the East African leaders appointed a commission to draw up a list of industries which might be established to serve the entire East African market. This commission would suggest means of attracting foreign capital and of distributing industries equitably.

The reactions to the agreements on trade relations and distribution of industries were generally healthy. The crisis over the common market had passed, and a new optimism was apparent in East Africa. Not only had Nyerere's threat to withdraw from the common market largely succeeded in winning his country substantial economic concessions, but the discussions had been carried on in such good spirit on all sides that the agreement had provided a new impetus toward political federation. As Tanganyika's five-year plan had indicated, only a supranational power could readjust economic imbalances effectively over the long term. But could the "brotherly" spirit which had averted the common market crisis be carried over into the more far-reaching negotiations on federation? The next month was to provide much of the answer.

Increasing Back Bench Pressures for Federation

After the demonstrations in April, 1964, the KANU Parliamentary Group continued to press for ways to speed federation. In late April, the KANU Parliamentary Group committee on federation sent letters to the chief whips of each ruling party suggesting that each parliamentary group send up to ten M.P.s to a meeting at Nairobi on May 7. Although their hopes were given a jolt when it became known that Uganda would not be represented at the meeting, the KANU and TANU backbenchers and KADU members determinedly proceeded with their conference nonetheless. B. M. Kaggia, the chairman of the KANU Parliamentary Group committee on East African federation, described federation as "overdue" and stated, "All efforts must be made to effect it now, by a united action of us all." And on May 8 the parliamentarians approved resolutions setting out a timetable for the formation of a federation in East Africa. The backbenchers called upon the three heads of government to meet before May 20 in order to sign and publish a declaration stating their intention to federate and demanded that final ratification by the National Assemblies take place before budget day or by June 16, whichever came sooner. If Uganda refused to commit itself at this time, Kenya and Tanzania should go ahead on their own, said the parliamentarians, leaving the door open for Uganda to join later.

The three heads of government did not view these resolutions quite as the

Nairobi parliamentarians had anticipated. Nyerere restated Tanzania's willingness to enter an East African federation or a union with Kenya or Uganda alone, but he said that if the other parties were not prepared to make a full and unqualified commitment to federation, it was infinitely better that they should wait. Obote, from his side, expressed open indignation at the parliamentarians' initiative on federation. He accused the backbenchers of trying to push the East African leaders into federation before many important issues had been settled, and he declared that if Tanzania and Kenya wished to go ahead with federation, Uganda would wish them well but would not be forced into any hasty union. He also accused them of harming East African unity by displaying a lack of confidence in the Heads of Government. "It looks," he remarked resentfully, "as if you are yourselves deciding the fate of 25,000,000 people—or, as you put it, 18,000,000 people."

Finally, on May 11, 1964, the backbenchers received their most serious rebuff. Prime Minister Jomo Kenyatta declared that the parliamentarians' conference had been premature and their resolutions ill-timed. Kenyatta described backbench resolutions on a federation of Kenya and Tanzania without Uganda as "a grave disservice to the cause" of East African unity and insisted that "the whole pace towards federation must be the subject of governmental decisions working through the legislative bodies."

Yet despite these high-level rebuffs, the parliamentarians continued to press for an early federation. On May 12, 1964, the members of the KANU Parliamentary Group committee on federation denied that they had been disloyal to their governments and declared that it was their moral and constitutional right to uphold the public will. Speakers at the Central Legislative Assembly meeting in Nairobi at the end of May continued to press for unity, advocating, for example, an East African central bank, an increase in authority of the Central Legislative Assembly, the holding of a referendum on federation, and the release of information on the differences between governments on the federation issue. Thus on the eve of the final working party conference on federation, a large section of the elite public remained at odds with their governments as to the urgency and practicability of East African federation.

Conference Deadlock

The federal working party held its final two-day meeting in Kampala at the end of May, 1964. Early press releases were highly optimistic over the outcome. But it soon became apparent that the governments remained deeply divided on many crucial issues. Tanzania's Minister of External Affairs, Kambona, disclosed in Dar es Salaam that the delegates were in fact fundamentally divided in their approach to East African unity. To emphasize his point, he and his colleagues took the East African public fully into their confidence for the first time by publishing a detailed report of the Kampala meeting.

This report revealed substantial differences of opinion on the site of the federal capital, the powers of the Senate, and the division of powers between the federal government and the component parts. Uganda, differing from the others, generally sought to limit central authority in such fields as foreign affairs, citizenship, external borrowing, agriculture, marketing boards, animal husbandry, higher education, mines, and trade unions. Thus, whereas Nekyon insisted that foreign affairs be a state subject, Mboya and Kambona considered it essential that foreign relations be a central responsibility. Ugandans wanted external borrowing placed on the concurrent list; Kenyans said that the central government should be in a position to regulate such borrowing.

In view of these fundamental policy divergencies, Kambona asked the Uganda delegation whether it thought "that the Working Party should now write to the heads of Government and say that, in their view, a political federation was not feasible and that they should make recommendations to strengthen E.A.C.S.O."

The chairman of the Uganda delegation, Onama, agreed that this was the view of his group, and the working party deliberations came to an end.

Reactions to Failure

Reactions to the report of the Kampala working party meeting varied from country to country. In Kenya, the backbenchers kept up the pressure for federation and, refusing to be intimidated "from any quarter," B. M. Kaggia told a press conference on June 4, 1964, that the Kenya parliamentarians' stand on federation was vindicated and that his group would confer soon with TANU backbenchers on plans to effect immediate federation. A head-on clash with Kenyatta's government occurred soon afterward when the backbenchers gave enthusiastic support to a motion in the House of Representatives calling on the government to present instruments of East African federation for ratification by the National Assembly not later than August 15, 1964. During the debate, Kenyatta refused to set any timetable for the achievement of federation, declaring such an approach to be impracticable. However, on June 18, 1964, despite Kenyatta's commanding position in both Kenyan and African politics, the rebellious KANU backbenchers and their KADU allies, by a vote of 59 to 28, forced through the motion to speed up the negotiations on federation. Their action dealt Kenya's new government an unprecedented defeat.

Kenyatta moved swiftly to regain the initiative. He called for and received mass support for his leadership at a rally in Nairobi shortly after his parliamentary defeat, and at a meeting with the KANU Parliamentary Group on June 25, he also attempted to turn public attention from federation to more pressing national issues. On August 2, 1964, he seemed to be playing down the importance of achieving early federation and avoiding embarrassment when he told a Kisumu rally that the June 5 communiqué on federation was an "ingenious" means of hastening Kenya's independence. Because he considered Britain and the United States keen on East African federation, he alleged that the declaration had been a means of prodding Britain to speed Kenya's independence so as not to obstruct East African unity. As for Kenyatta's attitude on future negotiations, his statement at Kisumu, "We are now proceeding without haste," seemed to sum up his view on the matter.

Parliamentarians in Tanzania remained steadfast in the cause of federation. During a rousing debate in Parliament on June 23, 1964, the government felt called upon to give a full statement of its position on the question and Kambona stated, "We would prefer to federate with both of our East African neighbours, but we are prepared to federate with one or the other." He added, "We are not interested in a federation which is not a genuine political federation." At the debate's end, the National Assembly unanimously adopted a motion calling for immediate action to form an East African federation.

In Uganda, political leaders continued to be as hesitant about federation as ever. On June 26, 1964, Obote told a press conference that his country would not be hustled into an East African federation. "Uganda is not against federation," he stated, "but there are certain problems which are extremely important to Uganda and which must be settled before the federation comes into being." The same day, Minister of Planning Nekyon noted that in addition to differences already announced Uganda demanded that member states should be granted the right of secession from the federation, that there should be equal representation of member states in the Senate, and that the states should be permitted to place restrictions on freedom of movement within the federation. Moreover, unlike the other parliamentarians, those in Uganda gave full support to their government's cautious approach to the federation question.

Federation had come to a standstill. However, as Nekyon indicated at the Kampala working party meeting, there was much that could be salvaged from the breakdown in these negotiations. Nekyon's recommendation that EACSO should be strengthened showed a practical attitude toward gradually increasing joint action in the economic sphere. The goal of unity remained the same; yet, as with European union, the emphasis had moved from a political to a functional approach.

Conclusion

Region-building by consent, a complicated and tedious process at best, is, if anything, more difficult to attain now than ever before. In the past, as in the present, political, ethnic, or territorial fears appeared in one fashion or another with each attempt to integrate sovereign states into a single entity. Immediate national interests were frequently stressed to the detriment of broader, long-term regional interests, and many political leaders failed to recognize fully the potential benefits of wide territorial integration. Then as now, the objective conditions for union and the enhanced scope for joint action could only predispose toward closer association; they were no guarantees of success in themselves. In the last analysis, men must be willing to share political power; otherwise the best of negotiating teams will be helpless to overcome differences at the bargaining table. In brief, men are challenged to leap into the unknown for the greater good of their region as a whole. It is a risk from which many have drawn back.

If in all eras federations have proved difficult to weld together, are there special complications about integrating territories under present-day conditions? East Africa's experience may be helpful here. During the 1963–1964 debate over federation, East Africans became acutely aware of a wide gamut of political, territorial, and ethnic fears as well as sharply differing appraisals of both national interest and the need for haste. Yet such anxieties and variances of outlook are anything but unusual to the federation process. Consequently it is necessary to look elsewhere for answers.

At this point let us reexamine Nyerere's argument that federation should precede independence. Nyerere was supremely conscious of the need for speed. He urged East African countries and the British to act while the political situation remained fluid, for he assumed—and correctly—that once the territories gained independence separately, a host of vested interests would grow up within each sovereign state. In December, 1962, Nyerere could ask, "What is Tanganyika after all—East Africa makes more sense," but it would not be long after independence before territorial consciousness would supplant East African consciousness. Territorial borders, which were admittedly artificial prior to independence, would become firmer barriers after independence. What is more, different constitutional structures would inevitably evolve after decolonization, thereby militating against an effective East African unity.

Events following independence bore out Nyerere's analysis. As the British relinquished control in East Africa, the new African governments tackled the demanding tasks of nation-building and economic development. As a result, territorial consciousness developed and political systems diverged increasingly in the year after the June 5, 1963, declaration on federation was issued. Following the mutinies of January, 1964, Tanganyika took decisive steps to set up a legally sanctioned one-party system with a high degree of central control over various interest groups and activities in the society. Kenyans conceded *majimbo* (subregionalism) in order to speed the transfer of power, but the KANU-controlled government moved steadily toward unitary direction and control. In Uganda the tripartite constitutional system, including features of federalism, semifederalism, and unitary government, reflected the local power configurations existing in that country. The localism of Uganda politics, and in particular the power and determination of Buganda, circumscribed Obote's flexibility of movement. Thus Nyerere's fears of territorial consciousness and constitutional divergence were substantiated—to the detriment of an East African federation.

In addition, Nyerere's actions after Tanganyika had gained independence pointed to another basic complicating factor of the present era. From the time Tanganyika gained independence in December, 1961, until the army mutinies in January, 1964, Nyerere attempted to preserve as much flexibility as possible in his country's political system. Only after the mutinies made a tightening of the reins essential did Nyerere reluctantly increase control over the labor movement and establish a one-party state by law. His reluctance stemmed principally from his realization that such steps would harden the East African political situation. To create an East African labor movement or a federal political party would obviously be more difficult once highly centralized control came into operation within a territory. But it is just such voluntary area-wide movements of labor and political alignments which could give political federation the strength to stand up against separatist forces after constitutional unity had been established.

More fundamentally, twentieth-century welfare-state means and objectives increase the power of the state in every country. Because the center would normally have to take over most of these responsibilities in the event of federation, regional integration tends to involve a more extreme commitment than in earlier eras. Canadian and American federalists operated under easier conditions—capitalism was no respecter of boundaries, development plans were virtually unknown, and limited government was an accepted way of life. Today's situation places enormous responsibilities—and pressures—upon leaders to achieve immediate results. Consequently, these leaders must act at times according to their view of the national interest which may appear shortsighted to the detached observer. By February, 1964, immediate affairs of state had taken precedence in East Africa, and longer term objectives such as federation were laid aside.

East Africans have not decided for all time the final outcome of the federation question. That they have survived the common market crisis and preserved EACSO is a hopeful sign for the future. Such interterritorial institutions are likely to foster "social communication" among East Africa's political, economic, and technical elite, thereby helping to promote an East African consciousness. It remains to be seen whether East Africa's political leaders will think it worthwhile in time to surmount all the difficulties in the way of federation and take on the risks it involves. In the end, they may have to design a different integration model than any now existing; if they can do this, we will all be richer from studying their experience.

Study Questions

1. In 1960 President Nyerere argued that separate independence would complicate the task of East African unity. Does this case support his contention? And why did many observers argue that unless the three governments swiftly committed themselves to political unification in the period after decolonization, new strains would probably appear in the common market and common services organization?

2. What factors affected the negotiations on federation most adversely—ethnic or territorial fears? the leaders' ambitions? different foreign policy objectives? external pressures? divergent political and constitutional systems? the application of present-day methods to control the economy? conflicts of economic interest among the partners?

3. A veil of secrecy surrounded the early negotiations on East African federation. Although few observers argue that the task of region-building would be advanced by informing the public about negotiations while swift agreement is possible, there is wide disagreement on the advisability of leaving the public uninformed over a lengthy period of time. What are the dangers of leaving the public in a vacuum, and at what point would statesmen be advised to take their countrymen fully into their confidence?

4. Once it became clear in the 1963–64 period that federation involved a greater political commitment than East Africa's leaders seemed prepared to make, what other constitutional formulas might have been proposed that would have lessened their fears while at the same time preserved the most significant advantages of wide territorial integration?

5. Are supraregional federations a practical means of bringing about Pan-African unification? If not, does the surrender of sovereignty to a continental African government seem a feasible alternative?

Selected Bibliography

Major Sources

ADU, A. L. "Staffing and Training the Federal Civil Services," *University of East Africa Conferences on Public Policy 1963–64* (Nairobi), II (November, 1963).

BANFIELD, JANE. "Federation in East Africa," *International Journal,* XVIII (Spring, 1963), 181–93.

BELSHAW, D. G. R. "Agricultural Production and Trade in the East African Common Market," *University of East Africa Conferences on Public Policy 1963–64* (Nairobi), II (November, 1963).

CLARK, PAUL G. "Co-ordination of Development Plans in East Africa," *Proceedings of the East African Institute of Social Research Conference.* Kampala, January, 1964.

COLONIAL OFFICE. *East Africa: Report of the Economic and Fiscal Commission*

(Sir Jeremy Raisman, Chairman). Cmnd. 1279. London: Her Majesty's Stationery Office, 1961.

———. *The Future of East Africa High Commission Services*. Cmnd. 1433. London: Her Majesty's Stationery Office, 1961.

Daily Nation. Nairobi, 1961–64.

DAVIS, JOHN A., ed. *Pan-Africanism Reconsidered*. Berkeley: University of California Press, 1962.

EAST AFRICAN COMMON SERVICES ORGANIZATION. *Economic and Statistical Review*. Nairobi: Government Printer, 1963.

———. *Proceedings of the Central Legislative Assembly Debates*. Nairobi: Government Printer, 1962–64.

East African Standard. Nairobi, 1960–64.

FRANK, CHARLES R., JR. "The Production and Distribution of Sugar in East Africa," *Proceedings of the East African Institute of Social Research Conference*. Kampala, January, 1964.

GHAI, DHARAM. "Territorial Distribution of Benefits and Cost of the East African Customs Union," *University of East Africa Conferences on Public Policy 1963–64* (Nairobi), II (November, 1963).

HICKS, URSULA K., *et al. Federalism and Economic Growth in Underdeveloped Countries*. New York: Oxford University Press, 1961.

HUGHES, A. J. *East Africa: The Search for Unity*. Harmondsworth, Eng.: Penguin Books, 1963.

INTERNATIONAL BANK FOR RECONSTRUCTION AND DEVELOPMENT. *The Economic Development of Kenya*. Baltimore: The Johns Hopkins Press, 1963.

———. *The Economic Development of Tanganyika*. Baltimore: The Johns Hopkins Press, 1961.

———. *The Economic Development of Uganda*. Baltimore: The Johns Hopkins Press, 1962.

Kenya Weekly News. Nairobi, 1960–64.

MASSELL, BENTON F. *East African Economic Union: An Evaluation and Some Implications for Policy,* Memorandum RM–2880–RC. Santa Monica: The Rand Corporation, 1963.

MBOYA, T. J. "The Integration of Labour Policy," *University of East Africa Conferences on Public Policy 1963–64* (Nairobi), II (November, 1963).

MCKENZIE, BRUCE. "A Common East African Agricultural Policy," *University of East Africa Conferences on Public Policy 1963–64* (Nairobi), II (November, 1963).

NDEGWA, PHILIP. "Some Aspects of Inter-Territorial Trade in East Africa in Recent Years," *Proceedings of the East African Institute of Social Research Conference*. Kampala, January, 1964.

NYE, JOSEPH S., JR. "East African Economic Integration," *Journal of Modern African Studies,* I (1963), 475–502.

———. "Unification in Africa: Six Traps in Search of a Scholar," *Public Policy,* XIII. Cambridge, Mass.: Graduate School of Public Administration, Harvard University, 1964. Pp. 358–68.

Parliamentary Debates. Kenya, Tanganyika, Uganda, 1960–64.

Reporter. Nairobi, 1961–64.

ROSBERG, CARL G., JR., with AARON SEGAL. "An East African Federation," *International Conciliation,* 543 (May, 1963).

ROTHCHILD, DONALD. "East African Federation," *Transition,* III (Jan.–Feb., 1964), 39–42.

———. *Toward Unity in Africa: A Study of Federalism in British Africa.* Washington, D.C.: Public Affairs Press, 1960.

———. "Uganda and Federation," *Spearhead* (Dar es Salaam), I (September, 1962), 11–13.

Tanganyika Standard. Dar es Salaam, 1960–64.

Uganda Argus. Kampala, 1960–64.

UGANDA PROTECTORATE. *The East African Common Services Organization Ordinance 1961.* Entebbe: Government Printer, 1961.

VAN ARKADIE, BRIAN. "Central Bank in an East African Federation," *University of East Africa Conferences on Public Policy 1963–64* (Nairobi), II (November, 1963).

7

South Africa and the High Commission Territories

The Ganyile Case, 1961

Jeffrey Butler

On September 21, 1961, the left-wing weekly newspaper *New Age,* published in Cape Town and Johannesburg, gave half of its front page to a sensational story under a one-and-a-half inch headline:

S.A. POLICE KIDNAP PONDO LEADERS IN BASUTOLAND

ANDERSON GANYILE SEIZED AT DEAD OF NIGHT,

WHISKED ACROSS THE BORDER INTO S.A.

Prominently displayed was a photostatic copy of a handwritten note "smuggled by Mr. Ganyile . . . this week":

> Kidnapped in Basutoland on 26/8/61 at 10:30 P.M. by 6 policemen from the Union. We were three and we are now in K.D. and we appeal to friends. We know and can identify our kidnappers.
>
> Yours,
>
> *Powers*

The headline and the note require some explanation. *New Age* gave the following details: "K.D." stands for Kokstad, capital of the Mount Currie District, an area owned by white farmers. "Powers" is "the pseudonym used by Mr. Ganyile in correspondence with his friends in South Africa";

Anderson Khumani Ganyile was "the young Pondo leader who escaped last February [1961] from exile in Frenchdale concentration camp near Mafeking and was living at Qacha's Nek in Basutoland." Furthermore, South African terminology should be defined: the "Pondo" are a Bantu people living in the Transkei, an area in which almost all rural sections are reserved for the occupancy of Africans; "Bantu" is used by scholars to define a very large family of African languages, but in South African official terminology it is synonymous with "African"; "the Union" is a widely used colloquialism for the former Union of South Africa, which became the Republic on May 31, 1961, outside the Commonwealth of Nations. Finally, Basutoland, Bechuanaland Protectorate, and Swaziland are collectively known as the "High Commission Territories" or, inaccurately, as "the Protectorates." When South Africa left the Commonwealth, the title of British High Commissioner was changed to British Ambassador to South Africa except in relation to the territories. The latter also had their own British resident commissioners and varying types and degrees of local representation.

This case is both a political and legal problem. An independent government—South Africa—had been accused of kidnapping one of its own citizens who had sought and been given asylum in a dependency—Basutoland—of another independent government—Great Britain. A very rough analogy could be drawn if an American had gained asylum in, say, Canada in about 1830, fifty years after the independence of the United States, and had been kidnapped by a group of American officials. It is a problem involving an individual and his rights, in relation both to his own government and to the one which had given him asylum. The South African government stood accused of a violation of British territory.

How could this accusation be tested? And if it were proved that a violation had taken place, what action would the British government take? In more general terms, what moves governments to act in disputes of this kind, and to what extent can the rights of individuals be secured?

Anderson Ganyile: His Life and Times

Assuming that Ganyile had been taken by force across the boundary between the Transkei and Basutoland by police officers who were aware of what they were doing, why should he have been regarded by the South African government, or by some of its officers, as worthy of such drastic treatment? Both his connection with the African nationalist movement and the area from which he came—the Transkei—seem highly relevant to what had developed.

The Transkei and Basutoland

The Transkei is the largest and most homogeneous of South Africa's African reserve territories and the first one to be granted so-called Bantus-

Eastern South Africa, 1961

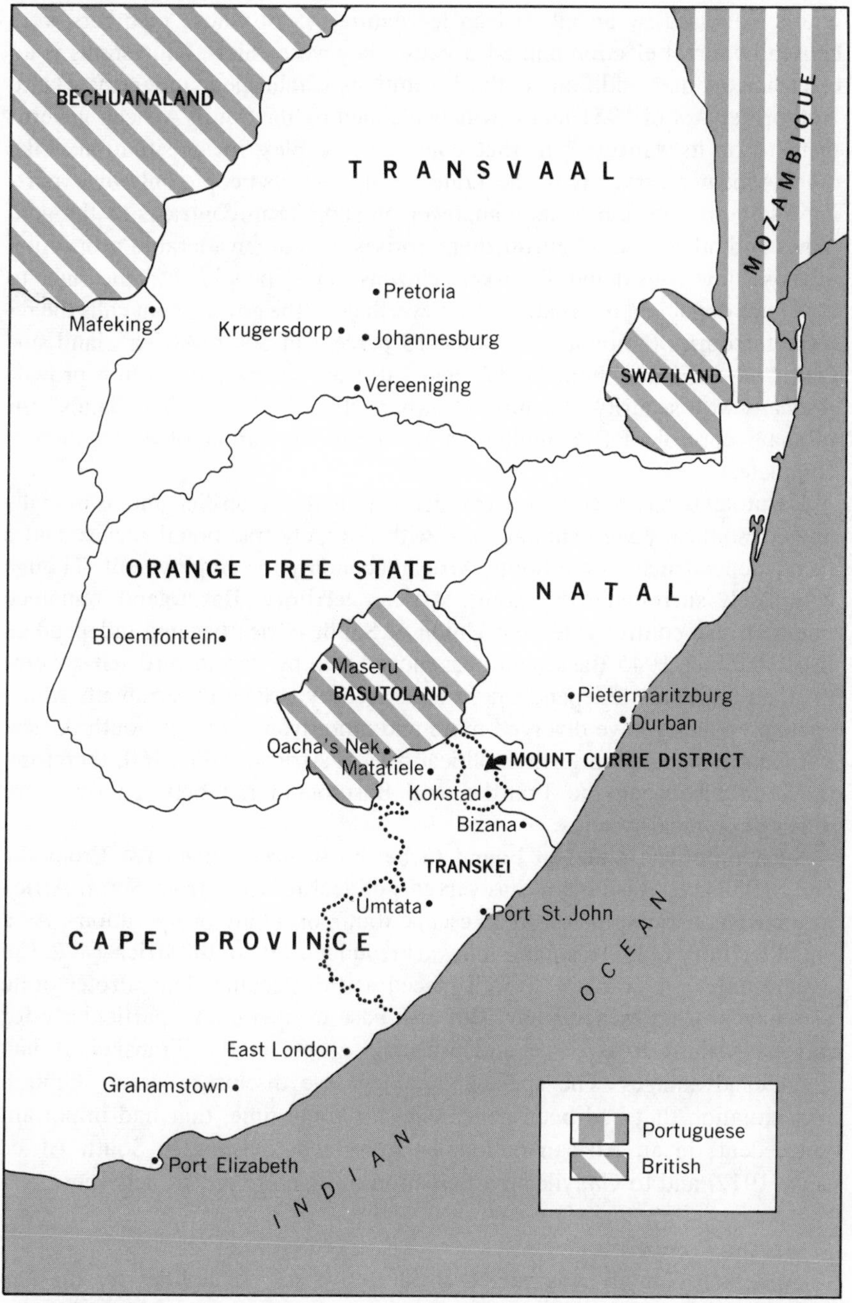
BECHUANALAND
TRANSVAAL
MOZAMBIQUE
Pretoria
Mafeking
Krugersdorp
Johannesburg
Vereeniging
SWAZILAND
ORANGE FREE STATE
NATAL
Bloemfontein
Maseru
BASUTOLAND
Pietermaritzburg
Durban
Qacha's Nek
Matatiele
MOUNT CURRIE DISTRICT
Kokstad
Bizana
TRANSKEI
Umtata
Port St. John
CAPE PROVINCE
OCEAN
East London
Grahamstown
Portuguese
British
Port Elizabeth
INDIAN

tan status. In 1963, the Transkei received a measure of autonomy in local affairs exercised by an all-African legislature, 45 of whose members were chosen by direct election and 64 because they were chiefs. This status is an extension of and addition to the institutions established under the Bantu Authorities Act of 1951 and is widely claimed by the South African government to be its "answer" to that country's complex racial situation. Like other African reserve areas, the Transkei supports its people only by exporting a large proportion of its manpower on short-term contracts to the gold mines and other white-controlled enterprises, and a considerable proportion of those now considered Transkei "citizens" (i.e., people with the right to vote) are domiciled in urban areas. Nevertheless, the government calls the reserve territories (amounting to some 13 percent of South Africa's land surface) the African "homelands" and, at least in law, does not provide Africans with security of tenure elsewhere. Even in these "homelands" the ultimate control of 3½ million in the total population of 16 million is complete.

Basutoland has a common frontier within the Transkei and is socially and economically very similar to it, with a largely traditional society and a heavy dependence on the South African economy for employment. Though completely surrounded by South African territory, Basutoland remained under British control when the Union of South Africa became independent in 1910. Since 1945 Basutoland has moved step by step toward self-government and ultimate independence, encouraged by British governments whose "native" policies have diverged more and more from those of South Africa, particularly in relation to the political role of Africans. By 1960, therefore, the border between the Transkei and Basutoland ran between two very different political systems.

Such a border is almost bound to be the scene of incidents. From the early 1950s on, Basutoland has served political refugees from South Africa as a haven, a resting place on an escape route, or a base of operations. As a small territory (11,716 square miles) surrounded by South Africa (472,359 square miles), it was not so well placed as the Bechuanaland Protectorate as a haven or an escape route. But as a base of operations, particularly for anyone wishing to observe and influence events in the Transkei, it had definite advantages. The spectacular *New Age* disclosure drew attention to a situation that had been developing for some time, that had important antecedents in an African nationalist movement existing in South Africa since 1912, and to Ganyile's participation in its more recent activities.

African Protest

Anderson Ganyile was stirred to an active role in politics by the Defiance Campaign of 1952 and by the Bantu Education Act of 1953. The campaign was an attempt by the standard bearer of African nationalism, the African National Congress (ANC), to awaken the white conscience by passive resistance. The Bantu Education Act effected a major change in the control and content of African education, principally by converting missionary-run, state-aided schools into state institutions. Special curricula were drafted to make greater use of local African languages, to increase the use of Afrikaans—the language of South Africa's ruling political party—rather than English, and to relate the education of African children more closely to their expected subordinate position in South African society. In 1953, at seventeen, Ganyile joined the Youth League of the ANC, founded in 1944 by militant younger members of the Congress. While at a mission high school, Lovedale, Ganyile was in trouble both with the school authorities and with the Special (i.e., political and security) Branch of the South African police. In 1959 Ganyile went to Fort Hare University College which for long had been the only liberal arts college for Africans in South Africa, and which had recently been changed from an independent college into a state institution under the Department of Bantu Education. Government control over curricula, faculty, and students, became very strict, and expulsion was a frequent means of disciplining those students who were critical of state policy. Early in 1960 Ganyile was told that he would not be accepted back as a student; he then returned to his home in Pondoland in the Transkei.

Sharpeville

The government could hardly have chosen a more disturbed time at which to force a young, educated, and resentful African to return to a rural society. On February 3, 1960, in Cape Town, United Kingdom Prime Minister Harold Macmillan had made his celebrated "wind of change" speech. It was addressed to a far larger audience than the South African one, to demonstrate to the new African states that Great Britain was not condoning or supporting South African policies of racial discrimination in political and economic life. In the following month the Pan-Africanist Congress (called PAC), a militant group that had broken away from the African National Congress (ANC) in 1959, planned demonstrations against the laws under which Africans must carry passes. At Sharpeville, near Vereeniging in the Transvaal province, sixty-seven Africans were killed when the police opened fire during the first of these political demonstrations. The shots were indeed heard around the world: the Security Council was called into session on the grounds of a "threat to the peace," and the government of the United States rebuked the South African government in a press statement deploring the loss of life. There followed widespread work boycotts by Africans and also an acceleration of an already serious outflow of capital.

The South African government reacted vigorously. A state of emergency was declared, gatherings were prohibited, and both the African National Congress and the Pan-Africanist Congress were banned. A large number of people, both Africans and others politically suspect to the government because of their sympathies for Africans, were detained. On March 30, one week after Sharpeville, Ganyile was arrested, presumably in the Bizana district of Pondoland, and detained in East London. He was released on August 8, 1960, and returned to Bizana.

The Peasants' Revolt and Ganyile's Part in It

In retrospect, the willingness of the authorities to allow Ganyile to return to Pondoland in August is surprising. The disturbances in March had been urban phenomena and related to protests against the structure of white power. But in Pondoland, an entirely rural area, there had been considerable disorder from May onward in a form that suggested a "civil war" among Africans, those who supported and were paid by the government challenging those reacting against it. The conflict had been going on for over two months when he returned, and it continued for some months more. On May 26, *The Times* (London) reported that "detachments of heavily armed police were patrolling the Bizana and Lusikisiki districts of Pondoland"; there were stories of hut-burning at Bizana on June 20, and six days later the police opened fire at Nquisa hill, killing eleven Africans. Arson, almost entirely of African huts, became common.

Frequently chiefs were targets of this violence. The government appointed a commission to inquire into the cause of the unrest. In its report, published on October 11, the commission claimed that a major grievance had been the failure to allow tribal custom in the appointment of "Bantu Authorities." These authorities had been set up under the Bantu Authorities Act of 1951, a measure providing a system of local government in African areas under control of the chiefs and the South African government. The commission defended the substance of this policy, questioning only its application. This report, however, had little, if any, effect on the unrest: on November 8 Africans boycotted a meeting with the Chief Native Commissioner for the Transkei, and on November 30 the government declared a state of emergency in the Transkei.

Organs of protest soon developed in that area to challenge the government's policies. A "Pondo National Committee" drew up a memorandum of grievances, and Enoch Mbhele, a Pondo, left South Africa (almost certainly illegally) at the end of September, to present this memorandum to the United Nations. Ganyile was involved in an organization which in its brief life played a dramatic part in challenging white rule of the Transkei. A committee of Africans, known both as "The Hill" and as "The Congo," set itself up outside Bizana as a sort of "people's court." According to *New Age* on January 25, 1962, Ganyile "soon emerged as the Secretary of the famous 'Hill' Committee that coordinated the vast popular upswing against Bantu Authorities, passes and increased taxation." The government alleged that The Hill was responsible for attacks on chiefs and headmen whose power,

and indeed whose lives, depended on the support of the South African government. Bantu Education was also a target for The Hill, because the system was under government control and because it was replacing a world language, English, by a local one, Afrikaans. At the beginning of November, The Hill enforced a boycott of all shops in Bizana. However, the major issue remained a political one. As Ganyile said immediately after his arrest: "The people of Pondoland are demanding their inalienable birthright: freedom. Pondoland will be satisfied with nothing short of sending representatives to parliament."

Ganyile had been busy in other ways. At the end of October, cases of arson began to be tried in the courts of Pondoland, and Ganyile became, in his own words, "very actively involved in arranging legal assistance." Some of the accused were defended by Rowan Arenstein, a former Communist and lawyer from Durban who had been prohibited under the Riotous Assemblies Act of 1956 from leaving the Durban magisterial district for five years. He was given permission, however, to go to Pondoland to defend thirty-nine Africans. During the period of this trial, Ganyile assisted him as an interpreter. At the same time, Ganyile acted as a representative for *New Age*.

Arrest and Banishment

On November 7, 1960, while the boycott of shops was still in force, Ganyile was arrested in the streets of Bizana while selling *New Age*. His prominence as a political militant is clear enough from *The Times* (London) report on November 9:

> AFRICAN LEADER SEIZED IN STREET
>
> Security police at Bizana . . . yesterday [November 7] seized Mr. Anderson Ganyile, a prominent university-trained Pondo, as he was walking in a street, and took him to area police headquarters at Kokstad . . . . the indications are that he has been banished from the district.

Ganyile's arrest was part of an attempt to contain the unrest in Pondoland by arresting a large number of actual and potential leaders. By the middle of January, 1961, according to a reply by the Minister of Justice in the House of Assembly on January 27, 4,769 Africans had been detained. South African governments have long possessed extensive powers of arrest, detention, and banishment, particularly since the Native Administration Act, No. 38 of 1927, gave the state the right to arrest and banish without appeal to the courts. The key section of the act (as substituted by Section 20 of Act 56 of 1952 and amended by Section 3 of Act 42 of 1956) is as follows:

> 5(1)(b): The State-President may—whenever he deems it expedient in the general public interest without prior notice to any person concerned, order that . . . any native [i.e., African] shall withdraw from any place to any other place or to any district or province within the Union, and shall not at any time thereafter . . . return to the place from which the withdrawal is to be made . . . except with the written permission of the Secretary for Native Affairs.

There are several important features of this legislation. First, the Act applies to the whole area of the Republic, not just to the reserves. Moreover, it is not emergency legislation, in force only at specific times for slated periods. Second, the Act applies to "natives," not to whites, Coloreds, or Asians. Thus, like much of South African law, it is avowedly discriminatory. Third, the powers of the president, or of the responsible cabinet minister acting for him, are very wide indeed, giving him the right at his sole discretion, without giving notice to anyone and without scrutiny by the courts, to order a "native" (i.e., African) to move from "any place" to "any other place" within the Republic. Moreover, there is no possibility of an appeal, *either* to declare the legislation unconstitutional, *or* to appeal to a specific historic provision such as a bill of rights. The South African constitution in fact includes no bill of rights. It is also virtually impossible to appeal on the more limited grounds that the Act has not been properly enforced. Fourthly, although the Act provides a penalty for refusing to obey, it does not *require* that a "native" so refusing be charged: he can simply be arrested, detained, and removed without any recourse to the courts. It seems, indeed, that it is the practice to deport those who refuse without charging them. Finally, the precise limits within which the banished "native" must live are to be set out in an order.

Later, in the April 1962 issue of *Drum,* Ganyile gave this account of his arrest:

> I was taken to the Native Commissioner's Office in Bizana. He informed me that there was a Ministerial Order for me to be removed to Frenchdale [the banishment farm at Mafeking]. I asked whether I could inform my attorneys, but permission was refused. I asked whether I could see my aging mother to wish her goodbye, but the authorities said "No." Instead they asked me whether I was prepared to go to Frenchdale voluntarily. When I refused the head of the Special Branch from Kokstad produced a warrant and arrested me.

It will be noted that the matter was dealt with by the Special Branch, which is exclusively involved with security and political matters, and that no charge was brought against Ganyile. He was clearly being removed for political reasons. Furthermore, he was denied communication with anyone before leaving.

The matter was handled by the authorities with despatch. On the same day Ganyile was taken first to Kokstad, thirty miles away, and then to Pietermaritzburg, the capital of Natal province. While changing trains there, he saw "an old acquaintance and asked him to pass a message to friends in Johannesburg." Presumably as a result of this message, he was interviewed and photographed in Johannesburg by reporters from the African paper *The World,* and in Krugersdorp by representatives of the liberal weekly *Contact* and of *New Age,* while on the way to Frenchdale, a farm near Mafeking in Cape Province.

Escape and Exile

Frenchdale has long been used as a place of banishment for Africans; according to Ganyile, Chief Mopeli of the Orange Free State claimed to have been there for twelve years. Looking back on it Ganyile complained of the enforced idleness: "There is nothing whatever to do at Frenchdale. All the people can do is sit in their huts and rot."

Ganyile had not gone to Frenchdale in a submissive mood. In handcuffs and under guard in the train at Krugersdorp station, he showed that he was anything but cowed: "The barbarous deportation measure . . . will not change my character. My only crime is that I have allied myself with my people." (*New Age,* September 21, 1961.) It is not surprising, therefore, that he made his escape some time between December, 1960, and February, 1961, not, it should be noted, to the Bechuanaland Protectorate a few miles away from Mafeking, but via Johannesburg to Maseru in Basutoland, across about 280 miles of South African territory. In Basutoland he was granted a Residence Permit in the terms of the Basutoland Entry and Residence Proclamation of 1958, presumably on the grounds that the reasons for his detention at Frenchdale had been political; thus there were no charges against him on which the South African government could ask for his extradition under the Fugitive Offenders Act of 1881, which still applies to British colonies and former colonies. Before the end of December he moved east another ninety miles to the village of Qacha's Nek on the border of East Griqualand, the northern section of the Transkei, and about ninety miles from Bizana. A friend offered him the use of a deserted hut one mile from Qacha's Nek and exactly 638 yards from the South African border. There is no evidence that the South African government applied to the Basutoland authorities to execute a warrant for Ganyile's extradition.

Information is meager both on Ganyile's escape and on his activities in the next eight months. On January 7, 1961, a South African government official denied that Ganyile had left Frenchdale, but at the end of February *New Age* published a photograph of Ganyile in Maseru. It is probable that he had chosen Basutoland, and particularly Qacha's Nek, to reestablish his political contacts and to resume his opposition to the government, which was not slow in reacting to his activities. According to the article in the African monthly *Drum,* April, 1962, there were rumors in Qacha's Nek that South African agents had been in the village in July and August, 1961, immediately before the kidnapping, offering bribes for information on Ganyile. In an affidavit from an unnamed informer, submitted by the South African Minister of Justice in later legal proceedings, is the following account of Ganyile's activities:

> I found that another person had been staying at Qacha's Nek for a while but had returned to his home which is somewhere near . . . and has been instructed by Ganyile to organize sabotage . . . .
>
> During my stay there I found that they were planning the following:
> (a) Boycotting and killing of Chiefs.
> (b) Cutting of fences where [land] Rehabilitation Schemes had been established.
> (c) Cutting of telephone wires.
> (d) Damaging of bridges.
> (e) Other acts of sabotage like burning of Government buildings, like Magistrates Offices, Bantu Authority buildings, damaging of dipping tanks, etc.
> (f) Killing of Government informers and witnesses for the prosecution in the Pondo Unrest cases.
> (g) Any other acts which would harm the Government or other subversive activities.

It is difficult on internal evidence alone to establish the authenticity of the document or the accuracy of the reporting. However, the allegations against Ganyile were not implausible. He was by his own account in contact with friends in South Africa who helped him to "keep body and soul together" and sent him "reports from time to time of . . . the troubles of the Pondo people." A frequent companion was Jackson Nkosyane, the *New Age* reporter who went to the same hut in August. Ingleton Ganyile, a cousin who succeeded Anderson as a seller of *New Age* in Bizana, joined him at Qacha's Nek in May, 1961, and Mohlovu Mtseko, a Masotho from the Transkei, fled after the declaration of emergency in November, 1960, and joined Anderson and Ingleton some time later. Thus a group of exiles was forming on the border of the Transkei and, perhaps, was in frequent contact with groups in Pondoland.

Kidnap

It has been difficult to reconstruct what happened on August 26. Only one side of the story has been told at any length; the six South African policemen involved have yet to give their version of the events. None of the parties involved were cross-examined. Furthermore, for months little "hard fact" was available. The following account comes from an affidavit by Ganyile dated January 9, 1962, three and one-half months after the kidnapping took place, and published the next day. After telling how he reached Qacha's Nek, Ganyile described the events of August 26:

> At about 10:30 P.M. of that day, I was awakened by Ingleton Ganyile who informed me that there were people at the door. I asked who they were and a voice replied saying he was Ndaba. Ndaba is the name of the owner of the said hut.
>
> As Ndaba had never visited me at that hour of the night, I became suspicious . . . . After further conversation with the people outside I recognized one of the voices as being that of Constable du Toit of the South African Police. He was born and bred in Bizana and was well known to me.
>
> As soon as I realized that the party outside the hut included members of the South African Police I became most apprehensive because I knew they had no authority to operate without a proper warrant, and no mention had been made of any such document.
>
> I concluded that they were there for some very serious purpose which might include bringing about my death and I accordingly determined to defend myself.
>
> The party outside then commenced throwing stones at the door and windows of the hut. The windows were covered with cardboard which soon tore open, allowing the attackers to shine their torches into the hut. At that stage I was at the door of the hut, armed with an axe, whilst my companions were at the windows armed with bottles.
>
> I instructed my companions to do all in their power to resist this unlawful attack, and they commenced throwing bottles at the attackers. We also raised the alarm, shouted out that we were being attacked by members of the South African Police. When we started shouting, our attackers withdrew for a short distance, but when nobody came to our aid they returned.
>
> The attackers threw more stones and someone threw himself at the door. The door burst open, and as he entered the hut I struck at him with the axe. It was merely a glancing blow and I later recognized this person as the said du Toit. He was wearing civilian clothes and a balaclava cap.
>
> Others of the attackers entered the hut and after a violent struggle I and my companions were overcome and handcuffed. There were six people in the attacking party and I recognized five of them as members of the South African Police. . . .
>
> They were all in civilian clothes and were wearing scarves which had been wrapped around the lower half of their faces as masks. . . .
>
> I was able to see that I had injured Sergeant du Toit [earlier Ganyile referred to him as "Constable"] on the face. . . .
>
> After I had been handcuffed, I was struck a violent blow between the shoulders and pushed out of the hut.

When I reached the door I attempted to escape and was pursued, thrown to the ground and kicked. One of my assailants spoke to me in a low voice and warned me to keep quiet or they would shoot me.

There is a fence along the border and this point of the road from Matatiele to Qacha's Nek passes through a gate which is manned by a constable in the Basutoland Police. My attackers did not take me to this gate or to the road, but forced me to walk across country towards the fence which marks the border.

I continued struggling and shouting and then Sergeant Potgieter tied a scarf around my neck and Jan put a handkerchief in my mouth to gag me. I continued my struggles but was forced to the border. . . .

The three of us were then handcuffed together and taken towards one of two cars which were parked on the South African side of the border.

Durance Vile

Ganyile did not appear in court until December 22 and did not give his own account until January 9, 1962. According to that account, and to documents released by the Department of Justice, he was taken at once to Matatiele in the Transkei, the nearest town across the border, where he was questioned on the same night. On September 7 he was moved to Kokstad and it was from there that he smuggled out his note, clearly thinking that he was going to stay there. But he was moved at once to Umtata, and he remained in solitary confinement thereafter.

It might well be asked what was the alleged legal basis of Ganyile's detention. The police took no action during the two weeks between the kidnapping and the smuggling of the note either to charge Ganyile or to return him to his place of banishment. According to an affidavit signed by the Minister of Justice on January 10, 1962, Sergeant Hendrik Steyn of the

> South African Police was satisfied that certain offences in terms of Proclamation R400 of 1960 . . . had been committed . . . . The said Steyn had at all relevant times reasonable grounds to suspect the said Ganyile of taking part, or intending or having intended to take part in the offences or intended offences in question. . . . The aforesaid Ganyile failed to satisfy the said Steyn that he was answering the questions put to him fully and truthfully and he has been detained since 26th August, 1961, in terms of the Regulation 19 of the aforesaid Proclamation R400 of 1960, as amended.

On August 27, the day after the kidnapping, Sergeant Steyn signed a "*Warrant of Detention,* to the Keeper of Mount Fletcher Prison" requiring "you to detain him [Ganyile] until he has answered to my satisfaction fully and truthfully all questions. . . ."

Proclamation R400 was issued on November 30, 1960; it was the principal proclamation in the declaration of emergency on that day. It was not, however, an emergency provision in the sense that it had been proclaimed with a definite time limit, but was part of ordinary law, issued under an old statute, the Transkei Annexation Act of 1877, which delegated large powers to law enforcement officers to be used only in the Transkei. Regulations 19 and 20 are given below:

> 19. (1) Whenever a Native Commissioner or a commissioned or non-commissioned officer of the South African Police, is satisfied that any person has committed an offence . . . or whenever the said Native Commissioner or commissioned or non-commissioned officer has reason to suspect that any person has or had the intention to commit such an offence the said Native Commissioner or commissioned or non-commissioned officer may without warrant arrest or cause to be arrested any person whom he suspects upon reasonable grounds of having taken part or intending or having intended to take part in the offence or intended offence in question . . . may detain or cause him to be detained at any place which the said Native Commissioner or commissioned or non-commissioned officer deems suitable for the purpose until the said Native Commissioner or commissioned or non-commissioned officer is satisfied that the said person has answered fully and truthfully all questions put to him which have any bearing upon the said offence or intended offence. . . .
>
> . . .
>
> 20. No person who has been arrested and is being detained under regulation 19 shall, without the consent of the Minister or person acting under his authority, be allowed to consult with a legal adviser in connection with any matter relating to the arrest and detention of such person.

If this had been the final say of the law, Ganyile could have been detained indefinitely.

A Tight-lipped Government

One of the remarkable features of the Ganyile case is the small amount of information released by the South African government. The publication of the story in *New Age* on September 21, 1961, certainly appeared to place the ball in the government's court and the issue was taken up by *The Rand Daily Mail.* But *New Age* was a paper on the far left, in South African terms, given to sensationalism and with very small readership among South African whites. Parliament was not sitting, and it was not necessary, therefore, for ministers to answer probing questions. Of course, the whole case would have ended if Ganyile had been released, but the government chose not to release him. A confused period of denials and partial admissions followed. On September 24, Colonel W. Prinsloo, Chief of the Special Branch, told a *Cape Times* reporter that he knew nothing of the alleged kidnapping and had not ordered it. Far closer to the scene of action, Major Loxton, Commandant of the police at Kokstad, an area headquarters, denied all knowledge. But the London *Observer* on September 24 printed an account of an interview with a police official who admitted the detention of Ganyile but claimed that the arrest had been *on South African soil.* Even earlier, on September 22, a Johannesburg lawyer who was searching for Ganyile had obtained by telephone from a police sergeant in Kokstad the statement that "three Basuto [sic] were brought in about a fortnight ago" and later that Ganyile was being held "somewhere in the Transkei." On October 2 the government published an emphatic denial of kidnapping in the pro-government paper *Die Burger*—if Ganyile had been arrested, they said, he had been arrested on South African soil.

Preparing the Case

In most western countries there are ways in which the state can be called upon to justify the continued detention of a prisoner. On September 28, 1961, *New Age* called on the government to produce Ganyile in court:

WE DON'T WANT A LUMUMBA TRAGEDY HERE!

S.A. POLICE ADMIT GANYILE IS IN CUSTODY IN PONDOLAND. IF THEY DENY HE WAS KIDNAPPED, LET THEM

BRING GANYILE TO COURT TO TELL HIS OWN STORY

The South African police did not, however, move quickly to charge Ganyile; the first charges were laid only in December—and it remained for Ganyile's relatives and friends to raise the issue. The Congress Alliance, a loose group of antigovernment organizations containing representatives of the South African Indian Congress, the white, left-wing Congress of Democrats, the banned African National Congress, and others, came to the aid of the Ganyile family. Legal proceedings were begun to force the government to justify further detention.

Anderson Ganyile's mother became seriously ill on the day that she received the news of the kidnapping, September 22, and the task of instituting legal proceedings fell to an uncle, Siwele Ganyile. Rowan Arenstein, the lawyer from Durban who had employed Anderson Ganyile as an interpreter in the arson cases in Pondoland, undertook to prepare the case, and Siwele Ganyile went to Durban, where a petition was drawn up. Arenstein announced that he was going to engage a leading Queen's Counsel (i.e., senior lawyer) from Durban to plead for habeas corpus, that is, that a detained person should be brought to court with the charge against him made public. This is the major safeguard against arbitrary and prolonged imprisonment.

The South African court system is divided into an Appellate Division—the highest tribunal in the system—and a number of geographical divisions, each containing a large number of magisterial districts, the basic administrative and legal divisions of the country. The Eastern Cape Division has its headquarters in Grahamstown and has jurisdiction over the whole of the Transkei. An application such as Ganyile's would, therefore, have to be heard either by a judge "on circuit" (i.e., one of the members of the Supreme Court who regularly holds court in the districts) or in the court at Grahamstown.

Mr. Justice Wynne

The case came before the courts within two weeks of the preparation of the petition drawn up and signed in Durban by Siwele Ganyile on September 30. On October 5, *New Age* published a summary of this petition. It called for the government to produce Ganyile in court and to show cause why Ganyile should not be released and returned to Basutoland; *or,* if he was to be detained, why he was being detained without charge. On October 13 the application was heard before Mr. Justice Wynne.

Before going on the bench, Lieutenant Colonel George Wynne had been a lawyer in Port Elizabeth and had served in the South African forces in World War II. As an English-speaking South African he would, if he had acted like most of his contemporaries, have found a political home in the opposition United Party. But after World War II he became very active in the National Party, led by Dr. Daniel F. Malan. In 1949 he was an active campaigner, in 1951 he was elected to the "Head Committee" of the National Party in Cape Province, and in the same year he became a member of the South African Senate. In 1955 he became a judge of the South African Supreme Court in the Eastern Cape Division. In his questioning of the barrister, D. D. V. Kannemeyer, who appeared for Ganyile, Wynne showed some resentment at what he regarded as carelessness in the preparation of the application, and he queried the appearance of an uncle as the petitioner. Kannemeyer asked that the application be treated as an urgent one and suggested October 23 as the "return date" by which the government would have to release Ganyile or justify his further detention. On October 18 the court met briefly and judgment was reserved.

Ganyile's Friends Stand Up to Be Counted

By taking the matter to the courts, Ganyile's friends had imposed on a judicial organ of the South African state an obligation to take some action, if only to reject the petition. But there was no means of ensuring that such action would be taken soon, even though South African courts ordinarily deal with applications for habeas corpus rulings very rapidly, often the same day they are made. The beginning of legal proceedings, however, to some extent inhibited political action by Ganyile's friends, inside and outside South Africa. In a country with a British and Roman Dutch legal tradition, comment by politicians and others on matters before the courts is subject to the stringent legal and conventional limits of the *sub judice* doctrine; free comment on issues awaiting decision by a court can lead to prosecution for contempt.

Who were Ganyile's "friends" apart from his immediate relatives? The official opposition party, the United Party, did not take up the case. This may have been partly out of respect for the *sub judice* doctrine, but far more probably it was because South Africa was in the midst of a general election, held on October 18, the day Judge Wynne reserved judgment. The election led to the fourth consecutive victory by the National Party, with an increased majority in Parliament and, for the first time, apart from the republican referendum in 1960, an indisputable majority of South Africa's white electorate behind it. The strategy of the United Party since its first defeat in 1948 has been to argue that apartheid, or racial segregation, is not new in South African life, that it can be preserved as well by convention as by law, and that the United Party is better fitted than the National Party to maintain racial peace and economic advance along with segregated society and white supremacy. Though white supremacy and violation of frontiers are entirely different issues, there was little political capital for the United Party in the Ganyile case. Ganyile was hardly a figure for whom it could have much sympathy, with his demand for direct African representation in Parliament. Though the major English language newspapers, *The Cape Times* and *The Star,* reported the allegations and police denials and the more outspoken *Rand Daily Mail* pressed for explanations, the issue was dropped when no further startling developments took place.

But Ganyile was not friendless. *New Age,* in its scoop of September 21, had set out not merely to perform one of the worthy functions of a newspaper by providing accurate information, but to shock its readers as well. Jackson Nkosyane, who went to the hut "last week" (i.e., Monday, September 11, to Sunday, September 17), gave a lurid description of what he had found there. The hut was "in a shambles," he wrote. "SOME OF THE BLANKETS WERE COVERED WITH BLOOD. It was evident that the men had put up a fierce fight before they were overpowered and dragged away." Not content with mere observation, he had "immediately" reported the facts to the Basutoland mounted police at Qacha's Nek. The article concluded with a resounding appeal: "From all sides the demand must go up: Free this gallant freedom fighter! . . . Ganyile must be allowed to return to Basutoland!"

Three days later on September 24, the *Golden City Post,* a Johannesburg weekly newspaper written for Africans, published an article which contained a fuller reconstruction of events. According to this account, Jackson Nkosyane had last seen Ganyile and his companions in August. At about the time of the alleged kidnapping at the end of August, he had noticed that they had not been to the village of Qacha's Nek for some days. On hearing from a herd boy that the door of the hut was open, he went to investigate. In the meantime, and independently, the note from Ganyile had been sent to Joseph Matthews, a prominent ANC refugee living in Basutoland and the son of a distinguished African intellectual, Professor Z. K. Matthews, himself in voluntary exile. Joe Matthews, the article continued, had worked closely with Ganyile in the past. "Powers" had been a secret name between them ever since the trial in Russia of the American U2 spy pilot, Gary Powers. Matthews went to see the chief of the Basutoland police, Colonel Paul Kitson, and flew with him to Qacha's Nek on Tuesday, September 19. There they examined the hut with District Commissioner Lawrence and a policeman from Qacha's Nek. A photograph was taken in the hut by Peter Maqubane of *Drum,* showing Lawrence investigating while Nkosyane of *New Age* watched. Lawrence, according to the *Post* article, had said that "in his view the men had clearly been kidnapped."

Other groups inside South Africa, besides the African press, were also moving. The Congress Alliance which had helped with the legal proceedings organized a "placard parade" in Cape Town on September 23, by African, white, and Colored members, calling for the punishment of the kidnappers and the release of Ganyile. Duma Nokwe, an African barrister, wrote a report on the case for use in England, and sent it and telegrams of protest to Labor Party leader Hugh Gaitskell and to Hilary Marquand of the Labor front bench, who had a special responsibility for Commonwealth affairs. There was, however, little that people like Nokwe could do in South Africa. For one thing, they had no means of bringing pressure to bear on the South African government. For another, a large number of leaders like Chief Luthuli were under orders restricting their movements and activities. And Nokwe himself was charged under the Unlawful Organization Act on September 28 for taking part in the conference of African nationalists in Pietermaritzburg in August, 1961.

Pressure on Basutoland Authorities

All roads for Ganyile's friends seemed to lead to London. In Basutoland there were soon loud complaints that the local authorities were unwilling to act vigorously. According to Nkosyane's account, after reporting to the police he had immediately telephoned Joe Matthews and Robert Matji, a member of the Basutoland Legislative Council, commonly known as the

National Council. On September 22, the day after the *New Age* disclosure, Ntsu Mokhelele, president of the Basutoland Congress Party, asked in the Council whether the executive was aware that the South African police had seized "three refugees from the Republic of South Africa . . . ? Would the Government take measures both to prevent recurrence and to recover these people?" (*Golden City Post,* September 24, 1961.) The Leader of the House, British official G. M. Hector, denied any knowledge of the kidnapping but promised that an inquiry would be made. A day or two later, as reported in *The Star* on September 25, the resident commissioner went further: "Inquiries reveal that it is most unlikely that South African police entered Basutoland." This understandable caution on the part of officials was galling to those who had taken up Ganyile's case, especially since an article published in the *Golden City Post* had stated that the district commissioner—not a police official—believed that the men *had* been kidnapped.

The irritation of Ganyile's friends with local officials was most clearly shown in a long controversy over the bloodstained blankets found in the hut. These were sent to the South African Institute for Medical Research on October 7. Meanwhile, on October 3, Patrick Duncan, editor of the South African liberal weekly *Contact* and son of a former Governor General, went to Qacha's Nek and to Ganyile's hut, where he found a bloodstained piece of cardboard. He took steps to have the stains analyzed, also at the South African Institute of Medical Research. But the Institute, perhaps already aware of the deep political waters, refused to accept the cardboard without the express authority of Sir John Maud, the British High Commissioner for South Africa. Maud, however, had gone no further than to say that he had no objection to the work being done. This was not sufficient for the Institute and the piece of cardboard was then sent to England. On October 18, *New Age* published a statement by a group of South African refugees in Basutoland which accused the British High Commissioner's Office in Pretoria of "sabotaging" the attempt to have the blankets analyzed. On October 19, *Contact* criticized the Basutoland police for holding the blankets for three weeks. When this accusation was repeated in the House of Commons on November 16, Bernard Braine, Joint Undersecretary of State for Commonwealth Relations, warmly denied the charge. A report had been received by the British government: it was "being studied," he said. There was another exchange on December 7 when Hugh Frazer, Undersecretary of State for the Colonies—Basutoland was placed under the Colonial Office on December 1, 1961,—replied to two backbenchers, Jeremy Thorpe (Liberal) and Fenner Brockway (Labor), who were urging that Scotland Yard be called in to help the Basutoland police. Thorpe had the results of the analysis of the piece of cardboard with him—the police were overlooking evidence, he said. Brockway, in an article in the Socialist weekly *Tribune* on December 29, virtually suggested collusion: the Basutoland police, he wrote, "fraternize with the South African police."

Pressure on the British Government

Thorpe and Brockway, though from different parties, cooperated successfully in maintaining pressure on the government. Thorpe was an active young Liberal M.P., a frequent speaker on African issues, and a member of the Anti-Apartheid Movement (an "All-Party Protest Against Racial Discrimination"). Fenner Brockway (now Lord Brockway) was a veteran left-wing Socialist with a persistent interest in colonial issues, and one of the founders of the Movement for Colonial Freedom. Through these two organizations, Brockway and Thorpe were in touch with a large number of active people outside Parliament. Furthermore they were joined by members of the Africa Bureau directed by Rev. Michael Scott, another veteran of the struggle against colonialism and discrimination. It was to these groups that Patrick Duncan successfully appealed by attracting the attention of the High Commissioner's Office in South Africa, and in urging a more vigorous investigation in Basutoland. Some newspapers lent a hand: on September 24 both *The Observer* and *Reynolds News* gave some prominence to the story; from time to time in the following months *The Observer* reported on the progress of the case. And, finally African leaders outside South Africa appealed directly to the major opposition party, the Labor Party. Oliver Tambo, a founding member of the ANC Youth League and chairman of the short-lived United Front, a body that aimed to reconcile the conflicting policies of the rival Pan-Africanist Congress and African National Congress, and Joe Matthews in Basutoland had been in touch with Labor Party leaders directly after the publication of the story in *New Age*.

This group of people and organizations, not an aroused mass opinion, was what kept up the pressure on the British government. After the initial reports there was little discussion of the case in the newspapers or weekly reviews. Because the British Parliament was not sitting, the organizers of protest adopted a classic weapon to bring the issue directly to the attention of the minister: a deputation. On September 29, only eight days after the publication of the story in *New Age,* Brockway and Thorpe led a deputation to see Undersecretary of State Bernard Braine at the Commonwealth Relations Office. With the two M.P.'s went Tambo, representing the United Front, and representatives of the Anti-Apartheid Committee.

It was not an issue on which there was likely to be much party division: few members would take a violation of British territory lying down. Relations with South Africa were in a transitional state due to South Africa's departure from the Commonwealth on May 31, 1961, following criticism of South African racial policies by other members of the Commonwealth. In the debate on the South Africa (Temporary Provisions) Bill, 1961, the government had given explicit assurances that political refugees would *not* be handed over to the South African government if they were charged with offenses not regarded as crimes in the High Commission Territories. Though the South Africa (Temporary Provisions) Act of 1961 maintained in force for one year the Fugitive Offenders Act of 1881, which provided for the arrest and handing over of prisoners between British colonies and former colonies, the latter measure, of course, did not countenance kidnapping such as was alleged in Ganyile's case. It is not surprising, therefore, that Braine was able to satisfy the deputation that the government would take an active interest in the case. On October 11 the British Ambassador asked the South African government for information, a request repeated several times in the weeks that followed. Furthermore, on October 13, during the hearings of the petition in Grahamstown, an officer of the Basutoland police and an official from the British embassy were present in the court.

The Long Wait

Judge Wynne was to try the patience of Ganyile's friends. He gave no indication of when he would deliver judgment, though as noted the usual South African and British practice was to give a decision within a few days. As October ended and November appeared to be passing without a word from Grahamstown, Brockway and others became impatient.

In South Africa the left-wing papers could not attack Judge Wynne, but they could maintain their offensive against the Basutoland administration and the British government. On October 19, the day following the reservation of judgment, *New Age* published an article from Maseru headed *"British Suppressing Ganyile Inquiry:* Allegations by South African Refugees." According to the refugees, the British resident commissioner first ordered an inquiry and then quashed it; no investigation was taking place; "the rate at which the South African police . . . patrol the interior of the country of Basutoland has increased to an alarming extent. . . . *We have very strong reasons to believe that evidence is being suppressed."* The refugees appealed to "the British Government and the whole world" to acknowledge that their "security under the British Flag is threatened and the fundamental English Common Law is flagrantly being violated."

A similar line was taken by *Contact* on November 16. It concentrated its fire on the British government but particularly on the High Commissioner, Sir John Maud, and implied that Britain appeared to be "shielding" the South African "Security Branch." This could have "catastrophic" effects, it charged, on "British influence and even on British trade." Britain was already shielding South Africa at the United Nations, *Contact* continued: "No nation was so hostile to the idea of sanctions against apartheid as was Britain." If Britain were really to shield South Africa on these two issues, "Britain's reputation in Asia and Africa would stand lower than it has stood since Suez."

The British Parliament met on October 17. Two days later, the day after Judge Wynne reserved judgment, there was a general debate on Africa.

Thorpe thanked Braine for receiving the deputation and asked for further information; Brockway made a proposal that he and others were to repeat several times later, that a representative of the High Commissioner, preferably a lawyer, should be sent to interview Ganyile. "If this were done," he said, "we should be able to obtain the evidence to enable us to make the protests in a more public way." However, no reply was made by a minister in this debate. The issue then lapsed for nearly a month, a delay which did little to allay the resentment of interested members. On November 16, Brockway and Thorpe were joined by Dr. Alan Thompson (Labor) in asking for a statement; Marquand of the Labor front bench intervened to urge an early reply. The Joint Undersecretary of State for Commonwealth Relations, Bernard Braine, replied that he could say nothing: inquiries were proceeding, the British government had asked the South African government for information, and the matter was before the courts. This was not good enough for Brockway.

> MR. BROCKWAY: Is the hon. Gentleman aware that this alleged incident took place as far back as 26th August? Does he remember that he received a deputation consisting of a number of us on 29th September . . . ? Is he now aware of very disturbing evidence in South Africa of inactivity upon this matter? . . .
>
> MR. THORPE: . . . Is it that the South African Government are refusing to give it [i.e., information] or are claiming that the matter is *sub judice?* . . .
>
> MR. BRAINE: The South African Government have replied to the Ambassador that as the matter is before the South African courts it is *sub judice.* As Mr. Ganyile is a South African, was apprehended by the South African authorities and is held by them, only he and the South African authorities know precisely what took place. . . .
>
> DR. THOMPSON: Is the Minister aware that the first and most solemn duty of every Government is to protect their citizens from attack by foreign maurauders, whether their colour be black, yellow or white? . . . If the Minister persists in sheltering his officials, will he consider that only one honourable alternative remains to him? This is to uphold the high standards of the House in this matter by resigning.
>
> MR. BRAINE: I entirely repudiate the suggestion that we are not anxious to protect the interests of British subjects. . . . I suggest that instead of making extravagant remarks like that we should await the judgement and then consider our attitude.[1]

According to Braine, the British government was not going to abandon the legally and diplomatically "correct" posture. Ganyile, he persisted in reminding members, was a South African citizen. He did not define exactly what rights Ganyile possessed in the eyes of the British government as a person who had been given asylum on British soil. Furthermore, he would

[1] This and other extracts on the following pages are taken from speeches made in the British Parliament and are recorded in the official Parliamentary Debates.

not make a statement while Judge Wynne deliberated. The South African government was, apparently, taking full advantage of the judge's silence. At this point, no one attempted to distinguish between the circumstances of Ganyile's arrest and his continued detention. Both issues had, however, been raised in Siwele Ganyile's petition. The British government, it seems, saw no reason to define precisely the subjects affected by the *sub judice* doctrine, being willing to wait for the decision of the court. At that time the South African government would be bound to reply, whether a writ were granted or not.

This exchange attracted some attention in the English-language press in South Africa. *The Cape Times* gave two-thirds of a column to it on the following day, calling it "Another Commons Flare-up over Basuto 'Kidnap.' " This report and an editorial in *New Age* on November 23 stated that Braine had said that the ambassador had been "given the facts" by the South African government. (Presumably *New Age* obtained its facts from the same South African Press Association–Reuter dispatch as was used by *The Cape Times.*) However, according to the official report, Braine did not say this. The case, and others similar to it, continued to receive attention in *New Age,* which on November 30 published an article on John Itholeng, former chairman of the ANC in Kimberley, who, *New Age* alleged, had been lured back into South Africa from Basutoland by a "well known shebeen [speakeasy] queen" only to be arrested. Another article in the same issue told the story of three students who had fled to Swaziland from Turfloop, a "tribal" college like Fort Hare in the Transvaal; one of these students was quoted as saying: "I am afraid that what happened to Ganyile in Basutoland can also happen to us. We are being trailed by the South African police."

The matter was raised once more in the House of Commons before Wynne gave his decision. On December 7, Brockway and Thorpe pressed for details as to the "extent and nature of the search carried out by the Basutoland Police." Hugh Frazer, replying for the government, pointed out once more that because no report had been made for over three weeks, it had been difficult to investigate. Brockway was not prepared, however, to drop the matter. He protested that fourteen weeks had already passed since the kidnapping, and while he acknowledged that the delay was "predominantly due to the extraordinary postponement of any judgment in the court of the Republic," he drew attention to "very considerable criticism of the [Basutoland] police."

Judge Wynne Speaks

There the matter rested until judgment was given by Judge Wynne on December 11. The judgment, sixty-two pages long, rejected the application *"in toto."* Counsel had argued that escape from Frenchdale was a minor nonextraditable offense. On the contrary, argued the judge, under Section 5 of the Native Administration Act the legal consequences of escape were serious. The offense, he claimed, was one to which the Fugitive Offenders Act of 1881 could be applied: "The procedure of the backing of warrants . . . could lawfully be invoked to secure Ganyile's apprehension in Basutoland and his return to the Republic of South Africa as a fugitive offender . . . . " The whole basis of a habeas corpus plea fell away in his view because the powers taken by the state in Section 5 precluded any interference by any court. The order was unrevoked and Ganyile had no more right to claim relief than he would have if charged with murder. Moreover, it was an "inescapable inference that Ganyile, if in the Transkei, has been detained under these Emergency Regulations," particularly Proclamations R400 and R413 of 1960. Powers of detention under these regulations, as we have seen (p. 257), were very wide, giving to noncommissioned officers the right to detain without charge until questions had been satisfactorily answered.

Judge Wynne showed throughout his judgment an awareness of the political overtones of the case. Indeed, he complained of inaccurate press reports and of "agitation and pressure from certain sections of the Press." He had clearly leaned over backwards to give the executive the benefit of the doubt, throwing on the petitioners, rather than on the state, the burden of showing whether Ganyile's continued detention was lawful. He was not prepared to order the production of Ganyile *in person* in court; neither would he secure the laying of charges against him *or* the justification of further dentention without charge—all essential features of habeas corpus procedure.

Appeal to the Full Bench

An appeal was lodged at once. Wynne gave his judgment against the application on December 11. Four days later the full bench of three judges of the Eastern Cape Division heard the case and immediately and unanimously granted the appeal, in practically identical terms to those asked for, calling on the state to justify Ganyile's detention "in this court on 18 January, 1962."

The appeal had been made on eight grounds. Judge Heinrich de Villiers, judge president of the Eastern District Court, went directly to the issue of the continued detention by reading the first and seventh grounds of appeal together.

> The first is to the effect that: The learned Judge erred in law and in fact in holding that no *prima facie* case had been made out for the relief sought; and seventh, the learned Judge erred in law in holding that it has not *prima facie* been shown that the arrest and detention of the said Ganyile was

> unlawful. These two contentions cover the same ground and they seem to me to be most important grounds of appeal.

De Villiers then turned to the course of events since Ganyile's arrest. The banishment to Frenchdale had, *prima facie,* been lawful. Furthermore, in escaping, Ganyile had, *prima facie,* committed an offense, though without the order under the Native Administration Act before him, he could not say what other, if any, offenses Ganyile had committed. He pointed out, however, that

> The policy as well as the letter of the law demands that an arrested person charged with an offence shall be brought to trial without delay. If that had happened in Ganyile's case, it seems to us *prima facie* that he would either have been cautioned and discharged or reprimanded or fined or given a sentence of imprisonment. . . . If that had been done and he had paid his fine, or if he had been sentenced to imprisonment and had served his sentence, the authorities then could probably have taken him back to Frenchdale. But if he had been returned to that area they would have to let him loose and although his liberty would not be 100 percent he would not be incarcerated and kept in a cell.

De Villiers then examined Wynne's judgment. Wynne had argued that a person subject to a banishment order and found "at large" in the Republic had no "*prima facie* right to claim his liberty from the Courts of the country." De Villiers, though he agreed that the kidnapping was irrelevant, insisted that detention in a cell

> is justified only for so long as it is necessary to bring the person in question to trial and sentence. . . . All that we know now *prima facie* is that Ganyile was arrested and lodged in gaol on the 26 August, 1961, that on the 11 December, when judgement was given he was still in gaol *prima facie,* and is *prima facie* still under detention today. Where he is and what has happened to him we do not know.

Secondly, De Villiers would not accept the "inescapable inference" drawn by Wynne that "Ganyile, if in the Transkei, has been detained under these Emergency Regulations." As Kannemeyer, Ganyile's lawyer, had pointed out, the judge continued, Ganyile had been deported *before* the Emergency Regulations had come into force in the Transkei as a result of the declaration of emergency on November 30, 1960. "*Prima facie,* therefore, he had no opportunity of committing an offence which would justify action under the Emergency Regulations resulting in his detention." The Emergency Regulations, which give the police virtually unchecked and limitless powers of detention, could not be assumed to have been used in Ganyile's case because he had not been in the area to which they applied. De Villiers was arguing, in fact, that in spite of the immense powers of the police, habeas corpus still survived to the extent that the police could be ordered to produce the prisoner in court and state the legal basis of further detention, even if, under the Emergency Regulations, there was no need to have a speedy trial or to say on what grounds release was refused. The judge president concluded:

> If their [the government's] detention of Ganyile is lawful, if they can justify it, *cadit quaestio* [the discussion ends], but to refuse a rule [to order the production of Ganyile in court] may cause considerable hardship and injustice to Ganyile. From a practical point of view, therefore, I do not think the Court should be astute to find objections at this stage to the relief claimed. The Court should rather be astute to find a means of exercising its function and jurisdiction in the protection of a citizen from a potential inroad on his liberty.

It is interesting to note the differences in approach between the two judges. Wynne had gone out of his way to find reasons for supporting the government's action. He had been bitterly critical of the meager information in the petition, but, as De Villiers said, it was perfectly open to a judge to ask for further information. Also, Wynne had been in no hurry to deal with the case—and the long delay was nowhere explained in his judgment. De Villiers had not only deplored the delay, but decided to refrain from asking for further information because the delay had already been so long.

Reaction in the House of Commons

The court had now placed the onus on the South African Minister of Justice to act by January 18, 1962. Ganyile remained a prisoner, but it was becoming difficult to use the *sub judice* plea to refrain from giving any information. On December 18, a number of backbenchers and also the future leader of the Labor party, Harold Wilson, showed how impatient they were becoming. Brockway once more asked for an interview with Ganyile by a representative of the High Commissioner; Thorpe asked for a statement of the "representations" made to the South African government. Peter Thomas, Joint Undersecretary of State for Foreign Affairs,[2] replied that the British Ambassador in Pretoria "has made repeated requests for a reply, including two requests in the past week." Then, to the annoyance of some members, he persisted in explaining a lack of information by referring to the *sub judice* doctrine:

> MR. THORPE: Is the hon. Gentleman aware that the only matter that is *sub judice* is that the Republican Government must show cause by 18th January why these men should not now be released? . . .

[2] South African affairs were transferred to the Foreign Office from the Commonwealth Relations Office on December 1, 1961.

> Mr. Thomas: I think that Her Majesty's Government should await a reply from the South African Government.
>
> Mr. H. Wilson: Since this *sub judice* excuse has been used to drag this business on for over four months, and since there has been a certain amount of quibbling about whether these men were or were not British protected persons and this kidnapping was done on soil for which the House has responsibility, may I ask the hon. Gentleman whether he will not take the matter a little more seriously than he has done so far? Will he see that a complete investigation is made . . . to collect . . . all the evidence on this most wicked episode? Would the hon. Gentleman, having done all that, not feel in a much stronger position to talk to the South African Government in the way we think they ought to be talked to?
>
> Mr. Thomas: Investigation on Basutoland territory is a matter for my right hon. Friend the Colonial Secretary. We are anxious to find what information we can on whether or not this territory was violated. The matter was *sub judice* until last Friday, since when an order has been made reversing the decision, and we hope to have a reply from the South African Government.
>
> Mr. Wilson: But what was *sub judice* was the application for the release of these men under South African law. Is the hon. Gentleman aware that what was not *sub judice* was the simple question of fact whether British territory was violated by the South African raiders who undertook the operation? . . .
>
> Mr. Thomas: We have been asking for information for some time. Our concern was to find out whether or not this territory was violated. We hope now that we shall have a reply.

Next day Thorpe repeated Brockway's suggestion that Her Majesty's government request permission to send a representative to interview Ganyile and his two companions. However, Edward Heath, Lord Privy Seal, replied that the British government "have no grounds for asking to interview a South African citizen."

It is probable that the British government began to press insistently for information immediately after Wynne's judgment on December 11. At least one of the requests "in the last week" was probably made before the appeal. However legally correct the British government was prepared to be in sticking to its assertion that Ganyile was a South African citizen, it continued to show an interest in the case, sending representatives to the court in Grahamstown on both December 13 and 15, and again on January 10, when Ganyile finally appeared in court in Umtata. The British government was under increasing pressure in the House of Commons from those who naturally regarded De Villiers' judgment as a setback for the South African government. After December 15, therefore, the South African minister had to face both an increasingly impatient British government and the necessity to meet the return date of January 18 set by the Supreme Court in Grahamstown.

Ganyile Appears in Court

On December 22 Ganyile was brought to Umtata, capital of the Transkei. Only his account of this journey has been given in an affidavit dated January 9, 1962:

> On the 22nd day of December, 1961, I was brought to the Court in Umtata by members of the Special Branch. I was kept in their car whilst members of the public were cleared from the Court. . . . The case was remanded until the 5th day of January, 1962. I asked the Presiding Magistrate what the charge against me was and he informed me there were three, the first of failing to obey a Ministerial Order, and the second of incitement, and the third of attempted murder.
>
> At no stage prior to this had I been informed of any charge against me; I was never formally arrested, cautioned or charged; to the best of my knowledge and belief no warrant was ever issued authorising my arrest; I was not brought before a Magistrate or other judicial officer until the 22nd day of December, 1961.
>
> On the 22nd day of December, 1961, I was allowed for the first time to communicate with an Attorney.
>
> Before I appeared in Court on the 5th day of January, 1962, I was informed by the Gaoler that the Police were not proceeding with the first two charges against me but were charging me with attempted murder and incitement to murder.

This affidavit raises several questions about the action of the South African government. We can understand why Ganyile's first appearance in court was not reported in the press; Ganyile had not really appeared in "open" court. Why should the government have tried to hide this appearance in court? Perhaps a two-week respite to January 5 was regarded as valuable to government lawyers. Why did the government decide to drop the charge of disobeying an order, a charge which Judge de Villiers thought could probably be sustained? Here again, it may have been that the South African government wished to make use of the more serious charges like incitement to murder, and particularly attempted murder, both subject to legal penalties in South Africa and in Basutoland.

The State had gone a long way, however, toward meeting the court order. Ganyile had been brought before a court, charged, remanded, and allowed to see a lawyer, who immediately made an application for bail. As *Contact* pointed out on January 11, 1962, the government was "sidestepping" the court order. On January 10, the application for bail was heard before J. Potgieter, senior magistrate of Umtata. Ganyile presented his affidavit of January 9 to the court, giving the first detailed account of the events of August 26, 1961, and of his movements thereafter. After a narrative of the kidnapping, Ganyile stated that he had never been properly charged, but he presumed that he was now being charged for what happened during the kidnapping.

> I respectfully submit that if I on that occasion committed an offence—which I deny—the courts of this country do not have jurisdiction to try me for it.
>
> If I am granted bail I will stand my trial and will not interfere with any state witnesses. If the charges against me are based on the events of the 26th day of August, 1961, I respectfully point out that the State witnesses would all be members of the Police force.

The application for bail was opposed by J. J. Scholtenmeyer, an employee of the Department of Justice. For the first time, beyond the denials of knowledge by the police in October, the state gave an indication of the line it would follow. Ignoring the issue of kidnapping altogether, Scholtenmeyer refused to accept the account of events given by Ganyile, but he declined to give the state's version at that time. Ganyile, he said, had made "an unprovoked assault on a policeman who was doing his duty." Furthermore, he said, "The point that Ganyile had not been brought to trial in accordance with the provisions of the law would not have been hammered [i.e., emphasized] if it had been known that he was detained under the emergency regulations," the first time that an official had claimed such a ground for detention. (*Cape Times,* January 11, 1962.)

At this stage, the proceedings at Umtata had nothing directly to do with the order made by the court in Grahamstown, whose return date was exactly one week away. Ganyile was apparently to be tried for offenses committed in Basutoland—attacking the policeman with an axe—and for incitement to murder. If he had been liable to suspicion for incitement before he was banished, no charge had been brought against him. Thus the state appeared to want to ignore the illegality of the arrest—an issue on which officials gave no information or comment—to justify detention without charge by the Emergency Regulations, and to drop the charge of disobeying the order.

Release on Bail

Judgment on the application for bail was reserved by the magistrate until the following day. He decided to grant the application on deposit of two sureties (bonds) for R400 ($560.00). Potgieter did not, as Peter Charles wrote in the report for the International Commission of Jurists,[3] criticize the police for not bringing Ganyile to trial since his arrest in August. Ganyile had been detained under the Emergency Regulations, Potgieter said, "and the necessity to bring him to court in a specified time did not arise." However, he continued,

> It would appear that the State has had sufficient time in which to investigate the case, collect its evidence, collate it and bring the case to trial. . . .

[3] *South African Incident: The Ganyile Case* (Geneva, 1962), p. 16.

> It is, however, not clear to the Court what caused the delay since the accused's first appearance in court [on December 22].

Secondly, although Ganyile had disobeyed an administrative order and committed an offense at the time of his disappearance from Frenchdale, he was not facing a criminal charge, that is, a charge distinct from the proceedings at the time of his arrest. There was not sufficient evidence before the court to show that Ganyile would not stand trial if given bail. Moreover, he was prepared to take cognizance of Ganyile's claim that he had been acting in self-defense. (*Star,* January 11, 1962.)

"Desperate Hunt Before Ganyile Is Freed," wrote *The Cape Times* on January 12 describing the tense anxiety around the court while Ganyile's attorneys searched for, and found, two Africans in the Umtata area to stand surety for Ganyile for R200 ($280.00) each. This anxiety was more than tenseness over raising the sureties. An order for the detention of Ganyile under the Emergency Regulations was still in force, and when the magistrate signed the release order late in the afternoon of January 11, "there was an air of expectancy round the court as attorneys and newsmen waited to see if the police would act. Up to last night they had not done so." Ganyile was free to go subject to the conditions laid down by the magistrate. He had to remain in the urban area of Umtata and tell the police his address within forty-eight hours of his release; to report to the police station, Umtata, once a day between 10 A.M. and noon; and, finally, to make no attempt to communicate with state's witnesses. As all these were policemen, Ganyile was unlikely to try, as he pointed out in his affidavit. He was, then, due to appear on January 19 on a preliminary examination before a magistrate, for attempted murder and incitement to murder.

Cause Célèbre

The case was now attracting a great deal of attention inside and outside South Africa. The decision of the full bench of December 15 to some extent released participants from the restriction of the *sub judice* doctrine and deprived the South African government of one of its grounds for refusing to provide information. In South Africa, *The Cape Times* and *The Star* now treated the story as of the first importance. "Ganyile Case: The World Is Watching" was a headline in *The Cape Times* on January 12, reporting the arrival in Umtata on the day before of Peter Charles Q.C., a barrister from Southern Rhodesia and the author of the pamphlet referred to above. Charles had been retained to watch the case for the International Commission of Jurists, a body based in Geneva and dedicated to the maintenance of the rule of law.

Charles was no stranger to South African law and politics. He had only recently moved to Salisbury from Cape Town, where he had been an active member of the Liberal party and had unsuccessfully contested a parliamentary seat. After Ganyile's release, on January 12, Charles interviewed him and then gave a press conference in which he drew attention to what he regarded as unacceptable features of South African law, statements which he repeated in the report published by the International Commission of Jurists. Proclamation R400 was not an emergency proclamation, he pointed out. Some of its clauses were temporary, but the powers taken under clauses 19 and 20 were not temporary (see p. 257).

> Under this law a second class sergeant of police, if he has reason to suspect that a person, A, intends to commit any offence (say, the theft of a fowl) may arrest without warrant A and/or B who he thinks may have information about A's intended offence—and may keep A and B in jail indefinitely until they have answered all questions put to them about the intended offence to the satisfaction of the police sergeant. They need not be brought before any Court and they are not allowed to consult with a legal adviser without the consent of the Minister or a person acting with his authority.

Neither records of negotiations between South Africa and the United Kingdom nor the discussions within the South African government have been published. But it is obvious that the rising interest in the case, which Charles did his best to intensify, was becoming increasingly embarrassing to the South African government. Though it had been able to put the British government off with the *sub judice* plea, it was faced with the prospect of a searching cross-examination of the policemen who had kidnapped Ganyile, one of whom Ganyile was accused of attempting to murder. If the charge of attempted murder were proceeded with, the pleas of self-defense and lack of jurisdiction would certainly be used to justify the blow at Constable du Toit. It would quite clearly be impossible to keep the issue of the arrest and struggle *on British soil* out of the court. The evidence for which Brockway had asked in October "to enable us to make the protests in a more public way" would have been provided in abundance.

Release and Return to Exile

The South African government now moved rapidly to bring the episode to an end. The proceedings on bail, by giving Ganyile another limited triumph, only increased the interest and impatience of those who supported him. Umtata was full of journalists, lawyers, and others who would see to it that the preparatory examination was thoroughly reported and commented on. The government took virtually the only way out short of denying visitors access to the courts. On January 13, Ganyile's two companions, Ingleton Ganyile and Mohlovu Mtseko were freed, and the order authorizing their detention under Proclamation R400 was canceled. Then late on the night of January 17, apparently after a cabinet meeting, it was announced that Ganyile was to be freed the following day, and that all charges against him were to be dropped. (*The Cape Times,* January 19, 1962.)

The government issued one of its rare statements to explain this sudden action: "As it had now been established that the arrest of Anderson Ganyile had taken place within the borders of Basutoland, the Attorney General at Grahamstown had decided not to proceed against him." The Minister of Foreign Affairs had apologized to the British Ambassador for the incident. Then followed a brief statement of the events of August 26. The police had been searching for the murderers of "Bantu Captain Stanford" and had unwittingly crossed the border in heavy mist. Only after the incident had they established that Ganyile was one of those arrested, and he was afterwards detained under Proclamation R400. After an investigation by a senior police officer, the Attorney General was satisfied that the police had acted in "good faith." It was estimated by the police that they had overshot the border by 500 yards, but a surveyor had established that the distance was 638 yards. (*The Cape Times,* January 19, 1962.)

The significance of the reference to the exact number of yards was not immediately made clear. Ganyile appeared in court in Umtata on January 19, the day set down for the beginning of the preparatory examination. In announcing the dropping of the charges, Scholtenmeyer said:

> It has been established that Ganyile was arrested 638.86 yards from the boundary of the Republic in foreign territory [Basutoland]. Consequently Section 20 of the Fugitive Offenders Act has no application. For this reason only have I been instructed by the Attorney General not to proceed with the preparatory examination.

Section 20 reads:

> Where two British possessions adjoin, a person accused of an offence committed at or within a distance of 500 yards from the common boundary of such possessions may be apprehended, tried and punished in either of such possessions.

It seems, therefore, that the state was now claiming that its case would have rested on the proposition that the arrest had been lawful because the incitement to murder had taken place 500 yards from the frontier, and that in striking his blow with the axe, Ganyile was resisting a lawful arrest.

There remained the proceedings in Grahamstown consequent on the order by Judge de Villiers. On January 15 the Minister of Justice had filed an affidavit stating that Ganyile was being held under the Emergency Regulations on the basis of reports that he was inciting citizens to sabotage and murder. The Minister refused to consider the question of the kidnapping and asked that the order be dismissed with costs. The government now dropped the case and, on January 18, state attorneys got in touch with Ganyile's attorneys to offer to pay costs.

Aftermath

Ganyile returned to Basutoland on January 21 and on the same day announced that he intended to sue the South African Minister of Justice and other officials for R20,000 ($24,000). In addition, he intended to press criminal charges in Basutoland against the policemen concerned. On January 23, however, the names of all the policemen involved were given by the Minister of Justice in the House of Assembly, with the statement that no action was to be taken against them because no breaches of the Disciplinary Code had taken place.

In the House of Commons on January 29, many members heard with angry derision the claim by the South African government that the police had crossed the border by mistake. According to one member, Christopher Mayhew (Labor), it was "totally unconvincing." When pressed to support Ganyile's claim for compensation, Joseph Godber, Minister of State for Foreign Affairs, returned the assertion that Ganyile was a South African. This excuse did not go unchallenged.

> MR. H. WILSON: Since the Government are not as simple as the hon. Gentleman is making them appear, will he answer this question? . . . Will he make absolutely clear here and now that the apology we have had is not sufficient for everything that has happened and that the Government will firmly stand behind Mr. Ganyile in the matter of compensation for this quite illegal detention?
>
> MR. GODBER: I think the two points are separate. . . . We have made quite clear that we take a very serious view of what has taken place. As to Mr. Ganyile's application for compensation, I think it should go forward in the normal way. He is a South African citizen and should make his application through the courts.

Very little was said thereafter on the case either in Britain or in South Africa. On June 18 a member in the South African House of Assembly tried to raise the matter in a debate on the police, but he was ruled out of order because Ganyile's suit for damages was before the courts. There this particular case appears to have rested.

The Ganyile case was not, however, to be the last of its kind. A similar case occurred when Dr. Abrahams, a Colored doctor from South West Africa, was allegedly kidnapped on August 11, 1963, in the Bechuanaland Protectorate and taken across the border. On August 12 he was arrested by the South African police at Gobabis in South West Africa, taken to Cape

Town, and charged under the Suppression of Communism Act on August 16. The British government took up the case: On August 28 the South African Chargé d'Affaires in London was called to the Foreign Office on the matter. Habeas corpus proceedings were nevertheless started, and on August 20 the Supreme Court in Cape Town granted a rule requiring the Minister of Justice to show cause on September 5 why Abrahams should not be released and returned to Bechuanaland. On August 29 the Minister of Justice asked for the return day to be advanced to August 30, and on that day in court he personally announced the release of Abrahams, though denying that the police had crossed the border. In this case, the South African government, perhaps profiting from the Ganyile case, released Abrahams very quickly.

More recently, in August 1964, Dennis Higgs, a young Englishman who was wanted by the South African government in connection with a bomb explosion in the railroad station in Johannesburg early in 1964, was found bound and gagged in a park in Johannesburg. He had been kidnapped by a secret organization in Lusaka, Northern Rhodesia (now Zambia). The South African government immediately handed him over to the British government and then asked for his extradition to South Africa, which was refused.

One by-product of these and other incidents has been an elaboration of the security system on the borders, and a tightening of regulations governing the conduct of refugees in the Territories. The elaboration has taken two forms. First, the law has been changed. Though the South Africa Act, passed in Britain in 1962, to provide for South Africa leaving the Commonwealth, specifically excluded extradition for political offenses and for acts which would not be illegal in the Territories, the British government has been unwilling to allow its territory to be used as a base for subversion. Written permits of asylum are issued, but receivers of these permits have to give an undertaking not to engage in politics. In August, 1963, Jack Hodgson, a refugee from South Africa, was denied a permit to stay in Bechuanaland because he refused to give this promise. In the same month the Colonial Office was reported to be busy on the drafting of a "Protectorates formula" to establish criteria on which political asylum should be granted. A refugee was defined, according to *The Times,* August 27, as one who has "a well-founded fear of being persecuted for reasons of race, religion, nationality, membership of a particular social group or political opinion." This was based, wrote *The Times,* on normal British Home Office practice. However, the new formula aimed to prevent political asylum being granted to people who wanted to go overseas for training in subversion before reinfiltrating South Africa. The Basutoland Prevention of Violence Abroad Act, passed on August 24, 1963, provided for a three-year prison sentence for conspiring to commit acts abroad which, if committed in Basutoland, would be declared illegal. Similar legislation has been passed for Swaziland

and the Bechuanaland Protectorate, and in 1964 the High Commissioner issued a proclamation denying protection to those who used British territory for hostile acts against other states.

The second elaboration of the security system has been a tightening of the security apparatus on both sides of the borders. Better fences, twenty-four-hour border patrols, and control posts were established in August, 1963, between South Africa and the three Territories, though it is not clear precisely how complete the new system is. The South African government has instituted stringent control of flyover rights, most serious in the case of Basutoland and Swaziland. It has been said that travel documents will even be required for all except migrant laborers to the mines. But though this elaboration has been proceeding steadily since 1960, the flow of refugees had not been stopped. At the end of 1963 it was estimated that 1,200 refugees had "passed through" Bechuanaland alone since March, 1960.

Conclusion

Looking at the Ganyile case as a problem in intergovernmental relations, we can see that there are definite limits to the extent to which such disputes can be treated as legal ones. No international tribunal exists as yet to which such a dispute can be referred as a matter of course. The important issue for the British government, as a government, was the violation of its territory. When legal obstacles to raising the issue were removed by the judgment in Grahamstown, it insisted on a partial restoration of the situation existing before the kidnapping by the return of Ganyile to Basutoland. It was, however, only a partial restoration, for Ganyile had received no compensation for the long months of solitary confinement or the violence at the time of his illegal arrest. The British government insisted all along on a limited definition of its obligations toward Ganyile, though it is hardly surprising that it refused to act on the issue of compensation before legal process within South Africa had run its course. Presumably those on the Labor benches who were urging support for Ganyile's claim were thinking of a claim through diplomatic channels. Such a claim would probably have had to wait for a decision on Ganyile's suit in the South African courts. At the time, the British government had no obvious interest in pursuing the matter further, though it is, of course, possible to imagine a state of relations in which the British government would have insisted on greater satisfaction than the return of the prisoner and an apology. What would have happened if Ganyile had been a British subject is a nice but unanswerable question.

By establishing a republic outside the Commonwealth, South Africa's Afrikaner rulers have achieved a long-standing objective and one of the main goals of Afrikaner nationalism, but they have not thereby made a fundamental change in relations with Great Britain. By the South Africa Act of 1962, South Africa remains in the Commonwealth preference area for most commodities. British investment in South Africa is substantial and increasing. Defense relationships were a matter of bilateral agreement even while South Africa was in the Commonwealth. The issue of the incorporation of the economically dependent High Commission Territories in South Africa as envisaged in the South Africa Act of 1909 has been decided in favor of their separate independence, but their relation with South Africa is hardly solved. Though South Africa has left the Commonwealth, Britain has not "left" southern Africa, and it is the separate existence of the three Territories that makes its departure difficult.

British leaders of all parties, with few exceptions, sympathize with the aspirations in the High Commission Territories and with the refugees, not with the South African government. As statesmen, however, they are aware of the conflicting claims of the tangible, identifiable interests of trade, investment, and order on the one hand and the long-term, debatable, but nevertheless compelling, considerations of ideology and relations with new states on the other. Hence, they adopted an attitude which to Ganyile's friends appeared to be legalistic and perhaps even pusillanimous.

Joseph Godber, in the House of Commons on January 29, 1962, claimed that Ganyile had been released because of British representations on his behalf. If it be assumed that this was indeed the case, what sanctions, if any, did the British government employ to induce the South African government to release Ganyile and return him to Basutoland? The British government was certainly sensitive to the charge that it was failing in its duty to those living in Basutoland, and it had considerable interest in demonstrating to the new African states that Britain would not be defied by South Africa, a state virtually isolated on the continent and at the United Nations. Throughout this period—from August, 1961, to January, 1962,—the future relations between South Africa and Britain were under negotiation, including the future of the High Commission Territories. There were far greater interests at stake for South Africa than the fate of a young African leader who was hardly a major threat to the regime. The South Africa Bill of 1962 was about to be presented to the British Parliament—the debate on the second Reading, that is, on the general principle of the bill, took place on February 26. The settlement embodied in it was economically very favorable to South Africa and for that reason subjected to much criticism in the House. There was no interest for South Africa in making difficulties for the British minister responsible for piloting the bill in the House. The lame explanation implying it had taken the South African government five months to find out that Ganyile had been arrested more than 500 yards inside Basutoland was a small price for South Africa to pay. The South African government adopted the most effective method of ending the matter: release, apology, and a minimum of explanation.[4] Whether the British government had, in fact, to threaten to break off discussions on future relations to secure South African cooperation will be known only when the diplomatic record is published.

The South African legal system is shown by the Ganyile case to have some remarkable characteristics. A large and increasing number of laws are avowedly discriminatory between the various legally defined groups in the society, and particularly in respect to Africans. Much of that law originated before the National party came to power in 1948. The state possesses plenary powers of arrest, banishment, and confinement without trial and without access to counsel, sometimes on the authority of noncommissioned officers in the police. Yet even within such a legal structure, the South African judiciary has been able to perform many functions regarded as essential to a regime characterized by the phrase "rule of law." Though the remedy adopted in this case was political, not legal—Ganyile did not return to Basutoland because a judge ordered it—the court ultimately performed the essential function of forcing the executive to justify publicly the incarceration of a citizen, even one without political rights. Under the General Laws Amendment Act of 1963, the government could imprison any suspects for repeated ninety days at a time without charge and to the exclusion of any court process. (Use of this provision was suspended in January, 1965.) These powers appear on paper to be no greater than those possessed by police officers in the Transkei. It seems, therefore, that the prospect of cross-examination of police witnesses about a crime which took place on British soil, before an attentive international audience, was one which the South African government was not prepared to face. An acquittal of Ganyile or an order by the court for his return to Basutoland would have involved the government in a humiliation at least as great as the course actually followed.

In acting as he did, De Villiers was following the dominant theme in the conduct of South African judges in this century, particularly since 1948. As Peter Charles wrote in his report for the International Commission of Jurists:

> It must be said that the handling of the *habeas corpus* application by Mr. Justice Wynne was not in accordance with the high traditions of the South African Judiciary. . . . In every other respect, however, the South African judicial officers and legal practitioners . . . added lustre to the deservedly high reputation enjoyed by the South African Courts. . . . It is clear that despite the existence in South Africa of repressive laws . . . much can still be done and is being done to maintain the liberty of the subject by a vigilant and independent Bench and a courageous legal profession.

---

[4] The Anti-Apartheid Movement had urged the British government that "discussion . . . be suspended pending proper assurances." (Press Release, March, 1962.)

The existence of such plenary powers in the hands of the police, however, and especially of the Special Branch, raises a serious institutional problem. It will be some time before it is known if the crossing of the Basutoland boundary was ordered by superior officers, and if so by whom. Nor do we know the extent of cooperation between the Basutoland mounted police and the South African police. If Ganyile was using Qacha's Nek as a base of operations, the anxiety of the Basutoland police would be understandable. But if Ganyile's account is true, the South African police knew the name of the owner of the hut, and, according to the statement of their own informer, they knew that Ganyile was in Qacha's Nek. The course of events leads one to wonder what degree of control is exercised over sergeants in the course of their duties. To what extent was the kidnapping the result of rugged local initiative? When the *New Age* disclosure was made, did senior officers deny all knowledge of the matter until someone at a high (political?) level decided to detain Ganyile in spite of the circumstances of his arrest? The existence of such a battery of acts under which Africans can be arrested, detained, and banished may itself have led to a belief on the part of the police and the minister that they would be able to justify their conduct. Paradoxically, Judge Wynne's long and, probably, unprecedented delay, far from helping the government, only increased the sense of outrage felt by Ganyile's friends in the British House of Commons, and perhaps also the determination of the British government to gain satisfaction on the issue of the violation of British territory. This is *not,* of course, to suggest that there was collusion between Judge Wynne and the South African government.

The case suggests some general conclusions. First, the rights of individuals cannot be left confidently to the ordinary processes of law in any country. There is no guarantee that judges or juries will act on behalf of the individual, especially when political issues arise and where the processes of law are under such pressure as they have been in South Africa. The decision to prosecute or not is a political one and, in virtually all states, prosecuting officers have a considerable degree of discretion. A decision to prosecute can be reversed by making it politically expedient to do so. Opinion-forming bodies therefore play a crucial role in the legal as well as the political aspects of civil rights. Second, where the rights of an individual conflict with the interests which two states have in preserving intimate economic and strategic relations with each other, the rights of the individual may well be sacrificed. His fate may depend on the vigor with which the issue is taken up by the aggrieved party. In the beginning the British government was far more willing to accept the *sub judice* plea than it was toward the end, a reflection of a changing political climate. For, as Harold Wilson pointed out in December, the *sub judice* plea was to some extent irrelevant, for it was not the arrest of Ganyile which was *sub judice*. The British government could easily, at the very beginning, have insisted on a statement as to how Ganyile came to be in a South African prison. The *sub judice* plea was no better, and no worse, *after* Judge de Villiers' order than it had been before.

As a case in political behavior, the Ganyile story illustrates the importance of gaining the right allies in a nonparty issue, and in the right place—in Britain, not in South Africa. That *New Age* was articulate and active on Ganyile's behalf was hardly surprising because he had had a long connection with the paper. But *New Age* had few allies. It was the gaining of the help of the members of the non-Communist opposition in South Africa, and particularly of members of the British Parliament, that made it possible to move the British government to exert some, and possibly strong, pressure. Furthermore, even in a democratically governed society, dedicated to the rule of law, with an independent judiciary of high quality, the rights of an individual may go by default because there is no process that necessarily ensures that a case will be judged in such a way as to accord with the facts or, indeed, even come to court. The probability that an individual's rights will be protected may be further diminished if his case involves two governments rather than only one. Though in the west we regard *raison d'état*—a claim to special immunity on the part of the state—with an aversion that is almost instinctive, a government may well plead a "reason of state" for not insisting on full redress, even for one of its own citizens who has clearly suffered at the hands of another government. There are indeed limits to the actions which a government will take on behalf of an individual, limits that will be determined by the state of relations between the governments concerned, the amount of information available, the degree of mobilization of opinion, the power of the respective states and, even, the nerve of the diplomats and ministers involved. There is an African proverb: "When the elephants fight, it is the grass that gets trampled on." Paradoxically, however, in this case, it was precisely because the elephants fought that the grass was ultimately not trampled on.

Study Questions

1. Is it possible to draw an analogy between this case and the kidnapping of Eichmann? Why did the two cases have such different conclusions?

2. "When the elephants fight it is the grass that gets trampled on." In what precise sense does this African proverb apply to this case? Can you conceive of conditions when the very reverse is true; that is, it is only when states really "fight" that the rights of individuals are protected. Was this true in Ganyile's case?

3. If you had to justify the actions of the six policemen, how would you do so? If you had been the South African Minister of Justice how would you have dealt with the threat posed by Ganyile and his friends at Qacha's Nek?

4. Did the courts secure Ganyile's release and return to Basutoland? If not, what precise part did they play? What possible courses of action could a United States federal court have taken in an analogous situation?

5. What implications does the Ganyile case have concerning the proper relationship between public opinion and judicial proceedings in a society whose government is avowedly based on the rule of law?

Selected Bibliography

Carter, Gwendolen M. *The Politics of Inequality*. New York: Praeger, 1958.

Hailey, William M. H. *The Republic of South Africa and the High Commission Territories*. London: Oxford University Press, 1963.

Karis, Thomas G. "South Africa," in Gwendolen M. Carter, ed., *Five African States*. Ithaca, N.Y.: Cornell University Press, 1963.

Mbeki, Govan. *South Africa: The Peasants Revolt*. London: Penguin Books, 1964.

Munger, Edwin S. *Bechuanaland: Pan-African Outpost or Bantu Homeland?* London: Oxford University Press, 1965.

Acknowledgments

I thank many for help, but especially William Brown, Newell Stultz, Colin Legum, Edwin S. Munger, and Jacoba van Schaik.

A 6
B 7
C 8
D 9
E 0
F 1
G 2
H 3
I 4
J 5